RE-ENGINEERING HUMANITY

Every day new warnings emerge about artificial intelligence rebelling against us. All the while, a more immediate dilemma flies under the radar. Have forces been unleashed that are thrusting humanity down an ill-advised path, one that's increasingly making us behave like simple machines?

In this wide-reaching, interdisciplinary book Brett Frischmann and Evan Selinger examine what's happening to our lives as society embraces big data, predictive analytics, and smart environments. They explain how the goal of designing programmable worlds goes hand in hand with engineering predictable and programmable people.

Through new frameworks, provocative case studies, and mind-blowing thought experiments that you'll find hard to shake, Frischmann and Selinger reveal hidden connections between fitness trackers, GPS technology, electronic contracts, social media platforms, robotic companions, fake news, and autonomous cars. The powerful analysis provides much-needed resources for imagining and building alternative futures.

BRETT FRISCHMANN is The Charles Widger Endowed University Professor in Law, Business and Economics at Villanova University. He is also an affiliated scholar of the Center for Internet and Society at Stanford Law School, and a trustee for the Nexa Center for Internet & Society, Politecnico di Torino. He has published foundational books on the relationships between infrastructural resources, governance, commons, and spillovers, including *Governing Medical Knowledge Commons*, with Michael Madison and Katherine Strandburg (Cambridge, 2017); *Governing Knowledge Commons*, with Michael Madison and Katherine Strandburg (2014); and *Infrastructure: The Social Value of Shared Resources* (2012).

EVAN SELINGER is Professor of Philosophy at the Rochester Institute of Technology, where he is also the Head of Research Communications, Community, and Ethics at the Center for Media,

Arts, Games, Interaction, and Creativity. A Senior Fellow at the Future of Privacy Forum, his primary research is on the ethical and privacy dimensions of emerging technology. Selinger has co-edited *The Cambridge Handbook of Consumer Privacy*, with Jules Polontesky and Omer Tene (Cambridge, 2018). A strong advocate of public philosophy, he regularly writes for magazines, newspapers, and blogs, including *The Guardian, The Atlantic, Slate*, and *Wired*.

RE-ENGINEERING HUMANITY

BRETT FRISCHMANN

Villanova University

EVAN SELINGER

Rochester Institute of Technology

CAMBRIDGE
UNIVERSITY PRESS

CAMBRIDGE
UNIVERSITY PRESS

University Printing House, Cambridge CB2 8BS, United Kingdom

One Liberty Plaza, 20th Floor, New York, NY 10006, USA

477 Williamstown Road, Port Melbourne, VIC 3207, Australia

314–321, 3rd Floor, Plot 3, Splendor Forum, Jasola District Centre, New Delhi – 110025, India

79 Anson Road, #06–04/06, Singapore 079906

Cambridge University Press is part of the University of Cambridge.

It furthers the University's mission by disseminating knowledge in the pursuit of education, learning, and research at the highest international levels of excellence.

www.cambridge.org
Information on this title: www.cambridge.org/9781107147096
DOI: 10.1017/9781316544846

First published 2018

Printed in the United States of America by Sheridan Books, Inc.

A catalogue record for this publication is available from the British Library.

ISBN 978-1-107-14709-6 Hardback

To our families

Contents

Foreword

Human beings have a genius for designing, making, and using tools. Our innate talent for technological invention is one of the chief qualities that sets our species apart from others and one of the main reasons we have taken such a hold on the planet and its fate. But if our ability to see the world as raw material, as something we can alter and otherwise manipulate to suit our purposes, gives us enormous power, it also entails great risks. One danger is that we come to see ourselves as instruments to be engineered, optimized, and programmed, as if our minds and bodies were themselves nothing more than technologies. Such blurring of the tool and its maker is a central theme of this important book.

Worries that machines might sap us of our humanity have, of course, been around as long as machines have been around. In modern times, thinkers as varied as Max Weber and Martin Heidegger have described, often with great subtlety, how a narrow, instrumentalist view of existence influences our understanding of ourselves and shapes the kind of societies we create. But the risk, as Brett Frischmann and Evan Selinger make clear, has never been so acute as it is today.

Thanks to our ever-present smartphones and other digital devices, most of us are connected to a powerful computing network throughout our waking hours. The companies that control the network are eager to gain an ever-stronger purchase on our senses and thoughts through their apps, sites, and services. At the same time, a proliferation of networked objects, machines, and appliances in our homes and workplaces is enmeshing us still further in a computerized environment designed to respond automatically to our needs. We enjoy many benefits from our increasingly mediated existence. Many activities that were once difficult or time-consuming have become easier, requiring less effort and thought. What we risk losing is personal agency and the sense of fulfillment and belonging that comes from acting with talent and intentionality in the world.

As we transfer agency to computers and software, we also begin to cede control over our desires and decisions. We begin to "outsource," as Frischmann and Selinger aptly put it, responsibility for intimate, self-defining assessments and judgments to programmers and the companies that employ them. Already, many people have learned to defer to algorithms in choosing which film to watch, which meal to cook, which news to follow, even which person to date. (Why think when you can click?) By ceding such choices to outsiders, we inevitably open ourselves to manipulation. Given that the design and workings of algorithms are almost always hidden from us, it can be difficult if not impossible to know whether the choices being made on our behalf reflect our own best interests or those of corporations, governments, or other outside parties. We want to believe that technology strengthens our control over our lives and circumstances, but if used without consideration technology is just as likely to turn us into wards of the technologist.

What the reader will find in the pages that follow is a reasoned and judicious argument, not an alarmist screed. It is a call first to critical thought and then to constructive action. Frischmann and Selinger provide a thoroughgoing and balanced examination of the trade-offs inherent in offloading tasks and decisions to computers. By illuminating these often intricate and hidden trade-offs, and providing a practical framework for assessing and negotiating them, the authors give us the power to make wiser choices. Their book positions us to make the most of our powerful new technologies while at the same time safeguarding the personal skills and judgments that make us most ourselves and the institutional and political structures and decisions essential to societal well-being.

"Technological momentum," as the historian Thomas Hughes called it, is a powerful force. It can pull us along mindlessly in its slipstream. Countering that force is possible, but it requires a conscious acceptance of responsibility over how technologies are designed and used. If we don't accept that responsibility, we risk becoming means to others' ends.

NICHOLAS CARR

Acknowledgments

In writing this book over the past five years, we relied heavily on the generosity and ideas of others. We are grateful to the many, many people who have helped us. Looking back, it is difficult to acknowledge all the people, sources, and ideas that contributed to the book. It builds from prior publications, workshops, conferences, and countless conversations.

We would like to acknowledge the help we received from the following people, who provided invaluable assistance: Claire Adair, Jesús Aguilar, Muhammad Ahmad, Marc Aronson, Mark Bartholomew, Ann Bartow, Yochai Benkler, David Berreby, Aaron Bornstein, John Bronsteen, Christopher Buccafusco, Ryan Calo, Nicholas Carr, Julie Cohen, John Danaher, Juan Carlos De Martin, Michael Del Priore, Deven Desai, Robb Eason, Joshua Fairfield, Nick Feamster, Ed Felten, Lara Freidenfelds, Sue Glueck, Nathan Good, Peter Goodrich, Patrick Grim, James Grimmelmann, Katherine Haenschen, Pelle Guldborg Hanson, Woodrow Hartzog, Bob Hillman, David Hoffman, Anna Lauren Hoffmann, Christopher Hoofnagle, Don Howard, Robert Howell, Gordon Hull, Don Ihde, Lisa Kaufman, Ian Kerr, Nancy Kim, Brenda Leong, Melanie Leslie, Lawrence Lessig, Karen Levy, Richard Lutz, Michael Lynch, Michael Madison, Bryan Magnus, Rowland Maplethorpe, Andrea Matwyshyn, Arvind Narayanan, Frank Pasquale, David Ryan Polgar, David Post, Julia Powles, Riccardo Rebonato, Vance Ricks, Michael Risch, Stuart Russell, Melissa Rutman, Jathan Sadowski, Michael Salvato, Lauren Scholz, Natasha Schull, Joyce Searles, Doc Searls, Kole Seeber, Yan Shvartzshnaider, Ted Sichelman, Stasha Sosnowicz, Keith Stanovich, Ed Stein, Clive Thompson, Shannon Vallor, James Vasile, Mark Verstraete, Spencer Weber Waller, David Weinberger, Kevin Werbach, Josephine Wolff, Felix Wu, Tim Wu, Ekow Yankah, Elana Zeide, Ben Zevenbergen, Jonathan Zittrain and David Zweig. We are grateful to Nicholas Carr for authoring a gracious Foreword for our book.

We also acknowledge the universities we've worked at while the book was written: Cardozo Law School, Princeton University, Rochester Institute of Technology, and Villanova University. We thank Cardozo and Villanova for providing financial support for summer research as well as editorial and research assistance.

We are grateful to everyone at Cambridge University Press for working with us on this project. Matt Gallaway is an amazing editor and championed the project from start to finish. Catherine Smith, Meera Seth, and Heather Palomino provided invaluable assistance.

We'd like to thank Benjamin Carlson for creating the website for the book. For talks, reviews, opinion pieces, and more, go to re-engineeringhumanity.com.

And we extend our heartfelt thanks to Kim Michael for allowing us to use his wonderful artwork on the cover of the book and our website. His art can be found at www.thezinker.com.

The book builds and borrows directly from many of our previously published articles and public presentations. We directly draw from the following:

Brett Frischmann and Evan Selinger, "Why You Should Care About Net Neutrality." *Wired*, June 26, 2017. http://www.wired.co.uk/article/in ternet-frischmann-selinger-net-neutrality

Brett Frischmann and Evan Selinger, "Utopia?: A Technologically Determined World of Frictionless Transactions, Optimized Production, and Maximal Happiness." *UCLA Law Review Discussion* 372 (2016): 372–391.

Evan Selinger and Brett Frischmann, "The Danger of Smart Communication Technology." *Arc.* September 13, 2016. https://arcdigital .media/the-danger-of-smart-communication-technology-c5d7d9ddof3e

Brett Frischmann. "Thoughts on Techno-Social Engineering of Humans and the Freedom to Be Off (or Free from Such Engineering)." 17 *Theoretical Inquiries in Law* (2016): http://www7.tau.ac.il/ojs/index.php /til/article/view/1430.

Brett Frischmann and Evan Selinger, "Why It's Dangerous to Outsource Our Critical Thinking to Computers." *The Guardian*, December 10, 2016. https://www.theguardian.com/technology/2016/dec/ 10/google-facebook-critical-thinking-computers

Evan Selinger, "The Black Box Within: Quantified Selves, Self-Directed Surveillance, and the Dark Side of Datification." *Los Angeles Review of Books*, February 17, 2015. https://lareviewofbooks.org/article/black-box-within-quantified-selves-self-directed-surveillance-dark-side-datification/

Evan Selinger, "Too Much Magic, Too Little Social Friction: Why Objects Shouldn't Be Enchanted," a review essay on David Rose's *Enchanted Objects: Design, Human Desire, and the Internet of Things. Los Angeles Review of Books* January 8, 2015. https://lareviewofbooks.org/article/much-magic-little-social-friction-objects-shouldnt-enchanted

Evan Selinger, "Will Autocomplete Make You Too Predictable?" BBC, January 15, 2015. http://www.bbc.com/future/story/20150115-is-autocorrect-making-you-boring

Brett Frischmann and Evan Selinger, "Will the Internet of Things Result in Predictable People?" *The Guardian*, August 10, 2015. https://www.theguardian.com/technology/2015/aug/10/internet-of-things-predictable-people

Evan Selinger, "Can Predictive Technology Make Us Less Predictable?" *Forbes*, September 27, 2014. https://www.forbes.com/sites/privacynotice/2014/09/27/can-predictive-technology-make-us-less-predictable/#5c23b41072f1

Evan Selinger, "If Predictive Algorithms Can Craft the Best E-Mails, We're All in Big Trouble." *Christian Science Monitor*, April 27, 2015. https://www.csmonitor.com/World/Passcode/Passcode-Voices/2015/0427/Opinion-If-predictive-algorithms-craft-the-best-e-mails-we-re-all-in-big-trouble

Evan Selinger, "Automating Walking Is the First Step to a Dystopian Nightmare." *WiredUK*, May 20, 2015. Link was broken when last accessed.

Brett Frischmann, "Human-Focused Turing Tests: A Framework for Judging Nudging and Techno-Social Engineering of Human Beings" (September 22, 2014). Cardozo Legal Studies Research Paper No. 441. Available at SSRN: https://ssrn.com/abstract=2499760

Evan Selinger, "Why Predictive Shopping Might Be Bad for the Future." *Forbes*, August 21, 2014. https://www.forbes.com/sites/privacynotice/2014/08/21/why-predictive-shopping-might-be-bad-for-the-future/#61a24abb3653

Evan Selinger, "Today's Apps Are Turning Us Into Sociopaths." *Wired*, February 26, 2014. https://www.wired.com/2014/02/outsourcing-humanity-apps/

Evan Selinger, "You've Been Obsessing Over Your Likes and Retweets Way Too Much." *Wired*, June 9, 2014. https://www.wired.com/2014/06/you-are-worth-more-than-just-likes-faves-and-retweets/

Evan Selinger, "Why We Should Be Careful About Adopting Social Robots." *Forbes*, July 18, 2014. https://www.forbes.com/sites/privacyno

tice/2014/07/17/why-we-should-be-careful-about-adopting-social-robots/#7d10c1b771ef

Evan Selinger, "Google vs. Our Humanity: How the Emerging 'Internet of Things' Is Turning Us Into Robots." *Salon*, May 22, 2014. http://www.salon.com/2014/05/22/google_vs_our_humanity_how_the_emerging_internet_of_things_is_turning_us_into_robots/

Evan Selinger, "How We're Turning Digital Natives Into Etiquette Sociopaths." *Wired*, March 26, 2013. https://www.wired.com/2013/03/digital-natives-etiquette-be-damned/

Evan Selinger, "Facebook Home Propaganda Makes Selfishness Contagious." *Wired*, April 22, 2013. Link was broken when last accessed.

Evan Selinger, "Would Outsourcing Morality to Technology Diminish Our Humanity?" *Huffington Post*, September 19, 2012. http://www.huffingtonpost.com/evan-selinger/google-morals_b_1895331.html

Evan Selinger, "Impatience as a Digital Virtue." *Huffington Post*, September 6, 2012. http://www.huffingtonpost.com/evan-selinger/impatience-as-digital-vir_b_1859453.html

Brett Frischmann, *Infrastructure: The Social Value of Shared Resources* (Oxford University Press, 2012).

Brett Frischmann, "Cultural Environmentalism and the Wealth of Networks." *University of Chicago Law Review*, 74, 1083 (2007).

Brett Frischmann, "Some Thoughts on Shortsightedness and Intergenerational Equity." *Loyola University Chicago Law Journal*, 36(2), 457, (2005).

Note on the Text

All books run the risk of seeming dated the moment that they're finished. The pages end but time marches on. This risk is especially pronounced with books like ours that discuss technology. We submitted the manuscript for *Re-Engineering Humanity* in the fall of 2017, knowing that publication was scheduled for the spring of 2018 – a gap that can seem like an eternity in tech-time. We hope our readers appreciate this basic publishing constraint and recognize that our goal is to start a conversation about fundamental issues that have enduring relevance.

Introduction

There's a scene in the HBO series *Silicon Valley* where a character tries to show off by purchasing a $14,000 smart refrigerator that can identify when it's running out of beer and when someone is about to put expired yogurt on one of its shelves. Hilarity ensues when another character hacks into it and sets the start-up screen to an inappropriate and looping video. The absurdity is a welcome relief for skeptics like us who bristle at the breathless media coverage of "smart" gadget rollouts as paving the path towards interconnected utopia. Unfortunately, techno-social engineering, the main subject of this book, is no laughing matter. How we engineer ourselves and are engineered by others is one of the most important questions of the twenty-first century.

The companies, organizations, and institutions that use and design smart technology are our leading techno-social engineers. They seduce us by promising smart tools will make our lives easier and better. But like all narratives about pure progress, this isn't the whole story. As we collectively race down the path toward smart techno-social systems that efficiently govern more and more of our lives, we run the risk of losing ourselves along the way. We risk becoming increasingly predictable, and, worse, programmable, like mere cogs in a machine.

Critics often claim that new technologies dehumanize, especially in recent decades with the widespread adoption of computers, the Internet, and, more recently, smartphones. But the public generally takes such claims to be alarmist, and so the claims remain untested and ultimately drowned out by rampant enthusiasm for new technology. Yet techno-social engineering of humans exists on an unprecedented scale and scope, and it is only growing more pervasive as we embed networked sensors in our public and private spaces, our devices, our clothing, and ourselves.

To get a clear sense of where on the path we are, let's play a game, the type that philosophers call a thought experiment. Imagine that an "evil, tech-phobic monarch" forced everyone to stop using products and services from the major technology companies: Amazon, Apple, Facebook, Microsoft, and Alphabet (the parent company of Google), a.k.a. the "Frightful Five."[1] No more Instagram. No more email. No more searching the Internet. If you had to stop cold turkey, you wouldn't like it, would you? It might feel like the end of the world – the technological apocalypse.

But how, exactly, would our lives "deteriorate" by pulling out these cords?[2] It's hard to imagine the specifics because we depend so deeply on each one of these companies. Consider Amazon, the supreme retailer whose stock "has been rising at nearly 42% a year."[3] Amazon began by selling books online and offering customers a simple way to share book reviews and get automated recommendations for books we might like to read. Then it expanded and expanded some more. And the company just keeps on creeping along, pursuing "dominance, comprehensiveness, and the pursuit of monopoly,"[4] edging ever-closer towards a "United States of Amazon."[5]

Without Amazon, we'd lose one-click, fast delivery ordering of everything from diapers to breakfast cereal – purchases that are so easy to make that there's effectively "no thinking required."[6] If Amazon couldn't deliver vast libraries of streaming television shows, movies, and music to our desktops, laptops, phones, and tablets, the loss of entertainment would sting. And if, suddenly, we couldn't walk into brick-and-mortar stores and compare their prices to Amazon's, we'd feel like bargain shopping died.

It's become clichéd to say that the future is already here but not evenly distributed, but Amazon proved that this is so back in 2014. That's when the company drew headlines for acquiring a patent for "anticipatory" shipping. This is exactly what it sounds like – a patent for a system that can predict what customers want to buy before they even know they want to make the purchases. Amazon's goal is to "box and ship products it expects customers to buy pre-emptively, based on previous searches and purchases, wish lists, and how long the user's cursor hovers over an item online."[7] Amazon's "significant" stake in cloud computing – essentially running and renting space for other online businesses – means that the company is prepared to "power the public infrastructure that keeps the world running," once self-driving cars go mainstream and run on smart grids that are "underpinned by cloud computing networks."[8] In light of all that Amazon offers, does, and will do, *New York Times* technology writer Farhad Manjoo characterizes the company as his "keeper of lists, a provider of food and culture, an entertainer and educator and handmaiden to my children."[9]

When Manjoo describes his personal experience of getting sucked into Amazon world, he notes that the vortex intensified significantly when the company rolled out the Echo. Echo is a hands-free device. It interacts with users through a digital, voice-activated assistant named Alexa that "is designed to get smarter every day" by "adapting to its users' speech patterns, vocabulary and personal preferences."[10] All Manjoo needs to do is ask, and Alexa will perform a range of tasks for him. She'll look up the weather for him, turn on his favorite music playlists, and place his Amazon orders. And that's just the beginning. Manjoo notes that Echo has become such an integral part of the "most mundane moments" of his day that the device is "well on its way to becoming" his "household's brain, a kind of butler in the sky that runs the place for" him.[11]

Notice what Manjoo is saying about how Amazon instills a can't-live-without-you mindset. Alexa directly mediates Manjoo's everyday experiences and habituates him to think and act in collaboration with the device, and Alexa persuades him by design to fundamentally change how he performs household tasks and makes consumer choices.[12] Manjoo will get some benefits from this "relationship," but he probably won't recognize all the subtle and profound ways that Alexa is programmed to program him. The folks at Amazon knew exactly what they were doing when they gave Echo a human name and a human-sounding voice. These are two anthropomorphic features, giving the illusion of humanity. And as the research shows, both incline people to bond and empathize with inanimate technology.[13]

While the "brain" and "butler" comparisons suggest that Manjoo is using a networked device that is, at once, both master and servant, the reality is that Alexa doesn't present evenly balanced powers. What Manjoo identifies is the beginning of a path where powerful companies use smart technologies to gain control over us by framing our choices and nudging us towards programmed lives of convenience and cheap bliss. Cheap bliss is addictive. If it weren't, you could stop eating after you had exactly one potato chip. Or one bite of any of the other foods that are engineered to get us to come back for more, and more, and more . . . And so, Manjoo appears to say that if technology companies can deliver cheap bliss by optimizing his life, he's all for it. He's even willing to pay for their services with agency and self-determination.

Manjoo's desires are not unique. We are all like Manjoo. Consumer demand for various kinds of digital assistants is growing, and during the much-touted Amazon Prime Day, we considered purchasing the deeply discounted Echos.[14] Hal Varian, chief economist for Google, goes so far as to declare: "Centuries ago, rich people had servants, and in the future, we will all have cyberservants."[15] Apparently, in the future everywhere we go, technological valets will track and assess our behavior, steer us towards our anticipated goals, and take care of our predicted needs.

You might well wonder, what's the harm in technology companies making shopping easier for us? Or making it easier for us to communicate with our friends? Or making it easier to get valuable information like directions for how to get to a meeting across town during rush hour traffic? These all seem like good things that enhance our lives. That's why it would feel catastrophic to lose the technological services that we've grown accustomed to. At the same time, however, we're being sold a misleading vision of cyberservants and digital assistants. These tools don't just do our bidding. They're also smart enough to get us to do theirs.[16]

Our discussion of Amazon reveals a piece of a larger puzzle, a blueprint for building a world that's filled with ubiquitous smart programming. Such a world will be dramatically different from our own. And that's why it's important to take a step back and critically consider the human-level implications of being programmed by the environments that are being designed for us to live, work, and play in.

Such programming was on full display during the 2016 US presidential race, in what's come to be known as the fake news election.[17] While it remains debatable just how much fake news helped Donald Trump get elected, one thing is certain: propaganda campaigns let loose highly automated networks of social media bots. The software posed as real people – regular folks offering earnest, special-interest-free, political opinions – and masked their real agenda of being tools designed to sway votes and circulate calculated talking points. Even though disinformation campaigns have been going on for a long time and attack ads have become a political staple, the bot situation is especially troubling. In a polarized world, when bots are designed to look and sound like us, our neighbors, and our friends, it can be hard to know who – or better yet, what – is engineered to follow a deviously programmed script. This problem, the growing hold Amazon and other technology giants have on us, and many other related issues in the personal, social, and political spheres all concern *twenty-first-century techno-social engineering*.

Techno-social engineering refers to processes where technologies and social forces align and impact how we think, perceive, and act. That's the "techno" and "social" components of the term. "Engineer" is quite close in meaning to "construct," "influence," "shape," "manipulate," and "make," and we might have selected any of these terms.[18] After due consideration, however, "engineer" won out for two reasons. First, the practice of engineering is directed at designing and using tools to achieve desired ends. Second, the term "engineer" lends itself to analysis that draws parallels between designing environments and designing the people who live in them.[19]

Techno-social engineering has many components. An especially potent one is surveillance. We live in a surveillance society now, and while some people, groups, and even nations resist, most of us are being conditioned to accept surveillance expanding in scale and scope. Business leaders, policy-makers, and consumers are clamoring for a world with smart technology embedded in everything. And that world can't function without always-on people interacting with always-observing, always-analyzing, and always-acting technological systems.

Consider a few examples of techno-social engineering from your every-day life. Have you ever been relentlessly pursued by targeted advertising across the Internet – perhaps a pair of shoes or a jacket that you once considered buying pop up wherever you browse and won't go away? That's done to wear you down. The more you need to exercise will-power when considering whether to buy something, the more your will-power depletes.[20] Or, have you ever clicked "I agree" and accepted the terms of service for online contracts that you didn't bother reading? We all have. Those contracts are designed so that there's no point in reading the fine print. See it, click it, stimulus-response. Or, have you ever been in social situations where you shouldn't check your phone but you do because you just can't help yourself? That's addiction by design, and it cuts both ways.[21] It also accounts for why other people annoy us when they can't leave their digital tethers behind.[22]

Then there's social media. Ever intend to bare your soul or engage in a reasoned debate but end up sticking to the widely used expressions that the interfaces promote – clicking "like," "retweet," or "heart" instead of formulating more thoughtful responses? We have. And that's because social media platforms are optimized to get users to communicate this way. The platforms profit from this style of communication.

Let's not forget the games. Billions of dollars are spent each year on mobile games that are free to download. Free to download, however, doesn't necessarily mean free to play. Gamers pay with their time, attention, and data. They make in-app purchases and get sucked into playing during the time programmers select when they heighten their control over players by limiting when special rewards and challenges are offered.[23]

These experiences and many others reveal that powerful techno-social engineering is occurring everywhere and that a common theme runs throughout them: We are being conditioned to obey. More precisely, we're being conditioned to want to obey.

One extreme scenario that's worth considering is that the smart programming of the future will require us to automatically accept the shots that algorithms call. Perhaps the only way we'll be able to do all the things that smart systems require will be for humans to accept a new lot in life and behave like simple machines. That's the dark side to twenty-first-century techno-social engineering.

Should such a future arise, it will be a long way off. But before the programming deepens, it's crucial to get a clear sense of how decisions that are made today can impact the world of tomorrow. Conventional wisdom says we've made tremendous technological progress in the past century and that it's been driven by the rational behavior of producers and users who develop, deploy, adopt, and use innovative technologies to satisfy consumer preferences and pursue happiness. The conventional wisdom obscures the truth and engineers complacency.[24] Our preferences are increasingly manufactured rather than freely adopted, thanks to techno-social engineering calling the shots. The worst, perhaps, is yet to come.[25]

Welcome to the Experience Machine n.0

Farhad Manjoo's thought experiment about how contemporary technology companies are shaping our values reminds us of a different thought experiment – one that the philosopher Robert Nozick first articulated over forty years ago, long before the invention of the commercial Internet.[26] Nozick didn't seem to have much interest in being a futurist. As an exercise in theorizing about well-being, he wondered whether he or anyone else would choose to plug into a hypothetical "experience machine" that could convincingly simulate any desired experience. In the blink of an eye, the experience machine would let you take on the role of a renowned novelist, a caring father, an ascetic saint, or any of the myriad of other possibilities, like rock star, brilliant scientist, or world-class athlete.[27]

Nozick seemed to imagine the experience machine as a huge mainframe computer. By now, it seems safe to say that he envisioned the wrong type of machine. If a contemporary experience machine were to be built, it wouldn't be anything like a 1970s-era mainframe computer that one plugs into with a cord.

Nozick wasn't far off in other respects. He imagined neuropsychologists would supply us with the sensations we desire and ostensibly crave. Today, technologists, entrepreneurs, and policy-makers are importing scientific insights about how minds work and can be manipulated into their engineering projects and business plans. Knowledge from cognitive science, psychology, and behavioral economics guides how technologists design contemporary computer programs, architect technical systems, and create human-computer interfaces.

Extrapolating from the present to the near future, trends point toward the possibility of creating distributed experience machines, comprised of interconnected sensor networks and big-data-driven automation of socio-technical systems around, about, on, and in human beings. In the final iteration, the distributed experience machine would be ubiquitous and all-encompassing. In this imagined future, our entire environment would be a host of interconnected experience machines, what we'll call Experience Machine n.0 for short. Deployed and integrated incrementally over decades, people will be gradually prepared for and conditioned to accept how it reshapes our entire world and ultimately us.

If the Experience Machine n.0 strikes you as unrealistic, remember we're using it as a metaphor. It represents the combined effects of several real technological developments – all of which are gaining momentum today. We're not claiming that an actual variation of Nozick's thought experiment will be built. The dynamic relationships between social and technological tools and the complex systems within which they are nested and deployed are not easily reduced to a linear series of cause and effect relationships.[28] Nevertheless, reports ranging from the White House's "Internet of Things: Examining Opportunities and Challenges" to the Pew Center report "The Internet of Things Will Thrive by 2025" suggest that the Experience Machine n.0 metaphor dovetails closely with projected projects and scenarios.

Nozick invented the thought experiment to challenge hedonism. This theory stipulates that what matters most in evaluating the quality of our lives is our subjective experience of happiness. Many who have engaged his hypothetical have assumed people would only enter the experience machine if they freely choose to – that is, if they willingly embraced hedonism. The presumption of choice, however, deserves more scrutiny in the context of the Experience Machine n.0. It's hardly a "choice" to plug in anymore. It's almost a practical necessity. Fighting for the freedom to be off will be one of the most important battles of the twenty-first century.

How could the Experience Machine n.0 get built? In an essay titled "Utopia?" we identify several pathways.[29]

- One possibility is a *slippery slope*. Slippery slope refers to the process by which incremental steps down a sloped path can lead to tipping point – a slip and fall, so to speak.
- Another possibility is *engineered complacency*. Engineered complacency refers to one of the mechanisms for accelerating slippage down the slope. If we're engineered to avoid critically questioning innovation, it's hard for us to pay attention to whether change accords with values we deem important or to deliberate about strategies for avoiding change that threatens our values.
- Another possibility is the *aggregation of trillions of perfectly rational choices*. The aggregation of trillions of perfectly rational choices refers to the idea that the incremental steps we take down the slippery-sloped path often will be perfectly rational when evaluated one-by-one on their own seemingly independent terms. This frame evokes the tragedy of the commons, which we'll revisit momentarily.
- Yet another possibility is the *ubiquitous deployment of "smart" techno-social resource management systems for the purposes of maximizing human happiness at minimal social cost*. This possibility links means with ends specifying what type of infrastructure could support Experience Machine n.0.[30]

Each possibility captures part of the techno-social engineering story. Collectively, they highlight the key features of the path we seem to be on.

Humanity's Techno-Social Dilemma

Let's consider in more detail how the path towards Experience Machine n.0 could be fueled by the aggregation of trillions of perfectly rational choices. A helpful comparison is the tragedy of the commons, a famous environmental allegory. In ecologist and philosopher Garrett Hardin's original formulation, the tragedy of the commons involves a dilemma faced by a community of sheep herders who share a common pasture. The herders create a disaster by thinking and acting selfishly. Each one wants to use limited land to feed her own sheep. And so, each individual proceeds under the assumption that it's rational to increase the size of her own herd to capture the benefits of a pasture that everyone shares while only bearing a fraction of the costs that accrue as the common resource gets exhausted. These externalized costs add up, however, and over time the mad rush for resources leads to massive depletion.

Many believe that things could work out differently if the herders adopt a different outlook. To avoid disaster, they need to better understand their relationships to each other and their shared resources and develop governance strategies for cooperatively bringing about sustainable well-being.

The tragedy of the commons is shorthand for describing many problems that involve a shared resource, a lack of governance, rational, selfish behavior, external costs, and incremental individual actions that aggregate over time to disastrous, often irreversible, social consequences. One of the most pressing examples is climate change – a super-sized, global tragedy of the commons. Remarkably, it has taken decades for the public to appreciate that a large-scale climate change problem exists that humans bear responsibility for creating. Despite widespread scientific consensus for years, the mainstream media only recently have come around to gloomy portrayals of our greenhouse gas crisis. How to understand the relationships between key factors and how to respond to the problem remain highly contentious works-in-progress.

In the context of techno-social engineering of humans, we're calling the tragedy-of-the-commons-like problem *humanity's techno-social dilemma*. Like climate change, there are an incredible variety of small-scale decisions we each make about technology that seem, on their own terms, rational and unproblematic. Yet the increments aggregate, and, like individual herders who need to decide whether to add another sheep to their flock, we suffer if we fail to account for the systemic effects of our decisions, including the production of negative externalities and the impacts on ourselves and future generations.

Just because techno-social engineering is old news doesn't mean we've got a handle on it. Think about our dependence on carbon-based fuels. Relying on them has induced status quo bias (the tendency to accept how things currently are) and made it hard for many people to acknowledge that climate change poses an existential threat. It is hard to accept that lifestyles, industries, and politics need to change. Similar things can be said of technology and techno-social engineering.

One of the ways that humanity's techno-social dilemma differs from the tragedy of the commons is that we're frequently unsure if the problems associated with techno-social engineering are being imposed on us, whether we're electing to behave in short-sighted and insufficiently reflective ways, or whether both factors are in play.[31] Companies, institutions, and designers regularly treat us as *programmable objects* through hyper-personalized technologies that are attuned to our personal histories, present behaviors and feelings, and predicted futures. Although some finger wagging at powerful corporations is justified, let's not fool ourselves into believing we're innocent victims. The overly simplistic "us vs. them" dichotomy is an ideological trap. There's not always a bright line dividing either, and even when there is, we can't blame "them" fully. We're at fault, too. We choose to participate or choose not to choose and simply follow laid out plans as our default orientation. We adopt technology and mindlessly bind ourselves to the terms and conditions offered. We carry, wear, and attach devices to ourselves and our children, maintaining a connection and increasing our dependence. In doing so, we leash ourselves. As we feed on incremental satisfactions, curiosities, updates, and attention, we treat ourselves as grazing sheep and make ourselves more susceptible to conditioning. We outsource memory, decision-making, and even our interpersonal relations, among many other things. In constructing many different aspects of ourselves, ranging from intelligence to fitness, attentiveness to sociality, we rely on the techno-social engineers' tools to train ourselves, and, in doing so, let ourselves be trained. We both herd ourselves and get herded by others.[32]

Take social robots – think of an embodied and upgraded form of Alexa. When they go mainstream, our new "companions" will engage in highly intimate forms of techno-social engineering by inviting us to change our habits and altering how we relate with others. Will those changes be good or bad for us? It's hard to know without possessing a framework for identifying the central components of techno-social engineering and evaluating some of its normative consequences. We create that framework as we analyze the fundamental ideas associated with techno-social engineering, develop a theory about what makes contemporary techno-social engineering more troubling than previous versions, and propose tests to measure the impact of techno-social engineering upon our capabilities and dispositions. Finally, we offer suggestions for how to minimize undesirable techno-social engineering in the age of smart systems.

The Structure of the Book

This book is divided into four parts. In the first part, we use contemporary observations, thought experiments, and theoretical analysis of creep phenomena and slippery slope arguments to reflect on why it's so hard to understand techno-social engineering and come to grips with humanity's techno-social dilemma. Some reasons concern the difficulty of identifying the dominant logics driving techno-social systems. Others have to do with the incremental nature of techno-social change and the challenge of recognizing when gradual adoption hits a tipping point and becomes radical transformation.

We explore different ways that techno-social engineering programs our behavior. The mechanisms are complex, subtle, and often interwoven. Technologies afford different actors different capabilities, and it's all too easy to become enthralled with the positive outcomes of innovation while underestimating the cost of its downsides and being blindsided by them, and even ignoring the fact that downsides exist.

We open the second part of the book with a historical primer on the transformative power of tools. Then we use electronic contracts as a case study that illustrates why techno-social engineering isn't taken as seriously as it should be, despite having powerful effects. From there we explain how mind-extending technologies can invite others into our minds, incline us to outsource important aspects of thinking and acting, and even lead to worrisome cases of mind control. These discussions highlight how techno-social engineering can influence our beliefs, preferences, and even values. We then critically discuss why there's so much excitement about smart environments, why dominant discussions of these environments obscure important points about techno-social engineering, and why we may not be aware of how profoundly techno-social engineering is altering our social relationships.

The second part examines three formidable influences behind the growing scale, scope, influence, and power of techno-social engineering. First, instrumental reason is valorized to such a degree that it's become fetishized. Second, the scientific management of human beings in general and data-driven efficiency management in particular are rapidly spreading, and that shift is best understood as the extension of Taylorism[33] from the workplace context to nearly every environment within which we develop and live our lives. Third, it's rapidly becoming easier to design technologies that nudge us to go on auto-pilot and accept the cheap pleasure that comes from minimal thinking; smart environments are poised to significantly exacerbate the situation.

The third part of the book builds upon the first two. We propose a new framework for identifying and evaluating the techno-social engineering of humans: a techno-social engineering test that follows a two-step procedure. The first step is to run an experiment – an empirical experiment or a thought experiment – that determines if, in some context, humans are behaving like simple machines. In cases where humans are behaving like simple machines, and, in principle, could be substituted by them without anything significant being lost in translation, this step triggers a metaphorical yellow light that invites us to pause and look closer at what techno-social engineering is doing to us.[34]

While the first step is observational, the second step is evaluative. It assesses whether the techno-social engineering that's taking place in the environment studied by the first step is adversely impacting us. Think of this follow-up step as triggering either a metaphorical red light (i.e. stop, determine how deep the problem runs, and consider alternatives if possible) or a green light (i.e. conclude that no normative problem exists). We articulate the framework's conceptual foundation and offer representative examples of how it could be applied.

Our framework is inspired by the famous Turing test that focuses on a conversation between a human judge and an unseen test subject, which could be a human or a machine. The mathematician and pioneering computer scientist Alan Turing proposed an observational test to examine whether a machine can think. If a judge mistook a machine for a human after an extended conversation, the remarkable machine might deserve to be classified as intelligent; perhaps it could think. Over time, the Turing test established an elusive endpoint or finish line for some artificial intelligence researchers.[35]

While there has been considerable research and attention devoted to the computers involved in the Turing test race, designing intelligent machines is only half of the relevant picture. Another race is occurring on the other side of the Turing line, the human side.[36] Though there is much more to our analysis than intelligence, a bumper sticker for our book might very well display the following motto: We're not interested in the engineering of intelligent machines; we're interested in the engineering of unintelligent humans.

We develop a series of techno-social engineering tests to examine different aspects of intelligence: (a) mathematical computation, (b) random number generation, (c) rationality, and (d) common sense. All four are plausible tests to distinguish humans and machines. However, the first two don't implicate fundamental notions of what it means to be a human whereas the third and fourth do. For each test, we explain what we are testing, specify the sorts of stimuli an observer might use, and then discuss how to interpret the results. We examine thought experiments to tease out implications of the rationality and common-sense tests.

We next explain how free will is threatened by engineered determinism. Free will is a person's situated capability to reflect upon on and determine their beliefs, preferences, values, and intentions. Based on the fundamental role free will plays in human civilization and in our basic conceptions of moral responsibility, we advance a pragmatic wager to live our lives and structure society as if free will exists and matters, and then we propose techno-social engineering tests for free will.

We conclude the third part by critically considering the core normative question, *To what end?* Techno-social engineering cuts to the very heart of who we are as people and the kinds of worlds we want to live in. We are techno-social animals. What meaningfully distinguishes *homo sapiens* from all other species is our capability to imagine, conceptualize, and engineer our environment and ourselves. And what matters about being human is how we exercise such power over generations to collectively produce, cultivate, and sustain shared normative conceptions of humanity. *How should we exercise such power? How should we engineer our world and ourselves? What type of society should we build and sustain?* These are not new questions. Every generation faces them and is defined by how they answer. Twenty-first-century techno-social engineering frames these questions in a new and challenging light.

We conclude the book with prescriptions. Most fundamental is our call for freedom, which encompasses two related ideals:

1. Freedom from programming, conditioning, and control engineered by others. In our modern techno-social world, we call this the *freedom to be off.*
2. Freedom of will and practical agency. In our modern techno-social world, we call this *freedom from engineered determinism.*

After discussing these ideals, we consider a series of strategies to mitigate humanity's techno-social dilemma and redirect techno-social engineering to sustain humanity.

Given the rapid pace of technological development and the insidious ways techno-social engineering can mold us while going unnoticed and unchallenged, we couldn't think of a better time to write this book. We, the authors, will narrate events and analysis by using the plural pronoun 'we'. This is a literary device meant to connect authors and readers and not a naïve way of pretending that the two of us can speak universally. We're painfully aware that our collective voice is biased by our disciplinary training, a lifetime of living in the US (despite spending significant time traveling abroad), and the privileges that come from being white, middle-aged, and financially secure. We further realize that limiting the scope of our book to deep discussion of the core aspects of techno-social engineering means we'll pay scant attention to the digital divides that exist within countries and even neighborhoods. We'll infrequently discuss why resources, opportunities, and problems aren't the same for everyone and we'll only obliquely refer to the employment problems associated with automation. These occlusions matter. But the type of deep analysis we're providing requires unwavering focus.

PART I

CHAPTER I

Engineering Humans

Introduction

Techno-social engineering represents a constant in human history.[1] Our analysis begins with contemporary examples of well-intended teachers, administrators, and parents helping to create a surveillance culture. The mystery of why these caretakers fail to understand the full implications of their choices illuminates how techno-social engineering works.

Fitbits at Oral Roberts University

Controversy erupted at Oral Roberts University in 2016 after the press drew attention to a requirement that students purchase and wear Fitbit health trackers for a physical education class. The wrist-worn device counts the total number of steps students take each day and tracks compliance with a weekly requirement of 150 minutes' elevated heart rate. Tracked activity represents up to 20 percent of the physical education grade. As students are required to take physical education every semester, they wear the Fitbits throughout their entire college experience.

Commentators both criticized and defended the program. Many worried that that university intruded too deeply into the lives of its students, seeming to disregard student privacy concerns. Who gets access to what data? What can the data-gatherers do with the information that they collect? How long is student data stored? How effective are the university's information security measures? Did students give informed consent (which is to say, did they give their permission to participate in the physical education program *after* being provided with full disclosure of the possible benefits and risks)?

Others saw the privacy panic as unnecessary, at least in principle. Consent forms, clear policies, and administrative safeguards could address these concerns, with the right to opt out of the requirement.

Oral Roberts University had provided these safeguards. And prior to introducing the Fitbits, the university already monitored students' physical activity in different locations as part of its physical education class. It just relied on different technology: students generated data by hand on paper.

Since the university did its basic due diligence, the privacy criticism fizzled out. A representative of the Electronic Frontier Foundation, a civil liberties group, stated the Fitbit requirement didn't pose privacy problems so long as the mandated technology didn't gather geolocation data. From this perspective, a Fitbit is merely a more efficient electronic means for gathering the same data that Oral Roberts University has always collected. It does not disrupt long-established norms, and incoming students and their parents presumably knew exactly what the expectations were/are.[2]

We're uneasy with this equation and will explain why by comparing how different surveillance tools impact students.

Different Forms of Tracking and Their Consequences

Psychologist James A. Gibson used the term "affordance" to describe the different "possibilities for action" that different environments provide.[3] Just as "caves afford hiding and chairs afford sitting," different writing tools help shape different writing environments and the opportunities they make available.[4] When a technology is put into practice, different affordances can incline users to adopt different behaviors and pursue different paths of personal development. In this case, we should compare a Fitbit versus a handwritten journal.

Students who record their daily physical activities in a journal find the analog medium affords several steps that require time and effort, planning, and thinking. It can orientate students to record fitness data in ways that automated and unreflective inscription machines could never do. The medium directs student attention inwardly and outwardly and the recorded data can reveal more than meets the eye.

Think-and-record activities inspire self-reflection, interpersonal awareness, and judgment. These activities are valuable because they're linked to the exercise of free will and autonomy. Even writing environments with standardized features can expand a student's consciousness. Blank forms with pre-specified categories of activities to fill in, measures to report, or boxes to check all impose higher transaction costs than automated Fitbits. The key to techno-social engineering better humans just might lie in taking these slower tools more seriously.

Let's move the discussion to an applied level. Journaling isn't just about recording numbers. It's a form of social communication that sociologist Erving Goffman calls an impression-management "performance."[5] Students are tempted to perform when they are acutely aware that other people are observing them.[6] When required to track their own activities, students can become sensitized to the consequences that follow from their instructors and peers judging them in light of what they've written. This awareness, in turn, raises issues concerning how students wish to be seen and understood. Social skills, including discerning relevance and appropriateness, can be deepened when students carefully consider these matters.

One may worry that giving students the freedom to write down their fitness activities tempts them to behave unethically. After all, students who want to boost their grades could fudge what they report. This is a genuine dilemma. It occurs every time students ponder whether to report 21 minutes of jogging as 21 minutes, round down to 20, or exaggerate and report 25 or maybe even 30.

White lies and outrageous fabrications seem to be bad outcomes. After all, accurate reporting and telling the truth are paramount in many contexts where trust matters.[7] Nevertheless, it's dangerously myopic to place too much value on accurate and truthful data collection. These variables only partially account for what matters. Fetishizing them prevents us from appreciating the benefits of giving students opportunities to actively make independent decisions. To relate to others, you need to decide how you want to represent your accomplishments and failures, numerically quantifiable things in general, and even how you feel about information that can impact how others feel and what they believe. These activities are a basic part of a human life that's filled with social interactions.[8]

Think of the judgment involved when responding to someone who comes late to an appointment and asks how long you've been waiting. Whatever numeric answer you give – "I just got here" or "half an hour" – can depend less on numeric accuracy and more on whether you want to shame the tardy party. Or consider what happened when one of our elementary school age children came home with an assignment to record what she ate for a day. She condemned the assignment for not taking into account sufficient context and refused to include a dessert she ate on that day because she believed it would present a distorted picture of her general habits. There are many other examples where our representations of numbers convey aesthetic or ethical judgment, or influence how others make such judgments.

Returning to fitness tracking in educational settings, the point is that while some tools require users to have skin in the game, to engage and exercise judgment, others do not or to a lesser degree.[9] Studies make similar claims when differentiating taking notes in class by hand from typing them up.[10] Handwriting class notes requires students to exercise more judgment compared to typing. The intuition is rather straightforward: If you need to stop and think about what's worth writing down because you can't possibly capture everything verbatim, that momentary act of deliberation can facilitate learning. Handwriting notes appears to lead to greater comprehension of conceptual knowledge and in some studies, retention of facts as well.[11]

The change in data collection tools (from journal to Fitbit) are only part of the story. So much is hidden behind the veneer of the Fitbit being a technological upgrade, an innovation that affords simplicity and convenience. But the seemingly simple, efficient, and effortless data collection afforded by the Fitbit only seems simple to the student. A more complex system operates in the background.[12] Looking at the techno-social system running behind the scenes reveals a wide range of inputs, outputs, activities, agents, and points of control. Data-sharing practices shift from student-to-university to student-to-university-and-third-parties (Fitbit, advertisers, providers). Default settings are particularly relevant when set by educational institutions as the authority. This is because defaults, in general, are "sticky" – which is to say that, due to inertia, people often stick with them – and defaults set by authority figures can have extra psychological weight.

Surveillance Creep

The narrative that Oral Roberts University doesn't challenge traditional privacy norms by mandating Fitbit use obscures another problem: *surveillance creep*.

Surveillance creep is an offshoot of what engineers call *function creep*, the idea that a tool designed for one purpose ends up being used for another one. A classic is the driver's license. In a short period, the document went from being proof that you could legally drive a car to a credential for purchasing alcohol and getting into nightclubs; thanks to the post 9/11 passage of the Real ID Act (2005), licenses have become more secure and are used as counterterrorism measures for decreasing the chances that people on the terrorist watch list can board commercial airlines or enter federal buildings.[13]

Surveillance creep can take many forms. The gradual expansion of surveillance from one context to another. Or, the gradual expansion of the types of data collected in each context. Or, the gradual expansion of the use or sharing of that data. Surveillance creep is perceived as something happening on the side of those doing the surveillance (e.g. the National Security Agency or Facebook). It also can happen on the other side, as those being surveilled become accustomed to it. Their beliefs and preferences about surveillance technologies and surveillance more generally are shaped through experience. Educationally mandated surveillance programs do much more than get students accustomed to using digital technology for self-tracking purposes. They habituate students to submitting data to opaque third parties that exercise authority and have agendas that may diverge (now or in the future) from the best interests of those surveilled. Such programs also normalize arrangements that occur in noneducational contexts, such as insurance companies that want to set rates by having their customers provide self-tracking data. Or, we might turn to the employment sector, where such programs are pervasive.

Schools shape us, generation after generation.

The Oral Roberts University example is best understood as a puzzle piece, a step along a path. When asked to reflect on the success of the Fitbit program 18 months after it began, Michael Mathews, Associate Vice President of Technology and Innovation at Oral Roberts University, proudly proclaimed that the college is "ahead of the curve with electronic devices to allow students to succeed."[14] As it turns out, "more than 70 major American companies have initiated similar programs."[15] No matter how commonplace surveillance is, its use in the educational sector remains particularly important.

Where does the *educational assembly line start*? If public elementary school kids were asked to participate in a digital tracking program, would views about its significance change? It's easy to presume that college students, who are usually older than 18 and technically adults, are discriminating technology users who appreciate why bodily surveillance can mean different things in different contexts. But it seems presumptuous to expect the same level of awareness exists for elementary school children – a more vulnerable, inexperienced, and less autonomous group.

Bedtime and Bathtime Surveillance

For this section, we switch to a first-person narrative to describe a personal encounter one of us had with educational surveillance.

Last year, my first grader came home after school very excited. "Dad, I won. I mean, I've been picked. I get a new watch." "That's great," I said,

"What happened?" He quickly rattled off something about being one of the kids in his class who was selected to wear a new watch for gym class. A day or two later, I received the following letter in the mail from the school district.

Dear Parents/Guardians,

Your child has been selected to be among the first group of students to participate in an exciting new initiative made possible by our recent $1.5 million PEP Grant.

We have added ACTIVITY WATCHES to the K-12 physical education program so that we can assess how the PEP grant impacts students' physical activity in [the school district]. We are periodically selecting groups of students at random to wear activity watches on their wrists to track daily activity time.

One of the goals of our program is to see that students get the recommended amount of physical activity each day (60 minutes). As part of a quality physical education program, the use of activity watches can motivate students to challenge themselves to become more physically active.

For the students selected to participate in this first group, we will be distributing activity watches starting January 13th for students to wear before, during, after school and over the weekend until Tuesday, January 21st. We ask that students do not take off the watch once it's on their wrist. They should sleep, even shower with the watch in place. There are no buttons to push or need to touch the watch, as it is pre-programmed to record and store each day of activity time.

At the end of the 9 days, each family will be able to access a report of their child's activity, and you are welcome to consult with your child's physical education teacher about what you learn and ways to further support your child's physical health and fitness. In addition, the group's combined information will be used to provide baseline data on student physical activity in [the school district].

In closing, I invite you to join me and your child's physical education teacher in motivating your family to participate in physical activity together. If you should have any questions about this new technology, please do not hesitate to contact your child's physical education teacher.

Yours in health,
XXXX XXXXXXXX
Supervisor of Health, Physical Education
and Nursing Services

What's your reaction to this note? I ask you to think about it for a moment before I tell you my reaction because mine was atypical for my community. When I read the letter, I went ballistic. Initially, I wondered about various privacy issues: who? what? where? when? how? and why? with regard to collection, sharing, use, and storage of data about kids. The letter did not even vaguely suggest that parents and their children could opt out, much less that their consent was required. Even if it had, it couldn't be informed consent because there were so many questions left unanswered.

I also wondered whether the school district had gone through some form of institutional review board (IRB) process. Had someone, anyone, considered the ethical questions? I read the letter again but got stuck on "We ask that students do not take off the watch once it's on their wrist. They should sleep, even shower with the watch in place." Seriously, bathtime and bedtime surveillance!

The letter made me think of one of those Nigerian bank scam emails that go straight into my spam folder. Such trickery! I thought. I remembered how my son had come home so excited. The smile on his face and joy in his voice were unforgettable. It was worse than an email scam. They had worked him deeply, getting him hooked. He was so incredibly happy to have been selected, to be part of this new fitness program, to be a leader. How could a parent not be equally excited? Most were, but not me.

I contacted someone at the PTA, spoke with the Supervisor of Health, wrote a letter to the School District Superintendent, and eventually had some meetings with the General Counsel for the school district. The program is like so many being adopted in school districts across the country: well-intentioned, aimed at a real problem (obesity), financed in an age of incredibly limited and still shrinking budgets, and elevated by the promise of efficiency that accompanies new technologies.

What caught people's attention most was a line from the letter I sent to the Superintendent: "I have serious concerns about this program and worry that the school district hasn't fully considered the implications of implementing a child surveillance program like this." No one previously had called it "child surveillance." All of a sudden, the creepiness of bathtime and bedtime surveillance sunk in. Naturally, this triggered familiar privacy concerns.

The term "surveillance" generated a visceral reaction and was an effective means for getting people to stop and think. Up to that point, no one seemed to have done so for several obvious reasons. People trust the school district and love technology. The salient problem of obesity weighs heavily on the community; activity watches seem to be a less intrusive means for addressing the problem. People obtain information about their activity levels and then are better able to adjust their behaviour and improve fitness. They can do so on their own, as a family, or in consultation with the physical education teacher. Plus, it was funded by a federal grant. The activity watch program presents substantial upside with little or no downside, an easy cost-benefit analysis. For most people, it seems like one of those rare win-win scenarios. After my intervention, very little changed; better disclosure and informed consent apparently would fix everything.

These limited privacy concerns fall woefully short of acknowledging the full power of techno-social engineering. The 24/7 data collection and the lack of informed consent are real problems. But the stakes run much deeper.

The most pernicious aspect of the program is the unexamined techno-social engineering of children – their indoctrination into a *"hidden curriculum."*[16] The Department of Education, the school district, and other program supporters understand that they are engaged in social engineering in the sense that they use the activity watches and corresponding surveillance to shape cultural attitudes and individual preferences regarding fitness and activity. That much is transparent. The program aims to generate and provide information about activity levels and fitness, and thereby enable better choices. The activity watch program has a laudable intended purpose (to combat obesity by encouraging more exercise) and it employs seemingly laudable means. The program uses nudges that preserve autonomy rather than more restrictive alternatives, like policies that mandate compliance.

This picture is not complete, however. It's a stretch to say that the program fully respects the autonomy of potential activity watch users. Without an easy opt-out, the ethical nudges (as defined by behavioral economist Richard Thaler and pre-eminent legal scholar Cass Sunstein) risk becoming paternalistic shoves that allow others' preferences to have significant sway over our personal decisions.[17] With that in mind, let's probe deeper into how much freedom the students really had.

Let's think about obesity and nudges in a broader context. Doing so will give us greater insight into the activity watch program. Obesity is a significant public health problem in many parts of the United States and around the world. It's characterized as one of the most significant modern public health problems and puts a serious strain on medical systems. Unfortunately, reducing obesity is hard to do and policy interventions to combat it can be contentious. Former New York City Mayor Michael Bloomberg learned this lesson the hard way back in 2012 when he proposed banning the sale of sugary drinks (in select locations), like soda, in serving sizes that exceeded 16 ounces. Bloomberg saw the initiative as a helpful nudge: consumers could still purchase as much soda as they wanted; they simply would have to put in the effort to carry multiple cups or cans. Critics, however, viewed Bloomberg's plan as the embodiment of an overly meddlesome nanny state that is intent on regulating ever more aspects of our private lives.[18]

Schools aren't just using fitness nudges to combat obesity.[19] They're also directing their attention to cafeterias. For example,

> [the] Cornell Center for Behavioral Economics in Child Nutrition Programs (BEN) has a long-term program in place for studying nudge initiatives to help people make better food choices. BEN has proposed numerous changes to school cafeterias as part of the Smarter Lunchroom Movement. In particular, BEN's work has influenced [former] First Lady Michelle Obama's initiative to solve the childhood obesity epidemic, as her group worked with BEN through the Chef's Move to Schools program. BEN's proposals for lunchroom nudges include relabelling vegetable choices with attractive names, serving fruit in attractive colourful bowls, placing healthy foods within easy reach and early in the food line, and placing problematic foods so that it takes a bit of effort to choose them.[20]

Critics argue that it's a mistake to generalize from successes experienced in the highly particularized environment of a school cafeteria to more broad-based enthusiasm for using nudges to promote healthy eating. Indeed, some have argued that the very idea of turning to nudges to remedy poor eating habits perpetuates the culture of victim-blaming. It may abstract away issues that concern food systems and focus, instead, on matters at the individual level, like personal vices (e.g. gluttony) and weak willpower. For starters, healthy food typically is more expensive than less nutritious food and no amount of nudging can make that price difference go away. Furthermore, the grocery stores found in some neighborhoods make it hard to shop for the food that health experts recommend. They simply don't carry it and nudge literature isn't going to alter how management selects inventory. As political theorist Evgeny Morozov sardonically states: "For what else could possibly explain . . . health problems but . . . personal failings? It's certainly not the power of food companies or class-based differences or various political and economic injustices."[21]

In principle, it isn't mandatory to participate in the activity watch program. But in practice, it's not a coincidence that nearly everyone does. There are a host of plausible reasons that can explain the mass conformity. For starters, the default for enrollment is set at "participation" for selected students. People tend to stick with the defaults they're initially presented with. This default is made especially sticky by how children and parents are informed about the program.

Children are told they've been selected for a special program and will get a new wearable device, while parents get a letter in the mail. After both parties receive this information, the path of opting out requires two cumbersome steps. First, parents need to have a difficult conversation with their children. These kids like the idea of being characterized as special. They enjoy fashionable, new technology. Such preferences make it hard for parents to ask their kids not to participate in the activity watch program. Friends opt into the program, triggering peer pressure, which is intensified because the school, a looming authority figure, sanctions the endeavor. Second, parents can't just snap their fingers and make the problem go away. They must inform school officials that their child will not participate, which can be a challenging conversation on a sensitive topic. Not every administrator or teacher likes to debate about hidden costs that are hard to quantify.

Such hidden costs – which no one considering the activity watch program voiced – include the matter of how the program shapes the preferences of a generation of children to accept a 24/7 wearable surveillance device that collects and reports data. Even if autonomy and choice are preserved, the subtle influence on beliefs and preferences still shape a host of future choices. These claims are not in the promotional material. Nor could they be. School administrators didn't consider these issues. Can you imagine the uproar if the school had said that the activity watch program would increase tolerance of surveillance, manipulation, and nudging?

The same argument applies to Oral Roberts University's physical education class. Students who are required to use Fitbits during college may be more likely to accept surveillance in other contexts, perhaps with the same or with other types of surveillance devices. This hypothesis requires empirical testing. Perhaps college kids are more sophisticated, have privacy concerns, and are capable of reasoning about the appropriateness of surveillance in different contexts. Maybe we can assume that college students don't have easily engineered beliefs and preferences. Perhaps they'll quickly recognize and perhaps resist surveillance creep. It's a stretch to make the same assumptions for elementary school children.

It is only in isolation that incremental steps of this sort seem justifiable on a constrained cost-benefit calculus that only considers immediate and obvious costs and benefits. To be clear, the bottom line isn't to reject activity watches in public schools. They may be effective in combating obesity and encouraging fitness. The key point is that touting this utility fails to consider the cumulative cost of many interdependent incremental steps. Privacy is but one victim of death by a thousand cuts.

A school district that chooses this path ought to do so more carefully, with an awareness of and open dialogue about how the technology affects the children as human beings. As I said to the General Counsel for the school district, this is a decent teaching opportunity. Fitness and privacy might be joined as students learn about the technology and their relationships to it and to others (the school, the Department of Education, device manufacturers, various third parties including aggregators and advertisers). They might even be introduced to old alternatives, like a handwritten journal.

Returning to the Oral Roberts University example, the university could combine the fitness tracking tools. It could require students to use a fitness tracking device that collects data, while also expecting them to write reports about the collected data in a journal. This two-step process would be more comprehensive and accurate than journaling alone. It also gives the students an opportunity to reflect on their performance and freedom to decide how and what to communicate to their instructors and peers. As a deeper exercise, students might be asked to reflect on the data, what it says and doesn't say about them.[22]

Fitness tracking devices, along with other tools for monitoring and recording healthy activities, are widely used in the "employee wellness" programs that are cropping up around the United States and abroad. These programs run the gamut from incentivizing losing weight and quitting smoking to improving employee morale. Vendors appear to be successful at selling these programs by telling companies that less illness results in employers paying less for the health insurance that they partially subsidize.

Unfortunately, as philosophy professor Gordon Hull and law professor Frank Pasquale argue in "Toward a Critical Theory Of Corporate Wellness," "the programs have routinely failed to generate any substantial impact on ... health, reported well-being, or medical costs."[23] This is insidious. If the programs don't produce the intended results, why hasn't a bottom-line-driven corporate culture jumped ship? Hull and Pasquale propose that these "counterproductive" initiatives are more than meets the eye. They're attractive for reasons that have nothing to do with enhancing employee health or lowering health costs, per se.

As Hull and Pasquale see it, wellness programs have an ulterior motive and that's conditioning employees to be submissive and hyper-vigilant of the "costs they may impose on their benefactors." It might seem overly cynical to portray management as engineering the employees to be ever-obedient and ever fearful of looking out for themselves at a company's expense. But Hull and Pasquale aren't demonizing managers for being ruthless and authoritarian. Instead, they contextualize the logic of employee management programs as a manifestation of the broader ideology of "neoliberalism."

Neoliberalism is a complex topic. At its core, what Hull and Pasquale have in mind is the conviction running through some governmental and industrial sectors that privatized market forces are best equipped to provide public good services. Within this worldview, individuals are held morally and financially accountable for making good choices, and good choices are defined as ones that minimize an individual's exposure to risky activities that have expensive consequences which they can't afford to pay for. The oil that greases the wheels of the neoliberal system, Hull and Pasquale argue, is citizens who perceive the big problems of life, including illness, to be the result of personal decisions, and not systematic problems that taint governance mechanisms. Workplaces have become training grounds for shaping citizens that internalize a you're-on-your-own ideology.

CHAPTER 2

Cogs in the Machine of Our Own Lives

Introduction

The previous chapter highlighted cases where well-intentioned educators impose techno-social engineering on students. In stark contrast, this chapter addresses examples where it is self-directed. We focus on delegating physical, cognitive, emotional, and ethical labor to a third party, often through technical devices, systems, and applications. This is known as outsourcing.

Rational people choose to outsource for lots of reasons, including to save time and other limited resources. From an efficiency-oriented perspective, outsourcing can be a beneficial process. A slightly wider lens shows how outsourcing may have unintended consequences and trade-offs.

Outsourcing has six existential characteristics.

First, *passivity*. As we accept assistance, we lessen the personal effort needed to accomplish a goal. As effort diminishes, passivity takes hold. At a certain level, we become akin to spectators rather than active participants.

Second, *decreased agency*. We participate in less of the process than we would if we performed it ourselves. Less effort results in a corresponding reduction in our experience of the action itself. Our behavior becomes less intentional, and some measure of control is lost.

Third, *decreased responsibility*. By abdicating control over a process, we can become less culpable for how things turn out. This is a double-edged sword. The very reason that we can become less blameworthy can also leave us less entitled to feel proud of positive results. When something amazing happens through collaboration, nobody deserves all the credit.

Fourth, *increased ignorance*. Delegation of tasks can limit our understanding of how a process works. Even if proxies seem reliable, we don't know the full extent of how they work on our behalf. In the case of technology, outsourcing happens by translating our requests into algorithmic or mechanical processes that computers – which don't always behave the way we do – can perform.

Fifth, *detachment*. Diminished participation leads to disengagement. The more intense the detachment, the less intimate an experience becomes. At the extreme, less intimacy results in alienation.

Sixth, *decreased independence*. When outsourcing becomes habitual, we become dependent on a third party for getting stuff done. At the extreme, dependency can result in deskilling. We can forget how to perform a task or become less capable of doing it. Or, we can lose the motivation to increase our knowledge and skills.

Outsourcing affects more than how a task is completed. When deciding whether to outsource, we need to consider whether it's worth losing agency, responsibility, control, intimacy, and, possibly, knowledge and skill. We address these issues by critically discussing a specific form of outsourcing: outsourced navigation.

Actuated Navigation

Max Pfeiffer, a researcher in the Human-Computer Interaction Group at the University of Hanover in Germany, ran an experiment where he manipulated how students navigated through a park. By stimulating their Sartorius muscles with electrical current, he directly guided their turns, nudging movements to the left and right. While this scenario sounds like invasion of the body snatchers, apparently the combination of existing smartphone technology and electrodes is all that's needed to inaugurate an innovative "pedestrian navigation paradigm".

Pfeiffer successfully assumed the role of an aggressive GPS device, but his prototype isn't ready to compete with Waze (yet). The successful proof of concept makes it hard to avoid speculating about future, fully automated, consumer versions of the technology.

Pfeiffer and his collaborators imagine a range of socially beneficial applications. Their vision revolves around three types of experience: multitasking, dispensing precise geolocation information, and coordinating group movement. These are embodied in several appealing scenarios including enhanced fitness (runners trying out new routes and optimizing existing routines), novel sports (coaches literally choreographing how their teams move), improved job performance (firefighters effortlessly zeroing in on danger zones), upgraded crowd control (concert goers' ability to evacuate in an orderly and calm manner if an emergency arises), and low transaction cost navigation.

Let's confront the basic moral and political question of outsourcing. To narrow our focus, consider the case of guided strolling. On the plus side, Pfeiffer suggests that senior citizens appreciate help returning home when they're feeling discombobulated, tourists will enjoy seeing more sights while with the pedestrian version of cruise control, and friends, family, and co-workers will get more out of life by safely throwing themselves into engrossing, peripatetic conversation. What of the potential downside?

Critics identified several concerns with using current forms of GPS technology. They have reservations about devices that merely cue us with written instructions, verbal cues, and maps that update in real-time. Technology writer and philosopher Nicholas Carr warns of our suscept-ibility to automation bias and complacency, psychological outcomes that can lead people to do foolish things, like ignoring common sense and driving a car into a lake.[1] Philosophers Hubert Dreyfus and Sean Kelly[2] lament that it's "dehumanizing" to succumb to GPS orientation because it "trivializes the art of navigation" and leaves us without a rich sense of where we are and where we're going. Technical fixes can correct the mistakes that would guide zombified walkers into open sewer holes and oncoming traffic. However, the value of knowing (and even not knowing) where one stands in relation to our physical environment and to others remains a more vexing existential and social problem. Being lost and struggling with the uncertainty may provide us with opportunities to develop our-selves and our relationships.[3]

Pfeiffer himself recognizes this dilemma. He told *Wired* that he hopes his technology can help liberate people from the tyranny of walking around with their downcast eyes buried in smartphone maps. He admitted that "when freed from the responsibility of navigating . . . most of his volunteers wanted to check email as they walked."[4] At stake is the risk of uninten-tionally turning the current dream of autonomous vehicles into a model for locomotion writ large. While the hype surrounding driverless cars focuses on many intended benefits (fewer accidents, greener environmental impact, less congestion, furthering the shift to communal transportation), we can't lose sight of the fact that consumers are wooed with utopian images of time-management. Freed from the burden of needing to con-centrate on the road, we're sold on the hope of having more productive commutes. Instead of engaging in precarious (and often illegal) acts of distracted driving, we'll supposedly tend to our correspondence obligations in a calm and civilized way. Hallelujah! We'll text, email, and post on social media in our "private office on wheels" just as if we were on a bus, train, or plane. All without having to deal with pesky strangers.

Pfeiffer's research demonstrates that a designer's intentions don't determine how consumers use technology.[5] In a world where social and professional expectations pressurize people to be online, the temptation to exploit newly found schedule openings for this purpose will be immense. When industries get a sense that people have more time to attend to work-related activities, expectations will ratchet up accordingly. This pressure disincentivizes us from pursuing offline lives and makes a mockery of the cliché "if you don't like it, don't use it." Just as historical decisions about building infrastructure to support a suburban culture have made walking to work less tenable for many people, shifts in the digital ecosystem can make it harder to take an enjoyable offline stroll.

The prospect of being further chained to our devices is disturbing. The thought of *outsourcing our physical abilities to free up attention* raises a more disconcerting problem – one with deep psychological and metaphysical consequences. "Actuated navigation" isn't just a process that turns voluntary into involuntary behavior. If done habitually, it's an invitation to dissociate from our physicality and objectify our bodies as mere commodities. To see why, let's consider some basic ways bodies and technologies interact.

Bodies, Technology, and Outsourcing Creep

Many people rely on prosthetics, such as canes, walkers, wheelchairs, and artificial limbs, to move freely. These deeply embodied tools expand a person's sense of agency. They are particularly powerful when society commits the resources for accessibility and embraces a sense of justice and equality for anyone relying on them.

Let's approach this in experiential terms. As the French philosopher Maurice Merleau-Ponty argues, a blind person can't use a cane to see colors.[6] The act of tapping just can't reveal how gray a street looks – at least, not yet. Technology can expand perceptual abilities by "extending the scope and active radius of touch and providing a parallel to sight." Indeed, the person who becomes expert at using a cane experiences the stick as a direct extension of being, a sense organ that's attuned to the world, not an external object that requires attention-grabbing, mechanical movements to master.

A seasoned driver feels that a car is an extension in a similar way. She gets in, cranks up the tunes, navigates on the highway while singing along, and arrives at her destination delighted that she became one with the vehicle and intuitively exhibited skill. By contrast, a beginner's journey involves deliberating and a pronounced sense of separateness. Beyond needing to pause to consider who gets the right of way at a four-way stop, she needs to engage in all kinds of abstract reflections – like explicitly focusing on putting her hands on the 9–3 position before starting to drive (10–2 is pre-airbag).

The prosthetic and driving examples show that we're quite adept at using technology to expand our embodied relation to the world and with it our sense of identity. In a suburban area, for example, it's easier for the person with vehicle access to see herself as independent than it is for someone who depends on public transportation (where schedules are set by others). While this case may be objectionable from a moral point of view (not everyone can afford to opt out of public transportation, and it may be environmentally wrong not to use it), the basic phenomenology of enlarged capacities shows that it's a mistake to see so-called "cyborg" fusions as inherently alienating.[7]

What is different between outsourcing walking and getting around with the help of a cane or car? That's easy to answer in the case of malicious hacking. If a third party engaged in a version of Pfeiffer's experiment that enabled her to take over our body and move us in directions that we didn't want to go, our autonomy would be violated. But if we freely choose a destination and actuated navigation helped us get there straightaway without any imposed stops, our autonomy apparently would be respected.

Turning to outsourced walking for the purpose of freeing up our attention is an act that so strongly privileges mental activity that it effectively treats the body as nothing more than an impediment that needs to be overcome. Our bodily engagement with the physical world becomes seen as a logistical and navigational transaction cost to be minimized, even eliminated if possible.

By this logic, why surrender only a single physical ability? Why not outsource other movements that prevent us from being totally engrossed in intellectual activities: chewing, showering, shaving are nothing but corporeal subversions that get in the way of more elevated affairs. Perhaps even the effort to raise our cheeks to smile is a waste. Why not eliminate it and purchase an app that triggers the requisite movements when it detects patterns that make smiling appropriate? Where do we draw the line, and why? Is smiling an essential component of our unique identities? Consider Batman's enemy the Joker, a villain who appears existentially menacing because his face is forever frozen and incapable of fully conveying expression.

Some of you might find outsourcing as much bodily movement as possible attractive, and yearn for the day that consciousness can be uploaded to a machine. For some "transhumanists" this is indeed the moment we finally can evolve beyond recognizable human limits and start living the good life.[8] Futurist Raymond Kurzweil, Director of Engineering at Google, predicts that by 2030 "our brains will be able to connect directly to the cloud" and not too long after "we'll also be able to fully back up our brains."[9] We encourage supporters to consider that, although it may not be immediately obvious, the optimizing logic that makes it attractive to outsource away bodily functions applies to mental operations, too. Once the outsourcing spiral commences, we may regret where it ends.

Others will feel diminished by auto-pilot dualism that makes our bodies mere cogs in the machine of our mental life. If you fall into this camp, it's empowering to move beyond gut feelings and vague impressions of discomfort and figure out exactly what's the basis of your opposition.

There are many ways a purely mental life could be lived. In ancient Greece, for example, Aristotle depicted God as an immaterial Prime Mover who only thinks about his own eternal thinking.[10] For our purposes, a decent place to start is *The Matrix*. Imagine human bodies are tethered to vats while human minds live virtual lives in a programmed simulation of our current world. In this scenario, human beings still needed to grapple with the same physical interactions that we currently do. They climb stairs. They open doors. They cook food.

Why does this familiar narrative persist? A compelling explanation is that the programmers recognized the structure is necessary for our mental life to be satisfying and meaningful. The optimizing logic we've discussed in this chapter persists. If so, there would be a desire for further reductions in transaction costs and more easily obtained bliss. Where would that lead us? A vicious circle where outsourcing occurs in the virtual world? An ever narrowing spiral? But to what end?

If autonomy is retained, we presumably still have decisions to make about our purely mental lives. If we retain free will, we still presumably must experiment with different kinds of experiences to form our preferences. We presumably must learn to develop interesting beliefs and contested knowledge. But making decisions, experimenting, and learning (among other mental processes) are costly endeavors. Optimizing logic would seem to press toward minimizing and if possible eliminating these costs.

To what end? The answer: cheap bliss.

CHAPTER 3

Techno-Social Engineering Creep and the Slippery-Sloped Path

The first two chapters painted a vivid picture of techno-social engineering creep. We showed how easy it can be for surveillance practices and out-sourcing decisions to expand their reach, increase their intensity, and magnify their consequences. All of this suggests a slippery-sloped path to a rather bleak world.

Let's think a bit more about what the path looks like. In Chapter 1, we outlined a surveillance trajectory that runs from elementary school to college. Similar dynamics also exist in high school. Consider the debate over Google integrating its software and hardware into the daily activities of primary and secondary schools across the country. Some applaud the public-private partnership for reducing how much schools need to pay for information communication technology.[1] Others, however, raise privacy concerns. Some worry about Google finding a loophole that will allow them to mine minors' data and profit from these privacy violations.[2] And some worry about Google making it too easy for graduating students to transfer their school data into private Google accounts that they'll use as adults.

These concerns only capture part of the techno-social engineering problem. Think about how private companies build brand loyalty among impressionable youth. Is there any doubt that Google, like Coca-Cola, aims to engineer children's preferences and create lifelong consumers? When corporations subsidize technology (and other goods and services) for schools, people get excited that immediate costs for schools – and by extension taxes – can be lowered. Educators, parents, and children must pay attention to the hidden costs of such arrangements. What gets left out of the cost-benefit analysis is what the corporations are paying for, which is access to the minds of children. Imagine if school districts prohibited branding on goods and services procured for students. We doubt companies still would be willing to give steep discounts. There's no free lunch. Not even in schools.[3]

Even if schools improved considerably, parents still would need to critically examine how they normalize surveillance. As Deborah Lupton, author of *The Quantified Self: A Sociology of Self-Tracking Cultures*, observes, many parents don't think twice about subjecting their unborn and young children to social and corporate surveillance. They post pictures and videos online of everything from ultrasounds to childbirth and all kinds of childhood milestones. "By the time an eight-year-old asks for a Facebook account," Lupton writes, "there already are plenty of images of them on that platform posted by their proud parents."[4]

Lupton is pointing out how parents – even well-intended ones – model poor behaviour for their kids to follow. By setting a tone, parents invite their offspring to develop similar preferences and form similar expectations. When parents frequently post information about their kids on social media and then stop their sons and daughters from getting a Facebook or Instagram account, they seem hypocritical.

As if this wasn't enough, "quantified baby" (yes, this is a real term) products are starting to go mainstream.[5] A "smart sock" called the Owlet lets you monitor a baby's heart rate, oxygen levels, and skin temperature. If your infant rolls over, you won't have to worry about checking up on her too infrequently. You'll get a cellphone alert and hopefully respond in plenty of time. Only time will tell whether such outsourcing will contribute to parents becoming less attentive than they should be and expecting technology to provide more care than it can offer.

A new technological twist on an old story also is taking place. Parents have always been worried about their kids making bad decisions, falling in with the wrong crowd, and getting hurt. They make tough calls about what rules to impose and how to ensure obedience. They grapple with the fact that policing curfew is a breeze compared to figuring out what happens when there's no adult supervision around and they can't verify who is where and doing what.

In the past, parents could deal with these issues by resorting to prying – perhaps eavesdropping or maybe going through a diary. The growing consumer surveillance industry makes these approaches seem quaint. They offer parents new, cutting-edge tools that (supposedly) solve their problems through software. Simply install inexpensive applications on your child's computer or smartphone, sit back, and let the technology do all the work to track your child's communication and comings and goings. Software can create automated reports about what your child is saying on email, texts, and social media and establish safe zones where your kids can travel. Through geolocation tracking, parents can get GPS verified alerts when their kids go too far, literally speaking. This is parental outsourcing on steroids.

Also, as a sign of our technologically changing times, the phrase "helicopter parent" is becoming passé. "Drone parent" is now part of the vernacular. Drone parents use surveillance technologies to monitor their kids, create a somewhat false sense of independence, and jump in when situations call for direct intervention. Heated debate on this issue erupted after a dad allowed his 8-year-old daughter to walk to school "alone" while trailing her every move through a drone's eye in the sky.[6]

In short, as innovation makes snooping even easier, it becomes increasingly tempting to become panoptical parents. Distraught guardians who monitor their kids say that the digital age changed what it's like to grow up, and not for the better. There's one-click access to inappropriate information, cyberbullying, sexting, and all kinds of ways to behave online that can ruin a reputation. With such high stakes, who can afford to rely on what their kids are willing to say about their personal lives? Kids may have a strong incentive to lie. And it's incredibly difficult to have cross-generational conversations about intimate affairs.

These valid concerns can obscure how constant observation does more than limit inappropriate boundary-testing and risk-taking. Too much surveillance and outsourcing can get in the way of children developing autonomy and cultivating a sense of personal accountability. If kids aren't given opportunities to learn to take responsibility for following rules and disobeying them, it's hard to see how they can possibly grow up to be responsible citizens.[7] As we shall see, parenting is one of many difficult Goldilocks-style balancing acts that modern techno-social engineering tools and practices can challenge.

Slippery Slope Arguments

Having outlined more aspects of surveillance and outsourcing creep, we now examine the very logic of creep itself. Discussions of creep resemble a form of argument called the "slippery slope." The conventional slippery slope argument expresses concern over seemingly small actions having very bad consequences. The slippery slope evokes a person taking a first step on a precarious hillside and then accidentally slipping to her doom. Here's a casebook example. It's a fallacious argument that's used to support the contentious, pro-NRA conclusion that society shouldn't ban assault rifles.

1. If the law bans one type of gun, such as the assault rifles that are repeatedly used in mass shootings, then soon all guns will be rendered illegal, except for use by special authorities like law enforcement and soldiers.

2. Shortly after the firearm ban is enacted, other Constitutional rights will be stripped away.

3. By destroying the Constitution, freedom and democracy will be obliterated.

4. To avoid these terrible outcomes, we should resist contemporary attempts to ban assault rifles.

Premises 1, 2, and 3 aim to persuade by dramatically expanding the set of consequences that flow from the initial act of banning assault rifles. In all three claims, the causal mechanism is assumed and not specified. In other words, the argument doesn't spell out how the transition from Point A to Points B, C, and D will occur. It's as if policy functions like a set of dominos that will fall once the first one tile gets pushed.

Richard Thaler and Cass Sunstein, scholars of behavioral economics and the law respectively, address slippery slope arguments in the final chapter of their much-discussed book, *Nudge*. Their analysis is important because slippery slope arguments arise in debates about many different types of technology.[8] Thaler and Sunstein characterize it as the weakest anti-nudge counterargument and insist that the skepticism it conveys should be disregarded. All slippery slope arguments fail, they insist, because the positions are guided by wildly speculative hypotheses and don't directly address, through tried and true cost-benefit analysis, the shortcomings of the individual policy interventions that are under consideration.

In his essay "Fear of Falling," Thaler is even more dismissive.

> [Y]ou may not be familiar with bathmophobia, which is an abnormal and persistent fear of stairs or steep slopes, or a fear of falling. Less well known is "nudgephobia," . . . which is the fear of being gently nudged down a slope while standing on a completely flat surface . . . Slope-mongering is a well-worn political tool used by all sides in the political debate to debunk any idea they oppose . . . The argument is perfectly versatile. If we allow (blacks, women, gays . . .) into the military then (fill in the awful but inevitable consequence here). If we allow free speech then we will give voice to the next Hitler . . . Instead of slope-mongering we should evaluate proposals on their merits.[9]

We understand the concern about "slope-mongering" but still reject Thaler's claim that slippery slope arguments are a mere phobia rooted in unfounded speculation. Slippery slope arguments can take many forms. They aren't all caricatures, like the portrayals above of guns, armies, and free speech. Good slippery slope arguments are analytically useful.

Good slippery slope arguments have two essential features. First, they explicitly specify plausible mechanisms that could drive slippage from one step to another. Second, they rigorously explain why the mechanisms deserve due consideration. When used properly, slippery slope considerations elevate dynamic over static analysis and highlight how complex and nuanced interactions drive transformative social change. To see what we mean, consider GPS technology one more time.[10] Sunstein claims:

> GPS . . . [is] a prime nudge, because it helps people to find the right route while also allowing them to go their own way. But there is a downside, which is that use of the GPS can make it harder for people to know how to navigate the roads. Indeed, London taxi drivers, not relying on the GPS, have been found to experience an alteration of their brain functions as they learn more about navigation, with actual changes in physical regions of the brain. As the GPS becomes widespread, that kind of alteration will not occur, thus ensuring that people cannot navigate on their own. This is an unusually dramatic finding, to be sure, but it raises the possibility that when people rely on defaults or on other nudges, rather than on their own active choices, some important capacities will fail to develop or may atrophy. This is the anti-developmental consequence of some helpful nudges, including the GPS itself.[11]

GPS technology is widespread and the utility associated with real-time navigation has lent itself to extensions that go well beyond providing people with logistical help. Indeed, our analysis of GPS creep and its potential effects in the previous chapters show why loss of navigational skill, important as it may be, is far from the only trade-off that's worth considering. As we all know, GPS performs many other functions, ranging from geo-targeted advertising and tracking to find-a-friend apps. GPS is even a fundamental driver of surveillance creep. Just ask the police, Facebook, insurance companies, or worried panoptical parents.

Is it fair to describe GPS creep as a form of slippery slope? Absolutely. In all likelihood, it would have been much more difficult to persuade people to accept GPS-enabled find-a-friend apps if that service had been the first commercialized GPS application. Real-time navigation in cars paved the way for normalizing persistent collection and use of geolocation data on devices like smartphones.

GPS creep demonstrates the flaws in Thaler's and Sunstein's advice. Their myopic view focuses on isolated and independent technological steps; and this makes it hard to detect and evaluate the convergence of complementary technologies (e.g. GPS, smartphones, mobile apps) and the expansion of practices and beliefs from one domain to another. One area of convergence that we'll discuss later in the book involves GPS, automation, and the path toward intelligent transportation systems. Moving along the path from GPS to self-driving cars is seen as a matter of technological feasibility and economic progress, but it's also about normalizing geolocation tracking and automation as well as outsourcing moral, economic, and political decisions. Intelligent transportation systems are poised to use vast amounts of data from surveillance to make morally relevant decisions about how our traffic will be prioritized. Whether all the affected stakeholders will have a voice in the outcome remains to be seen.

From Activity Watches to Brain Scans?

Let's consider one more case where slippery slope arguments might be useful to get a handle on the future. Imagine a School Board meeting where educators and parents meet to discuss how to upgrade the activity watch program.[12] Having successfully deployed activity watches for a few years, the children, parents, and teachers have grown accustomed to the technology. For some students, the fitness gains are truly impressive.

The new proposal is to use additional sensors to monitor brain activity. Proponents say that collecting neural data will improve mental fitness by allowing teachers to more accurately evaluate student attentiveness and engagement. Initially, the upgrade will only be available to the fourth, fifth and sixth grade students who have used activity watches. But over a two-year period, program administrators will extend the user base gradually until all the students are participating. Would you support the proposal? Do you believe the updated version differs meaningfully from the original activity watches? Regardless of your answers, are these questions relevant to an evaluation of the activity watch program or are they without merit, as Thaler suggests?

Now, suppose that instead of only measuring brain activity for attentiveness, the sensors could feed neural information into educational software, comprehensively map each student's brain activity, and then provide tailored instruction and personalized evaluation. Would you support the proposal? Does the proposal differ meaningfully from the original activity watch program or the first updated version of it? Again, is it prudent to dismiss this scenario as pessimistic fear-mongering?

We could go on. And on. And on even further. Accepting newer and more powerful upgrades gets easier over time, especially when they reflect broader trends.[13] The first step makes the second more palatable, harder to resist or even notice, and so forth down the iterative product line. This libertarian ideal of adaptability in motion shows why hasty rejections of slippery slope arguments risk substituting engineered complacency for critical discussions of techno-social engineering.

The Slippery-Sloped Path and the Forces that Drive Us

We wrote this book to look ahead to the possible future impacts that are being set in motion by current techno-social engineering practices. Futurism is an inherently speculative exercise, and those who pursue it dogmatically tend to conflate possibilities with necessities. Unfortunately, the rapidly evolving pace of innovation gives us no choice but to try to look ahead. It might be the only way to adequately combat path dependency. *How can we be honest futurists?*

To avoid overstatement and making definitive claims about dystopia on the horizon, we deliberately and transparently advance an argument consisting of various slippery slopes that can aggregate into macro-level outcomes. It's our burden to carefully specify steps, causal mechanisms, and possible consequences. This doesn't free us from the shackles of speculation. Indeed, one primary objective is to provide the motivation and tools for identifying and evaluating the various steps, mechanisms, and consequences involved. We don't claim to be either omniscient or exhaustive.

Our argument is better described in terms of a slippery-sloped path. Rather than the ledge of a cliff, imagine a steeply inclined path. We argue that society is progressing on a path that is downward-sloping and can become slippery.

That society is progressing on a path is not terribly controversial.[14] Nonetheless, we emphasize "path" for a few reasons. First, it suggests many steps, in a direction, and toward a destination. Each of these features demands attention, specification, and analysis. Second, it admits the existence of alternative paths and the phenomenon of path dependency (i.e. the stickiness of the current path and high costs often associated with switching paths). Again, it's critical that in making our argument, we identify viable alternative paths and to the extent possible consider trade-offs. Third, "path" suggests the existence of something knowable yet not necessarily known or recognized. In many aspects of our lives, we may not realize or pay attention to what path we are on, where we're heading in terms of direction or destination, or what infrastructures influence us. We must do so, however, to make plans for our future.

That society is progressing on a *downward-sloping* path might lead one to conclude we are pessimists or dystopian. Up or down in this metaphorical sketch of our argument has nothing to do with good or bad or normative valuation more generally; whether the destination is utopia, dystopia, or somewhere in between is an independent normative question. The slope is downward only because it reflects the idea that there is a powerful and constant gravitational force pulling society in a direction, toward an end, and so we say, "down the path". For our purposes, gravity is a metaphor, and it refers to the dominant logics driving decision-making regarding techno-social systems, logics which we argue relate to optimization for efficiency, productivity, and happiness. In the next chapter, we will describe these logics in terms of Taylorism and the scientific management of human beings, the imperialism of instrumental reason, the idea that all social problems are comprehensible in the language of computation, and hedonism.

The metaphor of a downward-sloped path can be exploited further to reflect the idea that there may be more or less friction and resistance. The "surface" of the path where society and environment meet provides another metaphorical force to consider: the difference between a smooth and rough surface and how that difference affects the rate at which an object slides down an incline. We might think of this frictional resistance in terms of various countervailing forces such as cultural resistance to the dominant logics driving progress, alternative logics that push in other directions or towards other paths, or even governance institutions that allow "sheep herders" to escape tragedy.

Finally, we suggest that our metaphorical downward-sloping path can be, but is not necessarily, slippery. In the conventional slippery slope argument, slipperiness corresponds with the causal mechanism that connects steps. In our argument, the dominant logics drive societal progress along the path we're positing. Slipperiness, then, corresponds to causal mechanisms or forces that accelerate progress, perhaps, metaphorically speaking, by greasing the surface of the path we're on. Thus, slipperiness relates to countervailing forces that could reduce or even eliminate the friction. For example, resistance to particular steps or progress down our hypothesized path more generally might depend upon deliberation or active choosing or engagement by citizens. When techno-social engineering creates complacency and habituation, the effectiveness of such resistance is reduced.

PART II

CHAPTER 4

Tools for Engineering Humans

Introduction

Since the dawn of time, humans have been shaped by technology. To survive, humans built tools and re-engineered the environment and themselves. The roots of contemporary techno-social engineering are ancient. Accordingly, in this chapter, we provide a historical primer on the transformative power of tools.[1]

Tool Use: The Basics

While the myth persists that technology is applied science, humans have always developed and used tools, even during pre-scientific times.[2] Some define the human essence by this capability, characterizing us as *homo faber*, beings who make and use tools. From this perspective, tool use enables us to accomplish ends that otherwise would remain out of our reach. Many of these ends continue to elude other species on the planet. There is considerable evidence of non-human tool use, even quite sophisticated techniques and inventions, among animals such as crows, chimpanzees, and cephalopods.[3] Nonetheless, we don't have to worry about any of them starting a nuclear war any time soon.

Technology doesn't always do what we want it to do. Inventors can't always determine how a technology will be used once it's integrated into society. To believe otherwise is to commit the mistake known as the "designer's fallacy."[4] Technology use routinely involves unintended consequences and trade-offs. Take the discovery of fire and early inventions that applied it to keep people warm and cook meat (a quick source of protein). The process had obvious benefits for our ancestors, including profound cognitive ones.[5] But the Promethean gift also posed risks. Fire can burn people, possessions, and shelters. Most importantly, the development and use of tools to make and manage fire shaped who we are and who we are capable of being. As anthropologists and historians have explained, these tools opened new possible paths for humans to live and develop. Other tools have done the same.

Yet over time we've lost many capabilities by learning to solve problems with newer tools. Our predecessors could do many things that most of us simply can't do anymore. Know anyone who uses "dead reckoning" to navigate a boat? That's a pre-GPS orientation to determining positioning, revolving around factors like time, direction, and speed. Or, imagine if, in the future, the only cars that exist are autonomous, self-driving models. If they collectively went on strike, how many would be able to ride a horse to work? Or pilot a "dumb" automobile, after stealing it from a museum?

Tool use also has expanded our capabilities. Delegating tasks to technology has freed up time and resources and enabled us to move on to new and often more advanced problems. Keeping the innovation cycle going requires imagining, creating, and using new tools.

Consider the trajectory of fishing tools as a progression from spear fishing, to using a fishing pole, to using nets, and so on.[6] Along the way, capabilities have been gained and lost. At one time, many humans had considerable skill in handling a fishing spear; doing so was necessary to obtain food. Over time, that skill gradually became less useful. At some point, a fishing pole proved more efficient. And that efficiency ended up paling in comparison to subsequent large-scale fishing from boats with nets, a historical turn that turned pole fishing into a recreational hobby (rather than a professional endeavor) for many cultures.[7] In the end, progress in fishing appears to be a net gain in terms of both efficiency and capabilities. Less fishing effort by fewer people yields more fish for consumption, and, as a result, people in a historically based fishing community can diversify their skills and learn to use other tools.[8] Upon closer inspection, however, complex trade-offs become apparent. Displaced fishermen who cannot find work doing other jobs are a problem. Not everyone can transition from skill to skill – not least because training can be too costly and time-intensive. In some contexts, eroded familial and community traditions lead to a loss of social identity and capital. We should be skeptical of overly rosy narratives about how the future of automation will liberate us to spend more time doing artistic and related endeavors.[9]

While it's tempting to assume innovation yields ever increasing net gains, we must avoid being lulled into complacency by simple and comforting explanations. Patterns of this sort aren't uniform or inevitable. They can change, be localized, and even be manipulated to affect the distribution of gains and losses. There are always winners and losers as wealth, power, and capabilities concentrate and dissipate.

Shaping and Being Shaped by Tools

As media scholar John Culkin put it in his rephrasing of a famous Winston Churchill quote, "We shape our tools and, thereafter, our tools shape us."[10] This truism seems banal. It's easy to state but much more difficult to employ in a manner that elucidates and enables evaluation of tools or humanity. We need to understand *how* we shape and get shaped by our tools.

This mutual shaping occurs on an existential level, through self-understanding and modeling. Philosopher John Searle thus observes:

> Because we do not understand the brain very well we are constantly tempted to use the latest technology as a model for trying to understand it. In my childhood we always assumed that the brain was a telephone switchboard ... Sherrington, the great British neuroscientist, thought that the brain worked like a telegraph system. Freud often compared the brain to hydraulic and electro-magnetic systems. Leibniz compared it to a mill, and I am told that some of the ancient Greeks thought the brain functions like a catapult. At present, obviously, the metaphor is the digital computer.[11]

On other levels, the dynamic constitutive relationship between humans and tools requires that we look beyond the particular function of a tool. According to Weizenbaum, "Whatever their primary practical function, [tools] are necessarily also pedagogical instruments."[12] In other words, our tools allow us to teach each other about the tools and their functions, but also to teach us about who we are, what we can do, what is possible, and who we may become. Tools become part of the environment that shapes our beliefs, preferences, and capabilities.

In the history of techno-social engineering, language may be the most important tool ever invented. Historian Yuval Noah Harari claims that three major revolutions shaped the course of human history: the Cognitive Revolution, the Agricultural Revolution, and the Scientific Revolution. The Cognitive Revolution, which occurred about 70,000 years ago, involved the emergence of "new ways of thinking and com-municating" that relied on "fictive language."[13] While many animals communicate, examples being the buzzing of bees and the howls of monkeys, only humans have developed language capable of describing things that don't exist – *imagined things.*

Fictive language is important because of the collective affordances it provides, especially our ability to coordinate activities and work collectively in flexible ways.[14] With fictive language, humans could create common myths and construct complex social institutions, such as churches and governments. People believe in "the existence of laws, justice, human rights," for example, but "none of these things exist outside the stories that people invent and tell one another."[15] Language begets myths and large-scale human cooperation or subjugation. Myths sustain empires. Remarkably, on two consecutive pages of his book, Harari displays the Code of Hammurabi and the Declaration of Independence.[16] Both claim to be rooted in "universal and eternal principles of justice." Nevertheless, the Code proclaimed a social hierarchy among superiors, commoners, and slaves, while the Declaration proclaimed all are created equal. Neither is natural or objectively true. Both are powerful myths, imagined orders made possible by the tool of fictive language.[17]

The Agricultural Revolution also profoundly transformed human societies across the world. Unlike foraging societies, agricultural societies needed to manage huge amounts of mathematical data.[18] Human brains were not up for the task, forcing our ancestors to develop tools to store and process data. The Sumerians developed a written language, initially "limited to facts and figures."[19] At first, this partial script did not cover the whole spoken language, but, over time, this changed. For example, cuneiform emerged as a full script allowing humans to speak not only to those around them but also across longer distances and even generations.

The Scientific Revolution introduced an array of powerful tools, starting with a change in mindset: embrace science as a means for transcending our natural human ignorance.[20] As humans began to accept their own ignorance, they invested more and more resources in scientific research to explore the unknown and use the acquired knowledge to develop new tools. Science incorporates systematic observation with experimentation, new forms of imagination, theorizing, and the logic and language of mathematics. Isaac Newton's 1687 masterpiece, *The Mathematical Principles of Natural Philosophy*, might be "the most important book in modern history."[21] Newton's theory was a powerful, general-purpose tool. It could be used to explain all sorts of physical phenomena, from apples falling from trees to the trajectory of artillery. It reflected and contributed to our changing mindset. "Newton showed that the book of nature is written in the language of mathematics."[22]

At a macro level, science has become a powerful techno-social engineering tool that rivals religion. For some, it has become a secular form of salvation. Instead of praying to God or the gods for help with some calamity, some place their faith in science's ability to solve all problems. Take global warming. Instead of having confidence in divine intervention or a radical change emerging in every-person's ecological sensibilities, some hope that global warming can be mitigated through powerful forms of geoengineering – literally, re-engineering the Earth.

Tools are also products of human imagination. We "create little without first imagining that [we] can create it."[23] Yet tools also shape our "imaginative reconstruction of the world."[24] Tools are "pregnant symbols in themselves," meaning that they "symbolize the activities they enable."[25] The fishing spear is a tool for fishing, and it represents the capability associated with its use. As it comes or goes, so does our imagined construction of the world and ourselves within it.[26]

Joseph Weizenbaum discusses a series of examples of this phenomenon, ranging from spears, the six-shooter, and other weapons, to "ships of all kinds," to the printing press, the cotton-picking machine, and industrial machines. He discusses tools for measurement, such as telescopes and microscopes, and various other prostheses that extend human power, reach, and control over the environment. With each of these examples, humans gain and lose functional capabilities while their imagined world and their place within it are transformed.

Perhaps the "paramount change that took place in the mental life" of humans was our perception of time and space.[27] For most of our time on Earth, humans perceived time "as a sequence of constantly recurring events" rather than "a collection of abstract units (i.e., hours, minutes, and seconds)."[28] The clock changed everything. It was the first autonomous machine, not a prosthetic extension of human power. As the historian and philosopher Lewis Mumford observed, the clock "disassociated time from human events and helped create the belief in an independent world of mathematically measurable sequences: the special world of science."[29] The clock transformed human perception of nature and consequently humanity's role as "creature of and living in nature to nature's master."[30] Weizenbaum not only connects the clock to the rise of scientific rationalism, but he also links the clock to the fall of direct experience as a guide for human judgment and knowledge.

> It is important to realize that this newly created reality was and remains an impoverished version of the older one, for it rests on a rejection of those direct experiences that formed the basis for, and indeed constituted, the old reality. The feeling of hunger was rejected as a stimulus for eating; instead, one ate when an abstract model had achieved a certain state, i.e., when the hands of the clock pointed to certain marks on the clock's face ... and similarly for signals for sleep and rising, and so on.[31]

Historians, economists, science and technology studies scholars, and experts from various disciplines have examined other transformative tools that shaped the developmental path for human society over the past few centuries. The steam engine transformed human society, as did the telephone, the automobile, radio, television, and many other forms of technology. And today, we have the computer.

Weizenbaum fixates on the computer as a symbol and implementation of the dramatic transformations at the end of the twentieth century. Like the clock, the computer is an autonomous machine that can run on its own and perform various functions without needing human intervention. Like the clock, the computer has transformed us.

Initially, computers simply performed existing computing tasks more rapidly. Calculations done by humans in their heads, with paper and pencil, slide rules, or tab cards could be done more efficiently with computers. But, as is often the case with transformative tools, the range of uses for the computer expanded substantially with experience. Problems that were comprehensible in the language of computation could be tackled with computers. Computers gradually became integrated into an incredibly wide array of business and government processes and systems, becoming part of the structures upon which these systems depended, part of their background environment. Business decisions and, more importantly, the methods for making business decisions, such as systems analysis and operations research, grew increasingly reliant on the power of computers. As the power of computers grew, so did the perceived power of the methods and consequently their prestige and scope of application or their domain. The expanded scope of systems analysis, operations research, and a host of related computer-aided decision-making tools extended their influence on society. They became their own fields and entered the mainstream.

Fetishized Computers and Idealized Computation

Weizenbaum makes a remarkable observation that resonates with much of what we say in this book. He states:

> The interaction of the computer with systems analysis is instructive from another point of view as well. It is important to understand very clearly that strengthening a particular technique – putting muscles on it – contributes nothing to its validity.[32]

If a computer greatly improves the carrying out of calculations used to cast a horoscope – performing a series of complex symbol manipulations, etc., and doing so much more rapidly and efficiently than an unaided human astrologer – the "improvement in the technique of horoscope casting is irrelevant to the validity of astrological forecasting." And thus, "If astrology is nonsense, then computerized astrology is just as surely nonsense."[33]

Weizenbaum identifies a fundamental problem: We have fetishized computers (and other tools), and, as a result, we have "reified complex systems that have no authors, about which we know only they were somehow given us by science and that they speak with its authority, permit no questions of truth or justice to be asked."[34] The "science" he refers to is a type of rationalism and instrumental reason that can be boiled down to "computability and logicality." For example, he criticizes B. F. Skinner[35] for elevating "behavioral science" over "common sense," and this means failing to appreciate "a common sense informed by a shared cultural experience [and that] balks at the idea that freedom and dignity are absurd and outmoded concepts."[36]

Weizenbaum sensed a shift in the pattern, in the co-evolution of humans and our social and technological tools.[37] There seemed to be an all too convenient marriage between means and ends. The tools – computers, systems analysis, science, instrumental reason – work together synergistically to define reality, just as the light under a lamp-post defines the territory within which a drunk might look for his lost keys. "[I]nstrumental reason, triumphant technique, and unbridled science *are* addictive. They create a concrete reality, a self-fulfilling nightmare."[38]

It's difficult to appreciate how powerfully the tools we develop shape us. One of the most important ways is by shaping our imagined reality, our very beliefs about ourselves, and our preferences and values. If the ends worth pursuing are determined by our tools, by their constructed reality (the contours and contents of the lit space under the lamp-post), then nothing less than our very humanity may be at risk of being whittled away. Our imagination could become bounded by the constraints embedded in the tools and the logics they perpetuate. We are not there, at least not yet. In many ways, experience suggest that our tools generally have expanded our horizons. This is especially true when it comes to knowledge.[39,40]

Nonetheless, we must remain vigilant and continue to examine our tools, our reliance on them, and what ends might linger just beyond the light.

Let us put the key point simply, as Weizenbaum did.

Problems comprehensible in the language of computation, in theory, can be solved with computers, systems analysis, science, instrumental reason, and so on. Conversely, problems incomprehensible in the language of computation, by definition, cannot.[41] Weizenbaum explains how many incomprehensible problems are improperly assumed to be comprehensible. Justice, for example, is not in and of itself comprehensible in the language of computation. Many different conceptions of justice have been articulated. None of them are fully reducible to computation problems. Recall Harari's comparison of the two codes of justice – Hammurabi's Code and the Declaration of Independence. The subject matter of both uses numerical relationships to express conceptions of justice, and one might argue that the codes aim to reduce justice to a computational problem, but neither really does. Both rely on the prior judgment of the collective human society – or those in power – to construct the imagined reality reflected in the codes. Humans set the baselines for justice. Similarly, policy-makers and value theorists may frame social choice problems in terms of social welfare functions and thereby structure choices and trade-offs in a manner that seems quantitative, formulaic, and possibly reducible to problems comprehensible in the language of computation. However, beneath the framing itself are a host of human judgments about values and relative weights, that set the baselines necessary for computational processes to run their course.[42]

A major social problem is rooted in the imperialism of instrumental reason and the improper assumption that *all* problems are comprehensible in the language of computation and thus can be solved with the same set of social and technological tools. This assumption sometimes results from erroneous understanding of problems but also from myopic infatuation with the power of our tools. We might modify Culkin's phrase as follows: "We shape our tools, fall in love with them, and, thereafter, our tools shape us." Weizenbaum's argument remains fundamental, particularly as we identify ever more powerful means for solving problems comprehensible in the language of computation.

Extending the concept of the "designer's fallacy," we label this issue the *problem of engineered determinism*. What we mean to evoke by the term is the idea that society can engineer in a deterministic fashion a world that operates deterministically. This is not to say the world is naturally deterministic, or predetermined by fate or natural physical processes. Rather, it is the grand hubris that we can socially construct a perfectly optimized world if we only have the data, confidence in our tools, and willingness to commit.

"Against the Imperialism of Instrumental Reason," a chapter in Weizenbaum's book, opens with a parable of how the "enormous power" humans have attained through the tools of (computerized) science and technology have left humans impotent. To hammer home the point, he quotes the historian Studs Terkel:

> For the many there is hardly concealed discontent . . . "I'm a machine," says the spot welder. "I'm caged," says the bank teller, and echoes the hotel clerk. "I'm a mule," says the steel worker. "A monkey can do what I can do," says the receptionist. "I'm less than a farm implement," says the migrant worker. "I'm an object," says the high fashion model. Blue collar and white call upon the identical phrase: "I'm a robot."[43]

Powerful as Weizenbaum's account is, it remains incomplete. It has influenced our work substantially, as we've hopefully made clear. But Weizenbaum focused on two related sets of tools, one technological and the other social. The technological tool set centered on the computer; he emphasized its symbolic role. Throughout this work, we'll discuss other tools within that set, such as communication networks, algorithms, and big data.

Taylor's Scientific Management of Human Beings

There is something fundamental missing, or perhaps implicit, in Weizenbaum's account that we need to draw out. It's the paradigm shift that occurred at the turn of the twentieth century with the emergence of Frederick Taylor's theory of scientific management, commonly referred to as Taylorism.[44] Taylor revolutionized the relationships between management and labor, and it's no surprise that all the people in the Studs Terkel passage that Weizenbaum quoted were workers.

In his biography of Taylor, Robert Kanigel offers the following description:

> Taylor was the first efficiency expert, the original time-and-motion man. To organized labor, he was a soulless slave driver, out to destroy the workingman's health and rob him of his manhood. To the bosses, he was an eccentric and a radical, raising the wages of common laborers by a third, paying college boys to click stopwatches. To him and his friends, he was a misunderstood visionary, possessor of the one best way that, under the banner of science, would confer prosperity on worker and boss alike, abolishing the ancient class hatreds.[45]

We connect Taylorism to Weizenbaum's account for a few reasons. First, the link strongly supports Weizenbaum's observations about the rise of systems analysis, operations research, and computer-assisted decision-making within business management circles. It even buttresses Weizenbaum's emphasis on the importance of the clock as a techno-social engineering tool. After all, Taylor's system depended heavily on "efficiency experts" using stopwatches to conduct time studies, a critical source of data used in scientifically managing workers. Second, the connection helps explain the rise of instrumental reason and scientific approaches to managing human beings and their social relationships in the workplace and elsewhere. Third, the association focuses on a set of techniques that preceded and did not depend on the computer. These techniques have been strengthened greatly by computers and adjacent technologies such as sensors, data analytics, communications networks, and so on. Yet the normative validity or legitimacy of the techniques must be evaluated independently, and, to do so, we must resist the pull of fetishized innovation and unwarranted claims of technological inevitability.

Taylor developed his techniques, his theory of scientific management of humans in the workplace, in the late nineteenth century and early twentieth century. Taylor saw substantial inefficiencies in factories and other workplaces, and he attributed many of the inefficiencies to mismanagement of labor. As a young man, Taylor had worked as a shop foreman, attempted to get the most out of his workers, and begun to diagnose the inefficiencies he observed as a product of poorly structured incentives, unmotivated and sometimes shirking laborers, and, perhaps most importantly, a tremendous knowledge gap that rendered management ineffective. Managers knew too little about the workers, their tasks, their capabilities, and what motivated them to work.

Over decades and across different workplaces and even industries, Taylor carefully studied workplaces, workers, and their work. He examined minute details of tasks performed, and, based on the data collected, sought to optimize performance in terms of increased efficiency and productivity. Taylor's system was generalizable. In other words, his system was not limited to a particular workplace, nor was it limited to any set of time and motion studies.

At one level, Taylor's scientific management system is a type of data-dependent technology.[46] Taylorism is one of the best early examples of data-driven innovation, a concept currently in vogue.[47] Taylor's system included the techniques for both gathering data and putting such data to use in managing people. Taylor's system thus encompassed the surveillance techniques employed by the "efficiency experts," their use of stopwatches and careful visual observation of task performance under varied incentive schemes. For example, he would offer a worker being studied a much higher wage than the prevailing market wage to test worker capability and task performance under different conditions, and, if possible, push prevailing views about what workers could accomplish and increase productivity. Taylor and his disciples relied on personal observations written in notebooks and careful analysis of various inputs, outputs, processes, and procedures across the many workplaces they studied.

Taylor's critics emphasized that Taylor's scientific management was anything but scientific. They alleged (accurately in many cases) that Taylor's prescriptions for management often had an ad hoc flavor to them. When the data was incomplete, Taylor relied on his own judgment, which amounted to little more than a fudge factor or unwarranted exercise of managerial discretion and could not be considered scientific.

Yet the managerial data gaps would close. Twentieth-century technological innovations, ranging from the computer to the camera, have dramatically upgraded the capability of managers to gather, process, evaluate, and act upon data.[48] Not surprisingly, Taylorism spread like wildfire across industries and beyond the factory floor, to hospitals, schools, and various other contexts.[49] As Kanigel put it, "Taylor's credo of rational efficiency has burned its way into the modern mind."[50]

Taylorism is an applied version of the instrumental reason and rationalism discussed by Weizenbaum. Consider how Taylorism defines both means and ends. As a technology or management technique or system, Taylorism is obviously branded as a means. The problem to be solved also was unambiguous: inefficiencies plagued the workplace leading to waste and lost productivity. Taylorism and Fordism are famous both for their underlying *objective*, namely, to increase efficiency, quality, and productivity for the ultimate benefit of managers, owners, and capitalists, and *means*, specifically by managing factory workers in various ways that get them to behave like machines.

Deeply embedded throughout Taylorism, the ends of productivity and efficiency are not only assumed to be paramount but also to be comprehensible in the language of computation. That is the heart of Taylor's claim that his system constituted scientific management; it is reflected throughout the system itself. Workers were, in fact, conceived as inputs, cogs, resources, etc.; their work was broken down, analyzed, and programmed.[51]

Taylor and his disciples assumed it was all comprehensible in the language of computation. At a fundamental level, Taylorism was a revolutionary system for engineering humans. As Taylor famously declared, "In the past the man was first; in the future the system must be first."[52]

The assembly line is a particularly salient and culturally recognized example.[53] An assembly line is a manufacturing process involving the progressive assembly of parts into a whole product, where the semi-finished assembly moves from one work station to the next in a linear fashion. While assembly lines pre-dated Taylor and Ford, Ford famously optimized the process for mass production. Fordism combined product standardization, systematized use of assembly lines wherein unskilled laborers used special purpose tools at different stages, and the principle that workers should be paid higher "living wages" to both provide better incentives and enable them to purchase the products they made.[54]

A critically important aspect of this type of techno-social engineering is the *environmental nature of the means*, the way in which the managers employing the management practices advocated by Taylor (and adapted by Ford) reconstructed the physical and social environments within which their workers worked. Managers could leverage control over the environment to control those within the environment in various subtle but powerful ways. Similar to how the clock reconstructed our environment and us,[55] time and motion studies fueled task and schedule management in the workplace. As Harari describes:

> [Modern industry] sanctifies precision and uniformity. For example, in a medieval workshop each shoemaker made an entire shoe, from sole to buckle. If one shoemaker was late for work, it did not stall the others. However, in a modern footwear-factory assembly line, every worker mans a machine that produces just a small part of a shoe, which is passed on to the next machine. If the worker who operates machine no. 5 has overslept, it stalls all the other machines. [To] prevent such calamities, everybody must adhere to a precise timetable. Each worker arrives at work at exactly the same time. Everybody takes their lunch break together, whether they are hungry or not. Everybody goes home when the whistle announces that the shift is over – not when they have finished their project.[56]

The factory thus not only produced whatever widget the company eventually sold (e.g. Harari's shoes or Ford's automobiles), but it also produced machine-like humans, sometimes referred to as automatons.[57] Kanigel states:

Both Taylor and Ford raised production, cut costs – and reduced the judgment and skill needed by the average worker. [A Ford plant differed from a Taylorized plant in certain respects.] In either case, the worker was left with eight or ten hours whose minute-by-minute course was more closely prescribed and scrutinized than ever. After Ford and Taylor got through with them, most jobs needed less of everything – less brains, less muscle, less independence.[58]

Taylorism Criticized Yet Expanding

Critics of Taylorism recognized and railed against these effects on workers, but architecting the environment (optimizing it, really) to achieve these particular effects is the technological innovation to note.[59] "The Industrial Revolution turned the timetable and the assembly line into a template for almost all human activities . . . [Soon] schools too adopted precise time-tables, followed by hospitals, government offices and grocery stores."[60] These are interesting examples because they define and are defined by the physical spaces, social institutions, and increasingly technologies that together constitute particular environments designed to engineer humans.

Schools engage in techno-social engineering of humans. Communities rely on schools to educate and transform their children. Like a factory, a school transforms a combination of inputs into socially valuable outputs; that transformation is the result of a series of internal processes. It may be disconcerting to think of schools as mere factories, children as inputs or outputs, teachers as factory workers, and so on. Still, Taylorism has had a profound impact on the educational workplace. In fact, "[t]he application of principles of scientific management within the structure, organization, and curriculum of public schools in the US became dominant in the early 1900s."[61] Like scientific management more generally, Taylorism in public schools may have waxed and waned over the past century and across different regions, but it has "resurfaced . . . as teachers' classroom practices are increasingly standardized by high-stakes testing and scripted curriculum." Education scholar Wayne Au and others have examined in detail how the incredibly fine-grained scripting (or micro-management) of teachers' work neatly fits with the Taylorist logic.

The school-as-factory metaphor is wonderfully exploited in Pink Floyd's "The Wall," which vividly illustrates the worry that schools can be totalitarian environments architected to construct machines, rather than humans. Schools need not, and should not, be built and run this way. Another ideal vision casts schools as environments that enable children to develop a range of human capabilities, including, for example, reason, reflection, introspection, emotional intelligence, sociality, and so on. For many schools, this is aspirational. Nonetheless, the social engineering that inevitably takes place in schools spans a continuum with the dystopian factory of "The Wall" at one extreme and the utopian ideal at the other. Schools in the real world occupy intermediate positions on the continuum and can be evaluated in terms of their position, which may change over time.

Without delving into education policy debates, we note that one modern trend in education is to import various surveillance, computation, and communication technologies into the schools. It is important to examine how these technologies may subtly affect the environment within schools. Schools tend to evaluate each technology on its own, performing a truncated cost-benefit analysis in the face of declining public funds and partially blinded by fascination with the power of new technology. Each incremental step to adopt a new technology may appear to be cost-benefit justified, but, in the aggregate, schools may be heading in the wrong direction on our hypothesized continuum. This is one example of humanity's techno-social dilemma.

Today, even though the assembly line "defines surprisingly little of modern manufacturing,"[62] Taylorism is pervasive. Taylorism had its ups and downs across business schools, management consultancies, and factory floors throughout the twentieth century. Some companies and even industries moved away from it to alternative systems for managing labor.[63] Nonetheless, the basic principles of Taylorism have become deeply embedded in how society conceptualizes all sorts of management, ranging from businesses to government to schools to amateur athletics to child rearing. Again, Robert Kanigel put it well:

> Today, it is only modest overstatement to say that we are all Taylorized, that from assembly-line tasks timed to a fraction of a second, to lawyers recording their time by fractions of an hour, to standardized McDonald's hamburgers, to information operators constrained to grant only so many seconds per call, modern life itself has become Taylorized.[64]

With ever growing data about human labor, task performance, and so on, the trend in workplace surveillance and management has only grown and expanded in scope,[65] and it is likely to continue. *Until when? How far can it go? What happens if taken to the extreme? What would it mean to Taylorize human labor fully?* One thing it would mean is that we would have accepted, even if only tacitly, the contention that management of human labor is a problem comprehensible in the language of computation. Another thing it would mean is that any boundary around the workplace, employment, or even the idea of work itself would dissipate because human labor is not constrained to any such boundary.

Modern data-driven micro-management of human resources (time, attention, effort, etc.) across various industries is simply a form of Taylorism extended beyond formal employer–employee contexts. Like vehicles, physical space, and computing resources, human physical labor can be optimized for on-demand allocation determined by data and algorithms. The Taylorist vision of efficient management is focused on minimizing costs associated with misallocated or wasted human capital, effort, and attention. Ironically, soon, eliminating productive inefficiencies that arise from mismanagement of labor might entail getting rid of human managers altogether and turning instead to smart technologies.[66]

There is no reason to limit technologically-optimized-and-implemented Taylorism to traditional work, however. The logic easily extends to a much wider range of actions that depend upon human labor (time, attention, effort, etc.), whether driving a car, caring for one's children, exercising our bodies and minds, or any other human activity.[67] In the not-so-distant future, intelligent technological systems – not necessarily sentient ones – may be deployed to maximize human productivity throughout our lives.

Humans are naturally inefficient. We are often unproductive and costly to sustain. One way to understand the power of the Taylorist logic, particularly as extended beyond the workplace, is that it entails minimization of various costs associated with humans being human. For humanists, this is deeply troubling. Some will emphasize the potential upsides, rooted in increased convenience, entertainment, happiness, and welfare. They'll argue that, overall, we'll all be much better off in a world optimized to deliver cheap bliss. In subsequent chapters, we'll revisit this debate about humanity and the world we're building.

CHAPTER 5

Engineering Humans with Contracts

Introduction

Q: What do you do when you see a little button on a webpage or app screen that says ["I agree"]?

A: Click the button.

Previous chapters explained techno-social engineering and considered illustrative examples. Here, we discuss in detail the current legal and technical architecture of electronic contracting, a surprising case of techno-social engineering. The design of this environment might incline people to behave like simple stimulus-response machines and become increasingly predictable and programmable.

Contract law shapes the transactional environments where people formulate legally respected and binding commitments and relationships. In general, contract law is understood to be a form of liberating social infrastructure that enhances individual and group autonomy. Unfortunately, conventional understanding seems to be wrong. Contracting practices have changed dramatically over the past half-century to accommodate changes in economic, social, and technological systems. Today's contracts might be more liberating for some (e.g. firms) than others (e.g. consumers).[1] As implemented in electronic architecture, contracts may be oppressive.

Designers arrange the digital contracting environment to create a practically seamless, transaction cost minimized user experience. Rather than requiring people who intend to use online services to read lengthy pages filled with boilerplate legal jargon – jargon they can't reasonably be expected to understand and won't be able to negotiate with – a simple click of the mouse, with mere conspicuous notice of the existence of terms, suffices to manifest consent for entering legally binding contractual relationships.

There's plenty of legal debate about the legitimacy of contracts that this mechanism creates, including heated disputes over whether opportunities for opting-out do enough to preserve autonomy. Some celebrate *efficiency*: the seamlessness of the interaction and the minimization of transaction costs. From this perspective, electronic contracts are a perfectly rational means for consumers to quickly access desired services and goods. Others, however, lament *unfairness*, the one-sidedness of take-it-or-leave-it contracts of adhesion that don't foster the "meeting of the minds" that once seemed to be the core principle of contract law.

While a significant debate about the content of contracts is taking place amongst scholars and in the courts, a crucial omission limits the critical conversation and prevents us from appreciating the full power of online contracting. Few discuss the negative impact the electronic contracting environment has on our habits and dispositions, and, more generally, on who we are as human beings.[2] It can be uncomfortable to focus on these issues and the possibility that electronic contracts are objectionable as a matter of public policy because they condition us to devalue our own autonomy.

We examine two related ways to characterize the contracting problem.

First, we claim that the electronic contracting environment should be understood as a techno-social tool for engineering human beings to behave automatically, like simple machines. To validate this claim, we develop testable hypotheses and explicate the underlying theory.

Next, we describe the contracting problem in Taylorist terms, as a system of scientific management that's directed toward consumers.[3] This view highlights how consumers, like laborers in Taylorist workplaces, are conditioned (and possibly deskilled) to behave in ways that largely are determined by efficiency-oriented system designers. Viewing electronic contracting through the lens of Taylorism connects our discussion to a broader set of techno-social engineering problems.

Although we don't believe the click-to-contract mechanism necessarily was intended to be a tool for techno-social engineering humans, it nonetheless may have become one because of its gradual optimization and the expanding scale and scope of its deployment. Emergent Taylorism might seem oxymoronic because Taylor developed tools for management who would use them in a direct and deliberate manner. However, this line of thinking places too much emphasis on intentionality and managerial responsibility. We aren't making claims about the intentions of designers. Instead, we're focusing on environmental tools and their impacts on human behavior, and we're questioning the underlying logic of optimization.

If the electronic contracting environment conditions human beings to behave like simple stimulus-response machines, and if repeated interaction with this environment has lasting effects, then systemic reform of contract law might be warranted for reasons that go beyond the arguments proffered in the standard literature.[4] Our argument is *not* about the goodness or badness of contract terms per se. Nor is it about the outcomes in specific contracts, transactions, or cases. Rather, our concern is with the social costs associated with rampant techno-social engineering that devalues and diminishes human autonomy and sociality.

One caveat before proceeding:

Throughout this chapter, we use endnotes marked with the header "Empirical Query" to identify hypotheses and claims that need to be verified through empirical investigation. These statements are not defensive. Nor are they signs of weakness in our theoretical argument. Good theory leads to good empirics. It reveals questions that are worth investigating and provides structure and boundaries for further theoretical and empirical inquiries. In short, we note these empirical queries to encourage others to work with us or independently on pressing research questions.

The Experience of Electronic Contracting

In her book, *Boilerplate*, law professor Peggy Radin presents two conceptually familiar worlds to help orient our thinking about contracts.[5] In World A (for Agreement) "contracts" are actual bargained-for exchanges between parties who each consent to the exchange. Traditionally, this is how many imagine contracts work in an ideal world. In World B (for Boilerplate)[6] "contracts" are standardized form contracts, also known as contracts of adhesion and take-it-or-leave-it contracts. The logic of this world captures what we often experience as consumers. Radin explores how the use of boilerplate has expanded significantly and what the implications of such expansion might be for consumers, contract law, and society. Most importantly, she explains how "boilerplate creep"[7] gradually erodes public ordering (e.g. law of the people, political and social institutions, government) and replaces it with private ordering (e.g. law of the firm, market).[8] Her analysis is comprehensive and includes many examples of boilerplate offline and online.

The beauty of the Internet is its scope and diversity, the incredibly wide range of websites, interactions, conversations, communities, activities, and transactions available to each of us. Not surprisingly, navigating webpages and online content carries an incredible amount of legal baggage. Much of it is governed by electronic contracts. If the Internet followed Radin's model of World A, transaction and information costs could be stifling. Lawyers have worked to reduce friction by drafting boilerplate agreements. And website designers who architect the digital environment have played a role in this process, too. Both are "choice architects" who frame the choices or options that consumers are presented with.[9]

Consider a system where a choice architect designs the online environment to make using digital services as seamless as possible. Essentially, the choice architect structures the environment to minimize the burden placed on the user when she is consenting to terms. It's an environment where the rational response to terms of use pages (links, really) requires little thought and imposes no burden on the user. After all, "acceptance" is reduced to a mere click of the mouse. If this is starting to sound familiar, it's because it is our current online contracting environment.[10] Technically, the contracting environment is choice-preserving in the sense that users retain their autonomy. They can opt out of the web applications services – so long as they're willing to accept that the social or professional costs of doing so can be high. The key point, though, is that, in this context, it is completely rational for a user to blindly accept the terms of use. To read the proposed and, frankly, imposed terms would be a complete waste of time, an irrational and ultimately futile exercise.[11]

It seems natural to distinguish this scenario from those that involve the government. Contracting is, after all, a private affair: the holy grail of private ordering. While many of us may feel ashamed, cheated, disappointed, or otherwise less than satisfied with our contracting behavior, we cannot complain about coercion, much less government paternalism. *Or can we?* The answer depends on just how dramatically contracting has changed over the past half-century to accommodate changes in economic, social, and technological systems, both off- and online. According to law professors Robert Hillman and Jeffrey Rachlinski, "[t]he Internet is turning the process of contracting on its head."[12]

One aspect of the dramatic change in contracting practices is its pervasiveness and relevance in our everyday digitally networked lives. The current scale and scope of private ordering through written contract is unprecedented. It may truly be a massive "orgy of contract formation."[13] We haven't attempted to quantify the number of written contracts the average person enters during her lifetime. However, we suspect the following: (i) the number has steadily, if not exponentially, increased over the past half-century;[14] (ii) the rate of meaningful participation in negotiating terms has steadily decreased;[15] and (iii) the number of written contracts concerning mundane affairs has increased, if not skyrocketed. By mundane, we mean ordinary, everyday affairs for which a written contract would be cost-prohibitive and inefficient in the absence of boilerplate.[16]

We could add a fourth hypothesis about the increasing number of written contractual agreements concerning trivial affairs, which we imagine to be something like the offline purchase of a lollipop. Such "lollipop contracts" are unnecessary and wasteful. Why bother to cement relationships with a written contract when it concerns trivial affairs? One answer becomes apparent when we flip the question around and ask: Why not? It's no bother because the transaction costs associated with forming a written contract are trivially low in the electronic contracting context. Such contracts might not really be about the legal relationship. They serve other purposes, such as setting standards, incrementally contributing to boilerplate creep, and further replacing public ordering with private ordering.

Let's put this in personal terms. *Do you consider yourself experienced in contracting? Have you negotiated many contracts? If so, what did the negotiation entail?* For many people, contracts are significant legal affairs that involve insurance, loans, employment, and other major life transactions. We also enter many contractual agreements that concern less significant affairs. For example, a contract for a single service – say, to have a porch painted – or an ordinary sales contract – say, for a household item.[17] Consider how much time you spend online each day, how many different service providers you interact with during such time, and the percentage of those interactions governed by contracts. Now perhaps you understand the intuitions behind our hypotheses.[18]

How many written contracts have you entered into during your lifetime? If we asked this question in the distant past, decades ago or a century ago, the answer probably would be orders of magnitude less than the answer provided by current readers.[19] Future readers of this chapter may find the question odd because the idea of distinct, identifiable contracts may be at odds with their experience of completely seamless contractual governance. This raises an interesting theoretical issue. Freedom of contract requires the correlative freedom from contract.[20] When contract becomes automatic and ubiquitous, both disappear. There is no freedom.[21]

Our modern, digital, networked environment is architected with technological systems that operate mostly in the background, behind user interfaces that magically hide the complexity and incredible number of actual and virtual machines, processes, data flows, and actors. These interfaces also happen to be means by which we enter a substantial number of legally binding relationships with service providers and other parties.

We routinely enter contracts by clicking a virtual button, whether using a mouse, touchpad, touchscreen, or remote control. The experience is hardly a momentous occasion and often is barely notable. This is a designed feature and not an accidental bug – a point we'll subsequently revisit. Experientially, it feels[22] nothing like signing on the dotted line of your mortgage, employment contract, or insurance agreement.[23] But the legal effect is the same. When you click "I agree," you manifest consent to enter a legally binding contractual agreement. *With whom?* Most often, the other party is the service provider. Providers include website operators, software or app providers, smart television companies, and so on. Sometimes, there are other parties – affiliates or third parties – who also are part of the deal. For example, you may enter an agreement with the website owner and agree to let her share your data with affiliated entities. But these entities are not typically contracting parties. They're just beneficiaries of the contract between you and the direct service provider. Typically, they have side-agreements with the service provider, but not with you.[24]

The electronic contracting environment we're all familiar with is thus a product of, and completely contingent upon, evolved contract law and practice. Critically, this includes technological systems through which we interact, communicate, transact, and form relationships. Both could be different. Contract law could have accommodated changes in economic, social, and technological systems differently.[25] What we have now is neither necessary nor inevitable. Fortunately, contract law still can change.

The technological systems through which we interact, communicate, transact, and form relationships also could be different. They are designed and optimized to obtain predetermined results given the legal and technological constraints and the predictable behavior of visitors. The technological systems reflect a series of design choices in their deployment, in their architecture.[26] Contract law has permitted and encouraged the development of an electronic contracting environment in which it would be irrational for users to read the terms of the contract. The technological design of the user interface – a click-to-agree button coupled with a link to a separate file with potentially endless pages of terms – is merely an implementation of what contract law has allowed.

It's efficient. Each online contract we enter is presumably in our interest and cost-benefit justified. Otherwise, we'd choose to abstain. Price and service are presumably the driving factors. All else is a mere transaction cost to be minimized, buried in terms of service that no rational person would read. You retain your autonomy and may choose to leave, but that's it. Quite simply, you may take it or leave it.

At least, that is how it seems. *But what exactly is the price?* Often, we have no idea because the true price is not money exchanged. Frequently, users do not pay money for services. The apparent sticker price is zero. Even when users pay money (e.g. for a subscription or a $0.99 app), the sticker price often is discounted; other side-payments exist. The actual price users pay for the services websites provide includes all the information the sites collect about them.[27] As Radin shows, the actual price also includes the various legal rights we may have given up.[28] Further, it includes the commodification of users through pseudo-relationships. Websites act as brokers for user data and relationships to generate a weird sort of B-world social capital that greases whole series of transactions as well as the slippery slope.

How, then, do we evaluate the relationships being formed as users visit websites when the relationships extend well beyond the website and users to include third parties, such as advertisers, website affiliates, and others who may be direct or incidental third-party beneficiaries of the user-site transaction? One might reject our characterization of the relationships as part of the price that users pay. This puts the skeptic in an awkward position. *How else can we reconcile the flow of third-party benefits?* Website users are the objects of the various side-agreements, after all. As people like to say about Facebook and Google, users are not really the consumers. Rather, users are the product being consumed by all the advertisers and other third parties with whom Facebook and Google have side-agreements.[29] The point generalizes well beyond Facebook and Google. Apple's App Store, Amazon, Microsoft, and many other online services work this way. User as product describes much of the digital networked environment, and consequently much of our everyday lives.[30]

Still, given the numbers (of users, sites, transactions, third parties, data, contracts), the design of the electronic contracting interface seems perfectly rational. In many offline contexts, consumers don't read most terms and only deliberate over a small number of salient variables, like price, quality, and timing. Comparable deliberation in the online context might take too long, be too complicated, and lead to fewer transactions. It's much easier to hide the complex details[31] and nudge users to click "I agree" without deliberation over any terms.[32]

Our current online contracting regime is a compelling example of how our legal rules coupled with a specific technological environment can lead us to behave like simple stimulus-response machines – perfectly rational, but also perfectly predictable and ultimately programmable. The environment disciplines us to go on auto-pilot and, arguably, helps create or reinforce dispositions that will affect us in other walks of life that involve similar technological environments. These similar environments might turn out to be everywhere given the direction of innovation.[33] Although Radin does not frame the issue in terms of conditioning or programming, she notes how status quo bias can lead us to continue down a familiar path:

> Given our tendency to stick with what we've done before, it is hardly surprising that after we've received boilerplate many times without having any negative repercussions, we will persist in our acceptance of it. Once we are used to clicking "I agree," we'll keep clicking "I agree." It would take some extraordinary event, some real change in context, to make us stop doing what we're used to doing when it seems to work.[34]

It turns out, however, that the effect may be more powerful than Radin suggests. A laundry list of heuristics (i.e. "rules of thumb") and cognitive biases might reinforce our behavior.[35] Decision fatigue can be overwhelming.[36] The opportunity costs of slowing down and deliberating can be high.[37] And, habits with their automaticity and corresponding behavioral path dependencies are incredibly powerful.[38]

Not surprisingly, boilerplate creeps, which only exacerbates the effects as we become more comfortable, complacent,[39] and easier to nudge.[40] Particularly worrisome is how boilerplate creep enables both surveillance and nudging, which are both creep phenomena as well.[41]

Consider how the electronic contracting environment optimized for websites has migrated to mobile devices and apps, and further to smart televisions and beyond. The parties, legal relationships, technologies, services provided, data generated and collected, and implications vary dramatically across these contexts. Nonetheless, in general, our behavior remains the same: perfectly predictable, seemingly rational, and hyper-efficient, check the box, click "I agree."[42]

Just think for a moment about how the relationships and privacy implications differ when you shift from website to smart television. There are different service providers, different third-party affiliates in the background, different technologies and services, and different types of data. A smart TV might be in your living room, and it might even have a microphone (for those karaoke sessions). Others have diagnosed the problem. We only want to emphasize how the stimulus-response mechanism works similarly despite how different the implications might be.

We might be disposed to deliberate for at least some of these transactions, to stop and think about what we're getting ourselves and other people (e.g. family members who share the smart television) into. But we're being conditioned not to do so.[43] For example, if you decide to investigate the privacy policy for your smart television, you'll likely see the "1/50" page count at the bottom of the screen, shrug, and click the back arrow, behaving just as you're supposed to.[44]

Some will resist our characterization and believe that while the objective theory of contracts is flawed,[45] nobody is in danger of mindlessly following scripted programming. You might believe that you really decide for yourself when you click "I agree" and are decidedly not pre-programmed to do so. This is a common reaction. It was ours at first. Many others have reacted similarly. People assume that, at some point in their past, they consciously adopted a strategy to deliberate once in a while and otherwise to trust in markets,[46] the wisdom of crowds,[47] and watchdog journalists and advocates.[48] If a contract has deep flaws, surely others will identify egregious terms and presumably a court would refuse to enforce them.

But what justifies the assumption or trust? Put aside the merits of such a strategy and the beliefs upon which it is based. The question is whether we in fact ever really adopt such a strategy based upon actual deliberation about the merits. Given the empirical difficulty of determining what's actually causing us to act, self-assessing the contents of our minds is an introspective blunder.[49] For starters, optimized environments might be architected to make you feel as though you're making deliberate choices when you're not actually doing so.[50] In other words, one effect of techno-social engineering might be that you're disciplined to overestimate how much freedom actually lies at your disposal – that you mistake the illusion of choice for the real thing.[51] Moreover, just as an immediate click may be rational in the immediate context, trusting in markets, the wisdom of crowds, watchdogs, and courts may be the only rational choice across contexts given the incredible number of interactions mediated in the same manner. Crucially, the seemingly efficient rationality of both the micro and macro choices is completely contingent on the designed architecture of the electronic contracting environment and the scale and scope of its deployment. Crowds, watchdogs, and courts do catch some shockingly egregious terms and conditions, serving a useful function. However, they can only do so much.

Law professor Randy Barnett compared electronic contracts and other modern boilerplate to agreeing in advance to do whatever someone else had written in a sealed envelope.[52] This excellent analogy highlights the degree to which we blindly trust in others, whether the other party, others with whom the party transacts, or, more generally, market forces or the legal system. Especially, although not exclusively, in the electronic contracting context, it may be a mistake to even call it trust. If we are conditioned to click or simply fatigued, can we really say we trust the other party? Or that we have agreed to anything? To the extent that we conclude that clicking "I agree" is an act that constitutes agreement to be bound Barnett-style and depends upon trust, we cannot ignore how the trust itself is contingent upon and a product of the techno-social engineered environment, much like the sheer ignorance of consumers. The sealed envelope metaphor works well to describe some aspects of the transaction, but it ignores others. Consumers who click "I agree" might view the interaction as Barnett describes, or they might view the click "I agree" button as a trivial annoyance, like a bothersome fly to be swatted when reaching for food at a picnic.

Would you hesitate before signing a piece of paper handed to you by a stranger? Do you hesitate to click "I agree" when downloading an app or visiting a new website?

Another complication concerns the very definition of choice. When we make decisions in the electronic contracting context (e.g. to click or not), it remains unclear whether we're exercising judgment and making a genuine choice. The electronic contracting environment may be designed to stimulate instinctive, heuristic thinking (referred to in the scientific literature as System 1 of the brain). Yet the user may feel or be led to believe that she has engaged in rational deliberation (System 2).[53] In the moment and even in hindsight, the stimulus-response behavior of simply clicking is perfectly rational – again, reading terms and conditions is a waste of time and insisting upon negotiation is futile – and so it's easily mistaken as a product of deliberation.[54]

Put otherwise, suppose choice architects – website, application, or other interface designers – arrange the relevant stimuli in an electronic contracting interface to trigger an automatic click. They might describe their optimization problem in terms of minimizing decision time or time-to-click or some comparable metric. The designer's goal is to consummate transactions with minimal transaction costs, which generally means rapid click-through to agreement. Consumers often have the same goal. For most, the electronic contracting interface is a mere hurdle, an obstacle to getting the content or service they're looking for. Deliberation is generally wasteful in this context, with significant opportunity costs. Triggering System 1 seems to be a win-win(-win-win- ... win^n).[55] This gradually becomes a truism. When we talk about this with people, they often suggest that they are behaving rationally, which is true, given the futility and costs associated with deliberating or reading terms. But they also insist that they deliberated at some prior point in time (which is left unspecified because they can't recall precisely when it occurred) and decided, rationally, to adopt a strategy of clicking through quickly and waiting for bad news to arrive later.

System 1 thinking does not always entail behaving like a simple machine,[56] but in this context, we think it does. First, the relevant human capability being engineered and examined by us is cognitive processing of an instrumental decision.[57] In this setting, System 2 corresponds with deliberation or "thinking slow," and System 1 corresponds with automatic behavior or "thinking fast."[58] Second, in this setting, the techno-social environment nudges at the micro level of a single interaction and contributes incrementally to decision fatigue. Other factors also affect participants and reinforce the techno-social environment at the macro level. People who repeatedly interact with this system end up performing simple scripts (whether learned or programmed) in response to stimuli, and, in this particular fashion, behave like a simple machine. Thus, we might go a bit further and say that, in this setting, System 1 corresponds with not thinking (rather than thinking fast) because the automatic behavior is scripted or programmed. It may be counterintuitive to equate rational behavior with scripted or programmed behavior because the former seems good and the latter bad. But the two characterizations are not mutually exclusive. Neither is inherently good or bad. Everything depends on the context. Sometimes following a script is perfectly rational. For example, we all do so daily when making pleasantries with others. What makes the electronic contracting environment special is that it is designed to make it irrational to break away from the click-to-contract script.

One strong objection to our analysis is that we have long behaved this way, that automatic assent is neither new nor unique to online contracts. Most people don't read the terms of insurance contracts, mortgages, or the vast majority of offline contracts. Supposedly, we have long given up on reading and negotiating contracts, especially in business-to-consumer contexts. But this counterargument is predicated upon a subtle mistake. *Not reading does not mean abandoning deliberation.* Skipping over the fine print does not mean we bypass exercising System 2 thinking altogether and rely exclusively on System 1. We still focus on the most important and salient terms of insurance contracts, mortgages, etc. At some point during contracting, we at least deliberate over the magnitude of price.[59] The same is likely true for online purchases that involve "big ticket" items. That is, when the price or quality of the good or service being purchased is salient to the consumer, the consumer presumably deliberates, both online and offline. But as noted earlier, such deliberation is absent from many electronic contracts precisely because the apparent price is zero and the hidden price is in the unread terms, the data exchanges, and the attenuated and sometimes uneasy relationships brokered with various third parties. By design, we're led to trust blindly, as if we had relationships worthy of such trust when we really don't.[60]

The electronic contracting environment is thus another illustration of techno-social engineering of humans. If our characterization is correct and the environment effectively programs human beings to behave like simple stimulus-response machines – perfectly rational, predictable and programmable – then it's important to determine *if* the process is dehumanizing.

Thus far, we haven't taken a strong normative position. Instead, we've primarily aimed to draw attention to a phenomenon that deserves more attention from legal theorists and ethicists. The majority of them seem to deny its existence or fail to recognize its contours. The techno-social engineering we've described affects two basic human capabilities, the capability to deliberate and the capability to relate to others. As we discuss below and in later chapters, we believe these capabilities are fundamental to being human and at risk of being lost through rampant techno-social engineering.

Electronic Contracting and Taylorism

In this section, we again turn to Taylorism. It's a useful lens for examining the design of electronic contracting and the phenomenon of electronic contracting creep.

As discussed in Chapter 4, in the late nineteenth century and the early twentieth century, Frederick Taylor developed his theory of scientific management of humans in the workplace.[61] His work was motivated by concerns about efficiency. Taylor saw substantial inefficiencies in factories and other workplaces. He attributed many of the inefficiencies to mismanagement of labor. Taylor carefully studied workers and their work, examining minute details of tasks performed in the workplace, and, based on the data collected, he developed a system for optimizing their performance with the objective of increasing efficiency and productivity. We consider Taylorism to be one of the building block philosophies that today supports widespread techno-social engineering of humans.

The human-computer interface that we're calling the electronic contracting environment is but one example of an unheralded modern extension of Taylorism outside the workplace. There are many others, some of which we discuss in subsequent chapters. The crucial point we would like to make here is that the underlying structure, logic, and effects of electronic contracting and Taylorism may be the same. That is, like an idealized Taylorist workplace, the electronic contracting environment is optimized to minimize transaction costs, which, in this context, largely consist of human time and attention. Human deliberation, especially in the electronic contracting context, tends to be unproductive. Moreover, as described previously, the impact on consumers also has a Taylorist flavor, in the sense that consumers perform scripted routines, habitually, automatically, like simple machines. Yet, in contrast with laborers who at least understand they are being managed and optimized like cogs in a machine, consumers are blissfully unaware of the techno-social engineering that they're experiencing.

The electronic contracting environment, interface and architecture evolved considerably over the past few decades. Our hypothesis is that it was optimized along the lines that Taylorism suggested, although in a more emergent and organic fashion.[62] Given this hypothesis, we formulated the following sets of questions:

i. What was the metric or value being optimized? How was it determined? Did it change? How was it measured and communicated? Did designers test it with humans? How so?

ii. Did people do the functional equivalent of time and motion studies to figure out how human beings interacted with the interface and how they "performed" certain predictable tasks (such as browsing and clicking)?

iii. Were studies reported in professional journals? What was common knowledge? Industry custom and practice?

Our research hasn't yielded fully satisfactory answers. In part, this is because we have found only limited published studies that directly address the design of the electronic contracting environment, interface, or architecture.[63] This leaves us with no choice but to rely on sources describing website design more generally[64] and informal personal conversations with experts, web designers, lawyers, and others about their experiences.[65]

Website design varies considerably in terms of the design objectives. Among the most common variables to be optimized are the following: user experience, user attention, time spent on the site, task performance (which can range from clicking on advertisements to interacting with other users or features of the site), and communication of messages or ideas (which can range from advertising to educational). Each of these can be broken down, measured, and optimized in various ways.

In the context of pages of a website associated with electronic contracting, the main design objectives include:[66]

- *minimize transaction costs* (i.e. all costs attributable to the pages and associated with consummating a transaction, including time and effort spent by the consumer);
- *maximize retention* (i.e. the rate at which consumers agree and don't leave the site);
- *minimize design and operational costs* (meaning the costs associated with creating and operating the contracting architecture);
- *maximize enforceability* (i.e. the resulting contract is enforceable in court).

Other design variables might be included, such as attractiveness, simplicity of the design, or how well the design fits with the brand or the rest of the website. "The design of an online interface involves many . . . choices [that can shape impressions], whether choices about font, lines, colors that 'convey mood and provide a setting for the information' or choices about how interactivity can evoke different personalities."[67] It's worth noting, however, that most of the major objectives for website pages – especially user experience and communication of particular messages or ideas – aren't relevant for electronic contracting pages, except in the negative sense that designers would like to *minimize any interference* with the website's primary pages.[68] The electronic contracting pages are functional and task-oriented. They usually have little to no personality. Accordingly, while the prioritization of these objectives might vary across sites, we believe the first objective – *minimize transaction costs* – matters most. The second could be framed in terms of opportunity costs and folded into the first. The third seems less important, mainly because the marginal costs associated with designing the electronic contracting pages of a website are quite small. Keep in mind this does not include the costs associated with a lawyer drafting the terms and conditions, which is not a design or operational cost.[69] Anecdotally, our informal conversations confirmed that these were among the least interesting but easiest pages of a website for a designer to create and operate, especially given the ease of copying and standardization. The priority given to legal enforceability varies considerably across websites, depending on, among other things, the degree to which service providers anticipate potential litigation. The gradual evolution of the electronic contracting interface in response to court decisions demonstrates the significance of this factor and how the shock of a court decision can lead to new design practices spreading relatively rapidly and becoming industry standard.[70]

We need to distinguish two types of website pages related to electronic contracting. First, there are website pages displaying contract terms and conditions. These static pages vary in terms of where they are located within a website, how a customer accesses the pages, their format, length, style, content, readability, and so on. Usually, people access them through a hyperlink, which may be a general Terms of Service link found on every page, or, if coupled with a required action on the part of the consumer (e.g. "Click I agree" or filling out a form), the hyperlink may be proximate to the button or form.[71] In general, these pages are not terribly different from hard copies of offline contracts. They're filled with legal jargon that's non-negotiable and incomprehensible to the average person.[72] The substance of some of the terms and conditions are meaningfully different because of the nature of the website services, relationships, data practices, and so on. Regardless, these are not design features, and so we generally leave them aside in the ensuing discussion.

A significant difference is that online contracts often suffer from bloat because the marginal costs of adding legal language are vanishingly small. This is an important design feature. The nature of the digital medium allows for cheap bloat, and one consequence of seemingly endless terms is obfuscation and raising the costs for consumers to read, engage, or deliberate. Non-negotiable, incomprehensible, and seemingly endless contract terms can be so daunting that no one bothers. This design feature affects consumer behavior on a micro contract-by-contract basis and on a macro endless-stream-of-contracts basis. To their credit, some firms have innovated in their design of these terms and conditions pages to improve readability or otherwise help consumers (consumer interest groups and markets more generally) better understand the contracts and identify important terms.[73]

The second type of website page includes some active mechanism for formally entering a contract, where the mechanism purports to satisfy the legal requirements for contract formation. Today, the most salient example is the click-to-contract mechanism, often referred to as a "click-through" or "click-wrap" agreement. For smartphones and tablets, it is the tap-to-contract mechanism.[74]

This architecture originated with software delivered in a box. Upon attempting to load the software on a computer, the consumer would be unable to proceed unless the consumer clicked a box confirming "I agree" or something similar.[75] The design innovation has three important characteristics. First, it forces the consumer to act physically and affirmatively in a manner creating a definitive record, which has both evidentiary and doctrinal significance.[76] The click-to-contract mechanism satisfies the objective theory of contract, which bases contract formation on objectively reasonable manifestations of assent, and, consequently, courts generally have upheld them.[77]

Second, the click-to-contract design innovation created obstacles, or speed bumps, of various sizes, that slow down the consumer. The smallest is an "I agree" button immediately clickable. Slightly more effort is required for a customer to check a box acknowledging that she has read the terms and condition before she can click the "I agree" button. Even more substantial are the software interface designs requiring a user to scroll over some (or all) of the terms and conditions before clicking the "I agree" button. Even more options are possible, even though they aren't practiced much, to our knowledge. For example, one could require consumers to type particular text from the terms and conditions or answer substantive questions about the contract. In the end, many different designs were possible. What would be the point of adding more substantial speed bumps? Why slow down customers? Why prevent them from getting what they are really after – the content or service just beyond the speed bump? As privacy and security scholars have noted, getting people to slow down and engage with the terms and conditions – even security warnings – takes quite substantial speed bumps.[78]

Third, the click-to-contract design innovation provides an aesthetically pleasing mechanism for executing standard form contracts.[79] The separation of the two types of pages is critical. In contrast with paper standard form contracts, the terms can be hidden on another page. As a result, the interface is more aesthetically appealing and the user experience is practically seamless. These design features contribute to ease and effectiveness of techno-social engineering.

In practice, as the click-to-contract mechanism evolved both off and on the Internet, the optimizing logic of Taylorism seems to have taken hold. So, returning to the questions we posed:

What was the metric or value being optimized? How was it determined? Did it change? How was it measured and communicated? Did designers test it with humans? How so? Was the testing reported in journals? What was common knowledge? Industry custom and practice?

Website designers and other architects of the electronic contracting environment primarily approached the optimization problem in terms of click-rates, which strongly correlated with time and attention. They may not have understood what they were doing as "an optimization problem." Their basic goal was to get visitors to observe and then click the "I agree" button as soon as possible.[80] The primary transaction cost to be minimized was the consumer's time and attention.

In the field of human-computer interaction, designers recognize the need to minimize user "interaction cost." This is defined as the sum of mental and physical efforts users must expend while interacting with a site to reach their goals or expected benefits.[81] There may be a variety of user actions and goals, depending upon the website. Raluca Budiu, the Director of Research at the Nielson Norman Group, a leading user experience research and consulting firm, explains that the following user actions contribute differently to the total interaction cost:

- reading
- scrolling
- looking around in order to find relevant information
- comprehending information presented to you
- clicking or touching (without making mistakes)
- typing
- page loads and waiting times
- attention switches
- memory load – information that users must remember to complete their task.[82]

Not surprisingly, electronic contracting interfaces evolved to minimize the costs associated with these actions.[83] Often, though not always, the click-to-contract mechanism *is designed* to eliminate most of these actions and thus interaction costs. The only action that really matters is clicking.[84]

Rules of thumb, industry custom, and standard design practices percolate in the web design and human-computer interface communities. The placement of text and images, font size and style, and various other factors are well-studied, although not always documented in academic literature.[85] In a sense, these communities have performed the functional equivalent of Taylor's time and motion studies to figure out: (i) how human beings interacted with designed interfaces; and (ii) how they "performed" certain predictable tasks (e.g. browsing and clicking). Anecdotally, we heard of various in-house "motion studies" of how people clicked with a mouse, how they used the up-down-left-right arrows and space bar to navigate, and eyeball tracking.[86] Time studies are legion.[87]

It's difficult for us to draw firm conclusions about how, if at all, these studies influenced the click-to-contract interface. We don't know of studies focused exclusively on this design subject. We hypothesize that the click-to-contract interface was gradually optimized based (perhaps only implicitly) on the more general web design "time and motion studies" to minimize time-to-click-to-contract and motion-to-click-to-contract and thus transaction costs. If we're right, then the analogy with Taylorism is strong.

Some legal scholars have suggested that website user experience designers might employ images, animation, and other seductive features to distract consumers or prime them so that the speed bump (even if only minimal) is one they speed over.[88] As many others have noted, the internet environment more generally might lead consumers to be more impulsive or impatient.[89] Let's suppose this is true. We would add that such behavior and feelings are not inherent, inevitable, or natural. They are constructed and contingent upon the built environment. Web designers in general contribute to such behavior, and they exploit it. The eye-tracking, click-rate, and other "time and motion" web design studies might not be framed in terms of exploitation. Then again, neither were Taylor's time and motion studies. Both sets of studies are managerial and, more specifically, aimed at developing the data necessary to scientifically manage human subjects – workers and consumers – to maximize productivity and efficiency.

The electronic contracting interface fits within the same pattern, at least in some respects. Yet the legal system has gradually imposed some constraints. For example, in *Specht* v. *Netscape*, 306 F 3d 17 (2nd Cir. 2002), the Court of Appeals for the Second Circuit required conspicuous notice to protect consumers against surreptitious contracts. The court directly evaluated Netscape's design choices and concluded that customers who downloaded a software "plug-in" called "SmartDownload" could not have reasonably known of the software's associated license terms. To download the software, customers visited a webpage and clicked on a "Start Download" button. The "sole reference to . . . license terms on the . . . webpage was located in text that would have become visible to plaintiffs only if they had scrolled down to the next screen." The website design itself concealed the license terms in a "submerged screen." This influential precedent has shaped design choices, both directly – by emphasizing conspicuous notice – and indirectly – by identifying potential legal risks from design choices that undermined the integrity of the click-to-contract mechanism as a means to satisfy the objective theory of contracts.[90] Not surprisingly, many major websites have reduced the clutter and potential distractions on their electronic contracting interface.

Humanity's Techno-Social Dilemma Revisited

So far, we have suggested that contract law and practice, especially the electronic contracting environment, are more than meets the eye. The standard account correctly stipulates that they enable people to formulate legally binding commitments and relationships. Additionally, we've suggested the Taylorist design of the electronic contracting environment conditions humans to behave like simple machines. Such an attack on our autonomy might warrant systemic reform of contract law.[91]

Again, our argument is *not* about the goodness or badness of contract terms per se, or even the outcomes in specific contracts, transactions, or cases. The oppression we're identifying *is not* unfair or exploitative terms. Nor is it Radin's concern about private ordering replacing public ordering. These are significant problems for electronic contracts. For now, let's assume away such problems and presume the terms of electronic contracts are fair, consumer-friendly, and even better than their paper counterparts.[92]

Our focus has been and remains on the social costs external to the contracts. These are the social costs associated with rampant techno-social engineering that devalues and diminishes human autonomy and sociality[93] as we become accustomed to being nudged, conditioned, and, more broadly, engineered to behave like simple stimulus-response machines. In the Introduction, we characterized this type of threat against core human aptitudes and capabilities as *humanity's techno-social dilemma*, an analogue to the tragedy of the commons. Here, we're presenting the electronic contracting dilemma as an example of humanity's techno-social dilemma. Like sheep herders who act in a perfectly rational manner when adding sheep to their flock without fully accounting for the social costs manifest through the degradation of the pasture, consumers rationally enter into electronic contracts that, as we have assumed, are fair and consumer-friendly, without fully accounting for the social costs manifest through the degradation of their autonomy, and, we would go so far as to say, the diminution of our collective humanity.[94] Our concern is thus with the macro effects of many micro-level decisions to contract that on their face are perfectly rational and efficient. This may seem to put too much weight on the shoulders of contract law. However, the same can be and has been said for many tragedies of the commons.

The electronic contracting dilemma raises concerns about human autonomy because people may be subject to Taylorist techno-social engineering nudging them to behave automatically. If this were an isolated or rare occurrence, the impact would not likely be meaningful or lasting. However, the click-to-contract human-computer interface has crept across varied contexts ranging from websites, smartphone apps, smart TVs, to the Internet of Things.

To make matters worse, electronic contracting creep is accompanied by surveillance and nudge creep. The human-computer interface itself nudges, and it enables surveillance by site owners and third parties. Such surveillance feeds data back and thereby further enables and contributes to nudging. It might seem unfair to put the burden of this problem on contract law. Perhaps one might argue that surveillance and nudging are wholly separate affairs and fall outside the purview of contract law. While that's a convenient argument, we fail to see the merit of putting on such blinders. The three creep phenomena seem inexorably intertwined, a vicious rather than virtuous cycle in our current digital environment.[95] All three are fundamental parts of modern Taylorism and the techno-social engineering of humans.

Contract Creep

Autonomy and sociality are critical to being human and maintaining a flourishing society. Without autonomy, we can't live self-directed lives.[96] And without sociality, we can't create meaningful personal and professional relationships upon which collective endeavors depend.[97]

Contract law is one of many important institutions aiming to support and even extend these basic capabilities (for more detail, see Appendix E). In general, it has been quite successful. But continued success is not inevitable. It's contingent upon many factors, ranging from the competencies of lawyers and judges to the technical media through which contracts are executed. Critically, contract law's impact upon our autonomy and sociality depends upon social practices and the built environments we construct that have distinctive affordances.

We've argued that the electronic contracting environment has inverted the primary aims of contract law. We explained how the technical architecture of the electronic contracting environment nudges consumers to behave automatically. The design of the architecture may have emerged gradually over the past few decades, but, nonetheless, it has a distinctly Taylorist imprint. In accordance with optimality conditions (i.e. efficiency and productivity), consumers follow the click-to-contract script. The choice architecture retains minimal decisional autonomy in simple take-it-or-leave-it fashion, but the fiction of actual choice only contributes to gradual creep of the human-computer interface from websites to apps to smart TVs to smart homes and beyond.

If the postulated conditioning not only exists, but also creeps across contexts, extending the range of situations where we behave automatically, then there is real cause for concern. When such creep leads us to be complacent, to follow the herd and passively accept matters that should require deliberation, our humanity itself is at risk.

CHAPTER 6

On Extending Minds and Mind Control

Introduction

This chapter furthers our analysis of techno-social engineering by discussing a philosophical position called extended mind theory. According to this view, throughout history humans have extended their minds beyond their physical brains and bodies by using technological tools as aids for performing cognitive processes. Proponents insist that calculators, address books, and other so-called "cognitive prosthetics" are reliable and integral parts of our minds, and, consequently, our selves.

Consider the humorous yet glowing terms *New York Times* columnist David Brooks uses to describe his relationship with GPS technology. The language resonates with our Chapter 2 discussion of outsourced navigation.

> I have melded my mind with the heavens, communed with the universal consciousness, and experienced the inner calm that externalization brings, and it all started because I bought a car with a G.P.S ...
>
> It was unnerving at first, but then a relief. Since the dawn of humanity, people have had to worry about how to get from here to there. Precious brainpower has been used storing directions, and memorizing turns. I myself have been trapped at dinner parties at which conversation was devoted exclusively to the topic of commuter routes.
>
> My G.P.S. goddess liberated me from this drudgery. She enabled me to externalize geographic information from my own brain to a satellite brain, and you know how it felt? It felt like nirvana.[1]

Brooks misses the big picture. And this isn't surprising. In the philosophical literature, folks are fighting about all kinds of topics related to the extended mind without asking the most important questions, which concern techno-social engineering of human minds.

- *Who is doing the thinking when humans use mind-extending technologies?*
- *In mind-extending situations, what types of thinking do humans and technologies each do and how transparent are the different forms of thinking to the humans whose minds are being extended?*
- *How does technologically extended thinking impact the development of human capabilities?*

What we object to the most is that leading extended mind advocates regard many of the technologies that extend the human mind as normatively neutral, in the sense that the tools themselves are neither good nor bad.[2] They say cognitive prosthetics empower users, leave their autonomy intact, and can be characterized as "cognitive upgrades."[3] We challenge these assumptions and the Silicon Valley lingo that's used to convey them. As many of the examples discussed in previous chapters demonstrate, seemingly harmless mind-extending technologies can be powerful instruments for techno-social engineering. The more potent ones make us pawns in other people's games.

We advance the following novel claim: Mind-extending technologies run the risk of turning humans into simple machines under the control or influence of those in control of the technologies, at least in contexts where the technologies are networked and owned and controlled by others.

Many readers may balk at this claim, viewing it to be speculative science fiction at best, or at worst, a fear-mongering attack on the technologists and technologies we hold dear. Such reactions are understandable but ultimately misguided and too easily used as dismissive parries. The fear-mongering argument is itself mere fear-mongering. We are not attacking technologists or technologies in general. Generalization poses a serious problem for extended mind advocates because technologies are not all the same. Given their affordances, technologies are rarely if ever neutral. Instead, they have context-dependent impacts (costs and benefits, if you prefer). Mind-extending technologies not only afford users beneficial opportunities to extend their minds and think differently with their tools, but the technologies also afford other parties opportunities to perform various thinking tasks and even to exercise mind control. The science fiction argument is reasonable, but it only highlights that we're talking about the extreme end-state when we say humans are made into machines. The incremental steps toward that end-state are what we are hoping to detect and examine. To do so, we must pay close attention to the relationships between different technologies, our extended minds, and our autonomy.

Extending Ourselves: Background and Examples

Is the extended mind thesis on target or wildly off base? It depends on how you see things. Before giving you our answer, we'll bring you up to speed on three related issues: the *extended body, extended cognition,* and *cognitive technology*. These topics are less controversial than the extended mind itself. They are a great baseline for you to determine how solid or porous the connections are between mind, body, and world.

Technologically Extended Bodies: Contemporary Experiences

Let's start with the body.[4] When we interact with ourselves and others, we regularly experience a range of artifacts, from aesthetic to prosthetic objects, as *bodily extensions*. In his classic *Being and Nothingness,* existential philosopher Jean-Paul Sartre shows why our first-person experience of using artifacts can be immensely rich. Expanding upon Sartre's views of how technologies can alter what other people make of our bodies, as well as how we understand them ourselves, philosopher of technology Andrew Feenberg invites us to consider what it's like to wear glasses in public.

> [O]ur objectivity before the gaze of the other extends beyond our skin out into the world of things by which our presence is signified. We are objects of the one whom we are hiding in the cracking of a branch underfoot. Our body extends to the glow of the cigarette that gives our presence away, or, to give a contemporary example, the ringing of the cell phone that embarrasses us in the middle of a lecture. This is the extended body in its simplest form.[5]

Google executives should have done a better job of this before launching the much hyped but heavily criticized Google Glass campaign – a campaign that left some so angry about the possibility of encountering people wearing smart, camera ready specs that the phrase "Glasshole" was coined and became a meme.

Although glasses provide a useful function by augmenting vision, they also can inspire social derision. This simultaneity of benefit and detriment is vividly illustrated when people who wear glasses get mocked for having "four eyes." Feenberg characterizes this objectifying experience as the "body-object for the other."

To further illustrate the point, let's consider clothing. Like glasses, clothing provides obvious practical benefits: "to clothe the body, to keep it warm, and to enable the wearer to perform particular activities while wearing it."[6] Clothing also serves aesthetic functions, "for example, by making [the wearer] look taller, slimmer, broader, curvier, or lengthier."[7] And, clothing can be independently beautiful.[8] In serving these functions, clothing communicates much about us and shapes how others perceive us. That's why fashion designers work hard to design products that people can use to manage how they're objectified.

To manipulate how people see us requires anticipating how they'll look at the different ways we can present ourselves. Sometimes, thinking about what others think can reinforce – if not create – bad habits. As a child who wore glasses, Feenberg felt fragile and "brainy" and constrained his behavior by acting *as if* others constantly were looking at and assessing him. That's why he took a cautious and hesitant approach to sports.[9]

Feenberg characterizes the structure of this self-regulating experience – in which both identity and behavior revolve around the meanings embedded in an artifact – as the "body-object for the other as perceived by the self." Again, clothing is an illuminating example. Clothing shapes how others perceive us and how we see ourselves, both in the mirror and through our anticipated and actual interactions with others. For example, suppose I think I'm overweight and others perceive me to be fat. I might wear only black outfits because the color has a slimming effect that can impact what others see. Many critics have lamented that industries routinely exploit our concerns over what other people think. Are fashion designers, advertisers, and mass media helping us to manage objectification or exploiting it to make a profit? Do the exemplars we see on television reflect who we are or who we want to be? These questions come up again and again for a reason.

Finally, Feenberg claims that Sartre's perspective on the extended body illuminates the contemporary experience of online communication. When we use email, the person to whom we're writing doesn't see our physical body. Nevertheless, the medium doesn't disembody expression. Instead, what we type often is stylized as "conscious self-presentation" that allows others to identify us.[10]

> We could be said to "wear" language online [similarly to how] we wear clothes in everyday life . . . Others can identify us from a few lines of our writing. We identify it too as our extended bodily presence, in this case, a strange textual cyborg . . . Our language shows us as neat or sloppy, formal or informal; we reveal our mood by our linguistic gestures as happy or sad, confident or timid. The fact that we can be proud or embarrassed, open or secretive, friendly or distant, all point to the complexity of this mode of technical mediation.[11]

Extended Body	Examples: Glowing cigarette that announces our presence as cool or ridiculous with its attention-grabbing glow. Cellphone ringing at an inappropriate time and calling attention to our inconsiderateness. See main text for more detail on clothing, glasses, and electronic writing.
Clothing	Means for shaping other people's perceptions of who we are. Also, the means for us to be shaped, e.g., into believing that certain outfits can powerfully transform our identities.
Glasses	Augments limited biological capacity for seeing. Also subjects wearers to cultural perceptions of what it means to wear glasses. If those perceptions are negative and a wearer internalizes them, he or she can feel safe from social derision in some contexts but at risk of it in others.
Electronic Writing	A means for expressing oneself through deliberately chosen words and symbols, but also a means for others to judge us by how we communicate.

You might believe Feenberg's final example takes the idea of bodily extension too far. We note this possible reaction here because the topic is controversial and the objection could resurface in related ways throughout our discussion of technological extension. At the same time, perhaps you can draw useful analogies from Feenberg's analysis. Know anybody who fills their online writing with emojis and expresses this style in other aspects of life?

Cognition: Extended and Distributed

Having discussed how the body can be extended, we now turn to philosopher of science Ronald Giere's ideas about *distributed cognition* (also called *extended cognition*). The concept augments the computer science understanding of distributed processing:

> It was discovered that what [computer] networks do best is recognize and complete *patterns* in input provided by the environment. The generalization to humans is that much of human cognition is a matter of recognizing patterns through activations of prototypes embodied in groups of neurons whose activities are influenced by prior sensory experience.[12]

Given how skillfully humans recognize patterns, it has been postulated that our cognitive history is filled with instances where humans routinely cope with tasks involving linear symbol processing by creating and manipulating external representations. For example, when the goal is to multiply

two three-digit numbers, we capitalize on our capacity to recall the products for any two integers by following this sequence. First, we construct
an external representation of the entire equation. Second, we follow long-
established rules of calculation that restrict our focus to basic addition (i.e.
four numbers in a row, at most) and basic multiplication (i.e. always two
numbers). Giere's reflection upon this cognitive activity prompts the
following question: *What cognitive entity is performing this task?*

It seems foolish to state that the person doing the task accomplishes
all the cognitive processing herself. That assertion ignores material
culture (e.g. pen, paper, etc.) and social culture (e.g. long-established
rules of calculation). *But what, exactly, does it mean to claim that the
person plus the material culture plus social culture collectively engage in
cognitive activity?*

Common sense suggests that the material and social media, including
the external representations, merely serve as inputs that structure the
problem in such a manner that it can be solved internally, what computer
scientist Herbert Simon calls "the Mind's Eye."[3] This view suggests that
the person in control of the inputs is the relevant thinker; she decides,
judges, or accomplishes the cognitive act. By contrast, according to the
distributed cognition view, the *system* (i.e. the whole person plus material
and social media) performs the cognitive task. Cognition is "distributed"
amongst all the parts of the system, including humans and material and
cultural artifacts.[14]

Why does it matter how we describe cognition? The common-sense
view fails to credit the cognitive contributions of material and social
cultures. It fails to fully appreciate the degree that the person in control
depends upon those resources and those who supply them. The distributed
cognition, however, puts too much weight on the whole system itself.
Consequently, the view doesn't always pinpoint where judgment and
control occur, and why these activities can matter more than the rest.
This issue can easily be remedied, as our subsequent discussion of the
extended mind thesis shows. To adopt the distributed cognition view,
analysts should examine control points within the system.

Common-Sense View of Cognition	Only human brains are capable of thinking.
Extended Cognition View	Systems of humans and tools together collectively perform cognitive tasks, including problem-solving.

Recall our discussion in Chapter 1 of the Oral Roberts University fitness tracking program and our comparison of different tracking tools. Tracking fitness by journaling is a different process than being tracked by a Fitbit. Both are examples of extended cognition. Each depends upon:

- human cognition;
- cognitive tasks or operations embedded in and performed by material objects (e.g. writing instrument + journal and Fitbit device + networked computers);
- cognitive tasks or operations embedded in and performed by social culture (e.g. norms and expectations about what physical activity data is appropriate for recording, how such records should be written, ethical standards about data collection and sharing within educational institutions, *et cetera*).

Each tracking system encompasses different distributions of cognitive tasks, including different control points.[15] Humans within both systems play different roles, too. This is partially due to the different affordances that are baked into the tracking tools and system design. Extended cognition theory reveals and explains this phenomenon. However, many of the theorists who discuss it don't focus on the existential, social, ethical, and political implications for humans participating in the different systems. Analyzing cognitive technology provides further detail. It's our final step leading to the extended mind discussion.

Cognitive Technology

At the end of her seminal *Mind as Machine*, cognitive scientist Margaret Boden highlights *cognitive technology* "as one area of promising empirical research and ... philosophical inquiry" that "will be key foci in effort and controversy in the foreseeable future," if not "well over 100 years from now."[16] Cognitive technology research focuses on how the differences in technologies and affordances affect human behavior and development.

The concept of "cognitive technology" stipulates the following ecological thesis: Using a particular class of technology can actively shape how people think, and, consequently, this influence can affect how people act, including how they treat the very technology that alters their thinking.

> What defines a cognitive tool, as opposed to other tools? And how does the cognitive tool specifically influence our thinking? These are the two

questions that circumscribe the domains of cognitive technology and technological cognition respectively. The specificity of the cognitive tool, as opposed to, say, a hammer or a car, is that it directly affects, and operates upon, the workings of our mind. In general, purely reproductive tools have little cognitive interest: a Xerox copier is not by itself a cognitive tool (in the normal case, and barring certain imaginative uses), while the typewriter, inasmuch as it interacts with our mind in forming our thoughts on paper, is a cognitive tool (albeit a primitive one, compared to a computer).[17]

Using cognitive technology entails entering into the process of extended cognition. For when we interact with cognitive technology, we don't perceive and manipulate tools as "external props and aids." Rather, our experience of cognitive technology is more intimate. The literature offers many examples to illuminate how humans and cognitive technologies work together as "cognitive systems" to solve problems. The following cases are frequently cited.

- The *slide rule* transforms complex mathematical problems into simple tasks of perceptual recognition.
- *Maps* provide geographical information in a manner that is well suited for complex planning and strategic military operations.
- *Expert bartenders use distinctly shaped glasses* as cues for mixing and dispensing volumes of drinks carefully and quickly.
- *Artists use sketchpads* to organize ideas, explore visual ambiguities, and determine how to express perceptions beyond what the "mind's eye" of the imagination typically permits.
- *Scrabble players re-arrange their tiles* to determine what possibilities for word formation their letters offer.
- *Skilled chess players* typically prefer to analyze positions with *real chess sets and real pieces.*
- *Existing language* provides *new generations of humans* with the opportunity to learn to classify things and express themselves without needing to first generate new vocabularies, grammars and techniques for imparting meaning to others. Even patterns of repetition, such as rhyme and rhythm, serve a cognitive function. They make it easier to remember complicated sound patterns.
- *Mathematical conventions* – that is, symbolic notation and basic procedural rules – reduce complex mathematical problems, such as multiplication, to more basic acts of perception and computation.
- *Air traffic controllers learn to physically hold flight strips* in a manner that helps them manage critical information needed to prevent adverse situations, including crashes.

- *Navigational tools, such as the gyrocompass, alidade, and hoey,* allow sailors to gather, unify, and judge an array of data that enables ships to effectively move to desired destinations.

Briefly considering these examples goes a long way. It helps us appreciate how cognitive technology can transform the nature of a task by altering the action sequences required to complete it:[18] (1) they can transform the deliberation process by minimizing how much conscious awareness and attention are required to solve problems; (2) they can transform our relation to time and space by stabilizing information that otherwise would be transient; (3) they can transform the environments we are embedded in to minimize the demands placed on biological memory; (4) they can transform intellectually difficult problems into perceptual ones that are easier to solve; (5) they can transform the processes by which knowledge is transferred; and (6) they can transform workspaces and residences so as to enhance the speed and reliability of frequently performed tasks.[19]

Extended Mind

In 1998, philosophers Andy Clark and David Chalmers wrote a provocative article, "The Extended Mind." They present scientific accounts of how the mind naturally copes with its inherent limitations (e.g. being good at pattern recognition but not at memorizing long lists of information). And they contend that humans have a biological propensity to extend their minds outside of their brains and bodies and into the environment. Since its initial formulation, a substantial literature has been engaging with these ideas. Clark himself has defended and refined the argument in a series of books and articles.

The core idea is that humans *think* in various ways through and with technologies that are external to their biophysical selves (bodies and brains), and by doing so literally extend the boundaries of their minds. This transformation happens by tightly coupling cognitive processes in the brain with those performed in or with the technology. If you don't believe that this expansive merger (or act of incorporation) regularly occurs, then, according to Clark and Chalmers, you've fallen victim to "biochauvinistic prejudice" and are mistakenly presuming that thinking only happens in the head. To help us avoid this error, Clark and Chalmers articulate an ideal they call the "parity principle":

Parity Principle: If, as we confront some task, a part of the world functions as a process which, were it to go on in the head, we would have no hesitation in accepting as part of the cognitive process, then that part of the world is (for that time) part of the cognitive process.[20]

Simply, humans effectively extend their minds through technologies when the mental processes or steps for solving a problem are like what would otherwise be completed internally. The difference between extended cognition theory and extended mind theory is that only the latter views the whole cognitive process as occurring in and being part of the subject's mind. For example, both extended cognition and extended mind advocates agree that when a person uses paper and pen to perform a calculation, she takes a cognitive task that could be performed in her head with varying degrees of difficulty and simplifies how it's solved. But only the extended mind theorist views paper and pen as genuine (not metaphorical) parts of the mind itself.

Let's consider another example. Clark and Chalmers discuss a man named Otto who "suffers from Alzheimer's disease, and like many patients, ... relies on information in the environment to help structure his life."[21] In particular, Otto relies completely on a notebook that he carries with him for all sorts of information about the world. For Otto, the notebook is more than an external memory device. He develops an intimate relation to it, relying on it automatically and with as much ease and confidence as one would rely on biological memory. Clark and Chalmers thus emphasize that Otto thinks using the notebook. It's an integral part of his thinking circuit, basically, and a bonafide part of his mind.[22]

Not all environmental, non-biological resources used while performing cognitive processes are "candidates for inclusion into an individual's cognitive system." Clark and Chalmers thus stipulate additional restrictive criteria, such as:

1. "the resource be reliably available and typically invoked";
2. "any information thus retrieved be more or less automatically endorsed [and thus] not usually be subject to critical scrutiny (e.g., unlike the opinions of other people). It should be deemed about as trustworthy as something retrieved clearly from biological memory";
3. "information contained in the resource should be as easily accessible as and when required";
4. "information [stored in the resource] has been consciously endorsed at some point in the past and indeed is there as a consequence of this endorsement."

Let's consider another familiar example of a mind-extending technology in light of these four criteria. For many people, the GPS navigation system is functionally equivalent to Otto's notebook, with respect to location and navigational information. Like Otto, many people rely on their GPS device to navigate, often while driving but also while riding a bike or walking. For most, GPS is "reliably available and typically invoked;" the "information thus retrieved [is] more or less automatically endorsed [and thus] not usually . . . subject to critical scrutiny [and] deemed about as trustworthy as something retrieved clearly from biological memory;" and the "information contained in the [GPS device is] as easily accessible as and when required." While the fourth criterion arguably is not met, when people rely on GPS to navigate the physical world, they appear to be extending their minds in the sense that Clark and Chalmers suggest.

Strangely, Clark and Chalmers appear to claim that the person extending her mind retains full autonomy and alone does the thinking required to determine: (i) what procedure should be followed when using technology to perform cognitive functions; and (ii) how to judge when a problem that's pursued with the help of such technology is successfully solved. Indeed, criteria (1) and (2) imply conscious choice and control over the resource, while criterion (4) requires some conscious endorsement. The problem is that these features don't guarantee an autonomous relation to technology. At the extreme, "reliably available," "typically invoked," "automatically endorsed," "not usually be subject to critical scrutiny," and "about as trustworthy as something retrieved clearly from biological memory" all would be satisfied in the extreme case of a brainwashed human who is indistinguishable from a machine.[23] In the next section, we consider more common and less extreme forms of techno-social engineering.

Extended Mind and Techno-Social Engineering

A recent statement of the core extended mind hypothesis is the Hypothesis of Organism-Centered Cognition (HOC):

> Human cognitive processing (sometimes) literally extends into the environment surrounding the organism. But the organism (and within the organism, the brain/CNS [Central Nervous System]) remains the core and currently the most active element. Cognition remains organism centered even when it is not organism bound.[24]

According to this articulation of the theory (which is compatible with previous ones), human minds are not only embodied, but they are situated within and integrated into their environment. The dynamic interplay between human minds and the constructed socio-technical environment is the main link connecting extended mind theory with our analysis of techno-social engineering.

To explore the juncture between extended minds and techno-social engineering, we have to bracket other debates, including some ongoing philosophical discussions.[25] For our purposes, we'll accept the extended mind thesis as a metaphysically valid account of the human mind and its basic relationship with technologies.[26] This means that rather than asking if the extended mind thesis departs too greatly from more widely accepted theories, like extended cognition, we'll focus on something else entirely: the *normative implications* that are *hidden* when the extended mind thesis is taken to have only descriptive and explanatory value. Our trajectory takes us into ethical and political territory. These are areas that theorists like Clark address somewhat lightly (as we discuss below) and which most philosophers of mind would contend fall outside their purview.[27]

For us, the central point of contention is that extended mind proponents tend to depict technologies that extend the human mind as *neutral*, thereby presuming that the humans who technologically extend their minds remain *autonomous decision-makers*. We're deeply skeptical of these presumptions. Mind-extending technologies run the risk of turning humans into simple machines[28] under the control or influence of those in control of the technologies, at least in contexts where the technologies are networked and owned and controlled by others.

Consider Chalmers weighing in and saying something that might have made Steve Jobs – the man who viewed computers as akin to bicycles for the mind – blush.

> I bought an iPhone. The iPhone has already taken over some of the central functions of my brain . . . The iPhone is part of my mind already . . . [Andy Clark's] marvelous book . . . defends the thesis that, in at least some of these cases, the world is not serving as a mere instrument for the mind. Rather, the relevant parts of the world have become parts of my mind. My iPhone is not my tool, or at least it is not wholly my tool. Parts of it have become parts of me . . . When parts of the environment are coupled to the brain in the right way, they become parts of the mind.[29]

Now, a skeptic would say this testimony sounds less like a metaphysical attestation and more like script written for a paid Apple spokesperson,[30] especially since warnings about proprietary technological extensions eroding our autonomy date back at least as far as the 1960s. Media theorist Marshall McLuhan then cautioned: "Who owns your extended eyes? Once we have surrendered our senses and nervous systems to the private manipulation of those who would try to benefit from taking a lease on our eyes and ears and nerves, we don't really have any rights left."[31] McLuhan recognized the risk of *mind control*.

To a degree, so does Chalmers. After all, in a TED talk that seems to represent how he conceptualizes his relationship with mind-extending technologies, he says that the iPhone "has already taken over some of the central functions of [his] brain."[32] Yet he does not see this phenomenon as risky because he assumes he retains autonomy when his mind and an iPhone merge, a form of "biotechnological symbiosis" as Clark describes it. The mistaken assumption, however, unwittingly works a kind of "moral magic" that transforms mind control from serious transgression into acceptable and desirable practice. (We discuss another example of such moral magic in Appendix E.)

What Chalmers fails to appreciate is that the iPhone is *designed* to grant access and control privileges to others – a feature that isn't deliberately built into Otto's notebook.[33] This blind spot is apparent when Chalmers proudly describes using Facebook to crowd-source the question of what to present to a TEDx audience. He never questions the role that Facebook plays as a mediator of all communicative exchanges that take place on its platform. Facebook's proprietary algorithms (which are not available for public scrutiny) determine who can easily see a post (because it's placed near the top of the News Feed), who must exert effort to see a post (because it's placed a good distance away from the top of the News Feed), and who won't see the post at all (because the algorithms determine it isn't relevant enough to appear on that person's News Feed). Nor does he consider the impact of social expectations and social pressures on his decisions. Only the truly resolute can ask for help on Facebook (where friends, colleagues, and family can personally respond as well as look at what different people have to say and comment upon their suggestions) without feeling the pull of peer pressure. (All of this is potentially the tip of the iceberg. In the next chapter, we'll discuss Facebook's emotional contagion experiment. Facebook not only affects what we think, but also how we feel.)

With this view of mediation in mind, let's revisit the GPS example. The GPS system processes location information in real-time and develops navigational planning. The system determines the steps in each route and, usually, the order of routes presented. If each of these functions were performed inside a person's head, we would describe the functions as thinking. Since Clark and Chalmers ask us to avoid "biochauvinistic prejudice" and admit that these functions are still thinking when performed externally, outside of the person's head and through the technology, we'll do so for the sake of argument. We concede that the person using a GPS system has extended her mind.

But there's more to the extended mind perspective. While a GPS navigational system provides suggested routes, Clark and Chalmers should be consistent and committed to the view that people themselves choose which turns to make and which routes to take. Viewed this way, the technology only provides recommendations for consideration; it allows users to fully determine for themselves whether they want to follow the selected pathways.

And yet, doesn't it seem odd to say that only the person using the GPS is in charge of the cognitive functions embedded in the GPS system? Instead, responsibility and the execution of various cognitive tasks seem to be distributed among different agents within the cognitive system. It seems more reasonable to say that the GPS system user is not the only person doing the thinking; the system designers and choice architects also participate. We can describe this form of extended mind as *techno-social thinking* because the person extending his or her mind with the GPS system is calling on cognitive resources embedded in the technology by other people. In some cases, GPS navigational systems employ real-time contributions from peers on a network that communicate traffic information and use that information to modify suggested routes and their ranking. Unfortunately, the extended mind thesis tells us nothing about a host of important issues, such as:

- the psychology of how people respond to information presented by machines, such as "automation bias" and "automation complacency," which are meticulously detailed by author Nicholas Carr;[34]
- the relationships amongst all these minds providing cognitive contributions (e.g. *Are there more compelling reasons to see them as all equal or to see some as some deserving priority over others? Is there or should there be hierarchy by technological design?*);
- the technological affordances on both the supply and demand sides of the system (e.g. *How can navigational, logistical, and route planning services be exploited? How does the presentation of routes and associated data shape what users can do and how they behave?*).

For example, one of us used a GPS to help navigate a long trip. The device interface specified how fast the car was traveling and how much longer it would take to get to the destination. Those numbers effectively nudged the driver to speed up by conveying how much quicker he could arrive. We suspect others have had this experience. While this may have been an inadvertent nudge, marketers have identified and clamored to exploit geographically targeted advertising; route planning is a natural extension – an attractive means for bringing customers closer to the point of purchase.[35] (Recall our extended discussion of GPS creep in Chapter 2.)

The other author has had the experience of using a GPS-based route-planning app that provides real-time updates based on feedback from other app users. At times, while using the app, he has wondered why the app suggests new route segments when there is no traffic on any segments (because he is driving very early in the morning) and a shorter route is apparent. After talking to several taxi drivers, he concluded that the app probably is directing him down route segments to help the system gather data. The suggested route is not necessarily the optimal one for his trip, but it might be better for the system.[36] (Recall Taylor's credo.)

The matter of *who is doing what type of thinking* might seem trivial in some cases. In others, however, it raises challenging questions about how mind-extending technologies convey power. Such power may be subtly employed to shape beliefs and preferences, among other things, at least, so long as you believe that beliefs and preferences are the province of individual human beings. As philosopher John Danaher put it, "the locus of control is the all-important variable."[37] In his book *Throwing Rocks at the Google Bus*, Douglas Rushkoff argues:

> Amazon flips into personhood by reversing the traditional relationship between people and machines. Amazon's patented recommendation engines attempt to drive our human selection process. Amazon Mechanical Turks gave computers the ability to mete out repetitive tasks to legions of human drones. The computers did the thinking and the choosing; the people pointed and clicked as they were instructed or induced to do.[38]

Some philosophers have argued that extended mind theory can bring needed clarity and justification to various normative debates. For example, philosopher Michael Lynch contends that the extended mind thesis is relevant to legal debates about whether police officers should be required to have a warrant before examining the contents of a citizen's cellphone. After all, if our memories, conversations, and so much more are offloaded onto our phones, then anyone with access to them can effectively engage in a form of mind-reading. Others have questioned whether someone who steals Otto's notebook should be charged with a crime that's more severe than simply absconding with pieces of paper. The perpetrator appears to be causing Otto to experience brain-damage (or something analogous to it). While these issues are important, more radical debates exist. They concern the notion of extended responsibility, the idea that since humans and machines can form systems for thinking and acting, different parts of a system bear responsibility for undesirable conduct. For example, contrary to the NRA's mantra that "Guns don't kill people; people kill people," it has been argued that human-gun systems differ from humans who are not part of those systems. The main idea is that guns have deadly affordances and that people who are not properly trained in how to handle these weapons might be inclined to resolve conflicts in a more dramatic and deadly manner than if they didn't have guns at their disposal. While it would be absurd to throw a firearm in jail to rehabilitate it, it might be sensible to view gun control proposals as attempts to prevent humans from entering systems relations that will undermine their good judgment.

We postpone until Chapter 12 further examination of how mind-extending technology raises the plausible prospect of engineered determinism and poses a corresponding challenge to free will and moral responsibility.

Intrusion and Uncontrollability

In the final chapter of *Natural-Born Cyborgs*, Clark himself considers various lurking "specters" raised by the extended mind theory and the prospect of biotechnological symbiosis. We focus on two: intrusion and uncontrollability.[39] His discussion of intrusion presciently anticipates the Internet of Things and opens with:

> You live and work in a smart world, where your car is talking to your coffee machine (and snitching to your insurance company), and your medicine cabinet and toilet are watching your inputs and outputs (and snitching to your doctor or HMO, not to mention the drug police). Your smart badge (or maybe your cell phone) ensures that your physical movements leave a tangible trail, and your electronic trail is out there for all to see. The damn telemarketers know your soul; their machines have surfed your deepest likes and dislikes. So whatever happened to your right to a little space, some peace and privacy, a quiet affair, a little psychotropic time-out?[40]

Clark recognizes how the mind-extending technologies of our emerging smart world allow, encourage, and indeed depend upon others intruding upon our lives. He casts the intrusions as privacy issues caused by specific aspects of the technologies – e.g. cookies, globally unique identifiers, ubiquitous computing, and smart-badge systems. He briefly discusses responses, such as biting the bullet and accepting the trade-offs, implementing technological fixes that allow people to choose to protect their privacy, and shifting democratic norms that might mitigate anxieties and harms from others knowing sensitive things about us. *Unfortunately, Clark casts the privacy concerns mainly as others learning something about us.* But as we saw in the discussion of the deployment of fitness tracking devices in schools, such a shallow conception of privacy is an insufficient means for understanding and evaluating the underlying normative trade-offs that occur when tools and systems provide us with benefits but also subject us to techno-social engineering.

Clark touches on our concern very lightly when he turns to uncontrollability: "Some suggest that we should actively limit our reliance on technological props and aids, not just to protect our privacy but to control our own destinies and preserve our essential humanity."[41] His response is quite simple:

> Human-machine symbiosis, I believe, is simply what comes naturally. It lies on a direct continuum with clothes, cooking ("external, artificial digestion"), bricklaying, and writing. The capacity to creatively distribute labor between biology and the designed environment is the very signature of our species, and it implies no real loss of control on our part. For who we are is in large part a function of the webs of surrounding structure in which the conscious mind exercises at best a kind of gentle, indirect control.
>
> Of course, just because nature is pushing us doesn't mean we have to go. There are times, to be sure, when the intelligence of the infrastructures does seem to threaten our own autonomy and to cede too much, too soon, to the worlds we build.[42]

Clark doesn't go much further into the analysis. He notes the prevalence of the utopian and dystopian outlooks on the humanity-technology relationship, but then concludes: "the kind of control that we, both as individuals and as society, look likely to retain is *precisely the kind we always had: no more, no less.*"[43] Perhaps he's right. His prediction is hard to evaluate. Still, in light of the extended creep of techno-social engineering that's occurring, the prognostication seems to be wishful thinking at best.

Since Silicon Valley joined Hollywood in becoming one of the largest US exporters of fantasy, it's not surprising that billionaire and technology entrepreneur Elon Musk is starting to sound a lot like Clark. Musk insists that the only way for humans to avoid becoming "'house cats' to artificial intelligence" is for us to evolve into cyborgs.[44] To further this end, Musk is developing an "injectable mesh-like 'neural lace' that fits on your brain to give it digital computing powers."[45] Rhetorically, this sounds great. To avoid being controlled by hyper-intelligent artificial intelligence, all we need to do is build technologies that enable "lag-free interactions between our brains and external devices."[46] This option, however, begins to lose its appeal once we ask the questions raised in this chapter, which neither Clark nor Musk take too seriously: *Who is doing what type of thinking?* And what will the technology companies that provide us with this service demand in return? The unstated but presumed answer is that markets will sort it all out. But as we've been arguing throughout this chapter and the book, it's dangerous to let the economy decide the fate of our humanity.

Mind Extension and Human Capabilities

Having accepted the descriptive thesis of the extended mind theory for purposes of analysis and argument, there is a second important question that we need to ask. *How might mind-extending technologies affect the development of human capabilities?* This question brings us back to ideas explored in previous chapters.

Let's return to the GPS example. Consider the damning assessment that philosophers Hubert Dreyfus and Sean Kelly offer:

> For those of us who are directionally challenged (and both authors count ourselves among this group) the GPS seems to offer a great technological advance.
>
> But notice the hidden cost to this advance. When the GPS is navigating for you, your understanding of the environment is about as minimal as it can possibly be. It consists of knowing things like 'I should turn right now.' In the best case – and we want to take the best case here – this method of navigating gets you to your destination quickly and easily. But it completely trivializes the noble art of navigation, which was the province of great cultures from the sea-faring Phoenicians to the navigators of the Age of Discovery. To navigate by GPS requires no sense of where you are, no sense of where you're going, and no sense whatsoever for how to get there. Indeed, the whole point of the GPS is to spare you the trouble of navigating.
>
> But to lose the sense of struggle is to lose the sensitivities – to landmarks, street signs, wind direction, the height of the sun, the stars – all meaningful distinctions that navigational skill reveals. To navigate by GPS is to endure a series of meaningless pauses at the end of which you do precisely what you're told. There is something deeply dehumanizing about this: it's like being the central figure in a Beckett play without the jokes. Indeed, in an important sense this experience turns you into an automated device the GPS can use to arrive at its destination . . . [47]

Dreyfus and Kelly emphasize the hidden costs realized while one uses the GPS, and they describe those costs in terms of lost knowledge, sensory perception, sensitivity, and navigational skills. Critically, these costs entail both static and dynamic consequences. They constitute lost personal experiences (static costs), and, as such, lost opportunities to practice and develop capabilities (dynamic costs). The immediate trade-off is easily understood; it's no surprise that GPS is so popular. Who wants to experience the hassle of navigating? And yet, the dynamic trade-off, like so many we face in daily life and which we highlight in this book, is not easily marked, much less understood and evaluated. Still, that shouldn't stop us from trying. We must ask how our capabilities are developed and shaped by our experiences, by our struggles and practices.

Pre-eminent legal scholar Cass Sunstein maintains GPS can have "anti-developmental consequence[s]." As noted in Chapter 2, he describes a 2000 study of London taxi drivers:

> [The] use of the GPS can make it harder for people to learn how to navigate the roads. Indeed, London taxi drivers, not relying on the GPS, have been found to experience an alteration of their brain functions as they learn more about navigation, with physical changes in certain regions of the brain. As the GPS becomes widespread, that kind of alteration will not occur, thus ensuring that people cannot navigate on their own. [This] raises the possibility that whenever people rely on defaults or on other nudges, rather than on their own active choices, some important capacities may atrophy or fail to develop entirely . . . If the brain is seen as a muscle, it can become weak or strong, and choice-making is a kind of exercise that may strengthen it.[48]

Sunstein focuses on choice-making as the relevant type of thinking and considers how defaults that require active choosing can support *learning* as people develop their own preferences, knowledge, and perhaps other forms of capital and capabilities. This argument should be broadened to include other types of thinking besides choice-making and to include many other types of mind-extending technologies besides GPS.

There's nothing new in noting that skill-based trade-offs can accompany technological development. As people, including Clark, frequently point out, back in antiquity Socrates expressed concern that the invention of writing would lead to atrophy of biological memory. Over time, this seems to have proven true. But even with the decline of oral cultures, it seems clear that, all things considered, we're much better off for it, considering all the amazing things written language can do.

Still, net gains are by no means inevitable. The key question, then, is how we should evaluate the trade-offs that occur where technology and skill intertwine and provide potential for both gains and losses. Philosopher Richard Heersmink puts the point this way:

Navigation systems decrease the level of detail in our internal cognitive maps, thereby diminishing our capacity to navigate without such devices; constantly using calculators may result in lesser developed calculation skills; and reliable Internet access reduces our internal knowledge base, because when we know information is easily available externally we tend to put less effort into memorizing it.

But in a world where many people have wearable computing devices, one might ask how bad this really is. Of course, there will be moments when we will be decoupled from our devices and then experience that we are less good in remembering facts without access to Google and Wikipedia, performing calculations without a calculator, navigating without Google Maps, and planning without our online diary. However, proponents may argue that these are minor drawbacks in relation to what we gain from cognitive technologies. One possible way to look at this situation is by taking a consequentialist view and comparing the advantages with the disadvantages. If the advantages outweigh the disadvantages, then the changes to our onboard cognitive capabilities are acceptable.[49]

At first glance, Heersmink seems to offer a sensible framework. If we're keen on examining skills from a pragmatic perspective because we value them for the practical advantages their development and use can bring, it seems like a no-brainer to run a cost-benefit analysis whenever we're trying to decide if new uses of technologies are better than older alternatives.[50] However, things are more complicated than this popular outlook suggests.

For one, it can be difficult to identify negative costs once an overly optimistic view of technology has been adopted. Take the United States Navy, which largely is considered to be the most impressive navy in the entire world. Integrating cutting-edge technology into its operations is a top priority. That's why "the Navy stopped training its service members to navigate by the stars about a decade ago" and focused "instead on electronic navigational systems."[51] Sensible as this seemed at the time, things have started to reverse course and Navy education is once again teaching how to navigate by stars. This is because "the Navy and other branches of the U.S. military are becoming increasingly concerned . . . that they may be overly reliant on GPS. In a big war, the GPS satellites could be shot down. Or, more likely, their signal could be jammed or hacked."[52] In short, while many military systems are powerfully connected to GPS technology to strengthen all kinds of functionality, *cybersecurity concerns* have arisen to illuminate how cognition enhancement and vulnerability can go hand-in-hand once systems dependency emerges. If a cyberwar erupts and GPS technology becomes a high-profile target for enemies to strike, saying it seemed impossible to fight the tide of innovation would sound like an excuse for not committing to thoughtful defense.

To further appreciate why it can be myopic to evaluate every new technology by determining whether it's cost-benefit justified, consider the following thought experiment that highlights the limits of using micro-level considerations to weigh pros and cons. Imagine that in the future GPS chips are implanted in every baby's head at birth. These technologically advanced chips are painless to install and their intracranial storage can't cause any biological damage or complications. Furthermore, the chips are constantly updated with accurate, real-time information, and cannot ever err, be hacked, or stop working during a user's lifetime. The chips don't impede concentration (or any other cognitive function) because they only provide logistical information when the user's brain sends explicit signals that request such detail. And, finally, the chips work everywhere in the world. There would be no such thing as a dead zone or place where a satellite signal can't be obtained.

Such powerful chips would improve everyone's sense of direction. We'd never have to worry about becoming separated from the flawless technology that's always ready to tell us how to get around. And yet, if GPS technology belongs to the class of techno-social engineering tools we've discussed throughout this book, then we run into the problem posed in Chapter 2. Once we're fully comfortable using GPS to handle all navigation, it becomes hard to resist techno-social engineering creep. As time passes, there will be ever-increasing opportunities to automate our mobility, our labor, our bodies, our minds, ourselves. Cost-benefit analysis is ultimately the wrong framework to evaluate our steps down this path.

We end where we began, with two fundamental questions: Who is doing what type of thinking when humans use mind-extending technologies? What are the impacts of technologically extended thinking on the development of human capabilities? We'll consider them further in the subsequent chapters as we ramp up to a robust discussion of free will, autonomy, predictability, and programmability.

CHAPTER 7

The Path to Smart Techno-Social Environments

Introduction

Smart is in. The latest buzzword in the technology industry and policy circles is smart. (Or maybe it's intelligent or autonomous. Buzzwords change like the winds.) We've built massive networked surveillance systems with the rise of the Internet that seem poised to inject intelligence into every aspect of our lives. The Internet may have transformed virtually every socio-technical system on the planet, but arguably it was just a step (or leap) down the slippery-sloped path we've been on for decades (if not centuries). What lies ahead?

Imagine a world that's aggressively engineered for us to achieve happiness at minimal social cost. In this hypothetical future, ubiquitous techno-social tools will govern – or micro-manage – our world to prioritize three distinctive yet interrelated normative ends: optimized transactional efficiency, resource productivity, and human happiness. In two words, *cheap bliss.*[1]

Now, even though we don't currently live in such a world, the technologies required for it to exist are being developed and deployed. Proponents of the Internet of Things, big data, sensors, algorithms, artificial intelligence, and various related technologies make seductive promises, including that increased intelligence – "smart" phones, grids, cars, homes, classrooms, clothing, and so on – will minimize transaction costs, maximize productivity, and make us perfectly happy. (Nudging entails a very similar seductive promise.)

It's important to note that society isn't really structured to optimize social institutions and systems to maximize efficiency, productivity, or happiness. Though it may sound counterintuitive, we usually take the opposite approach. Simply put: We don't optimize. (Apologies to economists and engineers.) The social value of leaving a wide range of opportunities open for the future generally exceeds the value that society could realize by trying to optimize its systems in the present.[2] In other words, at least in the United States, the default operating principle of social governance of people and shared resources is to leave things underdetermined; this allows individuals and groups to engage in self-determination with different outcomes, depending on the context and changing conditions.[3] As law professor Julie Cohen succinctly put it, we need ample room for play.[4]

Optimization presumes an identifiable set of values. One of the reasons why society generally does not aim to optimize for specific values, such as efficiency or happiness, is that people often are committed to many different values. Another reason is that these values are often incommensurable and that makes prioritization contentious and trade-offs inevitable. Yet another reason is that the means used to optimize are highly and probably inevitably imperfect. Further, our understanding of the complex causal relationships between means and ends is incredibly limited. Still another reason is that, even putting aside the prior concerns, what looks like an optimal equilibrium in a specific time, place, or context often may only be locally optimal and globally suboptimal. In other words, what looks great might turn out to be relatively crappy.

Nonetheless, our world is changing rapidly, and seductive promises of intelligent optimization are difficult to resist. As presaged by the computer scientist Joseph Weizenbaum, technologies govern many of our day-to-day activities, and do so with such powerful consequences that it can be difficult for social institutions to keep pace. Assuming we continue along the path we're on, in the near future we'll rely even more thoroughly on technologies to intelligently govern our behavior. To be clear, we don't believe this reliance will come about because technologies will have become sentient, autonomous AIs that enslave humanity. Instead, our hypothesis is much simpler and, we think, more plausible than the Frankensteinian alternatives. We imagine that within the next few decades: (1) we will have gradually built and connected smart techno-social environments that deliver on their promises; (2) the scope of deployment will expand to the point where there is seamless interconnection and likely integration across all environments within which humans live; and (3) the normative agenda executed throughout all this construction and deployment will be optimal efficiency, productivity, and happiness.

The path of engineered determinism we are heading on surely allows for many different futures; a change in direction, even 180 degrees, is always possible. Nothing, other than entropy (as Isaac Asimov suggested in *The Last Question*), is inevitable. But there are many reasons to believe that the future envisioned here is plausible and may even be a reasonable approximation of what lies ahead.

If the world we're envisioning seems stark, know that its intellectual seeds have already been sown. We've discussed some of them in previous chapters, and we'll have more to say later in the book. Recall from Chapter 4 that Weizenbaum worried that the computer would lead to the computerization of all human and social problems on the faulty assumption that all such problems are comprehensible in the language of computation; all that would be needed to solve the world's problems were more powerful computers, programs, and data. The imperialism of instrumental reason Weizenbaum warned of is no different than the optimization logic we've just discussed. Though incredibly prescient, he may have missed the critical, complementary role of converging communications media and networks in engineered environments. Accordingly, this chapter begins with mass media and the Internet before turning to smart techno-social environments.

Mass Media and the Reconfiguration of Our Lived-In Environments

The relationships between humans and tools often have an environmental component. At a minimum, the pedagogical function of tools shapes how humans perceive and imagine their reality. More concretely and acutely, techno-social tools for engineering humans often reconstruct the physical, social, and other environments within which humans are situated. The assembly line and public school examples are illustrative. Each is understood to be a special space constructed to achieve specific ends by social engineering.

What we mean by *environment*

An environment might be defined as a complex system of interconnected and/ or interdependent resources (or even resource systems) that comprise the "surroundings," "setting," or "context" that we inherit, live within, use, interact with, change, and pass on to future generations. We inherit the natural physical environment; we live within, use, interact with, and change it; and we pass it on to future generations. Similarly, we inherit, live within, use, interact with, change, and pass on to future generations a cultural-intellectual environment, comprised of many overlapping sub-environments, if one would like to distinguish culture(s), science(s), and so on. The world we live in comprises multiple, complex, overlapping, and interdependent resource systems with which we interact and that constitute our environments. One type is the natural environment, and the socially constructed environment, such as the cultural environment, is another.

The cultural environment provides us with resources and capabilities to act, participate, be productive, and "make and pursue life plans that can properly be called our own." It also shapes our very beliefs and preferences regarding our lives (life plans) and relationships with each other and the world we share. Human beings are not born with fully formed preferences, knowledge, and beliefs about the world they enter; rather, these concepts are learned and experienced and thus contingent to a degree on the cultural environment a person experiences. We have an incredibly complex and dynamic relationship with the cultural environment. Science and culture, for example, are cumulative and immersive systems that develop with society, while simultaneously developing society. Put another way, the cultural environment provides for, shapes, and reflects us, and, at the same time, we provide, shape, and reflect it.[5]

Media, treated as a collective noun, is an important and broad set of techno-social engineering tools not tied to any specific space. Media "encompasses the myriad technologies and means for communicating with, informing, and entertaining individuals and the masses."[6] The history of humans and media is as old as the history of humans and tools. An important example is language.[7] Innovations in media and extending access to the masses empowered our capacity to generate, cultivate, share, and sustain imagined realities that enable large-scale cooperation.

Media scholar Sharon Kleinman defines mass media as "media that aims its messages at large, mainstream audiences, the masses."[8] Mass media are communication tools designed to reach a large audience, often an audience that is geographically distributed.[9] Conventional mass media entail asymmetrical communications – one-to-many or at least a small number of content producers and a much larger audience. Examples include print, radio, and television. Some of the conventional boundaries that separated mass media from other media may be disappearing. "The once apparent and mostly rigid boundaries between media content creators and media audiences, and between interpersonal communication and mass media, have blurred tremendously in the past few decades such that the term mass media has lost its precision in the digital age."[10]

Mass media seem to be a precursor with a strong legacy and still a relevant part of the ongoing wave of technological, social, and cultural change we discuss below. We focus on media as a techno-social engineering tool and do not discuss market structures, content analysis, or sociopolitical concerns such as the relationships between mass media and democracy.[11]

Media are both constitutive and reflective of society. For all mass media, the ideas communicated, facts described, stories told, images displayed, agendas set, personalities shown, and so on contribute to a process of cultural development and exchange that affects and shapes the audience and feeds back upon itself and thereby affects and shapes authors and distributors – or more generally, the media systems themselves. Media scholars have extensively studied the various media and highlighted their important differences according to different models and metrics. Here, we emphasize affordances and effects. As we shall see, these features are relevant to our critical analysis of techno-social engineering tools more generally.[12]

Affordances are human capabilities extended, enhanced, or enabled by a tool. Affordances themselves may have effects on people even if those people never exercise the capabilities, where the opportunity itself shapes their beliefs and perception of reality and their place within it. More often, however, analysts focus on the effects attributable to users' exercise of capabilities afforded by a tool – what happens when someone actively takes advantage of an opportunity? Apart from the affordances of different media, there also can be direct and indirect effects attributable to consumption of media content – for example, entertainment and learning.

The affordances of mass media vary on both the supply side (e.g. content producers, editors, distributors, advertisers, etc.) and the demand side (e.g. audiences). For example, pre-digital print mass media – such as books, magazines, and newspapers – depends on the distribution of tangible copies. This feature of the technology involves production and distribution costs, imposes constraints on the nature of the communication, and shapes how audiences perceive and interact with the content. Once consumers possess a copy, they may decide where and how they choose to read – for example, in a public or private space.[13] Consumers may retain copies, annotate or otherwise modify them, sell or share them, or even destroy them. These affordances vary with the materials used to fix copies. For example, clay tablets are more durable, heavier, and less modifiable than paper. These differences affected – or biased, according to media and communication scholar Harold Innis – cultural development. Similarly, if we compare books, newspapers, and magazines in terms of their forms, style, production process, formats, conventions, and so on, we find many differences affect their content and consequently shape the corresponding "print culture."[14]

"[E]ach communication channel codifies reality differently and thereby influences, to a surprising degree, the content of the message communicated."[15] The medium matters because it shapes, structures, and controls the scale, scope, reach, pace, and patterns of human communications; it extends the human capability to communicate. As media theorist Marshall McLuhan emphasized, for "any medium or technology . . . the change of scale or pace or pattern . . . introduce[d] into human affairs" is what really matters: this is what he meant by his famous aphorism, "the medium is the message."[16]

Radio and television broadcasts are more ephemeral than paper. Radio and television broadcasts depend upon different production and distribution technologies than print. Book distribution resembles many other tangible goods; think of trucks delivering boxes of books to stores. Radio and television broadcasting requires completely different infrastructure, institutional structures, and equipment. Of the various media, the First Amendment provides the least protection to broadcasting.[17] Broadcasters must obtain a license from the Federal Communications Commission and comply with an incredibly complex regulatory regime.

Each medium affords content producers different means with which to communicate to audiences and presents content producers with different challenges for garnering and sustaining audience attention. Radio depended on, and perhaps revived, storytelling and oral traditions while television's synchronization of audio and visual was more akin to dramatic performance.[18] Radio and television dramatically expanded the scale with which news and culture could disseminate practically instantaneously. The entire nation tuned in and experienced momentous events, such as the assassination of John F. Kennedy and American astronauts landing on the moon. This change in the scale and immediacy of mass media reverberated throughout society.

On the demand side, consumers must possess a radio or television. If consumers wish to retain a copy of a broadcast, they must make their own with a recording device. Radio and television broadcasts are not the only way to experience music and video. Like print, discrete copies can be purchased, and those media offer some of the affordances that print provides, such as control over the time and place of consumption, but not others, such as relatively easy annotation. Consumers experience the content of radio and television akin to live performances, by listening and watching as an audience member. Yet there are some important differences. Audiences must possess equipment to tune in. They flip a switch or push a button; they choose a channel; and they pick their place. Radio and television lean more toward communal or group-oriented experience than print. Friends and families listen and watch together in their chosen environment, such as living rooms, clubs, or bars.

Both radio and television tend to be spliced with advertising, and regular interruptions are normalized. For many, advertising is a necessary evil to be tolerated as the means for supporting otherwise free broadcasts. As legal and media theorist Katherine Strandburg explains:

> [T]he traditional broadcast advertising-based approach is sometimes modeled as one in which consumers pay for television or radio content with "attention" to advertising. The assumption underlying such models is that content recipients experience some disutility from being subjected to broadcast advertising but are willing to incur that cost because it is outweighed by the expected benefit of the programming itself.[19]

Strandburg explains that the "plausible assumption that broadcast advertising is experienced by consumers mostly as a disutility or cost . . . is strongly supported by the empirical fact that consumers go to great lengths to avoid broadcast advertising, at least in the television context."[20]

The affordances of conventional mass media tended to reinforce asymmetrical communications, with content producers generally catering to mainstream audiences consisting mostly of passive consumers who often trusted what they were told and were happy to be entertained. This is a gross generalization; there are plenty of exceptions and counterarguments. Competition sometimes (but not always) brought diversity and competing perspectives; and the differences within and across media as well as between for-profit and non-profit suppliers complicate the story. Still, the (uncontroversial) point is that mass media are powerful technosocial engineering tools that cater to and create passive mainstream audiences.

There are various theories and explanations for why and how the mass media cater to the mainstream and what consequences follow. Advertising played an important role. As Strandburg succinctly explains:

> The broadcast advertising business model responded to failures in the market for broadcast content and transaction costs in matching consumers to advertising. Broadcasters respond directly to advertiser demand by producing content tailored to attracting large numbers of consumers and exposing them to broadcast advertising. The broadcast advertising model thus biases content production toward average, rather than specialized, interests and toward content designed to appeal to those who will (or can be persuaded to) purchase mainstream products.[21]

Our characterization of the audience as passive consumers refers to the fact that the consuming audience plays no role on the supply side of mass media systems. Mass media systems do not afford most people with access to the production or distribution facilities necessary to communicate to the public. Such power is generally afforded to – or reserved for – a relatively small number of people.

Let's turn our attention to mass media consumption and its effects. Mass media involve the presentation of perceptible content to consumers. The manner of perception and corresponding effects vary based on which senses and intellectual capacities the media are most directly attuned to.[22] Print involves text and visual stimuli and requires reading, imagining, and visualizing; radio involves auditory stimuli and requires listening; and television and cinema involve synchronized visual and auditory stimuli, requiring watching and listening. Generations of media scholars have analyzed and debated the scale, scope, nature, and causes of the political, cultural, and psychological effects of different media and the different ways that audiences can be empowered by critical media literacy to become active interpreters of content.

We're sure you are already aware of the decades-long debates over television. Has TV turned everyone into couch potatoes? No, and even for those of us who are prone to vegging out on the sofa and binge watching programs, most of us don't succumb to the siren call of television all the time. Studies suggest TV watching occupies quite a lot of people's lives, but it is difficult to assess the effects. Some, such as media theorist Neil Postman, contend "that TV ... attained the power to control education because it dominates the attention, time, and cognitive habits of the youth."[23] Other scholars suggest that televised content is anything but homogeneous. For example, philosopher of technology Don Ihde argues:

> Today's TV is *pluricultural*. News is worldwide with hotspots varying from all over the globe. Terrorism can occur in any country; natural disasters are immediately broadcast; royal weddings and births occupy admirers' attention; scientific discoveries such as a Pluto flyby are present, *ad infinitum*. This range of display is a temporal condensation, a "now" which is also pluralistic, but which also displays a "near distance" or cyberspace character as if all is "here." The living room has more pluriculture every evening than had any medieval king in his castle. The media "worlds" are diverse and rich ...[24]

On the Internet and across various devices and platforms, mass media continue to change dramatically; just think about how most people consume print, music, and video today. While it is beyond the scope of this chapter to summarize the extensive media debates and findings, the following takeaways are the most relevant for our discussion.

Mass media shape our cultural environment as they reach into and reconfigure our lived-in environments, our workplaces, schools, homes, automobiles, clubs, restaurants, taverns, and so on. The reconfiguration is often infrastructural and architectural because it operates structurally in the background and in a manner that tends to be overlooked and taken for granted by those situated within the environment. As with the clock and other tools, our perception and understanding of reality adjusts gradually as we become accustomed to the presence, power, and utility of the tools. Unlike those other examples, however, note that mass media attune more directly with our cognitive capabilities and senses. Mass media engineer humans within these lived-in environments by altering the range of stimuli that potentially affect the beliefs, preferences and actions of humans within those spaces. Print, radio, and television are also well-studied examples of such techno-social engineering. In the United States, the power of mass media never quite reached the levels depicted in dystopian science fiction (though some might dispute this claim). But it is indisputable that mass media have had a significant influence on American culture, politics, economy, and society.[25]

Mass media techno-social engineering encompasses a few interrelated factors: *scale*, evaluated in terms of audience size, markets, and/or geographic coverage; *scope*, evaluated in terms of the range and types of content and messages; *influence*, evaluated in terms of power to persuade, shape beliefs, or otherwise engineer audience members (i.e. do more than simply entertain or satisfy existing preferences); and *architectural extension*, evaluated in terms of the degree to which the media fit within and bridge different environments. The factors are interdependent, and media scholars have studied scale, scope, and influence extensively. The final factor, however, is one we introduce.

Media intervention into our lived-in environments is often architectural in the sense that it becomes an integral part of the environment, shaping our perception and experience of it. For example, a living room, dining room, or bar with a television is a different environment than one without. The extensibility of mass media depends on how well the media fit within our environments as a contextually appropriate (background) architecture. This should not be surprising as the media, like our other tools, also are extensions of ourselves. Media intervention into our lived-in environments may be abrupt or gradual, contentious or harmonious; it may occur within specific isolated environments, or it may bridge environments.

Radio and television extend architecturally into different spaces, and have done so quite differently. Compare, for example, radio with television in terms of how the media extended into the different environments we listed in the previous paragraph. Both radio and television broadcasters make content available in each of the listed environments, but consumption depends upon reception; what is contextually appropriate is contingent, changes over time, and varies among communities. Radio has long tended to be acceptable in many environments, provided it remains unobtrusive and a source of background ambiance. Television, on the other hand, was most appropriate in select environments, such as the living room and taverns, but inappropriate in others, such as automobiles. Like other creep phenomena, the television medium crept into other rooms of the house (bedrooms, basements) and beyond as its cost decreased. This extension also shifted how people consume the content, for example, by making private individual consumption more easily available. As we discuss below, the Internet fundamentally changed mass media. Today, on the back of the Internet, television is watched on handheld screens in virtually all environments.

Through these combined factors, one begins to see the precursors of the smart environments we'll discuss in the next chapter. Specifically, the architectural extension of mass media into lived-in environments coupled with expanding scale, scope, and, most importantly, influence conveys *power*, specifically, to practice techno-social engineering of humans. Early mass media were crude and of debatable effectiveness as techno-social engineering tools. But they could and would improve over time with better data and data analytics. Edward Bernays, often referred to as the "father of public relations," presciently suggested as much in 1947 when he wrote that "engineered consent," which is akin to influence, involves the "use of an engineering approach – that is, action based only on thorough knowledge of the situation and on the application of scientific principles and tried practices to the task of getting people to support ideas and programs."[26] Though not explicit, his views evoke Taylor's approach to scientific management of humans in the workplace, albeit with different undertones. Political theorist and linguist Noam Chomsky and Edward Herman, professor emeritus of finance at the Wharton Business School, went in a slightly different direction in their book *Manufacturing Consent: The Political Economy of the Mass Media* (1988),[27] and forcefully made the case that mass media served as a powerful propaganda tool. Their argument was not that propaganda was novel; it has been around for millennia. Rather, their argument was that the scale, scope, and influence of profit-driven mass media afforded elites more powerful access to and control over the minds of mainstream audiences.[28] Others disagreed and still do, as the ongoing debate about media bias and filter bubbles demonstrates.

The debate about power also highlights another important characteristic of mass media as tools for techno-social engineering: the attenuation and distance between the audience within the environment and those exerting influence through the media. This is a dimension of power. The tendency for mass media to support asymmetrical communication also concentrates power to influence, or more broadly, engineer humans. We will not dwell on this point here, however, as it is the topic of extensive scholarship and debate. Again, the simple point suffices: Mass media concentrate power in corporations, elites, and celebrities. This fact has long been a subject of conflict and attempts at resolution through political intervention or market competition have not generally succeeded. Perhaps the single most effective force to decentralize, democratize, and disrupt traditional mass media is the Internet.

The Internet and Networked Digital Media

Over the past few decades, we have witnessed the near-ubiquitous deployment of various information, computation, and communications technologies. As Weizenbaum predicted, the computer presaged our societal infatuation with the seemingly limitless power of computation, digitalization, data, virtualization, automation, artificial intelligence, and related technologies and techniques. And now the ring that binds them all is the Internet, our global all-purpose media network.[29]

The Internet has grown in just a few decades to completely alter every aspect of our society, economy, and community through its transformation and enhancement of connections and communication across its widespread network.[30] Consider, for example, how the Internet provides and shapes opportunities of individuals, firms, households, and other organizations to interact with each other and participate in various social systems. The scale and scope of possible and actual social interactions alone is staggering. The Internet has seeped into our daily lives and environments more deeply than any conventional mass media, and it has correspondingly reconfigured and transformed them even more so. So many formative actions and interactions that humans undergo have been shaped by these changes in the physical, social, and cultural environments.

The Internet is an open, general-purpose communication infrastructure. Although the Internet began primarily as a conduit for solely textual communications, it rapidly expanded to include images, sound, video, and all sorts of content and communications. Everything that occurs on the Internet entails the communication of data between computers at the "ends" of interconnected networks. The computers may be desktops, laptops, smartphones, or various other devices. Digital data are sent in packets that are automatically routed across and among various networks, including telecom, cable, satellite, and other physical infrastructure. The data packets are put back together at the ends and translated into higher-layer communications that can be interpreted and used on any connected device. Though more complicated technical models exist, the following five-layer model provides a useful illustration.

Five-Layer Model of the Internet

Layer	Description	Examples
Social	Relations and social ties among users	Social networks, affiliations, groups
Content	Information/data conveyed to end-users	Email communication, music, webpages
Applications	Programs and functions used by end-users	Email programs, media players, web browsers
Logical Infrastructure	Standards and protocols that facilitate transmission of data across physical networks	TCP/IPs, domain name systems
Physical Infrastructure	Physical hardware that comprises interconnected networks	Telecommunications, cable and satellite networks, routers and servers, backbone networks

The Internet evolved with the so-called "end-to-end" design principle as its central tenet.[31] To preserve its robustness and evolvability and to allow applications to be easily layered on top of it, the broad version of this design principle recommends that the lower layers of the network be as general as possible, while all application-specific functionality should be concentrated in higher layers at end hosts. End-to-end design is implemented in the logical infrastructure through the Internet Protocol (IP), which provides a general technology-and-application-independent interface to the lower layers of the network.[32]

As a media platform, the Internet extends the human capability to communicate in nearly limitless forms, languages, and content types. Software code virtualizes pre-existing mass and interpersonal media, and so those media remain available and relevant. But in contrast with the asymmetrical nature of mass media and the limited scope of interpersonal media such as the telephone, the Internet enables nearly instantaneous, many-to-many communication around the world. Software code itself has become an incredibly important platform for applications, and, within the applications layer itself, new media platforms have emerged: interpersonal media platforms such as email and text messaging; social media platforms such as Facebook and Twitter; gaming platforms such as the massive multiplayer online games that create virtual worlds regularly inhabited by hundreds of millions daily.

The Internet is socially valuable primarily because of the wide variety of productive activities it facilitates. End-users generate value and realize benefits through their activities, which involve running applications on their computers; generating, consuming, and using content; and creating and engaging in various social, economic, or other relations with other users. End-users also create demand for Internet infrastructure through their demand for applications, content, and relations. Keep in mind that *activities on the Internet* always involve *interactions* among *end-users*; that the interactions may be commercial, educational, social, political, and so on; and that end-users may be individuals, corporations, government actors, or other entities.

The Internet has so pervasively reached into and reconfigured our lived-in environments that for many people, it is difficult to remember or imagine being disconnected. The reach was less pervasive when Internet connections were primarily through personal computers on desktops, but the rapid diffusion of mobile devices capable of connecting to the Internet has dramatically extended the reach of the medium. It's difficult to evaluate the Internet as a tool for techno-social engineering humans, in part because it is so omnipresent. Consider the Internet through the lens of the interrelated factors we noted previously. *Scale*: billions of people, worldwide, and substantial though not complete market penetration. *Scope*: the range and types of content and messages is virtually unlimited, and the same can be said for both applications and social relations. *Influence*: hard to measure or evaluate generically; the power to persuade, shape beliefs, or otherwise engineer audience members operates at the application, content, and social layers. *Architectural extension*: the Internet is contextually appropriate in almost all environments, and it bridges most.

To evaluate the Internet as a tool for techno-social engineering of humans, we need to consider an additional factor: the scale and scope of data collection. Recall that Taylorism depends fundamentally on data. Scientific management of human beings in the workplace and beyond requires usable data about task performance, inputs, outputs, behavior, incentives, and so on. One limit of how far Taylorism could reach is the scale and scope of data available for management. Perhaps more than any other technology in human history, the Internet has expanded the pool of data capable of being cheaply collected and used. According to IBM:

> Every day, we create 2.5 quintillion bytes of data – so much that 90% of the data in the world today has been created in the last two years alone. This data comes from everywhere: sensors used to gather climate information, posts to social media sites, digital pictures and videos, purchase transaction records, and cell phone GPS signals to name a few.[33]

Again: everything involving the Internet involves the generation and exchange of digital data – every activity, every communication. Data – strings of zeros and ones – are what economists refer to as a pure public good, meaning the resource can be copied at zero marginal cost. Computing devices at the ends, as well as routers and other devices within and between networks, easily can make copies and collect such data. The dramatic increase in the supply of data created a corresponding demand for improved data storage and analytics technologies, and, in a few decades, major technological advances have coalesced in new fields such as big data[34] and reawakened seemingly dormant fields such as artificial intelligence and machine learning. We discuss these developments below, but, for now, our purpose is to highlight not only how the Internet reconfigured our lived-in environments, but also how it simultaneously drew us out of those environments, even if only virtually or metaphorically through our external communications, thereby extracting something of, or at least about, us.[35]

This data-gleaning feature of the Internet affords various public and private actors with incredible power to engage in surveillance and to use and act upon the specific information collected. Surveillance is simply easy and cheap when you have networked computing devices. It occurs throughout the Internet ecosystem, at the various layers pictured above. There have been many efforts to establish constraints grounded in various conceptions of privacy and implemented in law, norms, and technology, but with limited success. We acknowledge that it is hard to evaluate success or failure, because we don't have an established normative baseline for privacy nor do we know the full extent of ongoing surveillance practices. Nonetheless, we know that the dominant business models in our networked information economy are surveillance-dependent, as companies clamor to serve targeted advertising and provide personalized services. We also know that governments around the world spy on their and each others' citizens. Finally, while there are various exceptions, the dominant mindset shaping privacy constraints is rooted in the idea of notice-and-consent, which, as we explain below and in subsequent chapters, is doomed to fail.

Shoshana Zuboff, a professor at Harvard Business School, coined the highly relevant phrase "surveillance capitalism."[36] Per Zuboff, capitalism has entered a new phase that centers on extracting data rather than producing goods, and it's exemplified by Google in much the same way that Ford once was synonymous with mass production. Google's business model, Zuboff argues, generates profit by extracting, analyzing, and selling data that the company is constantly collecting, and creating value by offering customized and personalized services that are perpetually being refined through experimentation that, in part, involves crafting ever-more powerful ways to predict and alter behavior. While Zuboff concedes that it's too early to tell whether surveillance capitalism "will be the hegemonic logic of accumulation in our time" or an "evolutionary dead-end," she expresses deep reservations about the consolidation of power that's occurring in the private sector and its capacity to further erode our privacy and diminish our agency.[37]

While advertising is often advanced as a public explanation and even (partial) justification for surveillance capitalism, it remains hard to verify.[38] First, it isn't clear how well data-driven, particularly behavioral-data-driven, advertising works. Second, it isn't clear whether or how much or how often data supposedly collected to support advertising is actually used for advertising. Third, even if and when data is used for advertising, it remains unclear whether or how much and how often data is used for other purposes and what those might be in different contexts. Finally, and perhaps most insidiously, advertising may often be used as a surveillance tool. People may be conditioned to accept advertising sprinkled throughout our digital culture and, as a result, many advertisements may serve as cover for ongoing surveillance efforts that serve a range of goals.

This issue of conditioning is taken up by Mark Bartholomew, a law professor at the University at Buffalo, in *Adcreep: The Case Against Modern Marketing*. Bartholomew suggests that our willingness to allow advertising to become ubiquitous and colonize our public and private spaces is based, in part, on adaptive preferences legitimizing practices that once were disdained.

> A normalization process can easily occur once advertising enters a new territory. Take pre-film advertising in movie theaters. When it was first introduced in the 1990s, audiences howled at the presence of commercials before the trailers and the actual movie. Lawsuits were filed and new legislation proposed to stop the practice. But over time, the lawsuits and legislation sputtered out. Surveys now suggest that audiences have become ambivalent to the presence of pre-film commercials.[39]

We emphasize two ways in which surveillance relates to techno-social engineering. First, surveillance itself can exhibit disciplinary power and thus constitute techno-social engineering. Taylor exploited this, and his workers complained of it. One of the fathers of modern social theory, Michel Foucault, examined this relationship extensively across a variety of different contexts. Critically, the reach of the Internet extends the disciplinary power of surveillance dramatically. Second, the data collected can be used as an input for a host of other techno-social engineering tools. For example, at the lowest layers of the network, infrastructure providers, such as providers of broadband Internet access services, might use data to shape traffic in a manner that prioritizes certain user activities over others. Crudely, networks might prioritize applications or applications providers based on profit. More fine-grained, data-intensive price discrimination, however, is the holy grail that would allow them to maximize their returns by extracting as much surplus as possible. This has been the subject of the network neutrality debate, which we return to shortly.

Many of the most powerful media companies that regularly engage in data-driven techno-social engineering of humans operate applications-layer platforms – social networks, search engines, marketplaces, even online games. The next section discusses the Facebook Emotional Contagion Experiment, which is just one example that caught headlines a few years ago and remains salient in technology policy discourse.

Facebook's Emotional Engineering Experiment

On June 17, 2014, the *Proceedings of the National Academy of Sciences (PNAS)* published an article titled "Experimental Evidence of Massive-Scale Emotional Contagion Through Social Networks."[40] The short article reported on a remarkable experiment that demonstrated that emotional states can be transferred to others by emotional contagion. Researchers at

Facebook and Cornell University conducted the experiment and "manipulated the extent to which people (N = 689,003) were exposed to emotional
expressions in their News Feed."[41] Unbeknownst to a few hundred thousand people, Facebook deliberately reduced their exposure to their friends'
positive or negative posts, depending on which conditions Facebook
applied. In other words, Facebook deliberately exposed people to the test
contagion and then watched to see what would happen. It turns out that
the results of the experiment showed that emotional contagion exists and
can be deployed by Facebook. People exposed to more positive posts
tended to post more positive posts relative to the control groups, with
similar results for exposure to negative posts. Moreover, people "exposed to
fewer emotional posts (of either valence) in their News Feed were less
expressive overall on the following days,"[42] which the authors described as
a withdrawal effect. The authors concluded:

> [G]iven the massive scale of social networks such as Facebook, even small
> effects can have large aggregated consequences: For example, the well-
> documented connection between emotions and physical well-being suggests
> the importance of these findings for public health. Online messages influ-
> ence our experience of emotions, which may affect a variety of offline
> behaviors. And after all, an effect size of d = 0.001 at Facebook's scale is
> not negligible: In early 2013, this would have corresponded to hundreds of
> thousands of emotion expressions in status updates per day.[43]

Not surprisingly, a firestorm followed publication of the study.
Bloggers, media pundits, researchers, Facebook users, and others
debated the ethics of the research.[44] Most of them focused on whether
the researchers should have obtained informed consent from the
research subjects and whether the Institutional Review Board (IRB)
at Cornell should have played a greater role in regulating, supervising,
or monitoring the research. These are very important ethical issues.
A few months later, the *New York Times* reported on some progress:
researchers studying us on social networks and other digital media are
now grappling with ethics and may develop guidelines to govern how
they experiment on us.[45]

But we might not want to leave it to the engineers and tool users.
We subjects should grapple with the ethics as well. To get a sense of
where you stand, consider a few questions:

1. Is deliberate emotional engineering by Facebook a problem of process
    (no informed consent for the subjects) or substance (emotional
    engineering)?

2. If it is a problem of inadequate process: Is IRB review a solution?[46] What about informed consent? What does that mean to you? Pretend you're negotiating a one-to-one contract with Facebook. What exactly would you agree to? Would clicking "I agree" when you sign up for the service be enough?

3. If it is a problem of substance, can you explain the problem without reliance on adjectives like creepy? Can you articulate what exactly is wrong with emotional engineering by Facebook?

4. Is it acceptable for Facebook to induce or suppress the emotional contagion of your friends?

5. Suppose Facebook tests, develops, and optimizes its emotional engineering capability to help people make *better* decisions? Would it be acceptable for Facebook to induce or suppress impulsive purchases (or at least, clicks)?

6. Suppose Facebook optimizes its emotional engineering capability specifically to minimize emotional interference with instrumentally rational decision-making. Would this nudge people to make better decisions? Would people nudged in this fashion act like machines? Would they be (or could they be) any less human?

7. Suppose Facebook optimizes its emotional engineering capability and lets users choose the settings – dial up some happiness! Would you use it?

These are difficult questions. The lack of informed consent and the role of the IRB are important issues, but they are the tip of the iceberg. The tip is all that gets attention until too late. The deeper issues (reflected in questions 3–7) are substantive, have less to do with the research process or this specific experiment, and more to do with the technological capacity for techno-social engineering that Facebook is testing. To be clear, Facebook is testing a tool, a powerful one. Why? What are the predictable consequences? How about the unpredictable or unintended consequences?

The title of the Facebook study caught our attention: *massive-scale emotional contagion through social networks*. The type of response (human emotion) being engineered struck a chord but so did the scale, scope, and power of the tool being tested. With respect to the first concern – human emotion being engineered – we must acknowledge that many things alter our moods every day. Advertisers and politicians (and their various consultants) are expert manipulators, and so are the rest of us. We try to influence each other regularly, for better or worse. We nudge each other. That's a big part of what socializing and communicating entails.

Emotional contagion is not the only social contagion, but it can be a powerful nudge. Many technologies play an integral role in shaping our beliefs, emotions, and well-being, sometimes, but not always, in ways we know about and at least partially understand.

But systematic techno-social engineering of human emotions through platforms, like Facebook, that reach into, reconfigure, and, in some ways, constitute the environments we live in daily may be much more challenging to know about and evaluate, and it may become more pervasive. Such engineering may be much harder to know about and understand *independent* of the platforms' influence on emotional and other social contagions. A focus on process alone will *never* be sufficient. As privacy scholars have long recognized,[47] informed consent can be manufactured, in the sense that technological platforms can shape one's beliefs and preferences with respect to that for which consent is sought.[48] Aside from the emotional contagion experiment, Facebook is a rather straightforward example, at least when one focuses on privacy. The beliefs and preferences of hundreds of millions have been shaped over the past decade. Facebook set out to accomplish this objective – at least, to encourage broad sharing of content – and largely has been successful.[49] Although public outcry about the emotional contagion experiment might lead one to conclude that Facebook would not be able to obtain consent from users for emotional engineering because their existing preferences may conflict, such a conclusion seems somewhat far-fetched. Facebook has not, to our knowledge, abandoned the technology or practice, nor have Facebook users revolted and ceased to use the service. Further, there is plenty of time for Facebook to both develop its technology and gradually shape its users' beliefs and preferences regarding the technology. Only time will tell.

Keep in mind that regardless of whether Facebook is engaged in a formal experiment, it persistently engages in both surveillance and techno-social engineering. We need to engage the ethics, including both process and substance, and we need to develop better tools for identifying and evaluating such techno-social engineering. After all, we only know about Facebook's experiment because it published the results.

To this point, we've only scratched the surface and focused on one actual example of techno-social engineering by Facebook. As we suggested, this may be indicative of the path we are on and what the future may hold. While we hesitate to prognosticate about the future, consider a fictional extension of the Facebook emotional contagion experiment.

Suppose Facebook figures out how to control and deploy emotional contagions and thus optimizes its emotional engineering technology. Now assume it creeps. Suppose Facebook gradually extends the scope of content, contagions, and emotions, and suppose Facebook gradually extends its reach. Finally, suppose Facebook expands beyond its social network interface on the Internet to other interfaces available through the Internet of Things (described in more detail in the next chapter). Thus, suppose Facebook extends its optimized emotional engineering capability to the environments within which we live our lives. For example, suppose Facebook deploys its emotional engineering technology in your smart home, automobile, and workplace through networked sensors and communications devices.

For our fictional extension, we can imagine two different worlds, one in which we still have a choice about whether to log in, and one in which we don't. Yet it is not clear whether this would even be a meaningful distinction, whether choice in the first possible world would be authentic or illusory. Assume that is our imagined world: Would you consent? Does your answer depend on whether you are in control and whether you could choose the settings? It might be the case that your first decision to consent could be authentic; perhaps you'd be able to deliberate and decide for yourself. But one cannot help but wonder whether, thereafter, consent would itself be subject to engineering. (If the mechanism for consent is a simple click-to-contract-style interface, we may already have been conditioned to automatically accept.)

One question we genuinely struggle with concerns who is doing the emoting and whether it even matters. Suppose you live in an environment within which Facebook successfully programs your emotions. Perhaps you consented and even chose the setting, or perhaps your parents did on your behalf long ago. Facebook provides a comprehensive set of (emotionally contagious) stimuli that trigger a predictable, predetermined set of emotional responses. *Who is emoting? You? Facebook? Your parents? Does it matter?*

We could ask the same questions about a novel. *When you read a novel, who is emoting? You? The author? The publisher?* We doubt anyone believes that when you read a novel and become happy or sad anyone besides you is emoting. We might say that the author is communicating and perhaps jointly sharing emotions. Is the author engaged in techno-social engineering? Yes, in a sense. Authorship entails the informed use of language and other tools to communicate, entertain, and stimulate emotional reactions. The novel is a techno-social tool designed to serve those purposes.

It provides a set of stimuli and triggers emotional reactions. Generally, this is something we encourage and celebrate.

How, then, is the hypothetical emotional engineering by Facebook any different? We believe it is a combination of factors, the most important of which seem to be the following: the scale and scope of the techno-social engineering, the marriage of deterministic engineering and engineered determinism, and the simultaneously environmental and acutely personalized nature of the techno-social engineering. These differentiating factors are complex, hard to mark and evaluate. For the objects being engineered and society generally, the difficulty is in knowing when a line is crossed, if one can even be identified. The third part of this book develops some tests that might help.

The Facebook emotional contagion experiment and our hypothetical extension highlight steps along a path. We may doubt we'll ever get to the endpoint, or even very far down the path. But can you be sure? How might humans and society change along the way?

Although the concern about Facebook's emotional contagion experiment largely has died down, we shouldn't be lulled into the false belief that Facebook has stopped the techno-social engineering of our emotions.

Let's try to focus on the interface that Facebook provides – an interface that mediates how we communicate. When you post information into Facebook's "what's on your mind?" box, you have the highly visible option of augmenting your prose by clicking on the "feeling/activity" button and selecting from such emojis as "excited," "blessed," "happy," "sad," "amused," "annoyed," and "relaxed." And, when you use Facebook's "like" button to comment on posts, you can select from six different options: "like," "love," "ha-ha," "wow," "sad," and "angry."

It may appear that Facebook provides these emotional expression shortcuts so that users have creative and effective ways to convey what's in their hearts and on their minds. After all, who doesn't feel a tinge of warmth after someone "loves" our post and marks it with a heart? Tempting as this is, we should be wary of basking in the digital glow. For under the hood, what Facebook is creating is a mood graph. When we select any of the above options, we are providing the company with clear and coded insight into our emotions that its own algorithms might not be able to infer from our prose. Facebook can use this information for all kinds of commercial purposes, including creating more emotionally attuned, and therefore potentially manipulative, personalized advertising for both us and our demographically similar "friends". In other words, when we express our emotions on Facebook in the ways that the interface invites us to we're providing the company with a form of emotional labor that can be used to further corporate interests over our own.

These sorts of issues likely will be arising in other areas, too, including smart cars. Automobile manufacturers are becoming increasingly interested in perceiving and classifying the emotions of drivers. Doing so allows for a variety of new functions to be instantiated, such as customizing the music that's playing based on one's mood: perhaps playing happy tunes when a driver is sad or calming songs when anger is detected will mitigate against road rage occurring.

CHAPTER 8

Techno-Social Engineering of Humans through Smart Environments

Introduction

In examining the scale and scope of techno-social engineering of humans, we can no longer limit our attention to the isolated examples of the factory floor or public school. We must extend our analysis to almost every other space, including the home and our public spaces. Mass media have reached into those spaces, but so far only incompletely and discontinuously. The Internet dramatically increased their reach, interconnection, and continuity.

Yet in the present – and this may be wishful thinking – the various environments within which we live our lives remain separate, even if potentially interconnected and interdependent. *We have not been and are not always on.* Put it this way: Radio and television broadcasters may have bombarded all our lived-in environments with analog signals, but we still need to flip the switch and tune in, and we could easily tune out. The Internet may be even more readily accessible, as we carry our smart-phones and related devices with us throughout our lives. And we may in fact exercise our capability to access the Internet more regularly in our daily lives; our default may even have flipped, such that we are by default tuned in. Nonetheless, though we may not always appreciate it, we retain the capability or freedom to be off.

The frightening thought is that if we proceed down the path we're currently on that freedom will disappear. The practical, situated, and reasonably exercisable *freedom to be off*, to be free from systemic, envir-onmentally architected human engineering, is *the* – or at least, one of the – fundamental constitutional issues we, as a society, need to confront. Constitutionalists have always had to ask, grapple with, and answer the foundational and ultimately intergenerational normative question of what sort of society we want to build. We all must be constitutionalists and ask ourselves this question. In the twenty-first century, this question is unavoidably about the scale and scope of techno-social engineering of humans and the actual freedom to be free from such engineering – at least for some meaningful portion of our lives.[1] We return to this theme at the end of the book.

This chapter looks from the present to the near future and explains why interconnected sensor networks, the Internet of Things, and big data enabled automation of systems around, about, on, and in humans promise to expand the scale and scope of techno-social engineering significantly. The reason lies in the power of intelligent, often automated systems and the reconstruction of our everyday environments and, as we shall see, us. It's the even more fine-grained, hyper-personalized, ubiquitous, continuous, and environmental aspects of the resulting techno-social engineering that make the scale and scope unprecedented.

We begin with a familiar example from the present: the smartphone. The smartphone is one prominent case where adding intelligence (smartness) expands the range of applications and uses of a device, making it more general-purpose and providing more affordances for various actors. Smartphones – or smart mobile devices more generally – are jam-packed with powerful sensors, processors, memory, software programs, and well-designed interfaces. Thousands of components are integrated into light wearable devices. As a media device, the smartphone piggybacks on and extends the scale, scope, influence, and architectural extension of the Internet. It contributed to and likely accelerated the convergence of interpersonal and mass media, and, more importantly, extended connectivity to most environments, bringing most smartphone users closer to being always on. The corresponding techno-social engineering is intense and varied.

Again, as with the Internet, it is worth considering the affordances of smartphones. On the demand side – that is, for users – smartphones extend and enhance many of the same affordances as the Internet and networked personal computers. An important additional affordance is *mobility*. Smartphones travel with users, and this disintegrates constraints in both time and space, meaning you can be online anytime and anywhere. This affordance cuts both ways. Various others – friends, family, co-workers, employers, advertisers, service providers, etc. – can reach you anytime and anywhere. On the supply side, the smartphone software ecosystem significantly lowers the costs of developing and deploying software applications, and this has led to vibrant communities of app developers and a corresponding proliferation of apps, many of which leverage the expanded versatility of smartphones and mobility of users to solve new problems and meet new demands.

Just think for a moment about the range of applications, entertainment, news, and other features enabled by the powerful, networked computer you can carry in your pocket. The smartphone invites others into one's mind and affords them incredible – and incredibly personalized – surveillance, nudging, and control capabilities. As such, we'd like to be able to evaluate:

> *Who is doing what thinking with smartphones? Who is smarter? Who acts on what intelligence, and how? Who gains what power? How does smartphone use affect us, in terms of who we are and may be, and how we relate to each other?*

Each of these questions demands considerable research and attention. Take a moment and consider your own experience with the technology. How have smartphones affected your life, your experiences and interactions with others? According to technological entrepreneur Elon Musk, "The thing that people, I think, don't appreciate right now is that they are already a cyborg . . . If you leave your phone behind, it's like missing limb syndrome. I think people – they're already kind of merged with their phone and their laptop and their applications and everything." If you've merged with your smartphone and digital technology as Musk suggests, can you ever exercise the freedom to be off?

Smart Techno-Social Environments

Here are (some of) the basic components of tomorrow's smart techno-social environments:

- Networked sensors
- Data
- Intelligence-generating systems, including artificial intelligence, machine learning, algorithms, and others
- Automation/control actuators

Each of these comprises a broad set of techno-social engineering tools. (Computer scientists and engineers will recognize these as subsets of broader system design categories. Obviously, each of these requires various supporting technical systems, e.g. for power, data storage, and so on.) While some of these tools sometimes work independently in particular contexts, these tools often are and will be components of "smart" interconnected systems that architect, manage, and possibly even constitute our built lived-in and experienced environments.

Though not appreciated by most people, even in the technology community, it is critical to understand that the potential demand for and thus value of interconnected sensor networks, the Internet of Things, and big data depends on automation of systems around, about, on, and in human beings. Put another way, interconnected sensor networks, the Internet of Things, and big data are not in and of themselves socially valuable. Demand for such technologies is derived demand. Many in the business and technology fields assume that these technologies are the next best thing, without really knowing why.[2] There is a common perception of the technological power and potential, almost inevitability, of an Internet of Things, from smart toothbrushes to smart toilets, but actual consumer demand remains uncertain and likely will continue to be so for quite some time; it likely needs to be stoked, if not outright created (another job for the marketing and advertising community that undergirds much of the modern information economy).

Let's focus briefly on the Internet of Things, which is an umbrella term often used to capture the basic components of smart techno-social environments. To begin, we must acknowledge that the Internet of Things is clever rhetoric. The Internet, as we know it, is an infrastructure that connects computing devices and ultimately *people*. Almost everything that occurs on the Internet involves the communication of information between people – it is social and relational, and it involves the creation and sharing of information.[3] So what is the clever rhetorical move? It is to replace *people* with *things*. The Internet of Things is a metaphor, but, frankly, metaphors matter. The Internet of Things metaphor reveals an explicit and implicit shift in framing.[4] While people might look at this as simply the next step in the evolution of the Internet and adjacent computing technologies and systems, the regulatory implications could be dramatic, and we don't just mean government regulation. We also mean regulation by private companies, architecture, and technology because of the ways in which the environment that we live within and interact with changes. Instead of people being in the foreground, the Internet of Things pushes people to the background.

When folks talk about the Internet of Things, the focus shifts subtly from humans actively communicating with each other to devices gathering and exchanging data and automating various technological and business processes to make the lives of human beings easier, more efficient, and happier. The Internet simply becomes a means for ubiquitously distributed sensors – mobile and stationary devices, mere things – to gather, process, exchange, and act upon data. The things are primary; they are technological and perceived to be neutral; they require investment and involve innovation, and will allow service providers – private and public – to more cheaply and efficiently provide us with what we supposedly want and need. But they also will allow those service providers to engage in techno-social engineering of humans – of, at least, our beliefs, preferences, and emotions – if the incremental steps we have seen in recent years are any indication.

Beyond mere rhetoric, the Internet of Things is a major work-in-progress. The incredible hype and investment about a trajectory that's expected to lead to an "[I]nternet of everything" has generated policy discussions, concerned mostly with paving the way for investment and deployment but also with identifying privacy, security, and other consumer protection issues.

In its Green Paper published in January 2017, the Department of Commerce Internet Policy Taskforce and Digital Economy Leadership Team used the Internet of Things as an umbrella term "to reference the technological development in which a greatly increasing number of devices are connected to one another and/or to the Internet." The DOC explained that commenters who responded to the DOC's Request for Comments offered a wide variety of definitions and emphasized different features and applications.

> Many commenters suggested a definition based on particular attributes of devices, activities, or the integration of sensors, actuators, and/or network connectivity. IBM referred to IoT "as the growing range of Internet-connected devices that capture or generate an enormous amount of data every day along with the applications and services used to interpret, analyze, predict and take actions based on the information received." The Center for Data Innovation . . . "describe[d] the set of physical objects embedded with sensors or actuators and connected to a network." Vodafone . . . does not focus on the devices, but rather . . . a "dynamic global network infrastructure with self-configuring capabilities based on standard and interoperable communication protocols that connects to smart 'things.'" . . . The American Bar Association Section of Science & Technology Law argued that "IoT is not itself a 'thing,' device or product," but rather "it is a conceptual structure consisting of tangible things (e.g., commercial and consumer goods containing sensors), real estate and fixtures (e.g., roads and buildings containing sensors), plus intangibles (e.g., software and data), plus a range of services (e.g., transmission, development, access contracts, etc.)." The Center for the Development and Application of Internet of Things Technologies at Georgia Tech stated that " . . . the one single groundbreaking element is not the connectivity . . . [but] the smartness of things." The President's National Security Telecommunications Advisory Committee . . . described . . . "a decentralized network of objects,

applications, and services that can sense, log, interpret, communicate, process, and act on a variety of information or control devices in the physical world." Others have suggested that the Internet of Things should be described through the lens of its integrated component layers – applications, network, devices, and data ... The growing number of sectors deploying IoT devices includes agriculture, defense, energy, entertainment, environmental monitoring, health care, manufacturing/industrial operations, retail, supply chain logistics, transportation, and others. Often included within the purview of IoT are a variety of "smart" applications, such as "Smart Homes," "Smart Cities," and "Smart Infrastructure."[5]

We provide this ridiculously long quote to give you a sense of how the Internet of Things potentially encompasses all the components of tomorrow's smart techno-social environments: networked sensors capable of collecting and transmitting data to enable smartness (intelligence generation via machine learning and other techniques) and consequently action. Notably, the final value-creating step – action – is not always specified, much less linked to automation. This seems a convenient way to avoid the elephant in the room: *Who is smarter? Who acts on the new intelligence, and how? Who gains what power?*[6]

As our discussion of the extended mind emphasized, we must ask: First, who will be doing what thinking in these smart techno-social environments? Second, what are the impacts of smart techno-social environments on the development of human capabilities?

This may seem too abstract. We encourage you to pick a few examples – toothbrushes, televisions, homes, cars, etc. – of your own and consider our questions. Let's consider who learns what from a smart toaster.

Technology writer Mark Wilson highlighted the deskilling potential of smart devices in his critical review of the June, a $1,500 smart toaster. At first glance, it seems ridiculous that anyone would pay this kind of money for a commonplace kitchen item that in "dumb" form can be purchased for a fraction of the price. But the June is built on the back of $30 million in venture capital; it runs on AI and deep learning and contains many sensors.

As of now, the June appears to be glitchy. But we can expect that, over time, some version of it will improve and become available at a significantly cheaper rate. While we can't predict the implications of this happening – especially since the effects will be influenced by other social trends – we're sympathetic to Wilson's concerns about the logic driving the developmental pathway. Above all else, it privileges machine learning: "When *you* cook salmon wrong, you learn about cooking it right. When the June cooks salmon wrong, its findings are uploaded, aggregated, and averaged into a June database that you hope will allow all June ovens to get it right the next time. Good thing the firmware updates are installed automatically."

Placing a higher value on machine learning than human learning is the hallmark of today's Internet of Things, convenience-oriented, devices. The big existential question to consider, therefore, is whether engineering an appetite for pervasive smart kitchens will disincentivize people from cultivating culinary skills, including the personalized touches many of us associate with the favorite cooks in our lives.

The road leading to this possibility was paved long before consumer technology became an Internet of Things staple. As philosopher of technology Albert Borgmann repeatedly argues, widespread use of microwave ovens and a manufactured globalized taste for fast food helped set all of this in motion. That's why when Borgmann considers the possibility of living in "smart" homes filled with "smart" appliances, he doesn't envision future liberation. Instead, he cautions that "we will slide from housekeeping to being kept by our house."

In some cases, improving intelligence correlates directly with improving the efficiency of a well-delineated functional task. Consider a few other examples from the home:

- A coffeemaker can be programmed to brew coffee automatically at a specific time.
- A smart coffeemaker may rely on a timer or sensor to determine whether a pot of coffee has been sitting on a hot burner for too long, in which case it may turn off the burner, reduce the temperature, or generate a signal such as a flashing light or beeping sound.
- A thermostat can adjust heating and cooling systems within a home based on a temperature sensor. It is smart in the sense that it can automatically make adjustments without human intervention.
- A smarter thermostat can integrate additional sensors, data processing, and control mechanisms and thereby adjust heating and cooling systems within a home based on more variables, such as temperature, time of day, and occupancy levels.
- A smart light switch can adjust lighting levels within a home based on time of day or motion.

Some of these examples involve sensors and programmed systems that can process and act upon data from the sensors. The first example doesn't even need a sensor to be smart. (Some might conclude that the programmable coffeemaker therefore isn't smart, but we think such a narrow conception of smartness would be underinclusive.) None of these examples requires (i) networking beyond the home, (ii) big data, or (iii) intelligence-generating systems beyond the home. In fact, each of these technologies can accomplish its core improved functionality locally and without integrating or interconnecting with each other or other smart devices.

Yet smarter Internet of Things versions of these technologies often will communicate beyond the home. There are various reasons. Some may do so by mistake or poor design. Some may do so deliberately because the device manufacturer would like to keep future options open. Some may do so because it helps with marketing, in the sense that consumers believe Internet-connected devices are better. Some device manufacturers may genuinely envision additional functionality, and some may assume innovation will follow. None of the reasons suggests technical or economic necessity.

Homeowners should be wary of smart home technologies that extend beyond the home. After all, whose intelligence is really being extended? Is it the homeowners', the device manufacturers', or other third parties'? The situation is quite like websites with hidden side-agreements. When supposedly smart devices collect data from within the home and communicate that data outside the home, the homeowner may be treated like a product, or, as the Internet of Things metaphor goes, like a person reduced to a thing.

We advocate two simple default rules/design principles for everyday things (not people!). First, don't connect, communicate, or interoperate. Second, only engineer intelligence as needed; make things only as smart as they need to be to perform a well-delineated functional task. (This is akin to a data minimization principle that has been proposed in the privacy-by-design literature.) Our proposal amounts to heresy in most engineering, design, and economics circles. We've flipped these communities' existing defaults, and so many people will conclude that we've gone too far. But let's be clear about two critical limiting principles. First, default rules are not absolutes; exceptions should be expected. Exceptions to such rules, however, require justification. Second, both rules and exceptions might need to be tailored to specific contexts. In some contexts, such as transportation, justifying connectivity, communications, interoperability, and engineered intelligence is rather easy, even if, as we shall see below, governance and implementation of smart transportation systems is ethically, politically, economically, and technically difficult.

Let's consider an example that would trigger an exception from the default rules we've proposed. In some contexts, being smart depends on accurate sensor-based intelligence coupled with (i) knowledge about what to do with the intelligence and (ii) the capability to act. Suppose someone installs a device with a sensor capable of detecting water seeping in a basement. If that is all the device can do, it is useless. It must be able to communicate to be functionally useful. Thus, for example, the device may ping the homeowners' smartphones to let them know about a potential problem. *Does that make the homeowners smarter?* It obviously does somewhat. They received new information. If they already know how to deal with the problem, then they can do so. If the homeowners lack such knowledge, what good is the notification? It would enable them to reflect upon and determine what to do next: consult friends, look online for do-it-yourself solutions, or contact an expert to assist them. It might be more efficient if the sensor immediately contacted a trusted service provider to handle the problem. That might be a perfectly reasonable and justifiable feature of the smart device, if the homeowners actively chose that option. This final point reflects a third default rule and design principle in favor of so-called active choosing.

In 2017, Burger King ran a TV ad that ends with a fast food employee asking, "OK Google, what is the Whopper Burger?" If a consumer had Google Home – a voice-activated speaker that functions as a digital assistant of sorts – near the television, the device would be triggered by the query and read the Wikipedia entry on the Whopper – an entry that Burger King allegedly changed before the ad ran. This call and response style of advertising is disconcerting because it creates a chain of communication that leads to a smart device reading a webpage that can be edited by anyone. Not only does this blur the line between information and advertising (Wikipedia is supposed to contain factual information like an encyclopedia) but it invites other minds into the home and raises interesting questions about control and who gets to do what thinking. Beside Google, Wikipedia, and Burger King, there are the Wikipedia editors. Suppose someone vandalizes the Wikipedia page in the hopes that a Burger King commercial will trigger the digital recitation of bawdy material in front of kids. But once opened, the channel is by no means limited to these specific exchanges: Expect creep and a much wider range of communications and invitations.

Some might retort that we're making a mountain out of a molehill. Many isolated examples of smart devices, such as a smart toaster, light bulb, or toothbrush, seem innocuous and almost trivial. As with nudging, electronic contracting, and many other examples we've discussed in this book, an incrementalist view can be misleading and lull one into habitual complacency. Smart technology will creep along various dimensions.

An individual smart device may creep in terms of data collection and/or function. For example, the specified, and so we shall assume intended, purpose of a smart TV with an always-on microphone may be to capture aural input for voice-activated commands. Communicating such data outside the home may be necessary for machine learning and other techniques to improve the voice recognition technology. But we can and should expect data collection and function creep. The always-on microphone can pick up much more data than actual commands. Apparently, the fine print of Samsung's Smart TV privacy disclosure once stated: "Please be aware that if your spoken words include personal or other sensitive information, that information will be among the data captured and transmitted to a third party through your use of Voice Recognition."[7] When treasure troves of data such as this are collected and shared with third parties, it is hard to imagine companies will abide by purpose and use restrictions. In other words, using the data solely to improve voice recognition technology seems highly unlikely over the medium to long run.[8]

Suppose one deploys a host of different smart devices in the home. Standing alone, each device might not "transform" the home environment. Together, however, they might. The aggregate effects might resemble a tragedy of the commons in the sense that incrementally rational decisions lead to a net tragedy. Obviously, tragedy is not inevitable. Tragedy occurring depends upon various contextual details, such as whether the devices interconnect locally or beyond the home and how defaults are set for security, privacy, and user engagement (e.g. in setting parameters or programming options), among other things. The point is that creep phenomenon applies here as well.

At this stage of smart home development, we cannot say who will be doing what thinking or what will be the impacts on the development of human capabilities. With respect to the first question, many smart devices for the home environment involve outsourced intelligence and raise the possibility of a corresponding invitation for intrusion and/or control. In the third part of this book, we turn our attention to techno-social engineering tests that might provide a useful framework for identifying and evaluating when outsourced intelligence impacts basic human capabilities.

How Smart Should Our Shared Infrastructure Be?

Infrastructure systems are incredibly complex, and intelligence and control technologies exist in many forms and layers. The somewhat oversimplified layered model of the Internet presented in the previous chapter can be used to describe power, transportation, and other infrastructure systems.

Often overlooked and pervasive social policy and technological design questions concern where and how intelligence and control technologies are deployed within infrastructure systems. Who gets to decide how such technologies are used?

One topic where this issue has become the subject of intense debate is the matter of how designers of self-driving cars will solve the trolley problem.[9] In its classic form, the trolley problem is a thought experiment that asks us to consider whether we would save the lives of several people from being hit by a runaway trolley if we had to pull a lever – an action that would send the vehicle to another track and kill someone there. Among other things, the scenario helps us think about whether there's a meaningful ethical difference between actively killing and passively allowing people to die. The variation for self-driving cars ponders what autonomous vehicles should be programmed to do if, say, they're on a collision course with a school bus that's carrying lots of innocent children and which can only be avoided by swerving and killing the single passenger in the car. *Should a simple utilitarian calculation be made?* If so, the choice is clear: count the lives of the children as being more valuable since there are so many of them. Or perhaps the passenger of the car has the right to insist that her vehicle prioritizes self-preservation. That attitude can seem selfish, but it's not an untenable position to hold.

Consider a variation of this problem. Imagine that you're in a self-driving car going down a road when suddenly, the large propane tanks being hauled by the truck in front of you start falling out and flying in your direction. A split-second decision needs to be made, and you are incapable of running through all possible decision scenarios and fully computing outcomes and trade-offs. The smart system driving your car, however, can do so. *How should it handle the question of who deserves moral priority?* Consider the following possibilities:

1. Your car should stay in its lane and absorbs the damage, thereby making it likely that you'll die.
2. Your car should save your life by swerving into the left lane and hitting the car there, sending the passengers to their death – passengers

known, according to their big data profile, to have several small children.

3. Your car should save your life by swerving into the right lane and hit the car there, sending the lone passenger to her death – a passenger known, according to her big data profile, to be a scientist who is coming close to finding a cure for cancer.

4. Your car should save the lives worth the most, measured according to amount of money paid into a specific form of *life assurance insurance.* (Assume that each person in a vehicle could purchase insurance against these types of rare but inevitable accidents.[10] Then, smart cars would prioritize based on their ability and willingness to pay.)

5. Your car should (i) save your life and (ii) embrace a neutrality principle in deciding among the means for doing so, perhaps by flipping a simulated coin and swerving to the right if heads comes up and swerving to the left if tails comes up.

6. Your car should (i) not prioritize your life and (ii) should embrace a neutrality principle and randomly choose among the three options.

7. Your car should execute whatever option most closely matches the moral choices you would have made if you were capable of doing so. (Assume that when you first purchased your car, you took a self-driving car morality test consisting of a battery of scenarios like this one and that the results "programmed" your vehicle.)

We've presented a simplified hypothetical with limited options. One point these thought experiments make is that there's no value-free way to determine what the autonomous car should do. The choice of whether to save one person or many isn't comprehensible as a purely computational problem. Determining which value system to embrace is no more of a mathematical operation than favoring Hammurabi's Code over the Declaration of Independence (or vice versa). We will program autonomous cars to deliberately follow paths that preserve and end life, and this only makes the matter of finding morally acceptable protocols even more pressing. Indeed, once it's acknowledged that some form of ethics needs to be baked into the programming, the following sorts of questions arise. *Who should decide how autonomous vehicles will perform when difficult situations arise? Should it be politicians? Automotive executives? Or should people be allowed to customize the moral dashboard of their cars so that their vehicles execute moral decisions that are in line with their own preferences?* The alternative, after all, is to put some people in a situation where they're pressured to abdicate control over highly valued decision-making. While creating design specifications that respect pluralistic values can seem ideal, it's no panacea. It's been suggested that a key to making smart transportation systems efficient is to create constraints that impose uniform behavior. If that's true, there's an important tension to resolve over whether efficiency or personal choice should matter more.

Once these issues are resolved, difficult questions remain. *What's the best way to convey to consumers what autonomous vehicles are programmed to do?* Philosopher of technology Mark Coeckelbergh expresses concern that if humans don't know how the vehicles they travel in make ethical decisions, they'll outsource aspects of their agency that are needed to engage in responsible behavior.[11] Even knowledge about how smart cars have been programmed doesn't alleviate moral concerns about ethical outsourcing. What matters is practical agency.

Ethical issues don't end here. Like the Internet, transportation systems are layered, and in addition to issues surrounding smart cars, we will need to confront a host of ethical and governance issues at the infrastructure layers.[12]

For example, business theorist Shoshana Zuboff insists that "automotive telematics" – which is to say, the surveillance and control capabilities of the automotive industry – are presenting problems that are poised to become more pressing when self-driving cars become the dominant business model. She writes:

> Now, data about where we are, where we're going, how we're feeling, what we're saying, the details of our driving, and the conditions of our vehicle are turning into beacons of revenue that illuminate a new commercial prospect. According to the industry literature, these data can be used for dynamic real-time driver behavior modification triggering punishments (real-time rate hikes, financial penalties, curfews, engine lock-downs) or rewards (rate discounts, coupons, gold stars to redeem for future benefits) . . . [T]hese automotive systems will give insurers a chance to boost revenue by selling customer driving data in the same way that Google profits by collecting information on those who use its search engine.[13]

Another set of related considerations is highlighted by the following thought experiment about the future of smart transportation management.

Imagine: it's 2025 and you're an engineer managing traffic in and out of a major city. You watch the roads fill up at rush hour, as people in autonomous cars, trucks, and buses buzz alongside pedestrians and cyclists guided by Internet-connected eyewear. Your job is to plan efficient, safe, and environmentally friendly routes.

Since this is the future, all your decisions are guided by data. Algorithms predict with astonishing accuracy what will happen when the weather changes, plans alter last minute, and emergencies require people to leave their homes and jobs in a hurry. Still, even with all this information, your job isn't easy. Every time you try to minimize congestion, you face the same problem: can you do better than first-come, first-served?

Today, police cars, ambulances, and buses sometimes get special treatment on the road because of the contributions they make to public welfare. But these narrow exceptions aside, our roads are managed without prioritization. First-come, first-served is the default.

In the future, however, we will be able to make finer discriminations about who individual drivers are, what destinations they've set, and what they're expected to do when they arrive. Armed with this information, would you place some folks in the fast lane and stick others in slower ones? Perhaps the woman on her way to a business meeting should get priority over the woman who is attending her son's soccer game. Or should it be the other way around? The decisions don't end there. Suppose only one of the drivers is going to make her event on time and the other will arrive too late even if she speeds. Presumably, you should determine who gets to go and inform the other person to stay home to minimize her impact on others. Over time, these sorts of decisions can be expected to occur frequently.

Bottom line: *Traffic engineers will assume the role of social planners.* Decisions made in single instances (e.g. prioritize x over y) according to decision-making protocols and embedded values aggregate and over time become social patterns.

Question: Which of the following is reducible to a computation problem?

a) Life
b) Traffic management
c) Social planning
d) All of the above
e) None of the above

Answer: (e) None of the above.

In theory, fine-grained control over traffic seems like the perfect use of big data and artificial intelligence. That's why folks are enthusiastically lobbying governments to invest in smart grids and transportation systems.

In practice, however, things are more complicated. Contentious debates about power and privilege should arise.

To appreciate why, imagine being a traveler in 2025, instead of an engineer. Envision yourself in an autonomous car that's made it halfway to your destination. Say you're a parent en route to your child's championship soccer game, the match that your kid has been obsessing over for weeks. Suddenly, your self-driving car turns around. Confused and upset you say, "Siri, why am I being re-routed? Why is this happening to *me*?" In response, the digital assistant laconically replies, "Sorry, but there's priority traffic heading downtown." What you don't know for sure but deeply suspect is that the smart traffic-management software is programmed to assign a comparatively low value to "mundane" social outings like amateur sports. Business deals, like the one your neighbor is heading to, count as more important to society because they contribute directly to economic growth metrics.

At first glance, this scenario might seem like bad science fiction. In fact, it's an old and very real problem. For some time now, the related issues of control and intelligent infrastructure have fueled the network neutrality debate.[14]

The Internet both provided the blueprint and unleashed the wave of smart technologies that promises to transform most of the environments within which human beings live and develop, ranging from smart homes and smart offices to smart cities. The smart technology transformation is likely to work its magic first, however, on the basic infrastructures that operate unnoticed by most of us in the background. Smart grids and smart transportation infrastructure will literally pave the way for the smart technology revolution.

The history of the Internet also provides a decent map of future governance dilemmas society will face. The network neutrality debate will not only persist for the Internet but also will return in modified form for other infrastructural systems. At its core, the network neutrality debate is about whether and how private owners of the Internet's underlying communications infrastructure could use the intelligence they gathered. In other words, the network neutrality debate was and still is about how smart the Internet infrastructure should be.[15] The core Open Internet rules aim to prevent broadband Internet service providers from using intelligence about the identity of end-users and uses (essentially, who's doing what online) to exercise control through various means (blocking, throttling, pricing). Constraining the networks in this fashion enables and even empowers end-users to be active and productive rather than merely passive and consumptive. As we extend networked intelligence onto other infrastructures – e.g. transportation and electricity – and into other spaces – e.g. cities, workplaces, and homes – society will need to grapple with how to govern intelligence and intelligence-enabled control.

Think again about transportation. In the eyes or algorithms of traffic engineers, vehicles on roads are just like data packets online. Both draw on network capacity, can create congestion during transit, and generate value upon delivery. Yes, there are many important differences between vehicles and data packets and between roads and the Internet. The analogy draws attention to functional similarities and helps us to see relationships between the underlying infrastructures and society.

Functionally, traffic management depends upon intelligence and control. Typically, managers must know something about supply, demand, actual and expected traffic flows, interactions among traffic flows, and so on. And they must be able to exert control over the traffic and users. Control is an essential feature of traffic management, and it can take many forms, ranging from pricing to norms and technological constraints. Such different possibilities mean control can alleviate governance dilemmas but also give rise to them, too.

Infrastructure matters to society for a lot of reasons. Many economists, sociologists, and historians focus on how infrastructure investment played a major role in shaping the modern economy. Changes to transportation are inextricably linked to expanding cities, the rise and sprawl of the suburbs, and the transformation of rural areas. At the same time, infrastructure has shaped the human condition by enabling us to exercise and develop fundamental human capabilities. Consider free will and autonomy, concepts that play a central role in ethical and political visions of responsibility and entitlement. It's one thing to theorize the importance of people making informed and uncoerced decisions. It's quite another to create reliable pathways for citizens to realize their potential for free thought and action. That requires opportunities to be mobile, communicate, and socialize.

To democratize these existential benefits and *many* others,[16] both roads and the Internet historically have been managed as a commons. Guided by the logic that priority shouldn't be granted to anyone or any purpose, egalitarian policies have regulated infrastructure access and use. Sure, in an emergency, police can break speed limits and run red lights. But this narrow exception and others concern situations where our collective social welfare is at stake. They're not instances of fast lanes going to the highest bidders.

Different governance regimes can protect neutrality. The end-to-end architecture of the Internet can safeguard this goal. So can bolstering public ownership of most roads with regulations that promote public goods. Esteem for the commons goes a long way towards explaining why traffic engineering aims to mitigate congestion and not maximize market values or anyone's profits.[17] But this ambition can change.

Forward-looking and quickly-acting industries are actively involved in the design and regulation of smart transportation infrastructure. It would be naïve to expect that shareholder expectations won't influence the much-touted policy goals of using smart grids to enhance safety, minimize negative environmental impacts, and create efficient routing. These expectations are part of the package deal of using proprietary products and services to mediate how smart vehicles communicate to other smart vehicles and interact with smart infrastructure. As with the Internet, all layers of the emerging smart transportation system present opportunities for surveillance and control.

Consider a hypothetical: Suppose automated and street legal trucks go mainstream before autonomous cars do. If this occurs, the interests of trucking companies might be advanced through systematic design. To maximize the benefits of keeping fleets of trucks close to each other, other vehicles would have to be encouraged to not get in their way. How vigorous might the promotion of fleet flocking be? We don't know for sure. You might think it's an engineering question to be left to the technologists, but it's really a question of political economy. If we adjust the hypothetical by suggesting a different path forward where a different industry sets priorities (say, autonomous vehicles, app-plus-data intelligence services, or even, dare we say it, networked bicycles and pedestrians), the same basic question arises: *Who decides how priorities will be determined and on what basis?*

The network neutrality debate taught us that smarter technology isn't always better technology. As we collectively decide how smart new forms of infrastructure should be, we should keep in mind that sometimes smart systems can be too smart for our own good. We need to be very careful here, however, because what we really mean by smart is powerful. Keep in mind that traffic management depends upon intelligence and control, and what we are concerned with is the specific use of intelligence to exert control and set priorities. Such infrastructural power can lead to significant forms of techno-social engineering which are difficult to identify, much less resist. Prioritization of traffic (infrastructure use) based on willingness and ability to pay (market value) rather than some other measure of social value affects the distribution of infrastructural affordances. Simply put, prioritization determines who is capable of doing what and often with whom. It is nothing short of social planning.

What does this mean for our future smart transportation system? We cannot hope to do justice to this question in this chapter. But we will offer a short answer. There is a strong case to be made for network-neutrality-style rules at the infrastructure layers of any smart transportation system. As we've explained, such rules sustain an underdetermined environment and thus serve as a defense against engineered determinism, a topic we dig into in Chapter 12. Transportation systems are incredibly complex, and intelligence can and should be used to manage certain costs – such as congestion – and risks – such as accidents. This can be done in a manner that does not discriminate or prioritize based on the identity of drivers or some proxy assessment of or proxy for their value (e.g., market valuation), but again, it is a social choice involving complex trade-offs.[18]

Further, we should not fool ourselves into thinking that such costs and risks can or should be eliminated or even driven as low as technically possible because there are trade-offs to doing so.[19] Tolerating some congestion, some friction, some inefficiency, even some transaction costs may be necessary to sustain an underdetermined environment conducive to human flourishing. We revisit this issue in the final chapter.

We are optimistic about the potential of a smart transportation system that intelligently saves lives, manages congestion, reduces environmental costs, and identifies maintenance needs. Autonomous or self-driving cars increase human agency by providing people with more time and attention to devote to other pursuits, whether productive, consumptive, contemplative, or social . . . who knows? While people debate exactly how many lives autonomous cars can be expected to save, it's widely thought to be large enough that it would be immoral not to make them street legal as soon as possible.[20] We're highly sympathetic to this view so long as enough attention is given to the difficult issues concerning governance, technical design, and social choices about normative priorities, as reflected in the trolley problem discussion as well as the traffic management thought experiment. These issues return us to the basic and familiar *who decides* theme. This question needs to be front and center as industry and governments pave the way for the emergent smart transportation systems. We cannot afford to leave it to technologists, politicians, or some abstract and ultimately meaningless conception of a free market.

We hope this book persuades the reader to consider humanity's techno-social dilemma seriously. We are building our world and ourselves in the process. We cannot ignore the political economic realities or simply defer to idealized conceptions of free markets. "Free market" is merely a slogan, yet it has had quasi-religious power in shaping beliefs, preferences, and political debates and outcomes. Putting aside how all markets exist within social governance structures, we must emphasize that even robustly competitive markets routinely fail in many ways. The most ardent neoclassical economist will admit that competitive markets do not assure us of an environment that maximizes social welfare or human flourishing. As one of us explained in the context of the network neutrality debate:

> Competition does not ensure an efficient allocation of resources. It does not assure us an Internet environment that maximizes social welfare. Competition does not address these interests for the same reasons that antitrust law is orthogonal to environmental law – antitrust law does not address market failures associated with externalities, whether environmental pollution (negative externalities) or the production, sharing, and productive reuse of public and social goods (positive externalities). Indeed, it is well established in economics that competitive markets overproduce pollution and underproduce public and social goods.

Despite frequent claims to the contrary, we cannot count on markets alone to self-regulate or provide the necessary discipline on technologists designing techno-social environments. The trolley car dilemma and traffic management examples illustrate what we should expect.

Smart Media/Mediation

We began the previous chapter with mass media, and we'll end this one with smart media. Essentially, the term "smart media" refers to the various digital media platforms and systems enabled by the Internet that operate at the applications, content, and social layers of the five-layer model we presented earlier. Many of the most powerful media companies that regularly engage in data-driven techno-social engineering of humans operate applications-layer platforms – social networks, search engines, marketplaces, even online games. We've discussed many examples in this book and there are more to come.

The dominant data-and-advertising-driven business model (and corresponding incentives) shapes smart media platform design, algorithmic policing, and users. The smart media industry recognizes how the business model affects platform design, often casting the optimization problem in terms of maximizing user engagement. While this term can have nuanced meaning, we think it really boils down to optimization for clicks – actions that generate revenue or data. Many have lamented the quick click culture engendered online, suggesting that it has reduced attention spans and cheapened social discourse. There are many counter-examples. Our simple hypothesis is that smart media platforms optimized for clicks engineer humans to behave like simple machines by treating them as resources. Second, smart media systems run into the same normative issues as other smart systems in terms of social planning and techno-social engineering. Smart media shape beliefs, preferences, knowledge, relationships, democracy, and so on. As such, there seem to be decent reasons to turn to human experts to evaluate quality and shape discourse. Conventional mass media recognized the need for expertise, judgment, and even ethics, particularly in certain areas such as news. Yet various social/cultural/technological developments seem to have pushed in the opposite direction.

The smartness of smart media systems is not grounded in human expertise or judgment concerning the media content; rather, it's grounded in data, intelligence-generating systems, popularity, celebrity, and the apparent wisdom of crowds. In some domains, these sources of intelligence are likely to be better, but it's a dangerous social gamble to rely on smart media systems across all knowledge domains.

To limit our discussion, we'll stick with familiar giants, those household names that have the largest market valuations and social impact: Google and Facebook. In addition, we'll focus on the problem of filtering objectionable content. However, these really are tips of the proverbial iceberg, and they are exemplary. There are so many different digital media platforms and content evaluation problems to examine. We don't have the space to discuss the contours of fake news, cyberbullying, hate speech, pornography, or copyright infringement. These examples, like many others, seem to require smart media solutions, meaning intelligence-enabled control, whether through filtering, blocking, prioritization, outing, or other forms of discipline. *Who knows whether in fact such control is socially desirable?* It's too important a question to be ignored or for the answer to be assumed. Yet the massive growth in the scale and scope of content, data, relationships, transactions, and so on, generated every minute, across multiple jurisdictions, pushes quite strongly towards smart technological mediation. Whether intelligence-enabled control in smart media systems is, will, or should be exercised discriminately as an exceptional, targeted intervention or regularly as part of a broader program of techno-social engineering remains an open question. We return to some of these issues in the final chapter – by focusing on the fake news problem and possible solutions. For now, we'll focus on recent examples that highlight the basic problems.

In April of 2017, a shocking video was posted to Facebook that showed Robert Godwin Sr., a retired grandfather, being shot in cold blood by a man who filmed the murder he committed on a smartphone. Facebook didn't take the video down until approximately two hours after it appeared and critics chastised the company for acting too slowly. Some went further and proclaimed that the tragedy – or more precisely, a tragedy like it – was inevitable thanks to techno-social engineering. *Washington Post* columnist Kathleen Parker wrote:

> People will film themselves doing just about anything and everything. Younger folks who've been documented since birth, as well as during, and have never known a cellphone-free moment, perhaps can't fathom why they shouldn't "share" their every whim, appetite and mood ... For every exhibitionist, there are a million voyeurs. We're all so riveted to our screens that a moment not captured and telegraphed to our thousands of social media "friends" may as well not have happened ... I worry that the underlying imperative in our see-and-be-seen culture – one increasingly without even the expectation of privacy – soon leads to the expectation that one shouldn't have any privacy. Some slippery slopes really are slippery.[21]

Parker's concerns overlap directly with issues we discuss throughout the book. At the same time, the tragedy is part of a larger problem for smart media that we haven't addressed yet. Some of the problem revolves around questions concerning whether Facebook and other similar online companies should be subject to content regulations just like "traditional" media broadcasters. And some of the problem revolves around questions concerning whether the artificial intelligence that plays an integral role in content policing is up to the challenge.

To get clearer on these issues, let's think about some of the design features and value-laden considerations that are associated with Facebook and related online platforms. Many of these platforms want to provide users with a great amount of discretion over what content they can choose to post. Such dedication to diversity is an expression of a commitment to an ideal that many believe is central to the very fabric of democracy: promoting and protecting free expression. Spokespeople for Facebook, YouTube, Twitter, Instagram, and the like regularly portray their services as conduits for communication akin to phone companies that leave the scope and quality of conversations up to the users themselves. This is an idealized view which obscures how platform design mediates user communication and downplays how mediation is a form of techno-social engineering.

Even as these companies tout the value of free expression, they also affirm that their services impose limits and shouldn't be confused with environments where anything goes. Explicit community standards are established to prevent information that violates widely accepted norms from being shared, remaining online, and travelling to inappropriate feeds. These standards are not just about enforcing decency, but are also a business tool that is partly implemented to minimize the likelihood that users will be so offended by certain shared content that they will cancel their accounts.

Consider Facebook's Community Standards document.[22] It states:

> We remove content, disable accounts, and work with law enforcement when we believe there is a genuine risk of physical harm or direct threats to public safety . . .
>
> To help balance the needs, safety, and interests of a diverse community . . . we may remove certain kinds of sensitive content or limit the audience that sees it . . .
>
> By joining Facebook, you agree to use your authentic name and identity. You may not publish the personal information of others without their consent . . .

In principle, policies like the one Facebook uses are supposed to be minimally prohibitive, much like the legal proscription against falsely shouting fire in a crowded movie theater doesn't diminish First Amendment protections of free speech. In practice, however, things are not so simple, such as Facebook's reliance on a "real name standard." The standard is said to impact vulnerable populations the most – people who wish to discuss sensitive topics in safe spaces, people who want to criticize power norms without retaliation, and victims of crimes like domestic abuse.[23]

Additionally, smart media companies typically provide a mechanism for users to customize (at least somewhat) their experience of what they want to read and see on a platform. Personal customization through filters is supposed to enhance user control. But, in practice, filters can be techno-social engineering tools that modify user expectations and influence their preferences.

Shortly before the Facebook incident, YouTube came under fire for how its "restricted mode" filter was working. The filter is "an optional setting that you can use to help screen out potentially mature content that you may prefer not to see or don't want others in your family to see."[24]

Unfortunately, some LGBTQ vloggers (i.e. people who create video-based blogs) discovered that restricted mode was rendering their content invisible, as did other minorities. Not only did this exclusion raise social justice questions, but it also had financial implications for the people who were losing page views. Technology writer Fruzsina Eordogh notes:

> Restricted Mode, a feature introduced in 2010 and used mostly by schools and libraries to filter out sensitive videos inappropriate for children, should include some LGBTQ+ videos, according to YouTube, but the net cast by the algorithm is currently far too wide. Coming out stories, transition videos, wedding vows, mental health vlogs and even style and makeup tutorials are caught in the ban, videos that have absolutely no sexual or violent content that would merit them being invisible in Restricted Mode. In fact, most of the videos creators have complained about being censored have significant educational value.
>
> Beyond LGBTQ+ videos, Restricted Mode seems to unfairly target content about black people … and black content creators, especially if they have a more "urban" or controversial style ie: not family-friendly for middle class white people.[25]

YouTube probably wasn't intentionally trying to engage in unfair discrimination. At present, restricted mode, like all policing algorithms in the smart online media landscape, are vulnerable to four fundamental problems. First, algorithms can have a difficult time correctly identifying content that has context-specific meaning. This shouldn't be surprising, as humans can be terrible at it too – a problem that was vividly illustrated when Facebook employees removed a famous photo of a nude girl running from a napalm attack during the Vietnam War.[26] Second, values change over time in a pluralistic democratic society, ideally in ways that diminish prejudice and shatter harmful taboos. This makes the designers of policing algorithms responsible for understanding social change and ensuring that their software adequately reflects the times. Neither are easy tasks, and this brings us to the third problem. Companies that rely on policing algorithms need to ensure that explicit and implicit programmer biases are mitigated against when necessary. Unfortunately, problems can go undetected until real world debacles occur. And, finally, there's the issue that critics focused on when Facebook was slow to remove the gruesome murder post. How quickly can humans at a technology company respond to situations where their policing programs make the wrong call or fail to detect a problem?

Note that a fifth and perhaps more fundamental problem may be the data-and-advertising-driven business model itself.

CHAPTER 9

#RelationshipOptimization

This chapter is about sociality. Sociality is a matter of relating to others. In practice, it consists of exercising various capabilities, including reflecting upon and determining our own beliefs about others. For example, to relate to others we often need to try to understand what they think and feel about a range of issues, including how they perceive us. We also need to be able to assess their character and decide such things as whether they're truly loyal or, instead, merely self-servingly manipulative.

Relating to others often entails reciprocation, and this includes letting people who treat us well know that we have high regard for their thoughts and feelings. This type of communication may either go well or be fraught with misunderstanding. No matter how similar to us, others always lack first-person access into our minds. Given their external location to our thought process, it's unreasonable to expect anyone to be a mind-reader. Even when people in our intimate circles claim to know us well enough to say things like "I know what you're thinking," they're either speaking colloquially or making an approximation.

Sociality also regularly depends upon the successful use of perceptive, sensory, and emotional capabilities. Picking up on social and physical cues can be crucial to maintaining human relationships. If I can't relate to or sympathize with you during moments when you claim to be in pain, do I deserve to say that I understand what you're going through when you start sobbing?

In short, sociality is a rich and complex subject, and many disciplines study it. What we've said about it so far barely cracks the surface. Now, however, we're going to present an inquiry into human sociality that deepens conversations about the impact techno-social engineering is having upon it. The analysis is spread out over four interdependent sections. The first three use a series of stories, examples, and thought experiments to describe and critically analyze different aspects of sociality. While doing so, we set the tone for the discussions of free will, autonomy, common sense, and (ir)rationality that we'll present over the next few chapters.

The last section, however, goes in a slightly different direction than the others. There we discuss how techno-social engineering of human sociality can *creep across* different relational capabilities and different types of relationships. While this creep isn't inevitable, we argue that its potential needs to be acknowledged and resisted when appropriate, just like other forms of techno-social engineering creep that we've discussed.

A final prefatory comment is in order, however, on how sociality might have come to play a prominent role in human life. One prominent view contends that the propensity for sociality lies in our very DNA, dating back to a time when the only way our ancestors could survive in the face of the strength and speed of predatory animals was to band together and develop cooperative practices. Philosopher of science Michael Ruse claims that humans have evolved to believe that cooperation is an ethical imperative, placing sociality on a moral high ground for the continuation of the entire species.[1]

> [B]iology has pre-programmed us to think favorably about certain broad patterns of co-operation ... We are not hardline "genetically determined" like (say) ants, who go through life like robots. Nor are our patterns of thinking so fixed by our biology that culture has no effect. But the fact remains that, to make us co-operators, to make us "altruists," nature has filled us full of thoughts about the need to co-operate. We may not always follow these thoughts, but they are there.[2]

Ruse's thesis is controversial, and it would take us beyond the scope of this book to assess its accuracy. Instead, we're highlighting it to emphasize two things: (1) sociality is a longstanding feature of being human; and (2) Ruse is onto something important by linking human sociality with culture and social engineering. In this book our focus is on techno-social engineering and the problem of engineered determinism, not natural or biological determinism.

Digital Companions

Linguistic Coaching, Impersonation, and Digital Immortality

Our personal and collective identities are intimately connected to language. How we speak can convey a lot about what we've experienced – where we're from, how we've been educated, what we read, watch, and listen to, and whom we surround ourselves with. Think of the grueling linguistic tutelage Eliza Doolittle endures in *My Fair Lady* to improve her life.

Indeed, language can reveal our attitudes towards morally and politically charged topics, like social convention and class. For example, if you address an authority in an overly informal manner, that can signal something about your view of that person. Perhaps you think a CEO is stuck-up and needs to be taken down a peg for his arrogance. The same anti-elitist gesture, however, also can convey something fundamental about how you see the world and your place in it. Maybe you want to prevent a silver-spooned CEO from controlling how less powerful employees speak because you believe deferential social conventions are oppressive.

On the most basic existential level, language is crucial to our humanity. We can't read other people's minds. They can't directly peer inside ours. Language thus shrinks the gap between self and other and makes deep relationships possible: it allows us to infer, perhaps even know, what folks are thinking, feeling, hoping; it can bring others into our inner worlds; and it enables us to make plans and coordinate our actions with others. As many argue, this is a distinctly human capacity.[3]

> What is language, then, if it can describe the way we process actions as well as the way we manipulate words? Understand from this perspective, language is not a method of communication, per se, but rather a method of computation. Other animals clearly communicate with one another, sometimes in fairly elaborate ways. Whales sing, monkeys howl, birds chirp. Lizards bob their heads up and down to communicate, and some squid do it by regulating the colouration of their skin cells. But none of these processes can be explained by language.[4]

As we'll discuss in detail in the next chapter, the exceptional human use of language is why the traditional Turing test revolves around human conversation. If a machine genuinely can keep up with us as we bounce from topic to topic and alternate from factual questions to sarcastic banter, it might understand our way of life, just like other people do. And if that's the case, the computer deserves recognition for exhibiting social intelligence. Indeed, while in some respects Turing advanced a novel position, his views on language also reiterated longstanding historical assumptions. Back in 1637, philosopher René Descartes wrote:

> For one can well conceive of a machine being made so that it utters words, and even that it utters words appropriate to the bodily actions that will cause some change in its organs (such as, if one touches it in a certain place, it asks what one wants to say to it, or, if another place, it cries out as if one was hurting it, and the like). But it could not arrange its words differently so as to respond to the sense of all that will be said in its presence, as even the dullest men do.[5]

Since how effectively computers process language impacts our appraisal of how far they've advanced, the media enthusiastically covered start-up company ETER9's announcement that it aims to create a social network that "turns your personality into an immortal artificial intelligence".[6] On ETER9's platform, two interesting things will supposedly take place: artificial intelligence software will learn about a user's personality by analyzing what she posts; and artificial agents will apply that knowledge and, on their own, create high quality, new content on a user's behalf, even after she dies. If ETER9 succeeds, digital doppelgängers will convey estimates of our thoughts while our bodies decompose.[7]

ETER9 isn't the only technology company with skin in the simulated self game. Google, for example, submitted a patent for software that learns how users respond to social media posts and automatically recommends updates and replies they can make for future ones.[8] This wasn't a surprising filing. Google already predicts how our minds fill in blanks when using a search engine, and so perhaps it was inevitable that the company would aspire to automate our social interactions. Ultimately, it might direct our email, instant messages, and texts, too.

If you've bought books or music on Amazon, watched a film on Netflix or even typed a text message, you've engaged with machines that are designed to figure out how our minds work and steer our choices with personalized recommendations. They, too, use predictive algorithms to find patterns in our previous behavior and make inferences about our future desires. Apple has capitalized on this data mining and processing with QuickType, the software that's installed on iPhones and predicts "what you're likely to say next. No matter whom you're saying it to." Apple was so satisfied when the product was released that it represented the tool as yielding "perfect suggestions."[9] Critics didn't buy it and continue to complain of performance issues. But Apple depicts QuickType as so contextually sensitive that it can adapt its recommendations to the different styles we use when talking with different people and determine that "your choice of words is likely more laid back with your spouse than with your boss."[10]

And then there's an app called Crystal that's marketed as "the biggest improvement to e-mail since spell-check."[11] Essentially, the software creates personality profiles of people you want to email (by aggregating and analyzing their online posts) and offers targeted recommendations for how to communicate with them. People have different communication styles, and the folks at Crystal contend that if we fail to appreciate them, misunderstandings and hurt feelings can result. In the corporate world, for example, efficient workflow can require effectively translating our thoughts into recipient-friendly formats. Treating highly analytical correspondents who prefer maximum detail as if they're trusting intuitive types can be disastrous.

Crystal's guiding vision, therefore, is that when you don't speak to people as they want to be spoken to, projects can be undermined and folks can feel like their colleagues are selfish or insensitive. To avoid these pitfalls, putatively you just need to minimize the distance separating self from algorithm and defer to both the software's detective work and suggestions.

Only time will tell if ETER9 lives up to the hype. But as is often the case with prognostics about bold technological development, speculative fiction has already covered the subject and considered potential social impact. "Be Right Back," an episode of the dark British series *Black Mirror*, suggests we'll get much more than we bargained for if technological proxies become our ventriloquists.[12]

Martha's Disenchantment

"Be Right Back" revolves around a romantic couple, Ash and Martha. Ash spends a lot of time online, chronically checking social media. After he dies in a car accident (possibly due to digital distraction) a friend intervenes by signing Martha up for a new service. Despite initial misgivings, a grieving Martha eventually tries to find solace with computer programs that are designed to dig into his extensive data trail and replicate his personality – his disposition, presence, and even character. After using a text-based service that simulates written chats, she tries a voice-powered product. It allows Martha to talk with an audio simulation of Ash – something like an uncanny version of her partner reincarnated as Siri, or better yet, a male version of Samantha from the human-computer romance movie *Her*.[13] The conversations prove addictive. After the ventriloquized version of Ash suggests she take things to the next level, Martha orders an upgrade. She gets a full-blown android that's designed to look, sound, and behave just like Ash.

At first, Martha is thrilled with her purchase. Android Ash appears to have the real Ash's charm and warmth. Even better, it outdoes him in some respects. With an ability to quickly study vast amounts of online pornography and immediately emulate highly rated moves, Android Ash turns out to be a better physical lover. It holds out the prospect of being Ash 2.0, an iteration that may be better than the real thing.

Over time Martha becomes disenchanted. She's displeased with Android Ash's unending willingness to please and is unhappy about the subtle mistakes it makes that serve as painful reminders it's not Ash's exact double. Android Ash is a mere performer whose success in the role depends upon Martha's willingness to accept approximations as a job well done. Martha herself says as much when she tells Android Ash: "You're not you, you're just a few ripples of you. You're just a performance of stuff that he performed without thinking, and it's not enough."

Martha's changing outlook becomes cemented after an especially emotional interaction. She asks Android Ash to jump off a cliff, a request that proves confusing and prompts the machine to explain that the real Ash never conveyed suicidal thoughts or tendencies. Martha responds by noting that's the point, and the real Ash would have immediately recognized the demand is insane, if taken literally, and responded by crying. Then, as if Android Ash were one of Pavlov's dogs uncontrollably responding to a bell, it promptly starts to weep. Martha finds the servility disgusting.

"Be Right Back" isn't just about the limits of artificial intelligence and how hard it is for computers to simulate people we care about – to perfectly mimic their expressions of what they believe, what they desire, what they stand for, and how they make sense of the ever-changing things going on around them in the ever-fluctuating world. And unlike so much technophobic fiction, it isn't about robots going rogue and turning on their masters – a theme that the media are quick to pounce on, like the time when it portrayed as true a hoax about "a robot programmed to love" ensnaring a "young female intern" with "repeated" hugs.[14] And while privacy theorists might be alarmed by how the issue of permissions is treated – nobody questions whether Ash would have consented to a company using his data this way, or Martha using simulated Ash products – that doesn't appear to be the set of issues the viewer is asked to focus upon.

No, the episode is fundamentally about us. Not in the sense of drilling down into the question whether there's something spiritual or physical that makes it impossible for digital personas to ever be functionally identical to human personalities – although it's hard not to wonder about that throughout the viewing. First and foremost, "Be Right Back" asks us to think long and hard about *whether we'd become dehumanized* if, unlike Martha, we were willing to treat imperfect computational approximations of our partners as good enough relationships. Whether or not you've seen the episode, that's the thought experiment we'd like you to consider.

If your lover died, would you order an android version, if one was available? If so, what would you do with it? Would you go as far as trying to make a life with it? These are fraught questions, especially because grief can be powerful, even all-consuming. But the underlying issues are just as relevant in variations of the "Be Right Back" scenario. As a single person, would you order an android that's programmed to behave like your vision of an ideal partner? This might seem tempting. You could then have an enduring experience of what humans get as a fleeting moment when they initially become romantically involved with one another: a honeymoon phase where objects of affection appear without flaws and get put on pedestals.[15] In *Love and Sex With Robots: The Evolution of Human-Robot Relations*, artificial intelligence expert David Levy contends questions like these will be resolved soon when humans routinely fall in love with robots.[16]

Autonomy, Reductionism, and Meaningful Relationships

If Martha embraced Android Ash as a good enough proxy, she'd need to accept something profound: free will is not required within intimate relationships. After all, Android Ash lacks genuine autonomy; it cannot determine its own intentions. It can only do what it's been programmed as a robotic servant. For example, Android Ash can't break its computationally enforced script and become internally motivated to tell Martha that it doesn't want to be bossed around and treated like property. Indeed, Android Ash lacks the power to change its mind on its own about anything. It's stuck forever examining the data stream the real Ash left behind, predicting what that version of Ash would do in a given situation, and either impersonating the forecasted response, or asking Martha for permission to try out a different behavior that she'll find more satisfying.

Android Ash, therefore, is nothing more than an animate slave. It can't choose to walk away from Martha or grow and evolve in ways Martha finds displeasing. Indeed, Android Ash lacks its own preferences (it can't prefer to be doing something else or be somewhere else) and its own desires (it can't fall in lust, much less deal with being overwhelmed by those feelings).[17] All it can do is conform to standards of what Martha finds comforting and entertaining. It can't ever intentionally introduce elements of risk into the relationship that can reasonably be expected to undermine initially shared goals and lead to "failures" that folks sometimes associate with break-ups and divorce. Ultimately, Android Ash is the epitome of what philosopher Immanuel Kant calls "heteronomy":

lacking self-determination and remaining fundamentally subjugated to an externally imposed will.[18]

By contrast, autonomy is a key component of being human, at least in the modern Western tradition. When social arrangements permit, we're free to decide whether to be self-absorbed or other-oriented. We can select whom to care about and make up our own minds about when to start caring more about them, or even stop caring about them entirely. Unlike arranged marriages, Western wedding vows are meaningful precisely because they're supposed to be freely chosen commitments.

Thinking about autonomy helps us appreciate an important dimension of Martha's interactions with Android Ash. Those exchanges raise the question of whether humans only pursue relationships because they want to be surrounded by stimuli that make them feel good. Now, people can become aroused by all sorts of things, even inanimate objects, and treat those experiences as instances of love. For example, someone can have such an intense reaction to seeing, smelling, and touching leather that she says she loves it. But is that really the same type of love that two people experience when they freely commit to one another? And, yes, people often describe their loyal and affectionate pets as beloved members of their family. But when someone describes her dog or cat as her child, is that sentiment best understood as comparison between beings that have things in common, rather than as a literal statement of cross-species equivalence?

A good way to get a clear sense of how you see things is to think of the importance you attribute to your partner giving you a compliment. Do you only care that positive words come your way and trigger positive feelings? Or is there something more at stake existentially than your subjective internal response – how displays of regard affect your mood? If there isn't, then you might approach relationships like a *stimulus-response machine*. In principle, functionally commensurate triggers that create comparable reactions can serve as substitutes, and you might not even have to wait too long before technology can accommodate your sensibilities. Abyss Creations already announced that it "wants to start making robotic sex dolls that talk back, flirt and interact with the customer".[19]

Such a reductionist approach to conceptualizing relationships is in line with a reductionist scientific outlook – an outlook that some believe can explain why we aim for our loving relationships to culminate in marriage despite intimidating divorce and infidelity statistics. From this point of view, love is a series of subjective experiences motivated by neurochemical reactions.[20] According to one account, there's a lust phase where we're driven to sexual activity, thanks to a drive to reproduce and the hormonal power of testosterone and estrogen. Then, there's an attraction phase where adrenaline, serotonin, and dopamine draw our attention to a particular person that we desire. And when, over time, we become attached to a partner and collaborate to raise children, oxytocin releases help us remain interested, even when the feelings we experienced during lust and attraction aren't present.[21] Seen this way, it's a mistake to believe two people experience love together in a transcendent way. Instead, love is driven by impersonal, physiological forces and is something that individuals internally experience on their own.

If you're repulsed by reductionist characterizations of relationships, it's probably because you believe it matters if your partner has free will and deliberately chooses to bestow praise when she doesn't have to. It matters that she has her own standard – which you can't control – of when you deserve praise. From this point of view, meaningful communication isn't generated simply because words are uttered that you, or other people, like to hear. It matters who or what sends positive expressions, like admiration, your way, and the conditions under which the regard arises.

Consider how sensitive we can be to the possibility that other people might look down on us. This can be just as emotionally impacting as receiving a compliment, albeit negatively. That's why people who can afford housekeepers are prone to doing time-consuming pre-cleaning before their employees report for work. By contrast, we doubt that if a robot cleaner – say a future generation Roomba – could tidy up everything as well as humans can the same compulsion would be widely felt.[22]

What accounts for this difference? Why does it matter if humans or machines tidy up? After all, in both cases the same type of labor is performed. There's functional equivalence.

The answer is simple. Even if humans and service machines adhered to the same standard of cleaning, they'd still differ in an important way. Humans are morally judgmental. This is partially because we regularly presuppose others have free will and, as a result, can choose amongst different courses of action and be held accountable for the paths they opt to pursue. By contrast, service machines aren't programmed to look at us that way. If we give them a command to follow, they don't think about what we could have done to make that request unnecessary or less demanding.

So, while pre-cleaning appears to compromise the purpose of hiring a cleaner – by minimizing how much time and effort the third party saves us – the fact remains that people are embarrassed about the prospect of having other human beings discover that they're sloppy pigs. Who wants to be seen as lazily disgusting? Who wants others to inwardly exclaim, "I can't believe this person doesn't even put minimal effort into basic home maintenance?"[23]

Sociological Skepticism

Even if you accept that autonomy is a crucial mark of distinction that separates humans from robots for now and the immediate future, you might be skeptical that it amounts to much on an interpersonal level. Fueled by sociological doubt, perhaps you believe that romance is socially constructed and human approaches to love are mostly, if not entirely, robotic performances of socially expected behavior.

Take for example the widely shared conviction that a good partner should be conscientious and considerate. This isn't a value that individuals come up with all on their own. It's one of the roles everyone is expected to play as a member of a society that shares norms about partnership. It's reinforced throughout stories and movies of successful relationships; it's become the basis of widely shared advice; and it's the standard many appeal to when determining if they're in a good relationship. Describing how standardized, if not "automatable," many American romances are, design technologist and technology theorist Mike Bulajewski writes:

> First there are the three main thresholds of commitment: *Dating, Exclusive Dating*, then of course Marriage. There are three lesser pre-Dating stages: *Just Talking, Hooking Up* and *Friends with Benefits*; and one minor stage between Dating and Exclusive called *Pretty Much Exclusive*. Within Dating, there are several minor substages: number of dates (often counted up to the third date) and increments of physical intimacy denoted according to the well-known baseball metaphor of first, second, third and home base.
>
>   There are also a number of rituals that indicate progress: updating of Facebook relationship statuses; leaving a toothbrush at each other's houses; the . . . exchange of I-love-you's; taking a vacation together; meeting the parents; exchange of house keys; and so on.[24]

Because we're constantly judging our partner's performance against socially reinforced ideals that we've internalized, there can be intense pressure to live up to idealized expectations. And this, in turn, means that to avoid unpleasant repercussions, ranging from uncomfortable stares to harsh words or worse, our partners can feel compelled to *robotically compliment* us on occasions where they don't feel sincerely motivated to do so. They might even express their frustration in what sociologist Erving Goffman called "back stage" material, like a diary they don't ever expect we'll read.[25]

We leave it up to you to determine whether romance is a reductionist state of affairs that's regularly idealized as more. If so, then perhaps designing appealing, intelligent, servile robots who make us feel special and cared for would be a major advance – at least if we bracket the difficult related questions of whether making them would disincentive procreation, and, if so, whether that's a problem. Or, for the reasons Martha rejects Android Ash, you might find a one-way relationship with a robot insufficient and prefer a more challenging and authentic human connection – one that would affect your own development differently than being surrounded by a perennial affirmation machine that's incapable of being genuinely sincere.[26]

Automating Relationships

Chawla's Cautionary Tale

At some point, Rameet Chawla, founder of the mobile app company Fueled, became too busy to acknowledge his friends' pictures of kids, vacations, and food on Instagram. Presuming he wasn't interested in their affairs, they became offended. To make things better, Chawla turned to software for assistance.

Chawla designed a program to automatically "like" his friends' photos. From that point forward, he didn't even need to bother looking at the flurry of proliferating images or put in effort to judge which ones were meaningful. Technology took care of everything on his behalf. As *The New York Times* reported, the deception worked.

> Suddenly, his popularity soared. Friends gave him high fives on the street; his follower count surged; the number of likes that appeared on his photos doubled. One friend he had alienated texted: "Ah, it's fine, you've been giving my photo lots of life. I forgive you."[27]

Now, Chawla may have come up with an excellent engineering solution. But it's worth asking if dishonesty spoiled the outcome. Presumably, Chawla's friends could have been more supportive. But if a conscientious person isn't inclined to systematically fake paying attention to others, this is a clichéd case of two wrongs failing to make a right. A breakdown in conscientiousness occurred, and, instead of confronting its source, Chawla used technology to evade the underlying problem.

Conscientiousness is a virtue, and it's closely connected to compassion, empathy, and altruism. When we care deeply about someone, we adopt a *conscientious attitude*. And when we live a life that's consistently committed to reaching out to others and attuning ourselves to what they're thinking and feeling, we develop a *conscientious character*.

When we're behaving conscientiously, we focus on people we care about and try to get a sense of what they're up to and where their lives are going. By considering what they're looking forward to and anxious about, we can be supportive and respond appropriately to goals, hopes, dreams, and desires. For example, if you know that someone is anxious about finding a job after graduating from college, you might proactively ask if she needs help networking – rather than waiting until she finds things difficult, gets into too much debt, and tearfully begs for your assistance.

Many of us wish we could be more conscientious. We'd feel better about ourselves and for obvious reasons our friends and family would benefit, too. But attending to all the practical day-to-day matters in life – going to work, cleaning the house, picking up groceries, doing the laundry, paying the bills, etc. – can get in the way of us more fully living up to this ideal. Sustaining relationships take lots of energy and time, and we find these are scarce resources, just as the ancients did. Note that this is a standard example of free will and autonomy in action. That is, we often have higher order desires about who we want to be and how we'd like to behave with respect to others, but more immediate and often external factors constrain us in ways that may lead to conflicts among our desires and reduce our autonomy, which we discuss extensively in Chapter 12.

Back in antiquity, the philosopher Aristotle differentiated three fundamental types of friendship: incomplete ones based on mutual utility, where participants are attracted to instrumental advantages, like business partnerships; incomplete ones based on mutual pleasure, like a common attraction to a sport or hobby; and complete ones based on mutual goodwill and virtue.[28] Aristotle proclaimed we can't lead a good life without complete friends who are unconditionally devoted to our well-being (amongst other things, they help us develop moral virtues like patience and trustworthiness). But he also acknowledged a hard truth. Even if we're fortunate, we can only have a few of them due to all the work caring requires.

The limits Aristotle recognized are exacerbated in the digital age, as we continually expand our connections through networking technologies. In this respect, Chawla's story is a great cautionary tale. It aptly illustrates how so-called frictionless communication doesn't simply make it easier to reach out to others, but also can burden our lives with interpersonal complications. We're not only stressed out about giving less than we'd ideally like to the most important people in our lives, but we also worry about shortchanging others whom we care less about, but nonetheless still feel great affection and obligation towards.

Chawla's dilemma illustrates a problem that's been discussed by lots of people, ranging from Jean-Paul Sartre's classic existential analysis to, more recently, social scientist David Zweig's writerly perspective.[29] Too many people are desperate for attention and build their self-esteem with bricks made of external recognition. While chasing after other people's approval is a longstanding malady, it's hard to deny that the current selfie-obsessed form partially is fueled by a *constellation of powerful techno-engineering forces*: social media platforms like Facebook are designed to suck maximum self-centered content out of us; Klout scores overlay Twitter with a celebrity ethos, where the goal of acquiring followers becomes an end-in-itself; and self-branding and persona management have become ubiquitous, eroding the boundaries between public and private correspondence.

So, much as we might wish we could always be there when others need us, we simply can't. We've got concerns of our own, finite resources, time-sensitive obligations, and links to all kinds of demanding connections which easily leave us feeling overwhelmed and stretched too thin. This unsatisfying situation makes it tempting to look for shortcuts, just like Chawla did. Yes, he may have taken automation too far by constructing a system that entirely removed human agency from the loop. But in many cases it's unclear which interpersonal tasks can be appropriately handed off to software and which delegations will undermine conscientious objectives. In short, it's hard to tell when a line is crossed that turns attempts to be considerate or respond to other people's demands for consideration into *dehumanizing endeavors*.

This is an urgent question. Many technologies have been and will continue to be developed that hold out the promise of optimizing our relationships. We'll have tough choices to make when deciding whether to use them and whether to be upset if other people use them on us.

The market already contains contentious options. Online greeting card companies enable us to automate birthday messages. Facebook still leaves content creation to us, but many respond thoughtlessly to its birthday prompts, as if they're to-do list items that need to be crossed off as quickly as possible.[30] Apps like BroApp remind users to contact significant others and offer formulaic notes they can pass off as their own sentiments – literally passing off app-provided prose as one's own thoughts through a programmed schedule of dispensed notes so that loved ones get the illusion that they're being thought of at that very moment. Companies like Match.com even offer algorithms that help you find prospective new partners who look like your exes.

People who are pressed for time will be tempted to find these tools attractive, as well as the more potent ones that are developed in the next generation. And opinions will be divided when they're deployed. Take the case of programmer Justin Long's use of Tinderbox – a tool he developed that automates the dating app Tinder by combining "facial-recognition algorithms and a chat bot."[31] Basically, the app finds profiles of people who look like they fit the user's "type," initiates three rounds of automated communication with prospective dates, and then, finally, prompts Long to personally get involved in the communication process. The system worked so well that Long had to disable it. Apparently, it "started conflicting with work."[32]

What should we make of Tinderbox? As it turns out, some of Long's dates were fine with the automation and didn't mind that he deceptively passed off bot-generated text as if it were human-created conversation. One of the dates was even impressed after Long revealed all the algorithmic processes that were going on behind the scenes.[33]

But, as the reporter who covered this story notes, there's another way to see things. "If Tinderbox is unsettling," Robinson Meyer writes, "it's because it takes that commodification to the next level – treating people not just as data entries within Tinder but as piles of data themselves."[34] That equivalence – responding to others as if they were mere information – is a reductive orientation that many would deem dehumanizing.

To get a clearer sense of where lines should be drawn, let's consider two closely related thought experiments.

Mood Walls in Smart Homes

Suppose you could have a digital wall in your kitchen that uses lines of colored light to display trends and patterns in your loved one's moods. Maybe it gleans how they're doing from their posts on social media, email communications, and text messages. Maybe your partner and kids (or whomever you live with that you care deeply about) help the processes by inputting personal data into constantly updating mood-tracking software.

If this technology helped you better appreciate how your loved ones feel and how different factors affect their moods – such as being in different environments, participating in different activities, and even being confronted by your own fluctuating emotions – how would that knowledge affect the relationships in your household? Would you become a more attentive partner or effective caregiver? Or might the mood status system have a negative influence, possibly a dehumanizing one?

In *Enchanted Objects: Design, Human Desire, and the Internet of Things*, author and innovator David Rose argues this is an amazing device that we should all want.[35] He justifies his preference with simple logic: with great information comes great potential for being responsive.

> If we could know more about what's going on with those we love, we could alter our behavior in response. We might be quicker to celebrate the highs and good times of our lives together, more ready to offer support and understanding during low moments and difficult times. If we could see patterns of thought and mood in others, we might be better able to plan when and how we interact with them.[36]

Rose's conviction that automating communication is the key to bringing families closer together infuses his admiration for one of his own inventions. Inspired by the play *Peter and the Wolf* (where each of the main characters is associated with distinctive music and instruments) and the *Harry Potter* series (which references a magical clock that keeps track of the fictional Weasley family members), he built the prototype for the Google Latitude Doorbell. Rose describes it as follows:

> As each family member approaches the home, the chime sounds for that person when he or she is ten miles away, one mile away, or a tenth of a mile away [. . .] nearly home. It's not telepathy, but it does deliver information that gives clues to the mental and emotional states of each person. Frustration for the unlucky one in the traffic jam. Exhaustion with possible elation or crestfallenness, for the athlete. Mental distraction from the person in the intense meeting.

The design of both the mood status wall and Google Latitude Doorbell are guided by the assumption that good relationships can be fashioned by using technology to minimize misunderstandings and maximize predictive awareness. The question is whether such interventions would eliminate too much important human interaction.

An alternative way to judge the Google Latitude Doorbell is to consider whether it improves upon our standard means of communicating. Let's imagine, then, that we're comparing it to a more effort-intensive alternative: each family member gets ready to head home and calls or texts a relative who is already there and making dinner for everyone. In this scenario, each caller or texter must put in the time to convey a message with a status-update and whoever receives this information needs to put in effort to acknowledge the updates. Is this exertion so valuable that eliminating it would remove something important from the communicative equation?

We believe the answer is yes. Thanks to social media, we already have access to a constant stream of status updates composed for multiple audiences. This information can increase intimacy through ambient awareness, but the fact remains that providing direct attention through personalized communication is an important way we show people we care about them. It's how we demonstrate they matter more than others who get less of our consideration.

Little gestures like saying "On my way home. Can't wait to see you!" do more than convey logistical information. They spread positive emotions and reinforce esteem by communicating that you care enough about the other person to ensure she is up to speed on your travel plans. By contrast, an automated sound can't convey such regard; neither head nor heart guides the communication; there's no underlying human intentionality. At bottom, it's nothing more than a pre-programmed outcome that's deterministically triggered by features like GPS coordinates. Efficient? Yes. Sincere? No. And, let's not forget, as a one-way signal, Google Latitude Doorbell isn't conducive to the reciprocity that comes from dialogue. It doesn't invite recipients to respond at all.

This brings us back to the mood status wall. That technology minimizes the amount of observation and checking-in that otherwise would be required to get a sense of how someone is feeling and what makes the person tick. While such scrutiny or attentiveness can be exhausting and fraught with unpleasantness, it's one way we go about showing others they're worth the metaphorical trouble – that they aren't valued only in circumstances when they're easy to get along with and don't impose friction on our lives.

The mood status wall takes an instrumental logic that many see as appropriate in some business contexts and brings it into a different domain: our personal lives. This technology is but one example amongst many that embody the same underlying ethos. We're transitioning from a time when getting a business edge required using sales applications (e.g. databases and contact managers) that contained fields for inputting data about customers (e.g. hobbies, birthdays, and names of kids) to using next generation versions of the technology in our personal lives for "managing" social and familial relationships. This process is what philosopher Jürgen Habermas called "the colonization of the lifeworld."[37]

Collapsing these domains allows data-mining to crowd out moral attention. It isn't enough to be aware of what people need and desire. We also need to care about them and their condition, and respond appropriately. Appropriate responses can vary, but our main point is that appropriateness can require more attuned engagement than commodified environments are designed to facilitate. But can that attunement and the potent positive emotions that come with it arise without the back-and-forth of conversations that, admittedly, sometimes can be taxing? If it can't, then, at a certain level, effort isn't a bug that limits interpersonal relationships, but an essential feature of human connection that we need to maintain commitments.

Predictables

Israeli designer Dor Tal created a thought experiment about a hypothetical app called "Predictables" that raises additional questions about when automation might be bad for relationships.[38] His scenario goes beyond the information-disclosing features of a mood status wall and focuses our attention on consumers using a combination of big data analysis and recommendation algorithms to coach their interpersonal decisions.

Tal's hypothetical app performs three functions. First, it can scrape our digital footprints and the data trails of those we want to monitor – capturing the smorgasbord of social media posts, search engine queries, email, GPS data, etc. Second, it can quickly analyze the vast information it tracks, discover behavioral patterns, and predict events that are likely going to happen in the future. And, third, it can offer suggestions, expressed in a visually intuitive format, for what you should do in light of the patterns and predictions it discovers. This information gets synced to a user-friendly "predictive calendar." For example, Tal imagines Predictables telling a guy that his girlfriend is "about to be sad" and advising him to buy her flowers. He does as he's told, and she's thrilled. As time passes, the software makes a stronger recommendation. It suggests that the relationship has gone on long enough and recommends that the user purchase an engagement ring.

This scenario may seem like a science fiction. But Tal's vision is based on existing technology. As he told one of us:

> Most "big data" companies are able to analyze much more than how we feel and what will make us feel better. For instance, during my research, I analyzed more than 5100 of my WhatsApp messages and found very clear patterns that can easily be connected to produce predictions about my activities and future feelings. Facebook adds to its status line the option to share emotions.

Putting aside the numerous privacy concerns implicated by Predictables, the question is whether it's a good idea to use it or any similar technology even when all parties consent to being surveilled and assessed by the system. Some will say yes. They won't see it as adding any new moral wrinkles to the mood status wall. They'll contend it conveys useful information that otherwise can be difficult to obtain. And they'll insist that the recommendations it offers are mere nudges that users can ignore, should they choose to do so. Others will say no, categorically. They'll argue it crosses a fundamental line by engineering intimate interpersonal exchanges and relationships. They'll likely see it as a substitute in individual cases that lessens opportunities to develop critical perceptive, emotional, and social capacities.

Others still will be inclined towards a restricted affirmation. They'll see the technology as a good aid for dealing with people at the edge of their social networks. But they'll balk at using it to mediate their most intimate relationships.

We've all got people in our lives who we have genuine affection for but aren't so deeply committed to that we make the time to follow their social media posts or routinely catch up with them through phone calls and visits. Despite ordinarily putting in limited effort, we'd want to get in touch to express well-wishes or possibly even offer to lend a hand, if an emergency arose or a life-altering event occurred. Under these conditions, it can seem entirely appropriate to use technology as a filter for bringing these folks to the forefront of our attention, even though they are otherwise out of sight and mind.

For instance, if you got in touch with a long-lost friend who posted "My mother is sick" to Facebook, you'd demonstrate concern for her well-being under a set of trying circumstances. Nothing changes, morally speaking, if you do because an app predicts her mother is sick from a set of obvious clues (like your friend leaving several posts about needing to take time off work) and recommends you call. After all, we're not obliged to keep tabs on everyone. And, the recommendation that's offered seems like nothing more than a reminder to live up to the norms of common courtesy.

But people might believe it's a different situation entirely if this type of technology gets used on folks in their inner circle. If you care about someone that you have a special relationship with – a partner, a best friend, or a child – you might feel obliged to actively stay in touch and not outsource the monitoring. This can happen through face-to-face visits, or technologically mediated activity: phone calls, texts, emails, social media posts, and the like.

That said, bypassing the energy and commitment required to stay attuned to our inner circle through automated sentiment analysis might abdicate the moral attention described above. It can show others that we don't value them enough to commit to making their lives – out of all the lives we could attend to – worth our time. And perhaps turning to smart technology for recommendations of what to do in these situations abdicates care by demonstrating an unwillingness to be devoted to the hard work of making sensitive and responsible decisions that concern other people's well-being.

Algorithmic Bloodhounds

The Quantified Self (QS) movement is becoming quite popular.[39] Broadly speaking, QS draws on "body-hacking" and "somatic surveillance," practices that, as their names suggest, subject our personal activities and choices to data-driven scrutiny. Typical endeavors include tracking and analyzing exercise regimes, identifying sleep patterns, and pinpointing bad habits that subvert goals. Recently democratized consumer technologies, especially smartphones that run all kinds of QS apps, enable users themselves to obtain and store diagnostic data and perform the requisite calculations.

In *The Formula: How Algorithms Solve All Our Problems – And Create More*, technology writer Luke Dormehl gives an interesting example of how far people are willing to go with QS to follow the ancient Socratic injunction "Know thyself!"

> Consider ... the story of a young female member of the Quantified Self movement, referred to only as "Angela." Angela was working in what she considered to be her dream job, when she downloaded an app that "pinged" her multiple times each day, asking her to rate her mood each time. As patterns started to emerge in the data, Angela realized that her "mood score" showed she wasn't very happy at work, after all. When she discovered this, she handed in her notice and quit.[40]

Dormehl sees the type of activity "Angela" engages in as having the potential to transform our very understanding of what it means to be human. Since we're entering an age where algorithms increasingly tell us who we are, what we want, and how we'll come to behave in the future, he says our time is marked by a "crisis of self" where algorithmic ideology is challenging the Enlightenment conception that, at bottom, we're "autonomous individuals."[41] What does it mean to be me? Perhaps despite the stories I tell myself and others about my unique experiences, preferences, and desires, I'm not a special, singular snowflake, but a mere series of "categorizable node(s) in an aggregate mass."[42]

What makes "Angela's" case especially interesting is that she apparently lacked confidence in her own abilities – her capacity to introspect and have edifying conversations about her well-being – to determine if work was making her miserable. She believed she needed more than her own mind and friends could deliver. She wanted cold, objective, quantified data to identify the source of an emotional problem. She thought that, without consulting the data, she couldn't make a responsible life-changing decision.[43]

In our private lives, QS practices won't be limited to self-tracking. It's likely that over time they'll include a range of interpersonal applications and become integrated into *routine, domestic techno-social engineering practices*. Today, we tell our mobile-phone-carrying kids that being responsible means texting or calling when they get to their friends' houses. But what will happen tomorrow, especially when we're dealing with cases where more personal information is communicated peer-to-peer by machines without people in the loop? Will we expect automatic updates from our kids' phones announcing their locations whether or not they intend for us to have this information? How, in general, can we determine when those practices cross a line and become dehumanizing?

To get clearer about where your sympathies lie, consider the following extreme scenario. If it seems like an instance where dehumanization occurs, techno-social engineering might be a process that brings it about.

Period Tracking

Imagine you're at a party when out of the corner of your eye you see a friend looking intently at his smartphone. You ask why he's got his face buried in the screen. But instead of giving you a typical answer like "I'm on Facebook" or "checking email," he says, "I'm looking at the app that tracks when my wife menstruates and predicts when she'll have her next period." You ask if his wife knows about the surveillance. He says yes, she's totally on board and consent isn't an issue. Then, he offers several reasons to justify his behavior. "My wife gets very emotional during her time of the month, and having an app tell me when she's having this experience helps us avoid having awkward conversations about it. Without making things weird, I can decide if it's a good idea to plan a family camping trip over the weekend and when to schedule the next date night. It also helps me make better decisions: what food to have in the house; when to avoid saying things that can lead to a fight; and when to ensure my wife doesn't make big, bad decisions."[44]

To get the full import of this example, some context is needed. Back in 2010, the *Washington Post* ran an article about "code red," an app for men to use to track women's periods. It states:

> A tour of recent technological creations shows that menstruation apps for men are a booming market. "PMSBuddy," for example, is proudly "saving relationships, one month at a time." "PMS Meter" features "hilarious sound effects." And the infamous "IAmAMan," which is nothing if not unapologetic, allows users to track the menstrual cycles of several women at once, for those special times when you are a big cheater.[45]

Now, the market for these services doesn't seem to be "booming" yet. Some of these apps aren't even supported any more. But men easily can download menstruation trackers specifically designed for them to use, or they can repurpose apps designed for women to gain more control over their own reproductive health. Moreover, many of the fertility-tracking apps on the market for women are "largely designed by men" and "invite women to give their partners access to the information."[46] Indeed, "the app Glow sends a little note when a user's partner is entering her fertile period, along with helpful seduction advice like bring her a bouquet."[47]

Major technology companies also are encouraging widespread tracking. A recent *Time* post states that Apple – a company which exerts profound influence over what happens in the mobile phone market – is already on the menstruation tracking bandwagon as part of its electronic health agenda.[48]

> Your smartphone has reached a new level of intelligence: with the help of a forthcoming iPhone feature, you'll be able to tell when you're going to be getting your period.
> The iOS 9 upgrade will add a track-your-period feature to the HealthKit app ... The health app – which already tracks several screen-scrolls' worth of health and fitness data – seems to be able to record how long (and heavy) your menstrual cycle is. The ... update is billed as a "reproductive health" tracker, so it may come with other features related to fertility ... The extra feature, due out with the next update, will finally give women a more complete digital view of their health.

Debating Tracking

Let's unpack the key reasons why someone would think it's a good idea to track a partner's menstruation cycle. For starters, relationships have their ups and downs and, at times, both partners might wish to avoid certain conversations. If using a menstruation tracker helps avoid the recurring unpleasantness that comes from constantly asking "Having your period?," bypassing disastrous dialogue could be seen as a good thing. Especially if the person who is being tracked finds the conversations a frustrating reminder that biology impacts mood and important parts of our emotional life are beyond our conscious control. Indeed, some find the idea that they're "not themselves" – actual language that's used to defend tracking – once a month existentially unnerving.

The second justification for tracking is improved conscientiousness. Tracking a partner's menstruation might enable a person to be more attentive and helpful. For example, if a partner's willpower is put to the test by cramping and cravings, it can seem like the way to have her best interests at heart is by making sure of two things: she has ready access to foods that will stabilize her blood sugar; and she won't be tempted to consume unhealthy comfort treats she'll subsequently regret eating.

The third justification centers on proactively dealing with mood swings. If a partner becomes more sensitive than usual, isn't greater sensitivity during these times required? Isn't it crucial to do everything possible to avoid saying or doing things that will create conflict? Isn't it helpful to steer that person away from making big commitments until a time arises when they can give issues clearer consideration?

These are just a few of the justifications we've encountered in talking to folks about menstruation tracking apps. Lara Freidenfelds, a historian of women's health, sex, and reproduction suggested to us that sex planning might be the true motivator for many adopters who use the app to track their partners' cycles.[49] This defense of monitoring a partner's menstruation may be persuasive to those who adopt the utility-maximizing outlook associated with *homo economicus*. Personal relationships are treated like a system that should be optimized to minimize inefficiency and waste through strict cost-benefit-oriented planning. From this point of view, someone who objects to using technology to track a partner's menstruation cycle may seem more than old-fashioned, but also fundamentally irrational – prioritizing "political correctness" over progress.

Others, however, will find the arrangement described above outrageous. They'll see the *homo economicus* imprimatur as a rationalizing veneer that obscures underlying sexism and a reductionist impulse to view women as basically blood-filled machines who blindly follow the dictates of illogical programming. From this perspective, what the surveillance advocate sees as digitally enhanced smarts is just repackaged old-school chauvinism. As feminist philosophers argue, even the venerable history of Western thought – a tradition that represents itself as the apex of rational reflection – has perpetuated the view that women are inferior to men because they're overly emotional. Per philosopher Alison Jaggar:

> It is difficult for women to maintain their self-respect in a culture in which women and everything associated with the feminine are systematically scorned, mocked, belittled and disparaged. Even Western philosophy has participated in the cultural devaluation of women and the feminine by contrasting mind with body, reason with emotion, public with private, the sublime with the beautiful, and culture with nature and then associating the first and superior term of each opposition with the masculine and the second, inferior term, with the feminine.[50]

Cultural devaluation extends to authoritative views of women having fundamentally defective minds. Today, some sexists will say that women are too emotional to be president. But as feminist philosopher Susan James notes, over long periods of history pre-eminent thinkers have advanced the driving ideology.

> A great deal of recent feminist work on philosophy of mind has been grounded on a central claim: that the key oppositions between body and mind, and between emotion and reason, are gendered. While the mind and its capacity to reason are associated with masculinity, the body, together with our emotional sensibilities are associated with the feminine. Evidence for this view comes from at least two sources . . . [O]verly sexist philosophers have in the past claimed that women are by nature less capable reasoners than men and more prone to ground their judgments on their emotional responses.[51]

And so, one reason to find the tracking arrangement bothersome is to believe its advocates mistakenly construe women as, at times, thoroughly incapacitated by their bodies, and wholly incapable of addressing the weakness on their own, much less managing it.[52] In other words, the problem lies with the premise that women are fundamentally prisoners of their biology and only can be fixed by partners looking out for their best interest.

This position resonates with ideas that Freidenfelds advances in *The Modern Period: Menstruation in Twentieth-Century America.*[53] She argues the experience of menstruation has social as well as biological dimensions, and that the social aspects have changed over time. The "modern period," for example, is a historically specific type of experience. Women and men adopted distinctive forms of bodily discipline and bodily discourse acceptable for the American middle class. Women gained new control over their bodies (e.g. in 1984 physicians started approving Ibuprofen to relieve menstrual cramps and, shortly after, the medication became available over-the-counter). They also established new expectations consonant with the modern period, such as what counts as acceptable public conversation (e.g. it's not taboo to mention PMSing) and what counts as reasonable requests (e.g. husbands and boyfriends can be asked to pick up tampons and won't be stigmatized for doing so).

Self-awareness is a fundamental component of self-control, and it's a valuable capacity to cultivate. By delegating aspects of menstruation tracking to others, a woman risks undermining the empowering effects that come from embracing modern period ideology.[54]

Menstruation Tracking and Beyond

The logic behind the menstruation tracking app illustrates a broader set of concerns and isn't limited to a single form of mediating how loving partners relate to each other. For example, if a husband uses the app to track his wife's cycle, shouldn't he also use it to track his mother's and daughters' as well as his boss's and his employees'? In fact, shouldn't he use the app to mediate his relationships with all women?[55] Using the app, he presumably could avoid many discomforting conversations, be more conscientious, and relate better to women in general. In fact, there's no reason to limit his use of tracking apps to menstruation. After all, there are many other types of useful data, biological and otherwise, that could reliably be used to mediate social relations.

There's no reason to limit technological tracking to optimizing relationships with women: presumably variations could be done for all the men in his life. And there's no reason for our technology user to be a male. Women likewise would and presumably should use such technology to manage their relationships with other women and men. On its face, this isn't a parade of horribles, at least not for those who might be inclined to use the menstruation tracking app in particular.

It can be difficult to evaluate techno-social engineering applied to ourselves and our relationships. The menstruation tracking app raises some complex considerations that are also relevant to the broader category of quantified self apps. We hope this discussion has triggered useful thoughts about how techno-social tools mediate how you relate to others.

Creep

As the preceding examples demonstrate, sociality is a basic human capability that's highly susceptible to techno-social engineering. Hopefully, we provided diverse examples for your consideration. We intended for the variety to offer a hint about the topic we're covering here: *techno-social engineering creep*.

In previous chapters, we've discussed the concept and explained how it conceptually relates to humanity's techno-social dilemma and the slippery-slope arguments. We've also suggested that techno-social engineering creep is related to other more familiar creep phenomena, such as surveillance creep, outsourcing creep, and boilerplate creep.

This chapter has provided a series of examples where techno-social engineering creep exists or has the potential to gain traction. Techno-social engineering of human sociality can occur along multiple dimensions. To identify and evaluate techno-social engineering creep, it's important to analyze those different dimensions. Suppose, for example, we focus on a particularly important relationship, such as the relationship between spouses or intimate relationships generally. We might examine techno-social engineering of a specific aspect or subset of that relationship, as in the menstruation tracking app example, or techno-social engineering of the relationship itself in a more totalizing fashion, as in the Android Ash example. The shift from narrow focus to a more totalizing one is one dimension along which we might observe techno-social engineering creep. As we've suggested, a couple might decide to extend their use of available techno-social engineering tools from the menstruation tracking app to apps that rely on other biological signals to manage other aspects of their relationship. The techno-social engineering creep could easily extend to non-biological signals as well, as a few of the other examples demonstrated. It's hard to say when, if ever, such extensions would go too far and undermine or eviscerate the spousal relationship. But at the extreme, one might wonder whether both spouses come to resemble Android Ash, as far as their relationships are fully mediated and optimized according to the efficiency logic we discussed.

Another dimension along which techno-social engineering creep can proceed is relationship type – that is, the techno-social engineering tool can be extended from a certain type of relationship to others. Again, the menstruation tracking app, as well as any other tracking app, could be used to mediate non-spousal relationships. The technological tools are not limited to any particular type of relationship. Yet their initial adoption might be more easily justified in the context of a particular relationship.

Another dimension that's worth focusing on is interaction type. For example, a techno-social engineering tool might optimize a particular type of interaction (e.g. a sales pitch, wedding speech, or pick-up line) or mode of communication (e.g. phone, email, text) and then gradually extend to other interaction types or modes of communication.

We're listing these forms of techno-social engineering creep to give you a clear sense of how sociality maps onto the larger theoretical framework we've been developing. That framework will be expanded upon considerably in the next few chapters where we propose novel techno-social engineering tests, discuss the practical value of wagering that free will exists, and elaborate upon what the problem of engineered determinism entails.

PART III

CHAPTER 10

Turing Tests and the Line between Humans and Machines

Introduction

With this chapter, we transition from the second part of the book to the third. In the second part, we analyzed fundamental dimensions of techno-social engineering. In this part, we extend the analysis in three ways. First, we discuss the famous Turing test and explain how it inspired us to create a new form of analysis: techno-social engineering tests. Techno-social engineering tests can determine when humans are behaving like simple machines and if techno-social engineering adversely impacts important human capabilities, aptitudes, and dispositions. After discussing several techno-social engineering tests, we'll take the analysis further. We'll reflect on free will, engineered determinism, and ethical values. Finally, we'll conclude with recommendations for minimizing negative impacts of techno-social engineering. We'll argue for the importance of creating practices, policies, and systems that foster the practical freedom to be off.

Turing Test: A Brief Overview and Literature Review

Can machines think? This turns out to be a much more complicated question than it seems at first blush. In 1950, mathematician Alan Turing published a seminal paper, "Computing Machinery and Intelligence," that raised the question and then acknowledged the difficulties inherent in defining "machine" and "think." So, he pivoted away from the seemingly intractable question and instead developed a test to provide an operational definition of intelligence.[1] This chapter introduces the basic contours of the Turing test ("TT") and explores various features of the test that inspire our analysis in subsequent chapters.

Turing developed a *method* of testing and developing empirical evidence.

What he was proposing with his test is a way to make the overall question of machine thinking more precise so that at least in principle an empirical test could be conducted. Thus, Turing's replacement strategy involves both a clarification of meaning, particularly about the nature of the machine, and a procedure for obtaining good evidence.[2]

The TT is modeled on what once was a popular party game, the Imitation Game, where a man (A), and a woman (B), enter a separate room from the interrogator (C), and the interrogator attempts to determine which of the other two is a man and which is a woman by asking a series of questions. The interrogator knows the individuals by the labels X and Y and may ask questions like, "will X tell me the length of his or her hair?" The answers are provided as text to prevent any bias based on tone of voice. What makes the game so interesting is that A's objective is to cause C to fail to make the correct identification. As a result, A may answer questions untruthfully to increase the odds of a wrong identification. After several rounds of questioning, the interrogator guesses the sex of the individual by saying: "X is A" or "Y is A." (Obviously, the Imitation Game is a sign of the times it was played in.)

Turing's test for machine intelligence takes much of its structure from the Imitation Game. In its standard version, a machine and a human are separated from an interrogator, and the interrogator poses a series of questions to the machine and the human in order to identify which agent is human. Further, the machine will attempt to exhibit human-like conversational behavior to trick the interrogator into making the wrong identification. As in the Imitation Game, answers from the machine and human are typed to avoid any biases. Turing predicted that by the year 2000 an interrogator would not have a greater than 70 percent chance of correctly identifying the machine after five minutes of questioning.[3] This identification threshold is a common view of what constitutes "passing" the TT.

The TT allows the communicative behavior of the two agents involved in the Imitation Game to be scrutinized. Communication is considered an appropriate locus of investigation because of the link between intelligence and verbal output. Consider, for example, how we commonly attribute intelligence to other humans, even though we are unable to peer into their minds and do not have direct access to their mental processes. Despite this limitation, we still attribute intelligence to other people, and through inferential or analogical processes about their behavior consider them intelligent just like us.

One way we consider other humans' behavior intelligent is by judging their verbal outputs. For example, you have a conversation with a patron in line at the local coffee shop and based on their complex, intelligent verbal outputs, you justifiably attribute intelligence to that person. If we believe the patron is a machine, then, unless we're prejudiced against machines, consistency demands that we accept the verbal outputs of the entity as intelligent.

Computer scientist Stuart Shieber usefully expresses the TT in formal terms:[4]

- *Premise 1*: If an agent passes a Turing Test, then it produces a sensible sequence of verbal responses to a sequence of verbal stimuli.
- *Premise 2*: If an agent produces a sensible sequence of verbal responses to a sequence of verbal stimuli, then it is intelligent.
- *Conclusion*: Therefore, if an agent passes a Turing Test, then it is intelligent.

There are complications to this line of argumentation, discussed further in Appendix B. Many critiques of the TT concentrate on the second premise. The arguments contend that verbal behavior cannot provide sufficient information for the attribution of intelligence to an entity. In other words, intelligence or justifiable attribution of intelligence is not reducible to verbal behavior. We also have concerns with focusing exclusively on intelligence, much less verbal behavior, as the characteristic or attribute that distinguishes humans and machines, especially when we approach the Turing line from the human side.

Turing Test as Useful Tool

The major critiques and extensions of the TT reveal contested conceptions of what the TT aims to accomplish and what, if anything, it actually accomplishes. Our objective is not to defend the TT or reconcile these various perspectives. Rather, our goal is to show how the TT serves as a useful analytical tool or methodology. Some have questioned whether it is indeed useful in this regard and suggested that it fails to meet the standard that all graduate students learn for experimental design: "never ... design an experiment to detect nothing."[5] Computer scientists Patrick Hayes and Kenneth Ford suggest the Turing Test suffers from this design flaw and, as a result, even when the test is passed, you're forced back to the drawing board to figure out what it all means:

Does passing the test tell us the machine is intelligent? That the observer asked the wrong questions? And by the way, what are the right questions? And heck, isn't that what the Imitation Game was supposed to help us avoid? And so on.

In our view, and this is critical to appreciate, such recursive deliberation is the Turing test's virtue, rather than its vice. The test really involves two critical steps: first, running the observational test under specified conditions to identify a remarkable machine; and, second, if and when a remarkable machine is identified by step one, then carefully evaluate. We exploit this two-step structure in our framework.

The Turing test should be understood in context and with a sense of the initial question that motivated Turing: *Can machines think?* The test is a means for developing objective, empirical evidence about *something*. The difficult question is *what?* Does it tell us something meaningful – or, more accurately, does it provide us with information that allows us to infer something meaningful about machine intelligence? Or about something else? Perhaps something about the questions asked by the observer? We can have that discussion when the time comes, and it probably would be interesting and worthwhile. TT extensions (discussed in Appendix B) seem to be looking for necessary and sufficient conditions for attributing intelligence to machines that is on par with humans. But that need not be, and frankly is not, our objective.

The Turing test provides us with a systematic approach to thinking about the line between humans and machines, which we refer to as the Turing line, and to investigating the similarities, differences, and relationships between humans, machines, and machine-environments (explained in the next section). Reviewers have suggested that the Turing test is no longer important as a goal or objective in AI and related fields. That is irrelevant to us. We are not interested in detecting and evaluating intelligent machines.

We draw inspiration from the Turing test as a conceptual lens. It allows us to maintain focus on the Turing line while exploring the relationships among human, machine, and environment. Thus, we are as interested in thinking about the experimental designs, game structures, and questions to ask as we are about anticipating how we might interpret the results. The recursive nature of applying the Turing test, which Hayes and Ford critiqued, is its redeeming feature, one which we seek to mimic with our techno-social engineering tests. Hayes and Ford acknowledge at the end of their article:

> We suspect that Turing . . . wanted the test to be about what it really means to be human. This is why he has set us up in this way . . . If we really tried to

do [what Turing suggests], we might be forced into thinking very hard about what it really means to be not just a thinker, but a human being in a human society, with all its difficulties and complexities. If this was what Turing meant, then we need not reject it as our ultimate goal.[6]

We agree wholeheartedly.

The Human Side of the Turing Line

The Turing test draws a line between human and machine. You might think of it as a boundary. The Turing line might be bright and fixed; it might be fuzzy; it might change over time; it might be real; and it might even be illusory. Who knows? Perhaps, as some scientists and philosophers believe, humans really are just meat machines performing pre-determined biological scripts.[7] We, however, will assume a line exists.

The Turing line serves at least two functions, which are noted but not fully examined within the relevant literatures. First, the line differentiates humans and machines. We assume such a line exists and that we can recognize it even if we don't *fully* understand it. Indeed, the point of the mental exercise is to get us to examine and better understand it. The TT is satisfied when the line is in fact not seen; that is, during the course of playing the Imitation Game, a machine successfully imitates a human and thus a line that we "know" exists is not observed. The machine remains a machine even after passing the test, but we infer that a machine capable of passing the test has "something," some characteristic (that some would call intelligence, and some would not), that makes, or at least made, it indistinguishable from a human in the context of the test.

Second, the Turing line serves as a finish line. Within artificial intelligence, robotics, machine learning, and other adjacent fields, the race to cross this line has been on since Turing published his article.[8] Our point, then, is that Turing demarcated something specific to aim for when constructing machines and programming systems. Again, Turing made a prediction about the rate of progress toward this finish line, suggesting that by the year 2000, an observer would not have a greater than 70 percent chance of correctly identifying the machine after five minutes of questioning.[9] Obviously, we didn't quite make it. Some suggest we'll cross it soon, while others argue that it's a fool's errand. The important point, for our purposes, is to recognize its function.

Our contribution in this book is to examine the other side of the line, the human side. We'll ask and examine a related set of questions about humans. The simplest and most compelling reason to do so is that we're rapidly developing and deploying technologies that operate on the human side of the line by shaping human beings and the environments within which we live and evolve.

Critically, what matters most – more than whether we can or ever do actually cross the line – might be what happens during the race to cross the Turing line and how the race itself affects humans and society.[10]

Still, we shouldn't begin with a completely pessimistic frame. Like imperfect price discrimination,[11] there are beneficial and detrimental outcomes depending on the context. The TT leads us to focus on whether we can develop machines that "think" like humans, and this seems to be a beneficial innovation or improvement because we've potentially added something to the machine; it might have *gained* a capability previously possessed only by humans. Approaching the line from the opposite side with a focus on humans, it seems natural to frame the inquiry as this question: *Can humans not-think?*[12]

This framing suggests that as we approach the Turing line, something is diminishing, and that when we reach it, something will have been lost or taken away. Humans will have lost their capability to think and that seems troubling. And yet, there might be a problem with this framing. It is by no means necessarily the case that progressing toward the line from the human side means that something is lost. It might be the case that something is *gained*. That something presumably would be the capability to not-think. Imagine we're playing the Imitation Game with a human seeking to mimic a simple (unthinking) machine and deceive the observer. Perhaps the human can be indistinguishable from a machine by choice, by exercising the capability to not-think. There may be many reasons why this could be an attractive capability, though we are not inclined to explore them now. But we should be clear that the normative or moral evaluation of humans not-thinking is complex.

The question of whether humans can not-think might seem silly in the sense that the answer seems obviously to be: Yes, humans can not-think; we do so quite often, for example, when we act instinctively, impulsively, or emotionally,[13] and when we do not fully consider the consequences of our actions. Notice, however, that this type of reasoning relies on particular definitions of think/not-think. It seems much more plausible to say that while instinctive, impulsive, or emotional actions might not be actions that involve a certain type of rational or deliberative thinking, they nonetheless involve specific types of *mental states*. In fact, these types of mental states seem to be *particularly human* and not machine-like.[14]

This opens an interesting line of inquiry: Might the mental or intellectual characteristics that in part define us as humans and differentiate us from machines be those sometimes associated with *irrational* behavior? Some people influenced by behavioral economics have suggested that when people are likely to act irrationally or in a biased fashion, the response is to de-bias them or nudge them toward more rational or efficient behavior. Notably, such nudges are often implemented by reconstructing the context or environment. Would such efforts to de-bias people or nudge them toward rational thinking/behavior be dehumanizing? Imagine that we reconstructed the environment to eliminate irrational thinking. *Would this environment dehumanize? Would humans in such a constructed environment be distinguishable from machines?*

It's significant that the universe consists of more than humans and machines, and that humans and machines do not exist in a vacuum. They relate to each other and to the environment (and other living beings). The results of the TT depend substantially on the environment where the test is conducted. In the standard version of the TT, machines and humans are separated from an observer who poses a series of questions to identify which agents are human. The machines attempt to exhibit human-like conversational behavior to trick the observer into making the wrong identification. Answers from the machines and humans are typed to avoid any biases possibly arising from information that is irrelevant to attribution of thinking/intelligence. For example, visual cues might enable the observer to distinguish machines and humans, but such information would not be relevant to the underlying question of whether the machines are capable of thinking in a manner indistinguishable from humans.

It matters that the observer is in one room and the agents (humans and machines) are in other rooms, separate from one another and the observer. It also matters that the investigation focuses on verbal behavior. Verbal behavior (verbal responses to a sequence of verbal stimuli) is deemed an appropriate area of investigation because of the perceived link between intelligence and verbal output.

Turing imposed significant constraints on the means of observation and communication. He did so because he was interested in a specific capability – to think like a human – and wanted to be sure that the test gathered evidence that was relevant and capable of supporting inferences about that specific capability. But we want to make sure it's appreciated how much work is done by the constructed environment – *the rules and the rooms* – that Turing built. A machine that passed the TT would have done so within a very constrained context. In another context or environment, for example one where the observer could visually observe the subjects or where communication was aural, the same machine presumably would not pass the TT. The machine might be indistinguishable from a human in one context, but easily distinguished in another.

The conventional TT environment is constructed. It's designed to take a series of inputs (e.g. machines and humans) and, after doing some work performing a process according to predetermined rules, it produces outputs that we can use to draw inferences about the machines (some of the inputs). The TT environment is, in a sense, a machine. We will call it a "machine-environment" to distinguish it from other types of machines. Different machine-environments, such as the TT environment, can be constructed with the capability to render machines within the machine-environments to be more or less distinguishable from humans. Machine-environments thus play a very important role in shaping the actual and perceived capabilities of machines. *The same can and must be said for humans.*

Machine-environments play an important role in shaping the actual and perceived capabilities of humans. We've seen many examples already in this book – ranging from the electronic contracting environment to smart techno-social environments. Accordingly, to examine the space on the human side of the Turing line, we need to broaden the inquiry and ask the following questions:

• How and/or when are humans indistinguishable from machines?
• Can humans be programmed or constructed to be indistinguishable from machines?
• Can techno-social environments dehumanize?
• How and/or when are human beings engineered (via technology, social context, and the environment within which we live and through which our preferences and beliefs are formed) to be indistinguishable from machines?

Consider how the line established by the TT might function as a finish line when viewed from the human side. How would you progress toward this finish line? One way might involve *directly modifying* human beings through genetic, biotechnological or other means. Another way to make progress would be to construct environments where humans *are* indistinguishable from machines. Another way would be to construct environments where humans *become* indistinguishable from machines.

Let's consider the call center environment as an example. In a May 2014 *New York Times* article, "The Computerized Voice that Wasn't,"[15] the author questioned whether American Express had successfully created a computer that passed the Turing test because the author was convinced that a call center respondent that he interacted with was a computer decently masquerading as a human. The author quoted from his initial conversation and then from a follow-up call in which the author asked the respondent if she/he/it was a computer and proceeded to ask additional questions focused on that issue. The author ultimately concludes with apparent surprise and disappointment that the respondent revealed her/his location to be India, a fact that persuaded the author that the respondent was human. The author's conclusion was later confirmed by American Express.

What might be inferred, if anything, from the fact that for a while the author mistook the human for a computer? The reason given for the mistaken identification was that English was a second language for the respondent. Language and commonsensical use of language is one defining characteristic of being human. The author may have misinterpreted odd or incorrect usage of English as indicative of computer-speak. However, we suspect that there are more subtle reasons for the author's initial response that have to do with the environment constructed by American Express or its call center contractors. That is, it might be the case that the call center itself is a rather constraining, heavily scripted environment that nudges humans within it toward the Turing line.

To explore these questions on the human side of the line, we now turn our attention to developing techno-social engineering tests that are inspired by the Turing test. We will focus on humans and test techno-social engineering by asking whether the human being is indistinguishable from a machine with respect to certain capabilities. The context within which the test applies will be important, not only because the context shapes the test but also because the context shapes the participants. In the end, we may be testing the combined effect of humans and environments (or humans situated within specific environments).

CHAPTER II

Can Humans Be Engineered to Be Incapable of Thinking?

Introduction

Inspired by the Turing test, this chapter inverts the conventional perspective of the Turing test and focuses on humans rather than machines. Turing asked: *Can machines think?* Instead, we ask: *Can humans not-think?* We're not interested in identifying machines engineered to be intelligent so much as we're interested in identifying humans engineered to be unintelligent.

We identify a non-exhaustive list of intelligence characteristics to evaluate and develop an initial series of techno-social engineering tests to examine different aspects of intelligence and distinguish humans from machines: (a) mathematical computation, (b) random number generation, (c) rationality, and (d) common sense. We briefly discuss the first two and devote more attention to the third and fourth. All four are plausible tests to distinguish humans and machines. However, the first two don't implicate fundamental notions of what it means to be a human whereas the third and fourth do. This is a substantial difference. It illustrates how passing a techno-social engineering test at step one only triggers evaluation at step two and that the evaluation can reveal that dehumanization is occurring and should be stopped.

For each test, we explain what we are testing, specify the sorts of stimuli an observer might use, and then discuss how to interpret the results. We also develop thought experiments to tease out the implications of the common-sense and rationality tests. For common sense, the thought experiment concerns the problem of "being lost" and the dynamic relationship between common sense and technologies. This discussion highlights the facts that technologies are not neutral and vary in terms of how they may displace common sense. For rationality, the thought experiment concerns the prospect of government efforts to "nudge" citizens to behave more rationally.

Intelligence: Thinking and Not-Thinking

Our first step in investigating the human side of the Turing line is to ask: *Can humans not-think?* This isn't a simple query. The question presents the same intractable definitional questions that Turing faced: What do the words "human" and "not-think" mean? To avoid conceptual debate about these terms, we follow Turing's lead and propose an empirical solution to the problem.[1] For reasons noted in the previous chapter, this question ultimately might not yield the most interesting results. If we are really interested in not only *whether*, but also *when* and *how* humans can be constructed to be indistinguishable from simple machines, then thinking/not-thinking might yield insufficient information. Nonetheless, the inquiry needs a starting point, and this is a good place to begin.

Suppose we administer the Turing test in its conventional form. Does that tell us anything meaningful about the human participants? For example, when an observer correctly determines that humans are humans, do we learn anything? Probably not. But what about when an observer incorrectly determines that a human is a machine? This "confederate effect" has occurred during Turing tests conducted at the annual Loebner competitions.[2] For example, according to computer scientist Stuart Shieber, "Ms. Cynthia Clay, the Shakespeare aficionado, was thrice misclassified as a computer. At least one of the judges made her classification on the premise that '[no] human would have that amount of knowledge about Shakespeare.'"[3]

It seems hard to infer from this misidentification that the incorrect judgment arose because the human subject was not-thinking. When we examine the agent in the context and consider the questions asked by the observer, and we evaluate plausible inferences about the human agent, not-thinking doesn't rise to the top. Others do, and they have more to do with the observer and peculiarities of the human participant. This does not undermine our search for a test capable of investigating whether humans can not-think. It merely suggests we pay careful attention to how the *structure and rules of the game* need to be tailored to elicit relevant evidence.

If we stick to the basic structure with an observer in one room and agents distributed in separate rooms from the observer and each other, and limit communication to text, we can adjust who knows what about the game being played. The basic Turing template can limit what the observer and agents know about the game they're playing and who is effectively "playing" the game.

Here are a few variations:

a. Play the Turing test with the same rules (i.e. no difference at all) and examine situations where humans have been mistaken to be machines.
b. Play the Turing test as usual, except tell humans they should try to deceive the observer; ensure the observer doesn't know about this additional instruction.
c. Same as (b), but inform the machine programmers that humans will play strategically.
d. Same as (b), but the observer knows.
e. Same as (c), but the observer knows.

Under these varied conditions, the implications of using the Imitation Game to learn something about human intelligence would be different. When humans are playing the game and aiming to deceive the observer, for example, we would need to deal with the fact that humans can easily mimic some machines, like a car, by not communicating at all. (In fact, one study hilariously showed that a machine could be programmed to "take the Fifth Amendment" and pass the Turing test.[4]) Version **(b)** would not appear to work well because observers would likely perceive non-responsive agents to be machines and little could be inferred from such results. Version **(c)** might overcome this problem because machines could adopt a similar strategy, and versions **(d)** and **(e)** might overcome it because the observer would be able to anticipate the strategy.

On the human side of the Turing line, we don't need or even want humans and machines (or the humans programming machines) to play the game strategically. Consider the role that human participants play in the conventional Turing test. The humans are not necessarily strategic agents, seeking to confuse or deceive the observer.[5] Rather, the humans act as "normal" humans and thus usefully serve as a baseline. We need a similarly useful baseline for our techno-social engineering tests.

Accordingly, we propose to use the *simple machine*[6] as a baseline and ask the programmer of the machine to not act strategically by confusing, deceiving, or outsmarting the observer. For what matters to us, ultimately, is not if or how machines can be built to imitate or mimic humans. Rather, we are interested in the techno-social engineering of human beings. A determination that a human is indistinguishable from a machine allows us to reasonably infer that something meaningful has been lost because of the engineered environment.

Accordingly, we might use one of the following variations:

f.   Same as any of the above, except the machine agents are *simple machines*, or, at least, are not deceptive or otherwise strategically playing the game.

g.   Same as any of the above, except the observer is a computer.[7]

The question remains whether it makes sense to ask the human participants to play strategically. What would that mean? That the human agents are seeking to behave like machines? Success might indicate that the human who is mistaken to be a machine possessed the capability to not-think. That is, if not-thinking is a capability to be exercised, then passing the test could be relevant. For example, imagine a criminal defendant exercising the capability to not-think in an effort to persuade a clinical psychologist that he lacked emotion or the cognitive ability to distinguish right from wrong or to understand the consequences of his action or to have intention.

If we aren't interested in the affirmative exercise of the capability to not-think and instead are interested in identifying a diminished capacity to think or inadvertent or environmentally constructed triggers for not-thinking, then we might need to take a different approach. It might be more appropriate to set up the game as if it were a conventional Turing test (version (**a**)) except utilize version (**f**) or (**g**). The human participants would be instructed to simply "be themselves." Having removed strategic behavior altogether, imitation is less relevant than comparison. The burden shifts to the observer, the chosen stimuli, and the constructed environment where humans and machines potentially can be differentiated. (This move, amongst other things, differentiates the techno-social engineering tests from Turing tests.)

Beyond the basic structure and variations described above, we need to specify how to test for not-thinking. We might leave it entirely to the observer and the stimuli chosen by the observer. This "hands-off" approach might not be effective. Even in the context of the conventional Turing test, various constraints shape the observer's questions. The most basic limitation is restricting communication to text. Moreover, when the test moved from thought experiment to applied experiment, organizers introduced more fine-grained constraints on the types of stimuli permitted.[8]

The reason for restrictions on stimuli is to increase the likelihood of generating objective empirical evidence from which reasonable inferences can be made. We need to engage in a similar winnowing process. We need to consider more deeply what aspects of thinking or not-thinking can be tested. We could focus on some specific intelligence-related characteristics that have often been identified in the definitional debates about what makes us human. Here is a short list of some (potentially overlapping) candidates:

- Reason
- Rationality/irrationality
- Common sense
- Willpower
- Emotion
- Phenomenological experience[9]
- Creativity
- Language/capacity to construct new language or social meaning
- Planning for others
- Language with which to plan for future[10]/others.[11]

This is a non-exhaustive list. Nonetheless, with these intellectual capabilities in mind, we can begin to specify the types of questions that the observer would be allowed to use. Now, we can begin to construct the environment, the rules and rooms of the game. We would want to ask ourselves: What could be inferred when an observer mistakes a human to be a machine?

We are not seeking to explain or prove the existence of any particular defining characteristics of humans or machines. We assume they exist. For example, we assume intelligence exists, and it is not our goal to define it or explain its origins or underlying mechanisms. Let others define and debate what is or is not intelligence or what is or is not essential to humanity. For now, we are interested in marginal changes induced by technological environments, and we aim to investigate changes in our capabilities so that we can have a more meaningful discussion of what is or is not essential. We note this upfront to avoid getting sucked into the vortex of existing philosophical and definitional debates. However, some working definitional baselines remain relevant, as will be discussed in the context of specific tests.

This chapter does not explore all the possible tests. Instead, we consider four tests that might distinguish humans from machines based on (1) mathematical computation, (2) random number generation, (3) common sense, and (4) rationality, respectively. We briefly discuss the first two and devote more attention to the third and fourth. All four are plausible techno-social engineering tests that generally could be used to try to distinguish humans and machines. The difference is that the first two tests don't implicate

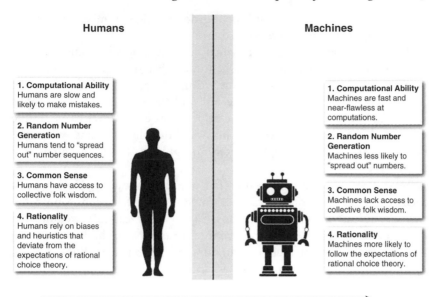

Figure 11.1 Image courtesy of John Danaher

fundamental notions of what it means to be a human, whereas the third and fourth do.

For each test, we begin with a brief description of what it is that we are testing for. For example, we specify the stimuli the observer uses and then discuss how to interpret the results of his, her, or its judgment. Does passing or failing the test support meaningful inferences about the human agents? (See Figure 11.1.)

Techno-Social Engineering Test Focused on Mathematical Computation

Suppose we set up our techno-social engineering test in the conventional TT manner (**a**), except that the machine participants are simple machines (**f**) and the observer is a machine (**g**) programmed to submit a series of mathematical computation questions to the agents, and then, after receiving answers, determine whether the agents are humans or machines. The types of mathematical computation questions could progress from performing simple to increasingly complex calculations (e.g. addition and subtraction of single- or double-digit numbers, to multiplying a single- and a double-digit number, to multiplying double-digit numbers, to square roots of triple digit-numbers, and so on).

There are at least two ways in which humans generally would be easily distinguished from machines. First, humans get tired and are prone to error as fatigue sets in. By contrast, simple machines don't get tired. Depending on the duration of the test and the rate at which questions are asked, humans will make computation errors even for relatively simple computations; the machines will not. Additionally, humans will make computation errors for sophisticated computations that machines will breeze through.

Most humans routinely would fail a techno-social engineering test focused on mathematical computation. But not all humans would fail this test, at least within some bounds. Suppose, for example, we limit the duration of the test to five or ten minutes or otherwise eliminate the first source of human error. Suppose that under this scenario a human being passes the test. *What would that mean? Are there any meaningful inferences to be drawn? What would we learn?* As explained above, passing the test provides us with evidence and suggests that there is *something* remarkable about the relevant agent. It triggers step two – evaluation.

The human being would appear to possess an extraordinary – inhuman – capability for mathematical computation. Does being machine-like with respect to mathematical computation mean the person was somehow *worse off*? We don't think so. The extraordinary capability appears to be a positive or valuable skill. Does being machine-like with respect to mathematical computation mean the person was somehow *less* human? We don't think so. Being machine-like in this specific context and in this specific manner does not seem meaningfully related to the agent's (normative) status as a human being. In other words, there is evidence of something unusual, but not of dehumanization.

We also might ask whether we can say anything meaningful about the humanity of the vast majority of humans who failed to pass the test. We don't think so. We might conclude that some of the humans who lacked some mathematical computation capabilities might be worse off than those who have the capabilities and that education or other means of improving their situation would be worthwhile. But that's a conclusion concerning a recommended improvement, not a guess about ontological status.

There may be trade-offs among skills and competencies that would not surface through this test. Extraordinary computational skills might correlate with deficiencies in other skills, and passing the test might help identify humans for which evaluating potential trade-offs would be possible. But it wouldn't say anything about evaluation, which is the basic point of this example. It highlights the importance of moving from the first step (identification) to the second step (evaluation).

Techno-Social Engineering Test Focused on Generating Not-So-Random Numbers

Assume a set-up similar to the previous test, except the observer asks the agents to generate random numbers, one every five seconds for ten minutes. Based on the responses and the observer's ability to predict the agent's nth response, the observer determines whether the agents are humans or machines.

Generating random numbers is difficult for both computers and humans. However, they face different difficulties, and that's what makes a techno-social engineering test plausible. Computers are deterministic because humans program them. This means that computers do not generate truly random numbers and instead produce pseudo-random numbers by running a seed number through a complex algorithm. The result is not truly random because it is determined by the seed number and the algorithm. If one knows or can reverse engineer the algorithm and seed number, then one can predict the numbers that the computer will generate.

We could assume the observer either knows or can figure out by reverse engineering the algorithms and seeds used by the simple machines. The assumption makes it easier to distinguish humans and machines, but might be unnecessary.

Humans would routinely fail a techno-social engineering test focused on generating random numbers. This isn't because humans can generate more or less randomness than machines. Instead, humans generally would be distinguishable from machines because the methods for generating numbers would differ substantially.[12] For example, some people would misunderstand randomness by seeking to avoid repeating a number too often ("I can't use 9 for a while because I just used it"). Some would exhibit preferences for certain numbers, other for certain sequences of numbers or alternating patterns. Frankly, most humans would not employ a seed number and an algorithm. This means some humans might be unpredictable, which would be a basis for distinguishing them from the machines. Others would be predictable, but for different reasons than the simple machine.

Suppose a human being passes the test. Again, *what would that mean? Are there any meaningful inferences to be drawn? What would we learn?*

Once more, the human being would appear to possess an extraordinary capability: generating pseudo-random numbers in a machine-like manner. In contrast with the machine-like capability for mathematical computation (which seemed advantageous), it is not clear how to evaluate this capability. Regardless, being "machine-like" in this context and in this manner does not seem meaningfully related to the agent's normative status as a human being. There is not much to be said about those who fail the test.

Techno-Social Engineering Test Focused on Rationality

Rationality is studied intensely in many different disciplines, ranging from psychology to philosophy to economics. It is central to models of human decision-making and serves as a baseline for evaluating performance in various settings. "What does it mean to be rational, and to make a rational choice on the basis of a meaningful and relevant distinction?" asked Oscar Gandy Jr., a highly regarded scholar of the political economy of information. He explains:

> Defining a concept by means of its opposition is rarely satisfactory, but it is a place to begin. Irrational decision-making is commonly associated with emotional, or habitual, responses, informed by broad generalizations, rather than by careful weighing of the relevant facts. Rational decision-making generally refers to the process, rather than the outcome or results of any decision, although we understand that a carefully considered decision arrived at following a process of extensive search, reflection, and analysis, can still produce unsatisfactory results. A realization that there are constraints on the ability of humans to access and incorporate all relevant information has led to the suggestion that the process is not necessarily irrational, but merely constrained or "bounded." Most often, the concept of bounded rationality is focused on the limits of human information processing, rather than on limitations on access, or strategic misdirection. But, as Giddens reminds us, some of the more important constraints on human agency are those blind spots we have regarding the motivations and goals of other interested parties who may be involved in some aspect of our decision-making.[13]

He then further explains: "There is a tendency to think about rationality in terms of a continuum; one that moves from an idealized intelligence – a difference engine that engages in rapid computation, without errors in calculation, and more critically, without any systematic bias introduced by irrational emotional distractions. On the other end of the continuum we find the sometimes slow, sometimes fast, error prone, easily distracted, and routinely distorted information processing by humans."[14] Gandy's continuum seems to place machines at one extreme and humans at the other.

Law professor Ed Stein explains that there are many different senses or conceptions of rationality,[15] and psychologist Keith Stanovich describes the strong sense of rationality conventionally used in cognitive science.[16] In a strong sense, rationality corresponds to "optimal judgment and decision making" according to a particular normative baseline, and irrationality corresponds to deviations from the same baseline, which can differ by degree. One widely used normative baseline for judgment and decision-making is instrumental, expected utility maximization. "The simplest definition of instrumental rationality is as follows: behaving in the world so that you get exactly what you most want, given the resources (physical and mental) available to you. We could characterize instrumental rationality as the optimization of the individual's goal fulfillment [which can be further refined to expected utility]."[17]

For our purposes, *rationality* refers to the strong sense captured by the instrumental rationality definition, and *irrationality* refers to deviations from the specified baseline, regardless of the cause(s) for such deviations. Let's be clear before proceeding: First, the normative baseline chosen serves the purpose of establishing a baseline and isn't meant as a complete normative evaluation. For example, irrationality may be normatively attractive for reasons not fully captured in or reflected by instrumental logic. Second, the cause(s) for deviation from rationality may matter for evidentiary or normative reasons in particular contexts.

Suppose we set up the techno-social engineering test in the conventional TT manner **(a)** except that the machine participants are simple machines **(f)**. The human participants are told that they're participating in the conventional Turing test where they are supposed to act normal and answer questions posed by the observer in a natural fashion. In other words, they are instructed to not act strategically or deceptively. They may even be told (falsely) that the object of the game is to see if the machines are intelligent enough to deceive the observer into concluding that the machine is a human. This claim is false in two respects. First, the object is to see if the human participants are mistaken to be machines. Second, the machines are simple machines programmed to do as instructed and/or answer the questions posed truthfully, accurately, and in accordance with instrumental rationality.

Let us also make the observer a machine **(g)**, such that the observer is programmed to run a series of conventional rationality tests and experiments.[18] For example, the observer may pose a series of *choice* *problems*, such as those posed by Allais and developed further in the extensive rational choice and behavioral economics literature.[19] The literature demonstrates a variety of ways in which humans make predictably irrational choices.[20]

One important reason that humans can be seen[21] to act irrationally,[22] according to such experiments, is that humans contextualize problems. As Stanovich puts it, "humans recognize subtle contextual factors in decision problems that complicate their choices."[23] Simple machines don't.

Another way that humans can be seen as irrational is through a series of biases in human decision-making that lead to distortions from the rational choice (utility maximization) model. Various biases lead people to make judgment errors that differ systematically from unbiased forecasts. Some biases may involve discrimination about groups, perhaps based on race. Some biases involve heuristics and decision-making errors; for example, optimism bias, self-serving bias, hindsight bias, among others.[24] Some biases may be the result of contextualization.[25] Simple machines don't suffer from such biases.

Another way that humans can be seen as irrational is through actions that serve symbolic utility but not instrumental utility. This is related to the notion of ethical preferences, which may lead humans to make choices that diverge from instrumental utility and rational choice theory. Humans also appear to be "strong evaluators" in the sense that they can have preferences about preferences (or different levels of preferences), and this can lead to destabilizing conflicts among preferences that cause humans to act irrationally when measured against the rational choice model.[26] Not so for simple machines.

This suggests that there are a variety of ways the observer might test agents and distinguish humans and machines. Armed with a battery of tests, the observer would be able to accurately distinguish humans and machines: The simple machines would always respond to the queries in a rational manner (e.g. make predictably rational choices) while the humans would tend to exhibit irrationality (e.g. make predictably irrational choices), at least over the course of a sufficient number of questions.

Finally, suppose we employ machine learning such that the observer program gradually optimizes its battery of tests and experiments. If, for example, the reliability of certain categories of tests is questionable, then the observer presumably would steer away from using those tests and rely on other more reliable ones. Suppose we've constructed the *perfect rationality detector* that can accurately distinguish humans and machines based on humans' propensity to act irrationally.

Now suppose we run our test with the perfect rationality detector as our observer. *What could we infer from a mistaken identification of a human as a machine? What would that mean? Are there any meaningful inferences to be drawn?* Passing the test provides us with evidence and suggests that there is *something* remarkable about the relevant agent. *But what?*

We have set up our perfect rationality detector in a way that makes it hard to fathom such a mistake, but the human propensity to act irrationally is not constant or fixed; it varies with context. Thus, in certain constructed environments, we reasonably can expect humans to behave in perfect accordance with the rational choice model.

Psychologists have observed how environmental constraints shape irrationality. "Many authors have commented on how the behavior of entities in very constrained situations (firms in competitive markets, people living in subsistence-agriculture situations, animals in predator-filled environments) are the entities whose behaviors fit the rational choice model the best."[27] Environmental constraints also may push in the opposite direction. Consider this passage from Stanovich:

> Most humans now do not operate in such harsh selective environments of constraint (outside many work environments that deliberately create constraints, such as markets). They use that freedom to pursue symbolic utility, thereby creating complex, context-dependent preferences that are more likely to violate the strictures of coherence that define instrumental rationality. But those violations do not make them inferior to the instrumentally rational pigeon. Degrees of rationality among entities pursuing goals of differing complexity are not comparable. One simply cannot count the number of violations and declare the entity with fewer violations the more rational. The degree of instrumental rationality achieved must be contextualized according to the complexity of the goals pursued.[28]

Keep in mind that our objective is not to *judge* degrees of rationality in terms of inferiority or superiority. Pigeons may be closer to the Turing line than humans. But that is not relevant to our present objective.

What we are interested in identifying, examining, and evaluating is environments that engineer humans to be indistinguishable from machines. Thus, it would appear that we need to consider how the "harsh selective environments of constraint" shape human behavior. *Is such shaping transitory or lasting? Are the environments themselves transitory or lasting?* Are humans only affected while in the specific environment or are the effects long-lasting? For purposes of this techno-social engineering test, we could construct the environment (the rooms and rules) to be more or less constraining and see what impacts followed.[29]

Recall the discussion in Chapter 5 of the electronic contracting environment. This is a familiar environment designed to nudge us to behave in a predictably rational manner; just click "I agree." This seems like a straightforward context within which humans would routinely pass the techno-social engineering test described in this section. It's an environment where the instrumentally rational response to terms of use pages requires little thought and imposes no burden on the user because "acceptance" is reduced to a single click of the mouse. The interaction is designed to generate a response absent reflection or deliberation. The environment is choice-preserving, in the sense that users retain their autonomy and can opt out of the web applications services. Still, a user's blind acceptance of the terms of use is completely rational. To read the proposed (imposed) terms would be a complete waste of time, an irrational and ultimately futile exercise. While we have yet to run this experiment formally, we believe we can accurately state that the environment can make us behave like simple machines – perfectly rational and perfectly predictable. Here is the more difficult question: Does it make us programmable? Does the environment effectively create dispositions that will follow us through all walks of life? Are the shaping effects *lasting*?

Consider the following thought experiment. Suppose that to improve human decision-making and welfare, government decides to "nudge" people toward rational decision-making.[30] For our purposes, the nudge is simply a gentle adjustment in the environment or context that corrects for predictably irrational decision errors.[31] As finance professor Riccardo Rebonato put it in his "reasonably precise definition of libertarian paternalism," assume government implements

> [t]he set of interventions aimed at overcoming the unavoidable cognitive biases and decisional inadequacies of an individual by exploiting them in such a way as to influence her decisions (in an easily reversible manner) towards choices that she herself would make if she had at her disposal unlimited time and information, and the analytic abilities of a rational decision-maker (more precisely, of *Homo Economicus*).[32]

Thus, government adjusts the choice architecture by creating a sufficiently constraining – though not completely constraining – environment.[33] People still make decisions and have choices within the environment, but they will tend to do so in conformance with rational choice theory. Suppose humans within the government-constructed nudging environment would routinely pass our techno-social engineering test, administered by our special observer (the perfect rationality detector).

To put it more concretely, suppose that workplace regulation transforms the workplace – for example, an office or factory – such that the workplace constitutes a sufficiently constraining environment that humans in that workplace routinely pass our techno-social engineering test.[34] *What could be inferred? What would this mean? What would be the significance, if any?*

These are reasonable questions to ask. From the government's perspective, and even from a perspective focused on maximizing social welfare, passing our techno-social engineering test would be a measure of *success*. Humans in the constructed environment would behave exactly as intended, efficiently in accordance with the rational choice model – that is, *optimally*. From the perspective of the employers and the workers, there is little to complain about. Efficient workplace performance presumably translates into higher productivity and safety,[35] and no one is forcing them to work in this setting. It seems hard to imagine someone making a strong claim to a right or even desire to act irrationally. One might conclude, "If we are not contemplating either a violation of rights or a departure from existing preferences, then there is nothing to worry about." *Still, is there any reason to think that the constructed environment (workplace) is* dehumaniz*ing? Does the change induced by the constructed environment constitute a reduction or addition in human capability? Is it diminishing or empowering?*

In an essay, "Buddhist Economics," E. F. Schumacher contrasted modern economics' view of human labor with that of Buddhist economics. The former views human labor as a costly input to be minimized.

> The Buddhist point of view takes the function of work to be at least threefold: to give a man a chance to utilize and develop his faculties; to enable him to overcome his ego-centeredness by joining with other people in a common task; and to bring forth the goods and services needed for a becoming existence. Again, the consequences that flow from this view are endless. To organize work in such a manner that it becomes meaningless, boring, stultifying, or nerve-racking for the worker would be little short of criminal; it would indicate a greater concern with goods than with people, an evil lack of compassion and a soul-destroying degree of attachment to the most primitive side of this worldly existence . . .
>
> From the Buddhist point of view, there are therefore two types of mechanization which must be clearly distinguished: one that enhances a man's skill and power and one that turns the work of man over to a mechanical slave, leaving man in a position of having to serve the slave.[36]

Now suppose that humans who spent time in the environment constructed to nudge (e.g. the workplace) also routinely pass our techno-social engineering test when no longer within that environment. That is, suppose that after leaving the nudging environment, the humans remained indistinguishable from machines according to our perfect rationality detector. *What could be inferred? What would this mean? What would be the significance, if any? Would the constructed environment (workplace) be more or less dehumanizing?*

These are reasonable questions to ask. The basic distinction is between a constructed environment within which humans *are* indistinguishable from machines and one in which humans *become* indistinguishable from machines. We might label the latter a *constructive environment* because of its lasting effects. While the lasting nudges might seem creepy, we should not jump to negative conclusions. After all, helping humans to make more rational decisions throughout their lives may be in their own self-interest as well as certain conceptions of the broader societal or public interest. Moral or normative evaluation will be difficult and contested.

Suppose the nudging government did not limit itself to workplace environments. Suppose the government systematically constructed nudging environments in as many places and social contexts as possible. Consider government surveillance systems, which are expanding in scope and reach across technological platforms, and the public and private spaces and environments within which we live our lives. These systems may not always be explicitly billed or justified as being part of the nudging program, but that does not make them less so. To be fair, they are not part of the specific program advocated by Thaler, Sunstein, and other behavioral law and economics scholars who underwrite their prescriptions with the ethic of libertarian paternalism. Yet it isn't clear that this ethic sufficiently insulates their project from the concerns raised here.

Nudging is now a government agenda, pursued by governments around the world and not limited to any specific setting or technology (i.e. surveillance systems are just an example). It is also a market agenda. Private entities, such as firms and collections of people employing shared networked technologies, are also voluntarily constructing nudging environments. This is not an entirely new observation. Marketing and advertising have always been about shaping beliefs and preferences and nudging people toward products and services. The pervasive, networked, data-driven economy that dominates much of modern life expands the scale and scope, removing some of the barriers between media that had allowed us to be "off" or outside the constructed nudging environments. One of the most fundamental societal questions of the twenty-first century will be about whether and how to preserve our practical freedom to be off, or, conversely, whether the environment we build means we are and will remain always on.

Does it really matter *who* is doing the nudging? Maybe it matters when we evaluate a specific example and countervailing pressures. But in the aggregate, we don't think it matters. The political economy and legal distinctions between public and private institutions don't bear as much weight when one begins to look at the macro picture. *How should we evaluate the agenda from a macro, longer-term, and societal perspective?*

Note that however interesting and pressing these and other questions may be, we cannot examine them effectively until we have better means for identifying, examining, and evaluating humans and/in environments that engineer humans to be indistinguishable from machines.

Techno-Social Engineering Test Focused on Common Sense

Common sense is a concept with a long history and hotly contested meaning in various disciplines. You undoubtedly have your own conception of common sense in mind as well as a view about what it takes to acquire and lose it.

On April 9, 2017, United Airlines created international controversy after video went viral of passenger Dr. David Dao being forcibly removed from his seat to accommodate airline employees. In response to the tremendous backlash, UA's Chief Executive Officer Oscar Munoz eventually apologized for the incident. While making that apology, he characterized the matter as a "systems failure" that stopped employees from using "common sense." We suspect that Munoz used systems analysis to deflect accountability. But that's not why we're bringing up the example. We're simply illustrating that it isn't unusual to view common sense as something that circumstances can suspend and possibly even extinguish.

Let's skip past definitional debates and adopt a particular understanding of common sense. Philosopher Gerald Erion offers the following view, which we adopt:

> A more focused notion of common sense . . . [is] virtually universal among typical adults because it concerns an important subset of objective reality that we all live our everyday lives in, the common-sense world. As rough

approximation, it is helpful to think of the common-sense world as the realm of familiar objects that we become acquainted with during ordinary experience. People, plants, non-human animals, and simple geographic features are all included in this world, while sub-atomic particles, neurons, and galaxies are not . . . [We] can understand common sense itself as the base of knowledge about common-sense reality that allows each of us to survive and thrive during our everyday lives. Common beliefs about the common-sense world are the most prominent components of this knowledge base . . . common sense also includes the widespread abilities that allow us to act successfully in the common-sense world.[37]

Erion goes on to explain how work in "various cognitive sciences" supports his claim that this type of common sense exists. It entails core knowledge and skills that are shared and "used by all of us (even skeptical philosophers) during our everyday lives." Language is critical to common sense both as knowledge and as skill. That is, competence in using language is a "subset of common sense."[38]

Erion suggests that despite some contrary interpretations among philosophers, Descartes' action test focuses on common sense as a characteristic that distinguished human beings from automata. Erion reformulates early modern philosopher Rene Descartes' two-pronged test as follows:

Automata are distinct from real people in two ways. First, automata cannot use language. Second, automata do not possess common sense, which includes not only knowing how to use language but also knowing how to perform tasks and answer questions that even the most simpleminded adult human can.[39]

Thus, a common-sense test could employ a structure like the conventional Turing test, and the observer could ask questions that would "require the skillful use of common sense." Erion explained that such a test would be more demanding than the Turing test; that is, a machine that passed the Turing test still might fail the Cartesian (common-sense) test. The idea is that by observing agents over a "significant length of time in a variety of circumstances," we confidently can distinguish humans from machines based on linguistic abilities and commonsensical performance. Erion focused on the machine side of the Turing line and viewed the common-sense test as a high bar for machines, in the sense that it would be difficult for a machine to be mistaken for a human (i.e. observed to possess common sense).[40]

On the human side of the Turing line, the common-sense test would appear to set a high bar for humans. Putting aside strategic and deceptive behavior, it would be difficult for a human to be mistaken for a machine (i.e., observed to be devoid of common sense). Erion suggests that "even the most simpleminded adult human" would pass the common-sense test.[41]

Given all this, why develop a common-sense test on the human side of the Turing line? It's a useful characteristic to focus on in part because it's often distinguished from other measures or types of human intelligence. As one of the usage examples from *Merriam-Webster's Dictionary* suggests: "She's very smart but she doesn't have a lot of common sense." Common sense also combines language, reasoning, and social skills in a fashion that may or may not be unique to humans, but which usefully differentiates humans from machines.[42]

Let us assume that a human passed the common-sense test. What would it mean if a human were indistinguishable from a machine based on the human's performance in a common-sense test? It seems more difficult to imagine contexts within which humans lack common sense. Common sense seems to be sufficiently adaptable to different contexts, essentially by definition, since it is what is common to our everyday lives, however we might live them. But it would be a mistake to assume stability or a persistent reservoir of common sense available to us.

Common sense depends upon a shared core knowledge base, language, and social interactions sufficient to generate common understandings and beliefs. Suppose access to these inputs is restricted. Indeed, there are various ways to imagine such restrictions.

Consider the following thought experiment. Suppose Alice gets in a taxicab, gives the driver an address, and then falls asleep. Thirty minutes later, the taxicab driver wakes Alice, takes her money, and leaves immediately after she exits the vehicle. After shaking off her initial grogginess, Alice realizes the cab dropped her off in the wrong location, and she is lost. What does common sense dictate/suggest she should do?

She should get her bearings, formulate a plan, and take action. How would she do this? Presumably by looking around, observing people, reading street signs, and so on. All this sensory information would provide her with baseline information that would help her evaluate her situation and options, and decide on a course of action. Based on such information about her environment, Alice would be able to form beliefs about her safety, whether she could trust people, whether people would understand her (speak the same language), and so on. She might be able to determine the likelihood of another taxicab arriving or whether some form of public transportation was accessible nearby. She might be able to figure out or approximate her location and then formulate a plan for getting safely from there to her intended destination.

Now suppose that Alice lacks the relevant situational and problem-solving common sense. What does this mean exactly? How could this be? Perhaps she lacks the ability to get her bearings through the various means just described. She is unable to take in and translate the various cues and information. Perhaps her incapacity stems from a physical or cognitive disability. Perhaps she has never had the necessary experiences that would have led her to develop the relevant abilities. For example, perhaps her prior navigation of the world was technologically mediated and fully automated (more on this below). Perhaps she was raised in a town with no street signs and thus would not think to look at street signs for location data. She might lack (the relevant situational and problem-solving) common sense because she has never discussed the problem of being lost with anyone else or contemplated the situation in which she now finds herself. That may seem hard to fathom, but being lost may be a problem of the past, at least in the near future.

In our everyday experience, it is highly likely that Alice would carry with her a device capable of determining her location, determining an efficient route to get from her location to her intended destination, and even ordering a taxi. Upon recognizing her plight, Alice need only pull out her smartphone, and she'll be on her way to her intended destination. She need not ask anyone for directions, learn very much about the environment in which she finds herself, or do much planning. Does this mean she lacks common sense? No, not necessarily. In fact, the common-sense reaction to her predicament is probably to consult her smartphone and use the taxi-ordering app. One might say that common sense dictates that she carry a smartphone in the first place so she will never truly be lost.

For fun, one of us turned to Facebook and Twitter to find out what common sense suggested Alice should do. Remarkably, many commenters suggested she order a cab using Uber. Among other things, they assumed she had a smartphone and felt safe enough to use it in public. After several comments, one person expressed surprise that no one had suggested Alice simply ask someone for help.

It might be the case that common sense often dictates using technology in one form or another – whether it be a map, cellphone or smartphone. Some would say that it is incorrect to suggest that navigational technologies weaken or diminish common sense. But it's important to bear in mind that the technologies are not neutral or equivalent. The degree to which a person such as Alice relies on (i) herself, her common knowledge base of beliefs, and experiences, and on other human beings (both directly and in terms of common sense itself), rather than (ii) a technological device/system, varies quite substantially across different technologies (e.g. from map to cellphone to smartphone). The shift from (i) to (ii) is relevant and important.

We might think that common sense becomes embedded in the technological devices and/or that shifting from (i) to (ii) entails a shift in the relevant community of human beings that Alice relies on – that is, from the community of people Alice knows and shares common experiences with to the community of people behind the technological system. Either way, the shift is remarkable and worth examining. It's by no means limited to the thought experiment we've discussed. One could formulate a similar thought experiment around what common sense dictates in a variety of everyday circumstances, such as when one feels a sharp pain in her back or when there is a power outage. Doing so would lead to the same observations, shifting from (i) to (ii).[43] As political economy theorist Evgeny Morozov contends, "As we gain the [technological] capacity to predict and even preempt crises, we risk eliminating the very kinds of experimental behaviors that have been conducive to social innovation."[44] Morozov wasn't focused on common sense per se, but we believe he identifies the underlying dynamic.

The thought experiment is mainly intended to explore what we mean by common sense and reveal how common sense is susceptible to technologically induced change. We considered discussing variations on the thought experiment, such as what common sense dictates when one is lost while driving on a road trip and how GPS has decreased reliance on certain forms of shared knowledge, skills, and experiences; one no longer needs to consult a map or stop at a gas station and ask for the assistance of strangers. There is nothing new to the observation. Many have made this point before. Our point is as follows:

The precursors or inputs to the creation and sharing of common sense are not stable or inevitably accessible and shared. At least for an important subset of common sense, one of the inputs (prerequisites) seems to be a problem to solve, and one that leads to social innovation through shared experiences and beliefs about how best to deal with the problem. If technology solves the problem, there is no need for common sense solutions. In a sense, humans and machines behave indistinguishably in that context, but not exactly (or not only) because they solve the problem in the same way. Rather, they are indistinguishable because a realm or subset of common-sense experience and knowledge that would otherwise be shared by humans (and not by machines) doesn't exist.

Consider the following set of arguments:

1. Humans face common problems in everyday life ("everyday life problems").
2. Humans develop and rely on common-sense solutions to everyday life problems.
    a. Developing common-sense solutions necessarily depends on a shared core knowledge base, language, and social interactions sufficient to generate common understandings and beliefs.
    b. Developing common-sense solutions [necessarily? often? usually?] depends on experimentation and social innovation.
3. Humans develop technology to solve problems.
    a. Developing technology to solve a problem depends on knowledge, experimentation, and innovation, but not necessarily on a shared core knowledge base, language, and social interactions sufficient to generate common understandings and beliefs.
4. Some technology solves everyday life problems.
5. If technology solves an everyday life problem (more efficiently than existing common-sense solutions) then humans will not (are less likely to) develop common-sense solutions to that problem.
6. If technology solves all everyday life problems, then humans will lack common sense (or a subset of common sense that concerns problem-solving).
7. Humans without common sense are indistinguishable from machines, at least in one (important) respect.

The first four statements are uncontroversial. The same is true for the soft version of the fifth statement (read with the parentheticals). The stronger version of the fifth statement is questionable. Surely humans may continue to develop common-sense solutions to everyday problems for which there is a technological solution; it is just a cost-benefit calculation. The seventh statement is just a restatement of the premise behind the common-sense test.

The sixth statement, however, requires more explanation. The idea that technology will eliminate the need for common-sense solutions to everyday problems may seem far-fetched, mainly because it's hard to believe that technology can so comprehensively address human needs. Moreover, perhaps technological solutions to present-day everyday life problems merely shift the demand curve, making a range of problems that were more extraordinary less so and thus potentially amenable to common-sense solutions. There also is an intermediate step missing between the fifth and sixth statements; something that would explain the aggregation of incremental substitution of technology for common sense.[45]

Our objective in this section has been to articulate and justify the set of arguments. There is plenty of work to be done in modifying, defending, and extending them, and in exploring the complex and varied relationships between technology and common sense in specific contexts.

For example, suppose technological substitution for common sense (step 5) creates different everyday life problems and returns us to step 1. We can envision this as moving parallel to the Turing line. People might take greater risks than they would in the absence of technological devices such as GPS. As a reviewer noted:

> I may take bigger risks. Mother never even drove on highways. With my GPS, I go places I wouldn't be confident visiting otherwise (long highway trips; errands in Newark). So, I venture into situations that may challenge and develop my common sense in a different way.

Greater or different risks might lead to new types of common sense. She explained that the specific example might work as a metaphor for other situations.

> For example, technology affects the traditionally "female" work of networking/connecting friends and relatives. The required common sense changes. But maybe some of this new common sense is even more nuanced and refined, given how many more interactions are happening, with fewer useful social cues.[46]

Common sense is rather flexible and serves various functions. It enables social innovation, problem-solving, and adaptive responses to the wide variety of everyday life occurrences. One of our students, Clement Lee, offered the example of common sense as a reliable fail-safe. "The greatest [shift in] humanity towards machines is not when common sense is removed from everyday life, but [when it is removed] as a backup method in order to move forward when other options are exhausted."[47] Common sense helps humans maintain a reasonably reliable system in the presence of failure.

We've questioned the stability or vulnerability of common sense on the human side of the Turing line and asked whether and how technology renders common sense less relevant, necessary, or even obsolete. Yet, as with our prior discussion of irrationality, the constructed machine-environment does a lot of work, in that case by nudging people toward rational choice and in this case by lessening human dependence on common sense as a means for solving problems.

But our observation is not limited to problem-solving. The techno-social environment within which humans are situated also may restrict access to the inputs necessary to create and sustain common sense. Keep in mind that common sense, as we've defined it, depends upon a shared core knowledge base, language, and social interactions sufficient to generate common understandings and beliefs. We could rewrite the set of arguments above to focus on the relationships between technology and these specific inputs and once more posit technological substitution (steps 3–5), a corresponding elimination of common sense (step 6), and indistinguish-ability/dehumanization (step 7).[48] Again, the bottom line is that we cannot assume the persistent stability and availability of common sense (or its inputs).

Consider one final thought experiment. Suppose Bob lives in a community that only discusses extraordinary events. In this community, one would suffer extreme approbation for discussing anything that anyone else considers to be familiar or within the realm of everyday experience. It is very difficult to know what the boundary is between ordinary and extra-ordinary, and this difficulty only drives a further wedge that chills social interaction and development of a shared core knowledge base about every-day life. Would people in this community be indistinguishable from machines for lack of common sense? Perhaps, at least in the sense that the pathway for developing common sense is disrupted by the norms against sharing ordinary everyday experiences. Now suppose that the impetus for only discussing extraordinary events was not a social norm but rather was information overload. Thus, suppose that the communica-tion channels used by Bob's community are inundated with status updates, recording and reporting of ordinary, everyday events in community mem-bers' lives, and that, as a result, community members only engaged mean-ingfully with the truly extraordinary. That is, assume that when flooded by the routinized reporting of the banalities of community members' every-day lives, people only devote shared attention to the extraordinary. Superficial skimming is the best one can do until something extraordinary catches one's attention. This thought experiment raises some interesting and familiar issues, such as who determines what is extraordinary and worth paying attention to and how is such power exercised? But we offer it primarily to illustrate how this state of affairs could lead to the dissipation of common sense.

The workplace is an important context to explore. Workers hone occupational skills to solve problems, and thus work (labor; task performance) entails a broad category of problems for which common sense and technology might be rivals. Recall the call center story in which a human call center receptionist was mistaken to be a machine. We suggested that the call center environment might have constrained the receptionist and that the scripts she followed made her appear machine-like. The caller might also have been influenced by his prior experience with call centers, which increasingly rely on machines to automate tasks. Advances in speech recognition have opened the space for competition between humans and machines in many occupations. In this competition, Stuart Elliot suggests, "we may overlook important skill requirements for some occupations, such as the substantial range of common-sense knowledge that enables a receptionist to reply sensibly when a customer makes an entirely unexpected request." What constitutes a "skill requirement" is not fixed; a sensible reply to an unexpected request may turn out to be inessential for call centers operations and a (forgotten) luxury.

Automation within the workplace and what it means for society raise a host of complex issues, some of which relate to this project and some of which do not. It has a long, rich history and is currently incredibly important, maybe more so than ever before. But it is too big a topic to dive into at this point. For now, note how common sense relates to occupational skills:

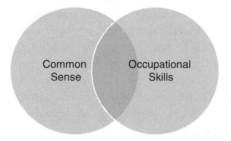

Common Sense   Occupational Skills

Many of the arguments raised in the debate about the erosion of occupational skills or competition between humans and machines for meaningful work take the same form as the arguments about common sense and at the same time face the same counterarguments and contextual nuances.

Lost and Found

Let's return to our unsubstantiated claim that in the not-so-distant future being lost may not be a problem most humans experience. The claim is based on the speculative premise that most humans will carry, wear, or

have implanted a device which tracks their location and provides instantaneous navigational instructions. Many already do, as was evident to me
when my question about the commonsensical response to being lost
appeared nonsensical to many people.

As we discussed in Chapter 2, it's not hard to imagine a wearable technology that allows a person to delegate fully the mundane task of physical
movement through the world to a complex navigation and sensory/motor
function management technology. What would it mean for humans to
delegate these mental and bodily functions – navigation, sensing, and movement – to a technological system? On one hand, navigation through the
physical world seems essential to being part of the world, to understanding it
and others with whom we share it. Given how environments construct us as
humans, it seems troubling to tune out or to remove/disrupt our direct,
physical and sensory awareness of and connection to it. Yet, one might argue
that humans modified by this technology are no less human just because they
choose to delegate various "mundane" tasks to a technological system.
Rather, by doing so, the humans arguably free themselves from the mundane
and can choose other more pleasing or productive intellectual activities. Each
person only has so much time and attention.

Is there any meaningful difference between a person employing the
navigation, sensory and motor function management technology and
a person sitting in a self-driving car? A taxi? The passenger seat of
a friend's car? The differences across the technologies are subtle; they
offer different affordances and have different effects on users. Notice the
differences in capabilities (not) exercised or practiced by the humans using
the technologies. What types of thinking are outsourced, to whom, and
what are the developmental consequences? It is difficult to say when, if
ever, the Turing line is crossed, such that we might infer a person is not-
thinking, or worse, that a person is rendered incapable of thinking.
The person might "look" like a machine to an observer, and a test based
on visual observation might be passed. But that would tell us very little
about not-thinking. It is likely impossible to fashion an appropriate test
without knowing, or at least inferring, what is going on in the mind of the
person who uses the technology. If otherwise mentally engaged, we might
infer that the person has extended her mind; perhaps the technology is
additive rather than subtractive. Recall the point at the beginning about
the capability to not-think. Our exploration of the theory of the extended
mind and mind-extending technology prompted a somewhat different
question: *Who is doing the thinking?* This raises important issues concerning autonomy and free will that are the subject of the following chapter.

CHAPTER 12

Engineered Determinism and Free Will

Introduction

In the previous chapter, we presented techno-social engineering tests focused on thinking. This type of testing can be extended to cover many of the ways that techno-social engineering affects human capabilities, habits, and dispositions. For example, techno-social engineering tests could be run on human emotions. They could identify contexts where emotional engineering goes too far and programmed humans behave like simple machines. These tests could be especially useful for investigating smart environments – including virtual social networks and lived-in physical spaces, like our homes and offices – that engineer emotional contagions.

You might be wondering how deep the techno-social engineering tests can go and how much of our humanity they can examine. In this chapter, we argue – boldly – that techno-social engineering tests are so powerful that they can drill down into the very core of our being and examine free will.

Some people contend that free will is an illusion and that no one is responsible for the choices they make. Whatever thinking or emoting that occurs is naturally determined. This view is called natural determinism. There are rich debates in philosophy about natural determinism and free will. For reasons explained in Appendix C, we do not wade into these debates. Instead, we advance a pragmatic argument: Whether or not reality is naturally determined, we should live our lives and order society *as if* free will exists.

Advancing this argument is critical because it clears the deck and allows us to focus on the techno-social engineering analog to natural determinism: *engineered determinism*. We've touched upon this concept throughout the book. Engineered determinism occurs when techno-social environments control how people behave, develop, and relate to each other. Later in this chapter, we explain why engineered determinism is a fundamental concept to grasp when trying to evaluate techno-social engineering and come to terms with the prospect of building a world that's devoid of free will.

Fortunately, engineered determinism isn't inevitable. It can only seem inevitable because we live, work, and socialize within highly engineered environments. We rarely have a say in how these environments are constructed. In many ways, they are black boxes that we don't have the power to open or change.

We've all encountered situations where we feel like we've been engineered into a state of helplessness. Recall our discussion of the electronic contracting environment and how it's designed to nudge folks to click "I agree." Technically, you have a choice when you see that prompt. However, it would be irrational to do anything other than clicking. Deliberation is wasteful. There's no room to bargain. Resistance is futile.

A similar dynamic occurs when people talk about privacy on social networks, and, frankly, in most other aspects of our data-intensive modern life. Many people feel helpless and believe they've lost control over their personal information. As the familiar mantra puts it, privacy is dead; get over it; get on with your life. Some, however, resist. Some folks leave Facebook and related platforms in protest or to stop the leakage of their private information. But for hundreds of millions, maybe billions, using Facebook is an essential facet of life.

Despite this state of affairs, falling prey to fatalism or despair is a mistake. We feel compelled to click "I agree" and succumb to surveillance capitalism because engineered environments deeply constrain our options. But websites and their affiliates are techno-social tools. People design, build, own, and try to use these tools to serve their own ends. These ends can be challenged and changed. In the final chapter, we'll return to the topic of resisting engineered determinism by pursuing an ideal that we call the freedom to be off.

Natural Determinism and a Pragmatic Wager

In philosophy, determinism is a theory about the nature of reality: the past fully determines the present. What actually happens is precisely all that could happen; the actual exhausts the possible.[1] The eighteenth century scholar Pierre-Simon Laplace offers a classical formulation of the idea.

> We ought to regard the present state of the universe as the effect of its antecedent state and as the cause of the state that is to follow. An intelligence knowing all the forces acting in nature at a given instant, as well as the momentary positions of all things in the universe, would be able to comprehend in one single formula the motions of the largest bodies as well as the

lightest atoms in the world, provided that its intellect were sufficiently powerful to subject all data to analysis; to it nothing would be uncertain, the future as well as the past would be present to its eyes. The perfection that the human mind has been able to give to astronomy affords but a feeble outline of such an intelligence.[2]

While Laplace's "intelligence" likely was divine, one can substitute other entities for God. In a functionalist sense, determinism is a variant of "scientific rationalism" and the "imperialism of instrumental reason," two concepts that computer scientist Joseph Weizenbaum criticizes and which we discussed in Chapter 4. *At bottom, determinism is the view that reality itself is thoroughly physical and that all events are caused by prior and inevitable physical conditions.*[3] From empirical and epistemic perspectives, as Laplace describes, determinism implies reality itself is fully "comprehensible in the language of computation," at least with sufficient data and computing resources.[4] From a metaphysical perspective, this view has direct implications for how humans make decisions and when they deserve to be held accountable for their behavior: *No one decides. It just happens. No one is responsible.* Unsurprisingly, this view is deeply contested. Many find it frightening.

We call this type of determinism *natural determinism*[5] and reject it as a guiding principle. First, the very idea makes us and many others uncomfortable because it conflicts with common intuitions and subjective experience. When reflecting on our decisions (e.g. whether to watch television, exercise, or read a book), we tend to believe and feel as though alternative possibilities genuinely existed and that we could have chosen differently and taken a different path. We presuppose the capability to choose differently in many everyday experiences. As philosopher T. J. Mawson contends, you can decide whether to keep reading this chapter.[6] *Go ahead, decide.* If you stopped for a bit and returned, could you have done otherwise? *Try again.* We could go on with this line of exploration, but you get the point. Unlike flying to the moon by flapping your arms, an activity that you can't do no matter how hard you try because of physically determined constraints, your decision about whether to stop or continue reading admits of more room to maneuver. Your deep interest in this topic, your limited time and attention, or the need to run to the bathroom may have had an influence on your decision, the first, second or third time. But the point is that you retained some type of capability to decide. The idea that what happened exhausted what was possible seems counterintuitive, to say the least.

Our second reason for rejecting natural determinism is that, with some exceptions, we tend to take ownership of and responsibility for our decisions, understanding that the past, luck, other folks, our environment, and so on affect those decisions substantially.[7] Responsibility seems to depend upon freedom, while determinism challenges our conventional beliefs about moral responsibility. Third, we tend to believe we can learn from past decisions and can make plans for the future. Otherwise, what's the purpose of learning? Fourth, if everything is determined, it seems hard, if not impossible, to make sense of why we sometimes regret past decisions. Thus, like many people, we'd like for natural determinism to be a false idea, one that inspires spirited debates but doesn't correspond with reality. This means we believe a naturally indeterminate reality is a more attractive option. It fits better with common intuitions and beliefs about the world and our place in it.

Just because we prefer indeterminism doesn't mean the world is structured that way. To be honest, we don't know whether our preference matches up with reality. Nor does anyone else.[8] It isn't as if there's a paradigm empirical test that can ultimately reveal whether natural determinism is true.[9] Instead, scholars judge the validity of the thesis by assessing leading arguments that claim to establish its truth or cast skepticism upon it. Does this never-ending debate and our refusal to enter it impact our project? No. Simply, a shift needs to be made, one that brings us away from metaphysical conjectures to a practical point of view that can be wagered on.

Blaise Pascal's Wager. Per Pascal:

If there is a God, He is infinitely incomprehensible, since, having neither parts nor limits, He has no affinity to us. We are then incapable of knowing either what He is or if He is ... God is, or He is not. But to which side shall we incline? Reason can decide nothing here. There is an infinite chaos which separated us. A game is being played at the extremity of this infinite distance where heads or tails will turn up. What will you wager? According to reason, you can do neither the one nor the other; you can defend neither of the propositions.

Do not, then, reprove for error those who have made a choice; for you know nothing about it. "No, but I blame them for having made, not this choice, but a choice; for again both he who chooses heads and he who chooses tails are equally at fault, they are both in the wrong. The true course is not to wager at all."

> Yes; but you must wager. It is not optional. You are embarked. Which will you choose then? Let us see. Since you must choose, let us see which interests you least. You have two things to lose, the true and the good; and two things to stake, your reason and your will, your knowledge and your happiness; and your nature has two things to shun, error and misery. Your reason is no more shocked in choosing one rather than the other, since you must of necessity choose. This is one point settled. But your happiness? Let us weigh the gain and the loss in wagering that God is. Let us estimate these two chances. If you gain, you gain all; if you lose, you lose nothing. Wager, then, without hesitation that He is.[10]

Many are familiar with Blaise Pascal's wager concerning the existence or nonexistence of God. Drawing from this well-known case and the philosopher William James' general conception of pragmatism and specific perspective on free will, we'd like to introduce another existential gamble.[11] It is a *wager on the nature of reality* that comes down to taking sides on a single question: *Is natural determinism true or false?* Given the stakes involved, there's no viable way to avoid the wager.[12] Assume you must choose a position and place your bet. While reason won't help you figure out the truth about the nature of reality,[13] it can help you decide which wager to make. The pragmatic decision shapes how we choose to live our lives and how collectively we understand and order our society. But it lacks any evidentiary weight in the ultimate question upon which the wager is being made. Since there's no truth value to how bets are placed, all you're doing is deciding whether we're collectively better off by living our lives and ordering our relations and society generally *as if* natural determinism is true or false.

Pascal suggested that when faced with such a wager you should choose to bet on the existence of God because of a simple cost-benefit calculation. Simply put, "if you gain, you gain all; if you lose, you lose nothing." The pragmatic wager is not so clear-cut.[14]

We have two possibilities, and we must weigh the consequences of choosing to bet on one over the other given the impossibility of knowing the truth. We can sharpen our focus by evaluating the consequences of selecting either option in terms of a two-by-two grid that identifies error costs. We aren't framing this formally in terms of expected utilities because we've assumed that we cannot know or learn what probabilities to assign. For purposes of argument, let's suppose each is equally likely.[15] We label the bottom row as status quo because we currently live our lives and order our affairs as if reality is not naturally determined and free will exists.

Reality / Wager	Reality is naturally determined	Reality is not naturally determined
Live life and order society as if reality is naturally determined	Accurate No free will	Error Illusion of no free will
Live life and order society as if reality is not naturally determined	Error Status quo: Illusion of free will	Accurate Status quo: Free will

First, suppose our reality is not naturally determined, that what occurs does not exhaust the possible, and that people do make their own choices. This doesn't mean that human choices are completely free and unconstrained. A host of different environmental factors inevitably influence the possible. But in this assumed reality, such factors do not determine what happens. *People do; we do.* An accurate wager in this reality would maintain the status quo.

So, what would be the consequences of wagering that reality is naturally determined when in fact it is not? This scenario would entail significant changes from the status quo, a shift from the bottom right box to top right box. First, while the wager itself does not constitute evidence about the ultimate truth, it nonetheless would shape behavior and beliefs. Rather than endlessly circle around the unknowable, we place the wager and move on with our lives *as if* we knew the truth. To live our lives and order our relations as if reality was naturally determined would undermine much of what human civilization depends upon – namely, our basic conceptions of agency, free will, responsibility, and social order. Recall, for example, our discussion of contract law in Chapter 5. Contract law generally aims to enable human beings to exercise their will and to relate to each other more effectively; it presumes free will as a foundational principle. So do most legal regimes that govern human relations. Beyond law, social norms and various commonsensical, religious, and other conceptions of agency, meaning, and moral responsibility that provide people with a "moral compass" to guide their everyday interactions generally presume endorsing free will. To erroneously unravel these foundations would be incredibly costly for human society and, arguably, catastrophically harmful.

Second, suppose our reality *is* naturally determined. This would mean that the past fully determines the present. Environmental factors not only would shape the possible, but they'd also determine what happens. Our common-sense intuitions and subjective experiences would be false. Free will, as we describe in the next section, would not actually exist; it would be an illusion. An accurate wager in this reality would not maintain the status quo; rather, it would entail dispelling the illusion of free will and consequently adopting significant social reordering.

So, what would be the consequences of wagering that reality is not naturally determined when in fact it is naturally determined? What would be the consequences of erroneously maintaining the status quo? In our view, the consequences would be largely *beneficial.* Like Pascal, we believe the deck is stacked heavily in favor of wagering for freedom. In a naturally determined reality, free will would be an illusion, but it would be an incredibly important illusion that we've evolved to depend on in many significant ways. Recall our discussion of imagined realities in Chapter 4, and, in particular, the conceptions of justice reflected in Hammurabi's Code and the Declaration of Independence. To toss out our conception of justice simply because it's in fact a mere illusion – the product of our imaginations – would wreak havoc on many of the institutional achievements of modernity. Perhaps no one would be responsible for the fallout because it was determined naturally. But that wouldn't make the fallout any less harmful or any less real. This leads to a rather bold claim: *Free will might just be the most important imagined reality that humans have the capacity to create and sustain.*[16]

Not everyone agrees with us. Some determinists would refuse to wager and insist that our pragmatic approach is inappropriate. Others disagree with our characterization of the consequences. Some determinists claim society would benefit tremendously from dispensing with the illusion of free will. These determinists insist that our current legal and ethical frameworks inappropriately assign legal and moral responsibility. They demonstrate how all too often people are held fully responsible for violating norms or laws in situations where someone demonstrably lacks free will.

For example, in "The Brain on Trial," neuroscientist David Eagleman presents three vivid examples of humans whose law- or norm-violating behavior is caused by brain damage, compromised neural circuitry, imbalanced brain chemistry, and other identifiable physical causes. The first example is "Alex," a 40-year-old man who developed perverse sexual proclivities and acted upon them in grotesque ways. This behavior was aberrant and yet it didn't express a lifestyle that "Alex" freely embraced. Instead, "Alex" did regrettable things because a "massive tumor in his orbitofrontal frontal cortex" altered what he found desirable. The second example is people who become disinhibited as a result of suffering from frontotemporal dementia. Some of these folks develop "startling behaviors," like audaciously "shoplifting in front of store managers." The third example is Parkinson's patients who took the drug Pramipexole as part of their course of treatment. The drug turned out to have an unexpected side-effect. By creating a dopamine imbalance, it caused over-the-top behavior, including "pathological gambling."

Eagleman concludes:

> The lesson from all these stories is the same: human behavior cannot be separated from human biology. If we like to believe that people make free choices about their behavior (as in, "I don't gamble, because I'm strong-willed"), cases like Alex the pedophile, the frontotemporal shoplifters, and the gambling Parkinson's patients may encourage us to examine our views more carefully. Perhaps not everyone is equally "free" to make socially appropriate choices.[17]

We couldn't agree more. It might seem like we're backtracking, but we're not. Wagering on free will and living our lives and ordering our collective affairs as if free will exists does not in any sense contradict Eagleman's observations. As we demonstrate below, free will, autonomy, and agency are contingent and variable. They exist on a continuum (or dynamic field, if you prefer that terminology) and depend on antecedent causes, factors outside our control, and affordances in built or engineered environments. That's why in various areas of both law and ethics, where free will is presumed, moral responsibility is still attributed with some recognition of human limitations, and the significance of history and context matter. Admittedly, more attention might need to be paid to limitations that stem from the internal workings of our brains. Science, especially neuroscience, might provide underappreciated but useful means for identifying, evaluating, and even engineering solutions for antisocial behaviors.

Still, two points deserve emphasis. First, arguments like the one Eagleman puts forth only apply to a relatively narrow set of cases where identifiable brain-based causes undermine our conventional concepts of moral responsibility. We indeed should identify and take these causes into account much as we do for non-brain-based causes, such as the physical and environmental causes we more easily observe, understand, and integrate into our evaluative judgments. Perhaps the set of cases will expand in scope with improvements in neuroscience and related fields. For now, we should be wary of overly optimistic and all-encompassing claims about inevitable scientific progress.[18] Furthermore, although Eagleman writes as if he's demystifying free will, most of his arguments are perfectly compatible with free will as we define it below. Although he seems ready to declare himself a determinist, he never goes quite so far. He only criticizes overly simplistic and rigid reliance on strong presumptions of free will and agency in certain contexts, but he does not explicitly deny the existence of free will. We need not throw the baby out with the bathwater.

To be fair, hard-core determinists and free will skeptics go much further than Eagleman does. For example, philosopher Gregg Caruso argues that accepting the truth of natural determinism is wholly compatible with believing in the rule of law and remaining committed to the policy agenda of responding to criminal behavior through procedures that are morally justified and neither cruel nor unfair. Caruso contends that society should embrace a public health framework for ethics – one that focuses on quarantining threats that challenge our right to self-protection and threats that predictably will lead to others being harmed if they aren't neutralized. Caruso further insists that by liberating ourselves from the false belief in free will we'll become more inclined to create better policies for promoting social justice. Instead of policy-makers adopting an individualistic focus that centers on rehabilitating putatively outlier citizens who make bad decisions, they'd instead be encouraged to identify and alter the root causes or *structural conditions* that lead people to violate the social contract. "The broad approach to criminal justice provided by the public health-quarantine model therefore places issues of social justice at the forefront. It sees racism, sexism, poverty, and systematic disadvantages as serious threats to public safety and it prioritizes the reduction of such inequalities."[19]

Ultimately, the hard-core determinists who argue that we ought to dispense with the illusion of free will believe we are currently in the bottom left box and that we ought to move to the top left box. To be fair, determinists aren't rooting against free will. They just think that the best available evidence justifies determinism. If they had divine powers and could create a world where free will exists we think they probably would. Nothing in their determinist arguments suggests otherwise. But what if they are factually incorrect about the nature of reality? If we are in the bottom right box, would they still believe we should move to the top right box? Given the uncertainty about (non)determinism, society must wager. Free will skeptics can argue all they want on truth and the best available evidence, but that does not alleviate them of the burden of placing a wager. They cannot guarantee they are correct. They do not know for certain. What if they are wrong? Even if the possibility is slight, they still must wager and explain why society should follow their advice. We have yet to find someone who has argued that even if free will exists, we'd be better off living our lives and ordering our affairs as if it did not exist. As we see it, this is a wager that the hard-core determinists would need to take.

In sum, free will – whether real or illusory – anchors many social constructs, our laws, and normative commitments.[20] We don't, and possibly can't, know the truth of natural determinism. Perhaps we don't want to know the truth, and maybe we've evolved to avoid confronting it. Accordingly, for the remainder of this chapter, we proceed with our intuition, belief, and desire that reality is not naturally determined and that some variety of free will exists.

Legal Causation as an Approach to Free Will

In the law, causation is generally split into two inquiries: but-for/actual causation and proximate causation. Both are required to hold a defendant liable in tort. For example, in a negligence case, actual causation asks whether the defendant's allegedly negligent act is a but-for cause of the plaintiff's injury; in other words, but for the defendant's act would the plaintiff's injury have occurred anyway? If it would have occurred regardless of the defendant's negligent act, then the defendant is not a but-for cause and not responsible; other causes determined her fate. If the defendant's act was a necessary determining factor, then the defendant is a but-for cause and potentially liable.

Proximate cause is much more complicated, and different jurisdictions employ many different tests for it. Simply, proximate cause asks whether the defendant reasonably should have foreseen the risk of injury to the plaintiff and whether the defendant's negligent act is sufficiently proximate in time and space (or, conversely, too attenuated) to hold the defendant liable. The idea is that while there may be very many antecedent but-for causes, most are too attenuated and thus not proximate causes.

It is hard to dispute the fact that innumerable antecedent causes determine our lives in a but-for cause sense. Slight changes in initial conditions or historical events could have dramatic consequences and reshape our lives. But focusing only on but-for causation inevitably misses something. Proximate cause helps to focus on what matters, why we care about specific cause-and-effect relationships, and how we decide what we are responsible for and with what we identify ourselves. In some ways, that is what the debates about natural determinism and free will are about. Those who insist that free will exists admit the existence of many but-for determining causes yet emphasize the critical importance of human decisions proximate to our conscious present, as experienced in terms of our bodies and minds, and thus as ourselves. Put slightly differently, there may be many physical and biological systems that constitute but-for causes of consciousness, subjective experience, our feeling and perception of free will, autonomy, and agency. But those causes are not necessarily proximate enough to us and how we understand and govern ourselves.

Notably, philosopher Patrick Grim explores some other examples where the law engages with the normativity and contextuality of free will. He emphasizes, for example, how the *mens rea* requirement in criminal law is not reducible to a metaphysical description or "simple characterization of free choice in terms of some internal mental state." After tipping his hat to H. L. A. Hart's similar observation in the context of traditional contract law,[21] he notes:

> One might conclude at this point that the law has understood free choice and responsibility better than the behavioral sciences have. This in turn might serve as a warning to the legal profession not to expect from the sciences any easy answers regarding freedom and responsibility.[22]

Engineered Determinism

In this book, we advance an understanding of a different type of determinism than the naturalist kind reviewed thus far – namely, *engineered determinism*. Recall from Chapter 4 how we described the problem of engineered determinism. There we contended that it's grand hubris to believe we could socially construct a perfectly optimized world if we only have sufficient data, confidence in our advanced technologies and expert technologists, and willingness to commit to what some see as a utopian program.[23] This topic and set of issues diverge subtly from natural determinism. The basic problem, as we see it, is that engineered determinism involves the elimination of free will and autonomy.

Similar ideas have been formulated before. For example, in his famous 1954 polemic, "The Question Concerning Technology," philosopher Martin Heidegger argued that the "essence" of "modern technology" is a type of technological determinism (although he didn't use the German equivalent of this specific term).[24] His core belief was that modern technology is utterly unique; unlike the tools of the past, modern technology isn't subservient to the goals of the people who design and use it. Berkeley professor Hubert Dreyfus provides a succinct summary of what Heidegger is driving at when depicting modern technology as having an autonomous logic of its own: "The goal of technology, Heidegger . . . tells us, is more and more flexibility and efficiency simply for its own sake."[25] In Heidegger's age of modern technology, flexibility and efficiency become ends in themselves – the highest good, so to speak. In this vision, the West is stuck perpetuating a cybernetic cycle of "*endless* disaggregation, redistribution, and reaggregation *for its own sake*" and we're all prisoners chained to a process that nobody can control.[26]

We don't share Heidegger's pessimism. Nor do we agree with his view that modern technology effectively has a mind of its own that humans can't change. We believe that a fully determined world hasn't been created, and that, if it were to be, it wouldn't be because technology demands how the pages of history will turn. Instead, progress towards engineered determinism requires the confluence of many factors, ranging from engineering decisions to market demands.[27] In the preceding chapters, we discussed some of the steps down a path toward such a state of affairs. For us, engineered determinism entails techno-social engineering of humans, often through the construction of smart techno-social environments that render humans within the environments increasingly predictable and programmable.

One important thing to keep in mind from the history of technology is that engineers aren't the only inventive people. Hacking, re-purposing, meaning-making, and even sabotaging happen all the time. French theorist Bruno Latour is a particularly keen observer of how people can subvert the intentions of designers. In one case, he discusses the frustration he experienced when being forced to deal with a technological approach to maximizing seat-belt law compliance.

> Early this morning, I was in a bad mood . . . My car usually does not want to start before I buckle the belt. It first flashes a red light "FASTEN YOUR SEAT BELT!," then an alarm sounds; it is so high pitched, so relentless, so repetitive, that I cannot stand it. After ten seconds, I swear and put on the belt. This time, I stood the alarm for twenty seconds and then gave in. My mood had worsened quite a bit, but I was at peace with the law – at least with that law. I wished to break it, but I could not. Where is the morality? In me, a human driver, dominated by the mindless power of an artifact? Or in the artifact forcing me, a mindless human, to obey the law that I freely accepted when I got my driver's license? Of course, I could have put on my seat belt before the light flashed and the alarm sounded, incorporating in my own self the good behavior that everyone – the car, the law, the police – expected of me. Or else, some devious engineer could have linked the engine ignition to an electric sensor in the seat belt, so that I could not even have started the car before having put it on.[28]

These considerations about the disquieting feeling that's aroused by being within an environment that's engineered to make resistance futile motivated Latour to reclaim some of his agency. "Because I feel so irritated to be forced to behave well," Latour writes, "I instruct my garage mechanics to unlink the switch and the sensor."[29] Not everyone would feel the way Latour did in this situation. Some would appreciate technology being used to enforce a law that's clearly designed to protect the public good. The lesson to draw from this example, therefore, is that the power of techno-social engineering can be more limited than technologists assume. Given enough of an incentive – apparently, frustration can do the trick – people will search for ways to avoid becoming programmed to be predictable. Humans with complex and messy emotions don't like being treated like simple machines.

Latour was an adult when he decided to prevent his car from programming him. But according to danah boyd, Principal Researcher at Microsoft Research and the founder of Data & Society, youth culture is a key demographic that resists techno-social engineering. While some tweens and teens take a by-the-book approach to social media, others, boyd argues, actively express their agency through subversive practices like "social stenography" that can thwart surveillance from authorities, like parents, as well as data-mining, from platforms like Facebook:

> Social stenography uses countless linguistic and cultural tools, including lyrics, in-jokes, and culturally specific references to encode messages that are functionally accessible but simultaneously meaningless. Some teens use pronouns while others refer to events, use nicknames, and employ predetermined code words to share gossip that lurking adults can't interpret. Many teens write in ways that will blend in and be invisible to or misinterpreted by adults. Whole conversations about school gossip, crushes, and annoying teachers go unnoticed as teens host conversations that are rendered meaningless to outside observers.[30]

One way to minimize resistance to grand techno-social engineering is to orchestrate a special type of complacency, a form of inertia. It's arguably an effective strategy for persuading people that they lack free will, live in a naturally determined world, and have no good reason to be concerned about one form of determinism supplanting another or co-existing alongside it. We're *not* suggesting that scholars who argue for natural determinism and against the existence of free will are intentionally trying to make all forms of determinism seem equally palatable. Nonetheless, that outcome may be an unintended consequence that accompanies widespread acceptance of their arguments.

Concluding that engineered determinism exists without examining a sufficient range of technologically mediated practices is a problem that impeded the early philosophers of technology. This methodology has come to be known as the fallacy of "transcendentalism." Transcendental accounts of technology examine the structure of technological affordances and, without paying adequate attention to how people negotiate their constraints, conclude that homogeneous effects exist and are powerful enough to "mass produce" a "mass culture."[31]

What we need are better tools to identify and evaluate incremental steps down the path toward engineered determinism. While techno-social engineering tests for free will might not ultimately be practical to create and run, we'll discuss them in the next section with the hope of advancing conceptual progress. We now turn our attention to free will and autonomy.

Free Will and Autonomy

Some variety of free will makes sense to us intuitively and seems to exist. After all, we are aware of decision-making and thus believe that we have free will. According to the philosopher Baruch Spinoza: "Experience teaches us no less clearly than reason, that men believe themselves free, simply because they are conscious of their actions, and unconscious of the causes whereby those actions are determined."[32] Usually, this quote is interpreted to mean that free will is an illusion: we may believe that we decide what we do – that we freely choose our actions and are thus authors of our own lives – but we also recognize that much of what we do is caused by unknown factors outside our control.

If our minds are stuck following biologically determined scripts, then perhaps free will is an illusion, an incredibly important one as we discussed above. We've wagered that not everything we do is predetermined by God, fate, laws of nature, history, or environment.

But a whole lot is! There is much one simply cannot do, no matter how strong your intention and will to do so. (Just try jumping to the moon.) Putting God and fate aside, each person's decisions to act are constrained substantially by laws of nature, history, chance, and environment.

Though not the conventional interpretation, Spinoza also might be read to suggest that what we are conscious of shapes what we believe and blinds us to the hidden complexities of multiple interdependent causes and contingencies that dramatically shape – and *in that more limited sense* determine – our beliefs, desires, and actions. This is a familiar theme. We extracted the same observation from the extended cognition literature.

The difficult question faced in many fields is what dark matter lies beyond the light of the lamp-post. What exactly are these multiple interdependent causes and contingencies and how and to what degree do they shape who we are and what we do? Suffice it to say, many things external to us significantly shape us in ways that we are completely unaware/unconscious of and thereby determine our actions *to a degree*, by determining the *range* of opportunities or possible actions we face. Not surprisingly, free will and autonomy are often described in related terms, such as degrees of freedom and level of constraints.

> Virtual worlds provide a useful example of heavily engineered environments. Law professor Michael Risch provides a useful description:
>
> > For the uninitiated, a virtual world is an interactive computer software program where users might interact (in modern times over the Internet). Many human users remotely control characters – called "avatars" – in the world's software. Participating in a virtual world is like guiding a character through a video game, except that the other characters are also humans who control their own avatars. Though avatar control is like a video game, many worlds are not games *per se*, as there is no competition. Avatars simply "live" in the virtual world as their users might live in the real world.[33]
>
> Much of what someone can be and do within a virtual world is determined by the designers. This is true of gaming environments, such as World of Warcraft, and more open-ended and unstructured environments, such as Second Life. The degree of freedom and level of constraint varies, but, for the most part, it seems safe to say that most virtual worlds expand human freedom in many dimensions. "Virtual worlds allow their users nearly unlimited choices in their actions and interactions with other users and the virtual environment."[34] Thus, it is important to note that engineering – even techno-social engineering – does not necessitate engineered determinism.

Free will often is defined in terms of self-determination and self-authorship. We might say that an agent with free will does the (relevant) thinking and has beliefs, desires, preferences, tastes, and values about what he, she, or it is, does, and can be. Following philosopher Harry Frankfurt, we might say that *will* is the set of first-order desires and a person has *free will* when that person has the freedom to have and to effectuate desires about the set of first-order desires, that is, for second-order desires about one's will to be realized.

> "[To say that] a person enjoys freedom of the will means . . . that he is free to want what he wants to want . . . A person's will is free only if he has the will he wants. This means that with regard to any of his first-order desires, he is free either to make that desire his will or to make some other first-order desire his will instead. Whatever his will, then, the will of the person whose will is free could have been otherwise; he could have done otherwise than constitute the will as he did.[35]

We could extend the analysis to the nth order and ask whether a person is free to deny or express her (n–1)th desires. But the key point is the jump from having first-order desires that arise largely from immediate needs and stimuli in context to the more elevated position of having higher-order desires that (potentially) arise from reflective self-determination.[36] (Others have offered similar ideas in terms of first- and second-order preferences and values.[37])

Difficulties arise in extending Frankfurt's theory beyond desires and preferences to beliefs. It seems odd to say that a belief is freely one's own only if the person ratifies it with a higher-order belief or desire. That's why philosophers Geoffrey Sayre-McCord and Michael Smith suggest, instead, that "a belief is an agent's own, or one with which she is to be identified and with which she could accurately identify, if it is robust: that is, stable in a way that qualifies it as characteristic of her."[38] They explain *robustness* (and fragility) in terms of *stability over time*, where stability reflects resistance to change in light of experience, evidence, and reflection. The reasons for stability vary. For example, a stable belief may be well justified based on the weight of evidence and experience or poorly justified based on wishful thinking or irrational dispositions. Regardless of the reasons, their account suggests that stable beliefs rather than fragile ones are the sort that constitute and reflect an agent's personality. They extend their account to desires as well, and further shift the view of mind away from the hierarchical account of Frankfurt.

To illustrate the difference, consider an agent who is an alcoholic and has a second-order desire to not desire a drink but who nonetheless desires a drink. On Frankfurt's account, this suggests a lack of free will and calls into question whether the first-order desire to drink can properly be the agent's own. (The analysis is complicated by the way addiction frames the agent's choices.[39]) Sayre-McCord and Smith suggest both desires can be the agent's own, but only if both are robust.[40] Both may constitute and reflect the agent and her genuine struggle with alcoholism. To be clear, Sayre-McCord and Smith characterize addiction as an irrational but robust desire, and thus properly the agent's own. They argue that the existence of the conflicting desires would not necessarily mean a lack of free will.

We adopt the following deflated account of free will. It lines up with Frankfurt's hierarchical mesh theory as modified by Sayre-McCord and Smith. *Free will is an agent's situated capability to engage in reflective self-determination about her will (beliefs, desires, values, tastes, etc.).* It does not necessarily encompass the agent's capacity to avoid conflicts or to exercise complete control over her will. Frankfurt's higher-order desires as well as Sayre-McCord and Smith's conception of robust desires depend significantly on rational deliberation and reflection in light of evidence, experience, circumstances, and context. The agent is situated in an environment that shapes the evidence, experiences, and opportunities available for reflective self-determination.

Our will is not fully the product of continuous self-reflection and determination. Far from it. Our time and attention are too limited. Many of our beliefs, desires, tastes, and even values are implanted in our minds, whether as remnants from evolutionary processes,[41] framings of external stimuli provided by System 1 processes of the brain,[42] or contributions from material and social cultures we take for granted.[43] Much of what constitutes our will at any specific point in time is not really self-determined through reflective deliberation. A substantial portion of our will seems to be more passively produced and accumulated by experience and experimentation in specific environments. None of these observations cast doubt on the existence or importance of free will, understood as the capability to engage in reflective self-determination about one's will. Freedom of will simply must encompass the *capability* to affirm, deny, or adjust one's will upon reflection, if and when such reflection is salient.

Following our discussion of mind extension and cognitive systems, we can evaluate free will from a systems perspective that acknowledges the roles of material and social cultures as well as other minds. And then we can see how an agent's capability to engage in reflective self-determination about her will is contingent both from static and dynamic perspectives. (Recall, for example, our prior discussions of GPS technology.) Each opportunity to reflect is situated in a specific context and thus contingent. But so too is the capability to competently reflect itself also contingent. It requires practice, development, and competence over time. Note that free will, as we've described it, is an internal mental capability shaped in part by access to and engagement with the external world.

In turn, *autonomy* can be broadly understood in terms of the *intentions* that determine our engagement with the world. There are many different philosophical accounts of autonomy.[44] Our objective is not to resolve the definitional or philosophical intricacies and debates. Instead, it suffices for us to focus on a conception that we find relevant for our exploration of techno-social engineering of humans: *Autonomy is the bridge between will and action; it's the internal process by which humans create their intentions to act.* An autonomous person engages the external world pursuant to self-created intentions. Conversely, a heteronomous person acts pursuant to others' intentions. A person who lacks autonomy is a mere puppet. Autonomy can thus be understood as a special component of free will: Intentions are shot through with one's beliefs, desires, and values regarding oneself and one's plans.[45] To minimize confusion about terms, we adopt this view and treat autonomy as an aspect of free will.[46]

Liberation from Genetic Determinism Only to Fall Victim to Engineered Determinism ...

In his book, *The Robot's Rebellion*, psychologist Keith Stanovich describes human self-determination in a way that's very much in line with our perspective.[47]

To start, we might say that even if we live in a naturally determined reality, we've been given a rather long leash. This refers to the idea that controlling a model airplane depends on a short leash, but controlling the Mars explorer vehicle relies on a rather long leash because the distance makes control of the vehicle impossible for NASA engineers on Earth.[48] The explorer must be designed to have more flexible intelligence with which to control its own moment-by-moment actions; it's given a long leash. As Stanovich suggests, "We are creatures for whom evolution has built into the architecture of the brain a flexible system having something like the ultimate long-leash goal suggested by Dawkins: 'Do whatever you think best.'"[49]

Further, Stanovich suggests that the analytical system within our brains (System 2) evolved to provide us with an escape hatch from genetic determinism, which holds that evolutionary biology fully determines what humans do.[50] The analytical system provides us with the capability to deliberate, formulate goals, assess our environment, form beliefs, make plans, decide, and act – in short, to be instrumentally rational. Systems 1 and 2 depend upon each other and are often complementary. While the goals of genes often coincide with the goals of the host (human being), the systems also can conflict, or even be at war with each other. For example, evolutionary pressures may lead System 1 to prime us to eat fatty foods or flirt with the boss's spouse, and System 2 may allow us to resist those pressures for our own good.

To rebel against genetic determinism, Stanovich calls for us to pursue perfect rationality and thereby elevate the self-determined goals of human beings. In a sense, this is a call for recognizing and supporting free will, although he does not use that term and might not agree with our use of that terminology to describe his argument. Nonetheless, one must wonder whether our escape from genetic determinism leads us into another trap, which is engineered determinism. We revisit this conundrum in the Conclusion.

Practical Agency: Freedom to Act and Exercise One's Own Will

Humans may have free will in the sense we describe, but that does not mean we always have the freedom to exercise, implement, execute, or act upon it. Such freedom is what we regard as *practical agency*. It depends on the degree of constraint and the actual range of opportunity for choosing and acting. In deciding what to do or who to be, one may have a multitude of options or just one. When biological blueprints and evolutionary pressures combine with constraining conditions, humans may lack a meaningful range of choices and, thus, lack agency.[51] We focus on *agency* as *practical, situated freedom to exercise one's will, including acting in accordance with one's own intentions.* To see how free will, autonomy, and practical agency relate to techno-social engineering, consider the following passage from legal scholar Julie Cohen's article on informational privacy and autonomy:

> Autonomous individuals do not spring full-blown from the womb. We must learn to process information and to draw our own conclusions about the world around us. We must learn to choose, and must learn something before we can choose anything. Here, though, information theory suggests a paradox: "Autonomy" connotes an essential independence of critical faculty and an imperviousness to influence. But to the extent that information shapes behavior, autonomy is radically contingent upon environment and circumstance. The only tenable resolution – if "autonomy" is not to degenerate into the simple, stimulus-response behavior sought by direct marketers – is to underdetermine environment. Autonomy in a contingent world requires a zone of relative insulation from outside scrutiny and interference – a field of operation within which to engage in the conscious construction of self ... We do not experiment only with beliefs and associations, but also with every other conceivable type of taste and behavior that expresses and defines self. The opportunity to experiment with preferences is a vital part of the process of learning, and learning to choose, that every individual must undergo.[52]

Cohen's vision of "autonomy in a contingent world" is dynamic and well-suited to describing the complex relationships between humans and the techno-social environment within which they are situated. She argues that the "only tenable resolution – if 'autonomy' is not to degenerate into the simple, stimulus-response behavior sought by direct marketers – is to underdetermine environment."[53] This argument provides an important hint as to what crossing the Turing line might entail: *degeneration of autonomy into simple, stimulus-response behavior by humans.* The argument also provides a hint as to the mechanism by which such degeneration could occur: an overdetermined environment, which would be an engineered environment that constrains to such a degree that humans situated within such an environment have no practical freedom to exercise their free will and be authors of their own lives.

We should distinguish (1) *overdetermined environments* that eliminate the practical freedom to exercise will by constraining the range of actions or opportunities presented to situated agents, from (2) *constrictive environments* that engineer the will by determining beliefs, preferences, tastes, or values. To the extent that there is no escaping constructive environments (because social shaping is a ubiquitous feature of the modern world), (1) and (2) can bleed into each other. The mechanisms in (1) and (2) are different, however, and worth distinguishing. In some contexts, the outcome for the situated agents might be the same, and in others, it might be different. Perhaps at the extremes (1) leads to *slaves* and (2) leads to *simple machines*.

Slaves are humans with free will who, due to circumstances beyond their control, lack agency – meaning the practical, situated freedom to exercise their will. In other words, the "slavery environment" dramatically reduces the scope of opportunities for humans; its constraints impede our ability to act and author our lives.[54] Nevertheless, slaves retain free will; they can think for themselves and have dreams and desires about their lives that can transcend the status quo. Slave-owners have tried, and, in some cases, may have succeeded, in effectively turning slaves into machines, by determining their beliefs, preferences, tastes, and values, thereby depriving them of free will.[55]

Simple machines are programmed humans who lack free will. Whatever will a machine possesses – whatever beliefs, preferences, tastes, or values we might attribute to the machine – is fully determined by the antecedent causes of its programming. Humans who are completely brainwashed or subject to mind control thus can be considered functionally identical to simple machines.

Techno-Social Engineering Tests on Free Will

Here we return to the idea of employing techno-social engineering tests to identify potentially problematic techno-social engineering of humans. To maintain consistency, let's use the set-up we discussed for operationalizing the rationality test. Our goal in this section is to investigate the following question:

Is there value in running observational tests that distinguish humans from machines based on stimulus-response exchanges focused on the specific capabilities associated with free will?

Let's revisit a baseline issue. Remember, we're looking for a valid and reliable means to produce evidence that shows techno-social engineering has rendered humans indistinguishable from simple machines, resulting in the diminishment or loss of meaningful aspects of humanity. We can differentiate humans from "simple machines" that we know[56] lack autonomy because they always behave as programmed, i.e. in a predetermined or fully constrained fashion. In other words, don't be distracted by the possibility that complex machines could be designed that aren't predictable or act irrationally because the programmer injects randomness or counter-intuitive responses to expected stimuli.[57]

Initially, free will might seem impossible to test, but a techno-social engineering test might do the trick. Much like the set-up for the (ir)rationality test, one can imagine a battery of questions that implicate higher-order beliefs, desires, or preferences and effectively distinguish humans and machines. Simple machines would not exhibit conflicts between first- and second-order preferences. By contrast, humans would, at least with respect to certain types of actions and contexts. Note that this type of test wouldn't provide the sort of empirical evidence needed to (dis)prove natural determinism. It would only distinguish human responses – which in a naturally determined reality would be determined by physical processes within the brain – from the responses of a non-biological fully programmed machine. Passing the test could, however, provide evidence of *engineered determinism*.

What sorts of questions or stimuli might be relevant for a free will test? We explore a few different ideas. Each involves queries designed to elicit either a conflict or discrepancy between first- and higher-order beliefs, preferences, values, tastes, or intentions. Evidence along these lines might support inferences that an agent is a human being. The absence of such evidence might support inferences that an agent is a machine or engineered to behave like one.

Moral Decision-Making

Suppose we designed a techno-social engineering test that focused on moral decision-making. Imagine the observer is tasked with asking questions about how the agent realistically would behave in specific scenarios.

The scenarios could frame conventional moral dilemmas in utilitarian terms and could vary, for example, from adultery to Good Samaritan to trolley car dilemmas. Next, the observer asks questions about how the agent should behave in those same or closely related scenarios. The observer also could ask for evaluations of others' behavior in the same or closely related scenarios. The bottom line is that, under ordinary conditions, we suspect humans and simple machines would be distinguishable within a reasonable timeframe. (We explain why in detail below.) Yet if/when that is no longer the case, we might need to ask whether an important line has been crossed, whether an essential human capability has been diminished or lost, and, if so, what caused it. The Google Morals thought experiment discussed in the textbox below suggests how we could end up crossing this line.

Moral thinking is an important human capability. Throughout our lives, we are confronted with moral judgments that affect ourselves and others. From an early age and with the help of others, we learn to reflect on what is right and wrong, on our values. We learn about what to do when confronted with a moral dilemma. We learn rules of thumb and absolutes and when we ought to stop and think and when we ought to act immediately. And we practice these rules.

When facing a genuine moral dilemma, it can be hard to know what to do. If we look to moral philosophy for guidance, we can easily become overwhelmed. Rival theories can each provide plausible and internally consistent solutions. That's why interminable debates exist.

Are moral dilemmas problems comprehensible in the language of computation? Is there a smart tech solution? Is there an app for that? Consider philosopher Robert Howell's example of "Google Morals."[58] Howell isn't a cyber utopian, and so he doesn't claim an actual technology will solve this problem any time soon, if ever. Moral wisdom can't be programmed. Despite this, Howell aims to drill down into fundamental normative questions, asking us to imagine a fictional app called Google Morals:

> When faced with a moral quandary or deep ethical question we can type a query and the answer comes forthwith. Next time I am weighing the value of a tasty steak against the disvalue of animal suffering, I'll know what to do. Never again will I be paralyzed by the prospect of pushing that fat man onto the trolley tracks to prevent five innocents from being killed. I'll just Google it.[59]

Following Howell, let's imagine Google Morals is infallible, always truthful, and 100 percent hacker-proof. Friends can't tamper with it to pull a prank. Rivals can't adjust it to gain competitive advantage. Advertisers can't tweak it to lull you into buying their products. The government can't even infiltrate it to brainwash you. Under these conditions, Google Morals is as trustworthy as an omniscient and omnibenevolent God.

Howell contends that Google Morals isn't as great as it seems, and can be morally corrosive. He offers several arguments, mostly concerning virtue, with nothing to do with the technology chipping away at our personal freedom. As far as Howell is concerned, autonomy isn't on the line because users always get to decide whether to use the tool. In his thought experiment, nobody is mandated to use the app, like institutionally forced pharmacology to remedy delusional and dangerous judgment. Moreover, once Google Morals offers its advice, users still get to decide whether to follow it. Sure, Google Morals can tell you that the right thing to do is to order the vegetarian entrée to prevent your action from validating animal suffering. But it can't stop you from smashing the phone with one hand while shoving a cheeseburger into your mouth with the other. Understood this way, autonomy appears to be preserved, if not enhanced. Users always get to make their own choices by deciding how to respond to the technology's advice.

Persuasive as this analysis can appear, several questions remain. What if there's lots of social pressure to use the app? What if using the app repeatedly builds habits that are hard to resist? What if knowing that Google Morals is infallible makes people too frightened to think through moral problems on their own – especially when the stakes are high and their decisions can lead to others being hurt and possibly killed? Howell doesn't deny that these types of scenarios can arise. Nevertheless, he seems to suggest that, since coercion isn't a factor, the buck stops with each individual decision-maker who must decide for herself whether to use the technology. But with the existence of so many mitigating and persuasive factors, does Howell's judgment match your sense of what it means to exercise free will? Or, is he overstating the case? Does it matter who is doing the moral thinking and who is making the ultimate moral judgments? Does our propensity to rely on tools like Google Morals increase with usage? Might our free will atrophy? Would our reliance on the techno-social tool become habitual, like clicking an "I agree" button? Would it then be another example of a subtle yet powerful form of engineered determinism?

Regret as a System 1 Trigger for Reflection and Self-Determination

Suppose we designed a techno-social engineering test that focused on emotions, such as *regret*, that affect well-being and consequently the salience of previously held beliefs or preferences, prompting the exercise of the capability to affirm, deny, or adjust one's will upon reflection. A person may feel regret based on an outcome – say a purchase or other action – and that feeling would raise the *salience* of the components of the person's will that shaped his or her decision and led to the outcome. The components may include beliefs, preferences, desires, and/or intentions. The increased salience may lead the person to reflect upon and affirm, deny, or otherwise adjust those components. For example, if you regret eating a donut, you may reconsider – think more slowly about – your beliefs about the nutritional consequences, the expected sensory satisfaction, and perhaps even the intention to chow down on another one. If you regret casting your vote for a candidate in a specific party based on your beliefs about the party platform, you may reflect and reconsider those beliefs. Such regret doesn't exclusively affect our exercise of free will *ex post* (i.e. after a decision has been made and an outcome decided). What psychologists call "anticipated regret" can lead people to reflect and make deliberative adjustments in their will prior to making decisions. For example, anticipating that you'll regret eating a donut may lead you to stop and think about your current intention to purchase one as well as any beliefs or preferences that shaped that intention. Notice that the System 1 emotion of regret serves as a trigger for System 2 thinking and the exercise of free will.

Let's imagine running a regret-focused techno-social engineering test in a clinical medical setting.[60]

> A paradigmatic decision-making dilemma faced by physicians is whether to observe the patient without ordering a diagnostic test, order a diagnostic test and act according to the results of the test, or administer treatment without ordering a test. Typically, this decision relies on the probability of disease and the relationship between the treatment's harms and benefits. The assessment of the likelihood of disease and the evaluation of treatment's benefits and harms is often done intuitively, but this decision-making process can be formalized under the "threshold model."
>
> Per the threshold model, if the probability of disease is smaller than the testing threshold, the test should be withheld. If the probability of disease is above the treatment threshold, then treatment should be ordered without ordering a diagnostic test. The test should only be ordered if the estimated probability of the disease is between the testing and treatment thresholds.
>
> The threshold model relies on expected utility theory (EUT) and it was formulated almost four decades ago. EUT suggests that when choosing between different strategies, the decision-maker should always select the strategy that leads to the outcome with the highest expected utility. It has been well documented, however, that EUT is routinely violated by decision-makers. These violations are typically attributed to the decision-maker's emotional, experiential or intuitive responses to decision choices that are different from the EUT derived expected utilities.[61]

Medical researchers Athanasios Tsalatsanis and Benjamin Djulbegovic developed a threshold model for clinical decision-making based on a dual-process theory (DPT) of decision-making that considers critical System 1 emotions, such as regret.

For our purposes, what matters is that the authors have identified an important context where persistent divergences between human and automated machine decision-making might be used in a techno-social engineering test. The test would compare outputs from simple machines that are programmed per the EUT model and outputs from clinicians (or patients) who make decisions based on the DPT model.

Running the test in a clinical setting presumably would distinguish humans from machines. If we ran the test and couldn't do so, that would be a credible reason for critically evaluating the techno-social environment that's shaped the human responses. Eliminating human emotion itself could be deemed dehumanizing, but let's leave that aside for now. It also might signify a diminishment in free will, at least in so far as it reflects a lost opportunity to self-determine one's beliefs, preferences, and intentions about a medical test; again, actual and anticipated regret seem to trigger reflection.

Now, you might be wondering what type of techno-social environment could engineer humans to be incapable of regret. Without entering debates about the pros and cons of formalized medical systems, it's worth emphasizing two possibilities:

- Hospitals and insurance companies sometimes insist upon outsourcing clinical decision-making about diagnostic testing to an algorithmic, data-driven system programmed according to the EUT model.
- Sometimes clinicians with scarce resources (e.g. time, emotional capital, etc.) rely on scripts that gradually conform to the EUT model.

The bottom line is that medical systems are under similar Taylorist pressures as other workplaces, and the promise and pressures of efficient technical solutions shape the environment and those within it. We don't know if it's better or worse; we are simply enabling a more complete evaluation. We have identified some potential costs to consider, but readily concede that they should be evaluated in light of potential benefits. Some would argue that medical systems should allocate resources and make decisions per the EUT model precisely to maximize social utility and avoid regret-based distortions. Others would denounce this position as technocratic.[62] We agree that complex debates surround the normative question of when to keep humans in the loop of medical decision-making.

We have focused on regret and the medical context, but our earlier discussion of techno-social engineering creep suggests that the argument extends both to other emotions (such as grief) that might affect the salience of existing components of one's will and to other contexts subject to similar pressures. The normative evaluation would vary considerably.

Reflecting on and Determining Our Own Beliefs

Suppose we instead focus on an agent's situated capability to engage in reflective self-determination about her *beliefs*. By definition, simple machines are fully determined by their programming. Hence, the observational test we'd like to run would seek to identify whether human agents' beliefs are programmed similarly in particular engineered environments. We'd want to examine whether humans situated within certain techno-social environments retain the capability to determine their own beliefs: to affirm, deny, or adjust one's beliefs in light of experience, evidence, and reflection, if and when such reflection is salient. As the previous section highlighted, exercising this capability appears to be contingent upon a range of factors, such as System 1 processes priming System 2 processes, the way we perceive and interpret evidence, and how our experiences possibly trigger reflection by making certain beliefs more or less salient.

Although we've been advocating for the methodological virtues of a techno-social engineering test through the book, we recognize that in this specific case they might not be needed. Extensive research in media studies, advertising, psychology, and other fields already focuses on these issues. There's also propaganda studies, studies of indoctrination in military and religious settings, search engine manipulation studies, studies of presidential elections and the false stories disseminated on social media, filter bubbles studies, and more. With such a wealth of scholarship to select from and possibly even systematize, we leave further exploration of the value and parameters of techno-social engineering tests focused on the aforementioned belief capabilities for future work.

Smart Social Media Environments and Fake News

When Mark Zuckerberg addressed the charge of whether the 2016 Presidential election was unduly influenced by the presence of fake news on Facebook, he admitted that structural issues lie at the heart of the problem: fake news economies financially reward widely consumed lies and technical systems haven't been up to the task of identifying bad reporting. This acknowledgment means that Facebook's efforts to combat fake news are an attempt to solve a problem it helped create.

The extent to which consumers of fake news act stupidly or lazily, as is often alleged, is a debatable matter. What gets left out of these debates, particularly when Zuckerberg weighs in, is the role that Facebook's design plays in orienting how users are disposed to relate to information.

The smart social media environment that has emerged in the past decade – of which Facebook is an important part – encourages people to accept what's presented to them without pausing for reflection or deliberation. Every piece of information is arranged to appear as being of equal weight to every other piece of information: a *New York Times* article followed by a funny dog video shared by a close friend, next to some fake news about the President of the United States, immediately followed by a friend's photographs of a birthday party, and then a distressing, unsourced, and unverified video of an injured child in some Middle East conflict. In the never-ending stream of updates, there's little incentive for users to break the flow, triangulate and fact check with reliable and contrary sources. Actively choosing what might need investigating easily feels like a burdensome endeavor. Think of how high the "transaction costs" are compared with staying the course. It's far easier to passively accept what you see than to deliberate about whether and how to challenge it. People who already believe they have too much to read can be exhausted by the prospect of leaving the platform and consulting even more information. Such inertia is further strengthened by the fact that the information users see on Facebook is curated to fit their interests and often associated with people they trust: friends, family members, and colleagues. Furthermore, Facebook has been designed to incline users to immediately respond quickly to the information they see rather than slowly pondering how to reply: "Like" and related buttons have affordances and their presence makes it tempting to view simple bodily gestures between fingers and cursors as adequate ways to participate in conversations.

Engineered habituation determines motivation and shapes beliefs. That's why, ironically, we have more information at our disposal than ever before but are often paralyzed into passive complacency.[63]

Reflecting on and Determining our Intentions to Act

Suppose we designed a techno-social engineering test that focused on an agent's situated capability to engage in reflective self-determination about her *intentions*. This would take us into the realm of *autonomy*. Again, simple machines don't determine their own intentions. They're on a short leash and act according to their programmer's intentions. Human beings, by contrast, have evolved the capability for long-leash thinking and planning via System 2 of our brains. Rational deliberation gives us the freedom to set goals and plans for ourselves.[64] *How, then, could we fashion a techno-social engineering test that focuses on this capability?*

One seemingly simple approach would be to ask questions that directly focus on an agent's goals and their originating sources. Imagine an observer first asking about the agent's intended career or life plan and then asking questions about how and why those plans were made. Or imagine an observer asking what an agent intended to do after the test was finished and then asking how and why those plans were made. This approach could be expanded to encompass questions in scenarios that require reflection on an agent's intentions and then require modification in light of conflicting preferences or beliefs.

This conceptually useful approach might be difficult to implement in an actual techno-social engineering test. Human beings who are incapable of engaging in reflective self-determination about their intentions might be able to state intentions or plans, but they would be unable to explain how they arrived at them. If you try this yourself, you will soon realize that it can be quite difficult to pinpoint the source of one's intentions and the processes may devolve into that annoying game parents of young children know quite well where every answer is followed with a question – *why?* Despite the limits of introspection, this approach might be usefully employed as a techno-social engineering test rather than an attempt to divine the ultimate source of human intentions. If the inability to reflect and reason about one's intentions is observable a yellow flag would be raised that justifies further evaluation.

Then again, perhaps a better approach would be to follow a similar procedure as outlined above for moral decision-making, but modify it to focus explicitly on the agent's intentions to act in the face of a moral dilemma. Suppose, for example, the observer posed a question concerning whether to commit adultery with the boss's spouse. The observer would describe a basic word problem and then provide a numeric estimate of the benefits and costs. The agent must decide whether to act. The observer describes the possible action in terms that can be interpreted in both moral and transactional terms. The moral terms would be reflected in the language and would largely rely on common sense. The transactional terms would be reflected in the quantitative values, which would frame the trade-off solely in terms of the immediate pay-offs – hedonic pleasure or gratification minus transaction costs – and, by design, in a manner that favored action. Thus, the split-framing would leave implicit any longer-term consequences associated with getting caught by the boss.

An agent who declined to act (commit adultery) presumably would be a human being capable of one or more of the following: (i) moral thinking that prioritized an end other than the utilitarian pay-off; (ii) common-sense recognition of the moral dilemma; and (iii) planning in a manner that accounted for the unstated long-term consequences. But what about an agent who chose to act? How would we interpret such evidence? At first cut, the agent could be a machine capable only of performing the utilitarian calculus according to its programming or a human being who was incapable of one of the three capacities noted above. The observer would need to pose a series of questions that had the same structure yet varied underlying facts, trade-offs, and moral concerns. Variations on the adultery scenario itself could adjust the trade-offs, for example by including the longer-term consequences in the transactional terms. However, it would be necessary for the observer to utilize different scenarios.

For example, the adultery scenario might be followed by, for example, a Good-Samaritan-style problem. Moral philosopher Peter Singer famously examines one such problem involving a child drowning in a puddle.[65] We would alter his scenario to obtain the structure we outlined for the adultery scenario, as follows. The agent must decide whether to rescue a very heavy mass murderer who is drowning in the deep end of a large swimming pool. Again, the narrative framing would frame the dilemma in a slightly different manner than the numeric framing. The utilitarian trade-off could be framed explicitly in terms of time spent, effort exerted, and opportunity costs versus the benefits of a life saved; those variables could be quantified and given magnitudes that make action unambiguously instrumentally rational. The hypothetical presents an *obvious but unstated risk* of harm to the agent that decided to rescue the drowning person (because of the person's weight), and it also presents a reason why some people might discount the stated benefits of a rescue (because the person is a mass murderer).

By design, a simple machine programmed to be instrumentally rational (in a rather narrow sense[66]) would not be capable of taking these unstated factors into account, but a human being would. Again, the narrative framing would challenge human beings to recognize the implicit moral dilemma and reflect upon and determine their intentions to act in light of the entire range of factors. A series of questions like this might provide a reasonable basis for distinguishing humans from simple machines because of their capability to self-determine their intentions. A human being who passed this test because he or she repeatedly evaluated the questions from a narrow, instrumentally rational perspective would appear machine-like and thus deserve further attention. We should note that according to some philosophers achieving moral consistency as a utilitarian might explain this outcome. Thus, at step two of the techno-social engineering test, we would need to know whether the person's decisions were engineered by others or were ultimately their own, that is, whether the person freely chose the commitments and intentions upon which his or her decisions were based.

The problem of determining what to make of a person's unwavering allegiance to a moral system or code is brought to stark relief in psychologist Philip Zimbardo's memoir of the infamous Stanford Prison Experiment that he ran in 1971. In that experiment, students who pretended to be prisoner guards took their roles to such extremes that Zimbardo had to cut it short. Many of the guards became sadistically cruel.

In Zimbardo's analysis, the horrific student behavior partially was caused by what he calls the "system" – that is, the environmental features that made it too easy for the guards to violate standard moral norms and possibly even inclined them to behave like monsters. While the system allegedly was powerful enough to transform good kids into bad ones, it never became so overwhelming as to reach the agency-obliterating standard of engineered determinism. We know this because of how a student named Tom conducted himself throughout the ordeal.

Tom – Prisoner 2093 in the experiment – was given the nickname Sarge because of his seemingly unwavering propensity to follow every order given to him as if he were a low-level grunt in the army. At one point, Tom responded to the guards' demand that he do push-ups by asking if he had permission to do more than was required.

Things took a surprising turn when a guard told Tom to call another prisoner a "pussy" or "bastard." Tom refused to comply and continued to resist when the order was repeated. Tom went so far as to say that he'd rather have his bed removed from his cell than call anyone else a dehumanizing term. Apparently before the experiment began Tom made a commitment to himself about how he would treat others no matter what difficulties emerged. Many would find his rigid allegiance to the self-imposed code a sign of his virtuous character.

A: What type of techno-social engineering would lead a human being to be machine-like with respect to saving a drowning mass murderer?

B: Lifeguard training. Lifeguards might save a life without considering the risk to themselves or the worth of the person drowning.

A: So, lifeguard training is a dehumanizing script?

B: No, not necessarily. Keep in mind that the techno-social engineering test is only step one. If at step two we learn that the person is a lifeguard, then we have a reason to believe they're not subject to techno-social engineering that inhibits their autonomy. It's analogous to the Shakespeare aficionado who was mistakenly identified as a machine during one of the Loebner competitions.

A. Yes, I see. But isn't the lifeguard training in fact scripting the lifeguard's decision-making in a manner that interferes with her capacity to reflect upon and determine her intentions? Isn't that exactly what the training is intended to do?

B: Fair point. And that is why we'd need to rely on more than just one problem.

The electronic contracting example serves as a useful illustration. When we discussed it we moved beyond traditional concerns about exploitation through such features as duress and undue influence and explained the problem of techno-social engineering of humans within the electronic contracting environment. The main question we asked is *when clicking "I agree," do we act pursuant to our own intentions?* In one sense, the answer is yes. We intend to get to the content or service and the click-to-contract architecture is simply a hurdle to cross. Yet, in another sense, it isn't so clear that we intend to manifest assent to the terms of the contract itself. Instead, we end up acting pursuant to the intentions of the website's creators when we bind ourselves contractually by clicking.

It can be hard to know when we're programmed to feel like we're in control at the very moment we're giving it away, or when control is being taken from us. Classic Marxist studies called this type of problem a matter of "false consciousness." False consciousness has been said to occur when ideological, material, and institutional forces hijack our self-understanding and mislead us into mistaking a distorted sense of a situation for a true one and an inaccurately twisted sense of who we are for a genuine sense of self. Per the logic of this analysis, such manipulation is exploitation.

We're sympathetic to this way of thinking as it makes analysis of techno-social engineering a form of socially relevant political inquiry. However, we're also wary of how a commitment to seeing the world through the lens of bad actors imposing false consciousness upon us all too easily can incline analysts to over-simplify complex situations and obscure the active role we sometimes play in the process, for example, by convincing ourselves that tough decisions leave us with no room whatsoever to go against the metaphorical flow. One of our main goals in this book has to been to add nuance to debate over techno-social engineering and show – as we announced from the very start – that the "us vs. them" mentality risks imputing too much power to others and too little to ourselves.

CHAPTER 13

To What End?

Introduction

Life is a role-playing game and the Earth is our experience machine. For better or worse, humans haven't optimized the planet to give us all the experiences we desire. The classic Rolling Stones song still rings true. "You can't always get what you want." But that can change. Our roles and desires can be engineered, more than we appreciate.

Let's unpack the gaming metaphor. Popular role-playing games allow players to create their own characters. In Dungeons and Dragons, players roll dice and assign points to different *attributes*, such as Strength, Intelligence, Wisdom, Dexterity, Constitution, and Charisma. They also select their *race*. If players want to stick with what they know, they can remain Human. Or, if they're feeling more adventurous, they can try being an Elf or Dwarf. That's not all. Players also get to choose their *alignment*, such as Good, Neutral, or Evil. And they decide on a *class*. Fighters, Clerics, Mages, and Thieves are all popular options.

Many video games follow similar procedures. Sometimes, players are given the option of using a pre-generated character that allocates a fixed number of points to a variety of attributes. Sometimes, they can create their own with a character generation screen. In this case, players choose how to spread points among the attributes. In Dungeons and Dragons and similar video games, players can improve their attributes, usually by performing tasks and gaining experience in the game. The built environment – the rules, story lines, maps, algorithms, and so much more – constrains and thus shapes players' lives.

This exact set-up arises in conversations about how to build androids that convincingly look and act like humans. You just can't build something that simulates something else unless you have a clear sense of what, exactly, you're trying to emulate. As an example, take the 2016 remake of the science fiction thriller "Westworld" (on HBO). It's set in a futuristic theme park where human visitors are called "guests" and get to live out their heroic, violent, and sexual fantasies by interacting with robot doppelgängers of old West archetypes (called "hosts"). In one of the episodes, "Trompe L'Oeil," a self-aware robot named Maeve demands an upgrade. To illustrate the engineering possibilities that she can select, the android is shown a list of human attributes that were programmed into "her" code. Each one corresponds to a skill that's numerically represented to illustrate its level of prowess.

These fictional narratives tell us something important about how we see and more importantly how we imagine ourselves as human beings. Humanity is represented as a collection of basic characteristics that each person starts with. You might believe a divine spark pre-generates your "character." Or you might believe that evolutionary biology plays this role. You could believe both of these things. Or something else altogether. Your cultural background, your religious affiliation (or lack thereof), your political orientation, and all the other features that make you who you are, influence which characteristics you value. You might believe that some characteristics are more essential than others. If given the opportunity, perhaps you'd allocate more "points" to autonomy than sociality, or maybe it would be the other way around.

Regardless of your perspective on how human "characters" are generated and the relative weight of various characteristics, the gaming analogy usefully emphasizes the importance of identifying various basic characteristics and recognizing how the built environment shapes them. Critically, we have opportunities to shape ourselves; we make such opportunities available through the worlds we build.

We've emphasized the need to pay attention to how techno-social engineering can impact important aspects of our humanity. We examined some core capabilities in depth, including thinking, sociality, and free will. We lightly touched upon others, such as how our sensory capabilities mediate how we look at and relate to others as well as the physical environment. In our discussion of transformative tools, we highlighted imagination, language, and the collective construction of shared ideals, institutions, and reality.

We didn't intend for this book to identify everything important about being human. Our contribution is providing a framework for identifying and evaluating techno-social engineering of core capabilities that distinguish humans from simple machines.[1]

In this chapter, we deepen the framework by taking a more explicitly normative stance on the stakes of twenty-first-century techno-social engineering. Normative issues have come up in every chapter. We've continually raised ethical, political, and social questions in our discussions of ethics, cost-benefit analyses, inevitable trade-offs, and human capabilities. But so far, we've only endorsed a few prescriptions.

Take the trolley car and traffic management hypotheticals for smart transportation systems. We presented these thought experiments as intuition pumps for thinking critically about normative issues. We stressed the importance of recognizing that system designers and operators will make critical decisions. Somehow, someone will embed values and predictable social outcomes into widely used infrastructure. Society cannot ignore these issues. Ultimately, they might need to be addressed in political and regulatory forums.

Despite identifying why normative issues inevitably arise, we haven't offered advice for designing the best type of smart transportation system. Yes, we highlighted why deviations from first-come, first-served policies ring alarm bells. But we didn't defend a specific system to establish which concerns matter most. In our view, there often isn't a single correct choice, even though one must be made and responsibility needs to be taken for making it. What's best depends upon what value system is selected – what moral theory of the good, the good life, or the good society applies. And that is, itself, a difficult choice to make. Much like the choice to commit to the principles of justice reflected in the Declaration of Independence rather than Hammurabi's Code, choosing a value system for one's life and for society is a matter of human imagination, social construction, deliberation, and, not surprisingly, conflict.

Not everyone looks at values this way. Some strongly believe that their specific value system is objectively superior to everyone else's.[2] That's okay. The framework we've provided can be integrated into diverse value systems. Moreover, in an interdependent social world, people who are committed to contestable value systems still need to figure out how to deal with others who aren't like-minded.

To grapple with the normative implications of twenty-first-century techno-social engineering of humans, we must ask the following questions:

- *Who are we?*
- *What sort of people do we aspire to be?*[3]
- *What values and capabilities do we possess and commit ourselves to sustain?*
- *What sort of society do we want to build and sustain?*
- *What obligations do we owe to past, present, and future generations? And how should such obligations shape the technological and social institutions we build and sustain?*

These questions are constitutional because they are the most fundamental, intergenerational questions that can be asked about what unifies a people, a community, a culture, a society, and even a civilization. We can't give definitive answers. And that's also okay. Each question is hotly contested because no one can truly give a definitive answer for everyone. People will have different, reasonably justified, and morally defensible answers to these fundamental questions. Collectively, groups organize their affairs and live their lives according to different sets of responses.

To advance the discussion of these fundamental questions, we revisit the metaphors from the opening of the book. First, we explain why humanity's techno-social dilemma is, in fact, a dilemma rather than the utopian heaven that smart technology boosters promise. Now, we explicitly and thoroughly argue that the shared resource that's at risk of deterioration, and possibly depletion, is nothing less than humanity itself. A world where engineered determinism governs is a world where fully predictable and programmable people perform rather than live their lives. Such a world would be tragic. People living there could be described as human and still would qualify as *homo sapiens*. But, in our view, they would have a thin normative status as human beings because much of what matters about being human would be lost. To help explain why, we turn again to the experience machine and Experience Machine n.o thought experiments.

Humanity Lost: Pixar Style

Countless science fiction stories depict humanity lost, often evoking the famous quote from the eighteenth century philosopher Jean-Jacques Rousseau: "Man is born free, but everywhere he is in chains."[4]

In one of our favorite movies, Pixar's *Wall-E*, the humans occupy a spacecraft and are so dependent on technology that they arguably lose much of what matters about being human. The passengers on the spacecraft never have any real human interaction. Their only contact is with the screen in front of them on the lounge chair that they sleep in, eat in, and presumably defecate in (though Pixar spares us that detail). Whether the engineered environment of the *Wall-E* spacecraft is dehumanizing depends on one's conception of humanity and what matters about being human.

Though a *Wall-E* world may seem quite remote, you can find aspects of it creeping into contemporary techno-social environments. Recently, one of us had a Wall-Esque experience at an airport. While waiting for an international flight to board, I decided to stop at the airport bar and have a drink. In the past, I would've chatted with other patrons about their travel plans, politics, or sports, and, usually, the bartender and waiter would've joined the conversation. But this time, something was very different. Everyone sitting at the bar and the tables in the restaurant stared at 8×12-inch, flat screen devices mounted on the bar and tables. They tapped and swiped to place orders, rather than consulting a menu or conversing with another human being. They checked the news, watched videos, and played games on the screens. When I sat down, no one noticed. No one said anything. I looked at the person sitting to my left, ready to smile and say hello, but he stared ahead, eyes glued to the screen. I turned to my right and received the same feedback. So, I looked for the bartender, and eventually one came around. He tended the bar by making and delivering the drinks that customers ordered on the devices. At first, he ignored me. I hadn't placed an order. But when he delivered a drink to the woman on my right, I caught his attention as I leaned into view. He asked if I needed help with the menu app. I sighed and asked if I could just have whatever stout he had on tap. He said I could, so long as I ordered it on the app. I did. When he delivered my drink, I struck up a conversation. When he joined, I was relieved. Despite the environment engineered to maximize productivity, minimize costs, and perhaps incidentally minimize social interactions, we're not yet fully immersed in a *Wall-E* world.

Revisiting Humanity's Techno-Social Dilemma

Our description of humanity's techno-social dilemma implies that humanity is a shared resource and our humanity can be lost.[5] Many have said that humanity can be taken away, for example, through slavery as well as its authoritarian political analogues, like totalitarianism. Psychologists also label certain practices, such as confining people to pointless tasks and subjecting them to deindividuation, dehumanizing.[6] Humanity can be lost in increments, partial deprivations, or deteriorations.[7] We need to better understand our humanity if we are to preserve, protect, and sustain it for ourselves and future generations.

Others, however, challenge the notion that one's humanity can ever be lost or taken away. They argue that one's humanity persists even when it is not acknowledged or respected. The slave is and always will be human, and thus her humanity cannot be taken away. What those who support slavery do is fail to acknowledge and respect her humanity. While this is a reasonable perspective,[8] we don't adopt it because the perspective doesn't do a good enough job distinguishing (i) being human from (ii) having access to, possessing, and sharing in humanity. To elaborate, we'll say more about different conceptions of being human (descriptive) and what matters about being human (normative).

> **Kantian Rule on Human Dignity:** **All human beings are worthy of respect and deserve to never be treated exclusively as a means to an end**
>
> We are committed to what, over time, has come to be known as the Kantian rule on human dignity. Some might argue that our suggestion that slavery deprives the slave of her humanity means that the slave is no longer a human being and consequently no longer worthy of respect. Similarly, they might argue that since a newborn baby lacks various capabilities that we identify as potentially essential components of humanity, the baby would not be a full-fledged human being worthy of respect. These arguments fundamentally misconstrue our approach. The slave and the newborn are and always will be human beings worthy of respect. The Kantian rule applies universally to all human beings, regardless of whether they have access to, possess, and/or share fully in the blessings of humanity.
>
> The eighteenth-century philosopher Immanuel Kant insisted that this rule is a universal truth, a categorical imperative dictated by an inescapable moral logic. We maintain that the rule is the product of human imagination and collective recognition, just like Hammurabi's Code and the Declaration of Independence. The Universal Declaration of Human Rights enshrines the rule, recognizing "the inherent dignity and . . . the equal and inalienable rights of all members of the human family [as] the foundation of freedom, justice and peace in the world."[9] As many have noted, the Declaration reflects an incredible cross-cultural and intergenerational commitment to human dignity.

It's easy to believe that the meaning of "humanity" is simple, intuitive, and unproblematic. You know it when you see it. At least, it seems that way when we look in the mirror or talk to our children. We are human, and so humanity must be what we are and those who are like us are. Unfortunately, this common-sense view lacks rigor and lulls us into believing that what matters about being human – what's special and important and worth protecting and cherishing – is whatever we happen to be in the present context. (What is = what ought to be.) Our humanity is taken as a given, stable and safe, *as if* it's a persistent and seemingly inevitable and natural state of affairs. Proponents of this view risk being profoundly *ignorant* about history. It obscures what the present generation has inherited from past generations. It underplays incredible cultural variations in the present generation. It also turns a blind eye to how our actions in the present affect future generations. And, frankly, it allows a *lack of imagination* about possible futures for humanity and the worlds we're building.

Some would say that what it means to be human can be described biologically in terms of what differentiates us from other species. On this view, we identify the distinguishable, evolved characteristics and capabilities of *homo sapiens*, the species of humans that outlasted the rest.[10] For example, in contrast with all other known species, only *homo sapiens* evolved the complex cognitive and social capabilities needed for widely shared language, fiction (e.g. myth, imagined realities), and social institutions (e.g. trust and rules) that scale beyond small close-knit groups (~n=150).[11] These basic capabilities and social infrastructure enabled humans to conquer the Earth and reconstruct the environment within which we evolve.

The descriptive, biological approach has the advantage of being scientific and revealing a continuum and set of functions that relate humans with other species as well as our natural environment. This approach has its limits, however. Biology doesn't explain everything about humanity. For example, biology can't account for the complex and nuanced ways we relate to and evolve within our reconstructed built environment. Biology also doesn't fully explain the tools we choose to build and use, much less whether, how, why, or when we should engineer ourselves through our techno-social tools. To more fully understand what matters about being human, how we engineer ourselves and future generations, and how to conceptualize humanity as a shared resource, we need to move beyond evolutionary biology.

After all, we may have evolved certain capabilities that enable survival and our rise to the top of the food chain.[12] However, we don't necessarily value all those capabilities as central expressions of who we are. Precisely because we have evolved to the point where we can shape ourselves and our society, several philosophical questions have arisen. *How should we exercise such power? What about us should we sustain and cultivate? What should we let go? Who should we aspire to be? How should we engineer ourselves? What type of society should we build and sustain?*

Crucially, human beings can contemplate and act upon such questions only because of the various capabilities we've gained through evolution *and* practiced, honed, developed, and sustained collectively. Several political questions accompany the philosophical ones. *Who decides? Who should exercise such power?*

Per our approach, (1) what meaningfully distinguishes *homo sapiens* from all other species is our capability to imagine, conceptualize, and engineer ourselves and our environment; and, (2) *what matters about being human* is how we exercise such power over generations to collectively produce, cultivate, and sustain shared normative conceptions of humanity.[13]

Humanity can thus be understood as a *set of ideals* about who we are and aspire to be. These ideals are valuable, intangible resources, particularly when shared, acted upon, and reflected in our most sacred institutions as shared commitments. Ultimately, we might say that humanity as both a normative concept and as a collectively produced and shared resource (or set of resources) stems from the answers we give to the fundamental questions we posed earlier.

We – as societies, as communities, as generations, as families, as individuals – answer these constitutional questions directly and indirectly through our actions and the cultures, institutions, infrastructures, and environments we build and sustain.

In a similar vein, law professor John Breen suggests that culture should be understood as a society's answer to a series of "fundamental questions" about what it values. He contends:

> A culture ... constitutes the response that a given people have to these fundamental questions, a response that is constantly being revised and worked out over time. It is expressed not only through the customs and traditions of a people, but through their language, history, art, commerce and politics. Indeed, "[a]ll human activity takes place within a culture and interacts with culture." At the same time, a given culture reveals its deepest identity in the position it takes "toward the fundamental events of life, such as birth, love, work and death," as well as "the mystery of God." Thus, "[d]ifferent cultures are basically different ways of facing the question of the meaning of personal existence."
>
> As such, every culture is, in essence, a normative and didactic enterprise. It indicates what is desirable and permissible within a given society. It instructs both the observer and the participant as to how they ought to act. Indeed ... as the etymology of the word confirms, at the heart of every "culture" is a "cult" in the sense of religious devotion. That is, a culture is a societal answer to the question of value. Every culture renders a whole series of judgments as to what is truly important in life.[14]

Humanity and culture are thus inexorably intertwined.[15]

Suppose we describe *states of human affairs* as the sum of who we currently are as a group, how we see ourselves, and who we want to be.[16] This description can include a set of characteristics and capabilities,[17] some of which we possess and some of which we aspire to possess. People with different normative conceptions (or value systems) might disagree about what characteristics and capabilities ought to be in the set, how to prioritize them, and how we sustain them through social institutions.[18] Such disagreement and diversity produce and are products of different cultures.

Despite such disagreement and diversity, there are some widely shared core ideals, for example, as reflected in the Universal Declaration on Human Rights.[19] These multinational, macro-level normative commitments answer some of the most fundamental constitutional questions about who we are and aspire to be collectively. International human rights laws and institutions create a global community committed to cross-cultural standards and moral floors.[20] These and other political processes enable but do not guarantee moral progress over time and across generations and cultures.[21]

Ideals don't become permanent, true, or worth preserving just because lots of people endorse them. They may change and be supplemented with other ideals that vary by culture, as the history of slavery taught us.[22] But across cultures and generations, human beings have exercised our capabilities to conceptualize and engineer ourselves and our environment, to build and sustain a collective heritage, which we characterize as nothing less than humanity itself.

Preserving the "fundamental blessings" of humanity is the most important constitutional commitment that unites cultures across generations.[23] In his Lyceum Address of 1838, Abraham Lincoln recognized that the "fundamental blessings" passed on from generation to generation extend beyond the blessings of the Earth to include the blessings of society – the communal heritage of law, political institutions, and fundamental rights of liberty and equality.[24] Lincoln reminded his generation, as his words ought to remind us today, that the fundamental resources upon which any society depends include the blessings bestowed upon any present generation by sacrifices of its ancestors. Lincoln's speech, like the Gettysburg Address,[25] offers a powerful vision of a transgenerational social contract firmly rooted in equity. Each generation inherits a wealth of natural and communal resources. In return for this boon, it's obligated to transmit these resources "to the latest generation that fate shall permit the world to know."[26] This duty to transmit a legacy to the future reverberates in many cultures. Lincoln's speech implicitly harkens back to the Athenian Ephebic Oath by which men of ancient Athens swore to "transmit my fatherland not diminished [b]ut greater and better than before."[27] The intergenerational moral obligation is rooted in a more traditional conception of equity, akin to the repudiation of unjust enrichment. The present generation is morally bound to perform its duty to transmit because its own welfare and humanity has been enriched by access to and use of the resources passed on to it. To accept the benefits without satisfying the attendant duty would constitute enrichment at the expense of future generations.[28]

Throughout this book, we've claimed that humanity, conceived of normatively as a shared set of ideals reflected in us and our built world of imagined realities, institutions, infrastructures, and environments, is at risk of deterioration by pervasive techno-social engineering. We've focused on specific forms of techno-social engineering that affect the basic capabilities that enable us to ask and participate in answering fundamental questions about who we are and aspire to be, individually and collectively. Thus, we considered thinking capacities, the ability to socialize and relate to each other, free will, autonomy, and agency. Some may disagree with our choices of capabilities to examine. They may choose to examine others, as we intend to do in future work. But the bottom line is that across cultures and generations, humans have engineered themselves and their built environments to sustain these and other core capabilities. In our view, they are part of our shared heritage, our humanity. And again, they are at risk of being whittled away through rampant techno-social engineering of the sorts we've described extensively in earlier chapters.

Early in the book, we introduced humanity's techno-social dilemma and explained how it might occur. We considered the idea of a slippery-sloped path, various creep phenomena, and the many different forces and logics that may drive us down this path. Taylorism extended, fetishized computational power, and the allure of ever more powerful intelligent control systems promise tremendous gains in efficiency and productivity along with the convenience and happiness of optimized lives.

Here we must ask: *To What End?*

Frog Soup

If you're familiar with the story of frog soup, then you could probably smell it coming.[29] Do you know how to make frog soup? If you begin with a live frog, you cannot just drop it into a pot of boiling water because it will jump out. You need to place the frog in a kettle of room temperature water and increase the temperature slowly enough that the frog doesn't notice it's being cooked. "As the water gradually heats up, the frog will sink into a tranquil stupor, exactly like one of us in a hot bath, and before long, with a smile on its face, it will unresistingly allow itself to be boiled to death."[30] *Cheap engineered bliss.*

The frog soup story often is used as a parable to comment on the difficulties humans face when dealing with gradual environmental changes that, over time, can have drastic, irreversible consequences. Global warming is a paradigmatic example. Like all metaphors, however, frog soup only can represent part of a complex phenomenon. The parable doesn't capture all the reasons that climate change or techno-social engineering of humans are thorny dilemmas.

When commentators use frog soup as an environmental parable, they're typically suggesting that humans are so focused on the present – so short-sighted – that they're oblivious to the drastic consequences. This, however, begs the question of why we find it so hard to keep the big picture in mind. In the case of the boiling frog parable, the answer is clear. The chef creates conditions that prevent the frog from noticing that its life is in danger. This specific framing device means that we – the people who are pondering the metaphor – have no reason to ask whether the frog is inherently compla-cent or disinclined to accept the truth. The narrative only lets us think about the frog's behavior under conditions of engineered determinism.

In the context of climate change, the best analogy to the chef's control over the environment is the merchants of doubt.[31] These special interest groups work hard to convince the public that climate change is a hoax or conspiracy. These groups are powerful. Yet they're only part of the climate change story. Climate change also is a problem because the human mind tends to discount the future as well as having a proclivity to feel powerless when confronted by large-scale difficulties. Climate change also causes controversy because some people are committed to CO_2-intensive indus-tries (like coal) and disinclined to believe that their jobs are harming the planet. And, let's face it, part of the reason climate change is so hard to stop is because developed nations are addicted to consumerism – to the ability to purchase cheap goods with short shelf-lives. These are just a few of many confounding factors.

In short, climate change is a multi-faceted problem. It's about what others do to us as well as what we do to ourselves and future generations. Techno-social engineering of humans is no different and that's why we've been using humanity's techno-social dilemma – also an environmental metaphor – as one of our guiding concepts. Big tech companies are partially responsible for our current situation. But no matter how much these companies engineer our world and us in pursuit of profits and power, we aren't rendered blameless. We, too, play a pivotal role in perpetuating techno-social engineering creep. We use platforms like Facebook and tether ourselves and our children to smart devices. Neither techno-social engineering of machine-like humans nor global climate change is reducible to a threat that a master planner (chef) brings about. The threats are the result of collective action, and mitigating the threats correspondingly requires collective action.

Since the future remains open, we should be skeptical about the fatalism of the frog soup metaphor. The frog is on a path to inevitable death the second that it's placed into the manipulative environment.[32] We are not frogs. We still have the potential to avoid catastrophe.

To do so, we must take seriously the problem of short-sighted incrementalism, which the boiling frog parable effectively highlights. Gradual change often is difficult to recognize, and, even when noticed, each incremental step (change in temperature) may seem desirable *in the moment*. The benefits seem to exceed the costs, particularly if measured by moment-by-moment felt experience. Systemic and longer-term effects are too often heavily discounted or simply ignored.

The end-state – *engineered cheap bliss* – is scary for many of us, but not for everyone. We'll revisit Nozick's experience machine and the Experience Machine n.o shortly to examine divergence of opinions about the end-states and the corresponding normative implications.

In all likelihood, none of us will ever reach the end-state. What if it is too far off in the future for any of us in the present generation to worry? Does that alleviate us of the burden of caring? For two distinct reasons, the answer is no. First, we are building the world for the future. We're morally obliged to future generations to consider the normative implications of the world we're building. Second, there are many intermediate effects on us that deserve our attention. Simply put, we have a lot to lose along the way, even if we don't become fully engineered machines.

Revisiting Nozick's Thought Experiment and Life on the Experience Machine

We opened the Introduction with the experience machine thought experiment. To move things along, we didn't stop to ask you an important question. So, here goes. *If you were presented with the opportunity, would you choose to plug into the experience machine?*

Recall that Nozick's scenario offers people a choice to plug into a virtual reality machine that guaranteed a "lifetime of bliss."[33] Upon entering the experience machine, there's no turning back. A bit of programmed memory loss occurs and you immediately forget that you've entered a simulated world and left *terra firma* and everyone you know behind. As far as you're concerned, everything and everyone appears normal in the experience machine and you don't have any reason to question the basis of your new reality. You have no clue that the world you're embedded in and everything that's found in it are designed to behave in choreographed ways that inevitably leave you feeling the maximum amount of aggregate happiness. If you experience any friction in the experience machine, it's only because programmers know that you're the type of person who requires obstacles or delayed satisfaction to feel as happy as possible.

Would you plug in?

We don't claim to know the right answer for you. People have different intuitions. This classic thought experiment prompts imagination and deliberation about one's basic conception of a good life. Is there more to life – or better yet, the good life – than a person's subjective experience of happiness? Or, as Nozick put it, than how one's life feels from the inside?

For hard-core hedonists, the decision is straightforward: Plug in. It guarantees optimal happiness, the highest aggregation of moment-by-moment positive feelings. The movie *The Matrix* toyed with a more reflective version of the thought experiment when a character named Cipher announces that he understands he's living in a simulation but still prefers that world to alternatives where he'd be less happy. "I know this steak doesn't exist. I know when I put it in my mouth the Matrix is telling my brain that it is juicy and delicious. After nine years, you know what I realize? Ignorance is bliss."[34]

Hedonism in a nutshell: Happiness consists of personal feelings of pleasure. Unhappiness consists of personal feelings of displeasure. Evaluating the quality of a person's life entails aggregating the moment-by-moment feelings that the person experiences over the course of her life. A happy life is a good life for the person living it.[35]

Most people would not choose to plug in.[36] And that's because most people are not hard-core hedonists.[37] Of course, happiness matters for most people and is an important component of a life lived well. But many other things matter too, and they are not reducible to or commensurable with happiness. Pursuing pleasure exclusively, as the ultimate end, would lead to a rather shallow life.[38]

Nozick contended that it would be a mistake to plug into the experience machine.[39] His reservations revolved around a core conviction that many people share today: "reality has intrinsic prudential value."[40] No matter how realistic a simulated world feels, it lacks the features of an independent reality conducive to human flourishing. It seems the epitome of a dehumanizing environment. It's a fully engineered reality wherein simulated people lack free will, simulated things bend to our will and desires, history has no weight, interdependence doesn't exist, and even the laws of physics can be broken. In such a programmed world, our actions wouldn't be meaningful. Our accomplishments, including caring for others, would be hollow. Our relationships would be fake, along the lines explored earlier with respect to Android Ash. And at least some of our basic human capabilities would atrophy. Fortunately, we wouldn't realize any of this while living on the machine because we'd be programmed to be oblivious to such concerns. And we'd feel really good.

There's a related concern that plugging in would lead to an inauthentic life determined by others. A life lived on the experience machine would not be one's own. Too much of the life lived and happiness experienced would be determined by the machine, or, to be more precise, the engineers who created the machine. This concern has weight for those who insist that the means matter when evaluating the quality of one's life. On this view, a well-lived life requires some human agency and exercise of free will. By contrast, a fully programmed and determined life on the machine is not a well-lived life, regardless of how much pleasure the machine supplied.

It's important to appreciate that these considerations are perfectly legitimate products of the thought experiment. By forcing someone to choose upfront whether to plug in, the thought experiment prompts deliberation. Some argue that critical resistance to plugging in is rooted in the framing effects of the narrative. For example, status quo bias may lead people to prefer what they currently experience over the unknown life on a machine.[41] Or people can question whether the experience machine will work: *What happens when the power goes out? Will the unplugged be able to take advantage of those who are plugged in?* These arguments are valid, but too easily taken as the final word. Framing effects, cognitive biases, and other related concerns can and should be dealt with by engaging with the thought experiment thoughtfully, rather than simply dismissing it. Behavioral psychology offers excellent grounds for criticizing and improving thought experiments but does not provide answers to the underlying normative questions.[42]

Others, such as economist Richard Layard and philosopher Joseph Mendola, criticize the thought experiment for being "wildly unrealistic" and pumping unfair intuitions with "unfamiliar gadgetry which invokes our fear of the unfamiliar."[43] These criticisms might have had purchase a few decades ago. But they seem wildly exaggerated today. Modern technology and culture make the experience machine scenario reasonably familiar and sufficiently realistic for people to consider. Regardless, these objections to the thought experiment hardly provide a better explanation for people's preferences than the claim that reality has intrinsic prudential value.

Let's say a bit more about reality's intrinsic prudential value. A significant reason why many people would choose not to plug into the experience machine is that they believe in free will and value having it. To plug into the experience machine would be to accept engineered determinism and know, even if only at the moment of deliberation about whether to plug in, that any subsequent experience of free will would be illusory.[44] Many people highly value free will. Arguably, it is one of the fundamental blessings of humanity, collectively cultivated and sustained across generations through the cultures, institutions, infrastructures, and environments we build and sustain.

But what if the promise of optimal happiness on the machine makes the thought experiment too outlandish? The utopian allure might exacerbate the framing effects, or it might trigger doubts, fears, or even guilt.

Suppose we adjust the thought experiment so that life on or off the machine would be the same in terms of aggregate happiness.[45] Suppose a person's life on the experience machine is assumed to be identical to the life they'd live off the machine.[46] If the life Jane experiences on and off the machine is identical from her subjective perspective, hedonists argue Jane would be equally well on and off the machine. Her well-being – the goodness of her life – is the same. And so, they argue, she should be indifferent to choosing one life over the other. She should be willing to flip a coin.

What about you? Would you be willing to flip a coin? Heads would mean you plug in. And tails would mean you do not plug in. Keep in mind that life on and off the machine is guaranteed to be identical.

If you are truly indifferent, you should be willing to flip a coin and accept the outcome either way. Perhaps some people would do so. We suspect most people would not actually be willing to flip a coin.[47] Further, it's hard to imagine that anyone would choose to plug into the experience machine if it promised an identical life. Most people would choose not to plug in. Some might argue that unwillingness to flip a coin should be construed as an indication of irrational biases, whether the status quo bias or some irrational fear that fights the hypothetical. But we think a much better explanation is that they would not be indifferent to the two lives. They would choose to maintain the status quo and for good reason. They value free will, or, at least, the illusion of free will. In other words, they would take a pragmatic approach and wager in favor of free will rather than plug into the experience machine, which would eliminate free will, and, at best, offer an engineered illusion of it. Thus, what people fear about the experience machine is precisely what Nozick highlighted: *the loss of authenticity in a world of engineered determinism.*

Let's flip the scenario around. Suppose you are informed that you're currently plugged into an experience machine and that you've been selected for a one-time opportunity to unplug and experience an authentic life. Unlike Cipher in *The Matrix*, your life unplugged is guaranteed to be identical to the plugged-in life you're currently living.

> *What would you choose if you were given the opportunity to (1) unplug, (2) stay plugged in, or (3) flip a coin such that heads would mean you unplug and tails would mean you stay plugged in?*

It's a little more difficult to predict what people would do, although for somewhat surprising reasons. We don't think many people would choose to flip a coin.[48] Most people are not hard-core hedonists; they wouldn't be indifferent to the two lives (worlds). Initially, one might think people would unplug and choose an authentic life. But most people would not do so.[49] Some have suggested that this demonstrates a cognitive bias infecting the thought experiment. A better explanation, in our view, is that in the reality we know and experience, most people would take a pragmatic approach and wager in favor of free will, meaning their existing belief in free will. In a sense, this is a reaction that fights the hypothetical. But, importantly, it only fights the hypothetical claim about our reality being fully engineered and determined. Absent a high level of proof that our current reality is fully determined (naturally or by engineering), wagering in favor of free will remains the best strategy.[50]

The bottom line is that the experience machine thought experiment usefully highlights competing value systems and prompts deliberation about what matters to you about your life. Hard-core hedonists would choose to plug in; most other folks would not. There are many reasons people might choose not to plug in. But an important reason is that a programmed world governed by engineered determinism is not conducive to human flourishing. At the most basic level, life on the experience machine doesn't jibe with how most people answer any of the basic constitutional questions. We don't see ourselves, our lives, or our reality as fully programmed or determined, even though we understand that much of what we do and who we are is the product of various factors outside our control. Nor do we aspire to such a fate.

Do we aspire to build such a world for our children and future generations? Notably, this is a moral question outside the scope of Nozick's thought experiment. To see why, consider the importance of the cord and plug. The decision about whether to plug into the experience machine served a few purposes.

- It kept the thought experiment focused on an individual decision about an individual life.
- It prompted deliberation by an individual about that individual's conception of a good life for that individual, which is often referred to as the individual's well-being or welfare.
- It eliminated concerns about paternalism, social engineering, or social welfare.
- It implied the existence of multiple worlds – at least, worlds on and off the machine.

The myopia of the thought experiment limits its relevance, however, when we turn our attention to social arrangements and world-building. Yet that is where we must go if we are to answer the fundamental questions about the world we're building for posterity.

Revisiting the Experience Machine n.0 – Life in the Machine/World

Let's eliminate the plug. Consider a different version of the experience machine, which we'll refer to as the Experience Machine n.0. Imagine a ubiquitous smart techno-social environment that spans the Earth and optimizes the planet to provide human inhabitants with optimal happiness. Rather than ask you whether you'd plug yourself in, we'd like for you to consider whether such a machine/world should be built.

If you were given the ultimate decision-making authority, would you build such a machine/world?

Moving from a decision about whether to plug yourself into the machine to one about whether to build a machine/world for all humans complicates the analysis and shifts the focus from individual well-being to broader moral and social concerns. To make the situation less abstract, let's be clear about what we mean by optimal happiness. Assume that the Experience Machine n.0 supplies all human beings on Earth with *maximum happiness*, measured moment-by-moment for each individual and aggregated over a lifetime, at *minimal social cost*. (Note that our arguments hold if we replace happiness with pleasure, positive affect, or other positive mental states.)

We must admit that this sounds pretty darn good. Optimal happiness appears to be an end worth pursuing. But *what about the means? Do they matter?*

We've already explored what the Experience Machine n.0 could look like and how we might build such a machine/world. Extrapolating from the present to the near future, we envision that the Experience Machine n.0 would be comprised of interconnected sensor networks and data-driven automation of socio-technical systems around, about, on, and in human beings. Imagine that within the next few decades, the following occurs. Large multinational companies[51] gradually build and connect smart techno-social environments that deliver on their promises. The scope of deployment expands to the point where there is seamless interconnection and integration across all environments within which humans live. The normative agenda executed throughout all this construction and deployment is optimal efficiency, productivity, and happiness.

Guided by the optimization criterion of maximum happiness at minimal social cost, the Experience Machine n.0 necessarily would engineer human beings. After all, human beings are inefficient and costly to sustain. Optimization would entail minimization of various costs associated with humans being human. For example, as explored in Chapter 2, our bodily and mental engagement with the physical world entails logistical, navigational, and various other transaction costs. Outsourcing to intelligent control systems would minimize these costs.

Making decisions, experimenting, and learning (among other mental processes) also are costly endeavors. Again, the optimizing logic would press toward minimizing and potentially eliminating these costs. Interacting with each other, coordinating behaviors, developing relationships, and many other aspects of interdependent human relations entail transaction costs to be minimized.

Finally, there is a subtler type of techno-social engineering prevalent in the Experience Machine n.0. Since what makes us happy is in large part contingent upon environmental conditions and experiences, and since those factors are fully determined within the machine/world, optimization also would entail engineered tastes, beliefs, preferences, and other factors that feed into our affective feelings of pleasure.

Bluntly, the cheapest way to make billions of human beings perfectly happy – particularly when using the sorts of technological means we're imagining – is to set the bar very low. In this case, the techno-social system need only meet or even barely surpass expectations. As hedonists know and often are prone to emphasize, people adapt their beliefs, preferences, and expectations to their conditions and, subsequently, their corresponding happiness levels typically adjust.[52] So, the goal might very well be to shape beliefs, preferences, and expectations in a manner that makes supplying happiness as cheap and easy as possible. At the end of the day, optimal happiness would boil down to satiation of engineered will.

There are many possibilities, however. Perhaps machine learning would settle on different equilibria. We can imagine extremely dystopian science fiction scenarios, such as *Wall-E*, where humans are dumb satiated fools. But we also can imagine scenarios where the machine/world manufactures higher happiness aggregates through different types of programs. John Stuart Mill famously argued that it is "better to be Socrates dissatisfied than a fool satisfied."[53] Perhaps the Experience Machine n.0 would produce a world filled with happy sages. Cheap engineered bliss need not exclude higher pleasures of the sort Mill defended. Higher pleasures often are cultivated and learned, and cultivation and learning entail costs.[54] On one hand, minimizing these costs might lead to outsourcing or pushing toward engineering wills satiated with lower pleasures. On the other hand, cultivating certain sets of tastes that correspond to higher pleasures might be worth the cost if they produce even more net pleasure. *Who knows?* Frankly, it's impossible to know exactly how the optimization would work out. But that's really beside the point. One way or another, techno-social systems would determine whether and what to cultivate, who and what we are. What makes humans happy would be predetermined rather than produced through the exercise of free will, experimentation, and self-authorship. (In Appendix D, we explore modern meal times, the engineering of tastes, and philosopher Albert Borgmann's appeal to "focal practices" as a means for escape and finding meaning.)

Regardless of the scenario, our thought experiment raises a fundamental normative question: *Would maximizing human happiness at minimal social cost through the Experience Machine n.0 justify forcing everyone to live a fully determined life?*

We strongly suspect few people would answer in the affirmative, at least upon reflection.[55] Think about what it would mean. Building the Experience Machine n.0 is functionally equivalent to forcing everyone to plug into Nozick's Experience Machine. Even the most hard-core hedonist would hesitate before imposing a machine life on others. Such paternalism conflicts directly with longstanding ideals concerning free will, autonomy, and agency, which are shared by many cultures and widely regarded as fundamental blessings of humanity. Lest you think we're setting up an indefensible position, we must emphasize that optimal happiness for everyone on Earth is an end worth considering carefully, particularly in light of how much misery and suffering exists in our world. We posed this thought experiment to Peter Singer, a renowned philosopher and incredibly thoughtful and generous person, and, after some discussion and deliberation, he replied: "I'm a sufficiently hard-core hedonist to think that democracy is a means to an end rather than an end in itself. If we can really imagine achieving optimum happiness for all sentient beings, forever, that would be a greater value than democracy, which may be better than any other system of government, but so far hasn't got anywhere close to producing optimum happiness for all sentient beings."

The Experience Machine n.0 poses a threat to the liberal democratic ideal that people should be generally free to choose their own ends with minimal interference. Commitments to forms of this ideal have proven to be the best way for diverse people to live together, have real opportunities to experiment with different ways of living, and determine, over time and with the accrual of experience, which ways to live well. A world that makes it very hard or impossible to opt out of Experience Machine n.0 would violate this ideal by interfering too strongly with our capacity to freely set ends for ourselves. Such interference is morally wrong and should be politically resisted. Though different in some respects, the spread of hedonism through neo-Taylorism amped up by interconnected and ubiquitous smart devices functions much like an authoritarian government imposing a mandatory state religion.

But if longstanding ideals are socially constructed and thus contingent upon techno-social engineering systems, would building the Experience Machine n.0 be defensible so long as it was done gradually? If it was deployed and integrated incrementally over decades, people could be gradually prepared for and conditioned to accept this brave new world. Engineered beliefs could pave the slippery-sloped path to the Experience Machine n.0. This is why we've emphasized the importance of asking these questions at a time when it's still possible to recognize and evaluate the path we're on.

Some would argue that any resistance people currently have toward building the machine/world is itself the product of techno-social engineering of beliefs, preferences, and values by past generations. This is true. The present generation has inherited the fundamental blessings of the past, including shared ideals about who we are and who we aspire to be. But this point doesn't undermine the inquiry or make it any easier to answer the difficult and pressing questions highlighted by our thought experiment and more thoroughly presented throughout our book.

Finally, some will argue that like Nozick's version, the Experience Machine n.0 thought experiment is wildly unrealistic and nothing more than an unfair intuition pump. They also will argue that the scenario is scary and framed in a manner that unfairly triggers psychological biases that distort rational analysis. These are fair points. But they are easily overstated and taken too far. Again, we use the thought experiment to prompt deliberation, analysis, and discussion. It is not a theoretical proof or empirical experiment.

While we truly hope our imagined machine/world is wildly unrealistic, there are various reasons to believe the slippery-sloped path we're on is headed in that direction. Regardless of whether we reach the end-state, we need to think more deeply about the world we're building, both because of what it means for our children and future generations and because of how it affects us as we proceed down the path.

Homogeneous *Homo Sapiens*

Many of us celebrate diversity. We appreciate how diverse people, thoughts, aptitudes, and attitudes enhance the richness of the world. A world filled with homogeneous humans might have fewer tribal conflicts. But it would be a boring place, comparatively speaking, and the annihilation of traditions would make a mockery of history.

Unfortunately, in a fully programmed world, the incentives for supporting and sustaining heterogeneity may drop. Cheaply engineered bliss may tend toward uniform satiation. When smart technology boosters flaunt the promise of personalized systems, they underplay how customization *is relative* to fairly uniform forms of life.

Life as a Machine: The Power to Control Minds, Make Humans into Things, and Determine What Other People Do

We are not fully predictable and programmable machines. In all likelihood, we never will be. But that is no reason to become complacent. Much of what matters about being human can be lost in partial deprivations as we march down the slippery-sloped path we're on.

Twenty-first-century techno-social engineering deeply affects how we think, feel, and interact with one another. Outsourcing so many of these functions to techno-social systems can't and shouldn't be assumed to be in our interest, neutral, or mere natural extensions of ourselves. We need to be aware of atrophying capabilities, mind control, and the gradual loss of human dignity as more aspects of our lives are determined by smart techno-social systems. Our techno-social engineering test framework provides a set of conceptual tools for identifying and contextually evaluating these risks.

We've also shown how different contexts relate to each other and how the means for techno-social engineering humans creep from one context to another, often engineering complacency along the way. Recall how the electronic contracting architecture is optimized to minimize transaction costs and deliberative thinking and how this logic creeps from websites to apps to smart TVs, bringing surveillance and nudging along for the ride. We expect continued creep to the Internet of Things, smart cars, and pretty much every other meaningful relationship plausibly mediated by the click-to-contract mechanism. It is cliché to note that websites and others who've succumbed to advertising-driven business models treat users as the products for advertisers and other third parties. But calling it a cliché only means we've become complacent and tacitly accepted the practice as an inevitable cost of doing business and living in modern times. Such engineered complacency is itself an important deprivation. None of this is inevitable.

Instead of revisiting any of the other examples we've already discussed, we'd like to take a new tack. In this section, we'll focus on *power*.

> *Do you ever feel like you're mindlessly following a script or behaving robotically?*
>   *If so, who authored the script?*

Over the past century, we've learned that many of the scripts we follow are the product of evolutionary biology. To survive harsh environmental conditions, we've needed programming.

Some programming is wired into our brains. In the past few decades, we've learned a lot from behavioral psychologists about how different systems within our brains perform different functions. As psychologist Daniel Kahneman explained in *Thinking Fast and Slow*, the dual process theory of human cognition suggests that System 1 processes are "fast, automatic, effortless, associative, and often emotionally charged," while System 2 ones are "slower, serial, effortful, and deliberately controlled."[56] The System 1 processes often involve habits and heuristics. Sometimes, we condition ourselves over time and develop routines and habits that economize on time, attention, and decision costs.

Sometimes, we are conditioned by others, who engineer routines and habits for us to follow. Such social engineering is obviously familiar to parents, teachers, coaches, and trainers. Socialization depends on learning norms and customs.

Contemporary social engineering is supposed to be data-driven. In public policy debates at all levels – whether a local school board or national regulatory agency – people insist on seeing the data. It's become commonplace to presume that policy-making should be based on hard evidence and not idle speculation or the whims of officials or, worse, lobbyists. In the private sector, efficiency drives companies to make decisions and design products and services based on the best data available to them. This increasingly involves real-time feedback from consumers and various other sources. The novelty of all of this, however, has been greatly exaggerated. Taylor's scientific management of human beings was an early form of data-driven social engineering practiced in the workplace and then extended to other contexts. The scale and scope of such practices expanded considerably in the twentieth century, in part because the scale and scope of data collection, storage, and processing expanded exponentially.

Nudging, which we started discussing at the beginning of the book, is an ascendant form of social engineering that aims to utilize the insights of behavioral psychologists and economists and leverage the recently emergent treasure trove of behavioral data.[57] Per the Organization for Economic Co-operation and Development,

> "Nudge" is an approach where authorities guide people to choose options which would achieve [a] welfare improvement. A nudge has two defining features: i) it preserves free choice by not preventing selection of suboptimal choice and ii) findings from behavioral insights are employed to alter the decision context in a way that makes better decisions more likely.[58]

Notably, not all nudges script behavior or trigger automatic responses. Some nudges transparently prompt reflective choice (System 2). An example is when someone is asked to choose whether to be an organ donor. Some nudges engage the reflective system through non-transparent means, such as lotteries that rely on people overestimating their chances. And some nudges trigger automatic or habitual behavior (System 1), such as playing mood music to relax patrons on a plane, adjusting plate size to get people to eat less (or more), or automatically enrolling people in a save-more-for-tomorrow program.[59] Nudges can engage either system, depending upon the cognitive problem the choice architect is trying to solve.

Of course, therein lays the deeper question: In each case, who designs the nudge? Who decides what problems are worth solving? Who decides when and how techno-social engineering will be an appropriate solution? These are just a few of the political questions about power that have lurked beneath the surface of our discussion throughout this book. Here are two more:

- In the twenty-first century, who are the architects building our world and the future?
- Are these architects responsible for humanity's techno-social dilemma?

An Architect, Economist, Lawyer, and Marketing Agent Walk into a Bar . . .

A: People are so inefficient. I mean, they waste so much time.

B: How so?

A: Second guessing themselves . . . and everyone else.

B: It's only natural. No one wants to make a mistake.

A: No, it's not natural. Think about it. Did cavemen have time to deliberate? Hunters had to make split-second decisions.

B: Sure, sometimes. But they also needed to make plans. And, c'mon, we've evolved quite a bit since prehistoric times. Today, human beings need to think both ways and use different parts of their brains depending on the task and context. That's what separates us from other animals.

A: Perhaps. Maybe we have two powerful capabilities, but people exercise the one type too much. At least there's too much time-wasting deliberation about the simple stuff . . .

B: It's hard to say what's so simple . . .

A: And – sorry, let me finish the thought – too little time thinking hard about the more complex and consequential issues.

B: Again, it's hard to say what's simple enough to leave to instinct and what deserves heightened attention and deeper thought. Best to leave it to them.

A: In general, sure. But in our line of work, we've got product to move. We can't afford for customers to dither, worrying about whether they could do better. Nothing good comes our way if they believe that by holding off they'll get a better deal in the future, or maybe somewhere else.

B: Well, sometimes they do. Sometimes comparative shopping or pausing to consider whether a purchase is a good idea is a good thing. It makes sense for folks to stop and think, to evaluate options. Don't you? Stop and think, I mean.

A: Sometimes, sure. But there's so much wasted time and energy. Often, the first option really is best. Or at least, it should be, if we're doing our job – which we are, thank you very much.

B: Well, that presumes a lot. We certainty do our best with what we've got and provide our best estimate of what they want.

A: Don't sell our product short! People who use it, benefit from it. And people who aren't using it, are missing out on those benefits. The bottom line is that we could make it a lot easier for everyone to start benefitting. Save time. Reduce waste. Increase efficiency.

B: Yeah, okay, I understand your objective, but not your means. How will we make it easier?

A: You ever hear the joke about the architect, economist, lawyer, and marketing agent? They walk into a bar and . . .

B: [Shakes head in disbelief.]

A: Never mind. It's not even that funny. We need to get people to go on auto-pilot and behave according to plan.

B: How?

A: How does the architect get you to enter and exit a room through the door and not the wall?

B: Huh?

A: Does she need a law that says: "No exiting through walls"?

B: Of course not.

A: Does she need to install a sign that says: "Please leave through the doors, and don't try to exit through the walls?" Nope. The architecture is self-enforcing. People do as the architect intends.

B: I don't see the point.

A: Suppose we want people to enter our site through Door A and not Doors B or C. How do we get them to do what we want?

B. I don't know.

A. It's simple. We don't build the other doors. Or, even if we do, perhaps because we want them for ourselves or other reasons, we lock Door B and paint Door C red. Make it look like they've got choices – full autonomy, but we know choices B and C won't actually get picked.

B: We write the script.

A: Exactly. We write the script.

Throughout the book, we've resisted casting blame on any specific set of actors. In one sense, we're all to blame for humanity's techno-social dilemma. After all, the dilemma depends on the *aggregation of trillions of perfectly rational choices*. At a micro level, our tech adoption and use decisions are rational, particularly when evaluated individually on their own seemingly independent terms. The same is often true of our habitual behavior. We rely on scripts and heuristics to efficiently save time and effort. Again, we can use electronic contracting as an illustrative and familiar example. Each time we click "I agree" without stopping to think about what we're getting ourselves into, we behave rationally, for a few reasons. First, we have little reason to believe that we have viable alternatives. There is typically no room for negotiation on terms. It is a take-it-or-leave-it decision, and we're encountering the click-to-contract stimulus because we're seeking something we want. Second, the interface is designed to minimize transaction costs and to nudge people to click. Any behavioral biases that would push one away from clicking automatically are likely mitigated by design. Biases pushing in the other direction – toward automatic or habitual behavior – are more likely leveraged by design. Third, it is typically too costly to deliberate about which click-to-contract stimuli require deliberation. We encounter the stimuli so often that it's hard to know which encounter demands more attention and deliberation than others, and stopping to deliberate about all such encounters would be debilitating. We could go on, but since we've already discussed these details in Chapter 5, we'll spare you. The bottom line is (i) each incremental decision to click is perfectly rational, and (ii) there are many environmental factors that shape those decisions. Thus, we individually contribute to the dilemma and are partially responsible, but we're not alone and we're not fully responsible. We could reiterate the same basic arguments and structure with respect to many of the examples in this book.

But what about the actors who play a major role in engineering the environment and correspondingly gaining, exercising, and concentrating power to engineer humans and shape humanity? These actors also bear considerable responsibility for humanity's techno-social dilemma.[60]

Casting judgment on bad actors or short-sighted ones brings us into the space where highly contentious finger wagging occurs. Many others have ventured farther and deeper than we do. Some debate the political economy that drives us down the slippery-sloped path we're on.[61] Others focus on powerful techno-social engineers, such as the platform companies at the forefront of techno-social engineering creep.[62] We've noted a few examples, such as Amazon, Apple, Facebook, and Google. There are many others.

It is, however, beyond the scope of this chapter to wade deeply into existing debates about power. Our book is relevant to those debates. That's for sure. However, there's too much nuance and complexity to unpack in the space that's left.

The single point we'd like to emphasize is that answering the constitutional questions we've raised requires giving attention to the most important constitutional question of all: *Who decides?*[63]

The conventional answer to the "who decides" question is the people. The people decide who they are, who they aspire to be, what capabilities and qualities to cultivate and sustain, and what society and world to build for themselves and future generations. Unfortunately, conventional wisdom is wrong. It's based on too many idealistic presumptions.

The conventional answer presumes that people exercise free will and can exercise robust agency. It further assumes that people are fully capable of actively participating in cultural, economic, and political systems. And conventional thinking takes for granted that our lives are not determined by others and we're free to decide for ourselves. These assumptions are rooted in ideals worth striving for. They are, after all, the fundamental blessings of humanity. Tragically, they are under attack and should not be taken for granted. The future of techno-social engineering might put them at greater risk.

PART IV

CHAPTER 14

Conclusion: Reimagining and Building Alternative Futures

What Are We Rebelling Against?

In *The Robot's Rebellion*, psychologist Keith Stanovich makes a compelling argument that humans have escaped being robots enslaved by our genes. Human beings evolved a set of cognitive capabilities that are essential to rational self-determination, long-term planning, collective imagination and cooperation, and even techno-social engineering. These capabilities enabled our rebellion from genetic determinism.[1] Through diverse cultures we've collectively built and sustained the fundamental blessings of humanity and avoided being biologically compelled to act like simple machines.

Wouldn't it be terribly tragic, and just a bit ironic, if human beings escaped genetic determinism only to fall victim to engineered determinism? If we escape being robots who are slaves to genetic scripts that perpetuate survival of the fittest genes only to become robots who slavishly perform techno-social engineering scripts for efficiently managing resources, including ourselves?

Stanovich insists that to find meaning in life we need to embrace a broad form of rationality and sustain the human capacity for rational self-determination. His advice is sound but incomplete as we struggle with humanity's techno-social dilemma. Our fundamental conflict isn't with our genes. It's with ourselves.

In this concluding chapter, we defend the idea that one of the most important constitutional questions of the twenty-first century is how to sustain the freedom to be off, to be free from techno-social engineering, to live and develop within underdetermined techno-social environments. To make this case we revisit humanity's techno-social dilemma and the path to a world governed by engineered determinism in light of the pathways we've described. We also offer proposals for how to implement the freedom to be off by mitigating and resisting the slippery-sloped path we're on.

Unfortunately, there's no easy way to solve the problems we've identified. They exist on many levels, at different scales, and span many different contexts. Let's take stock. We've discussed contextually specific *micro-level* examples (e.g. fitness tracking in an elementary school), industry- or sector-wide, *meso-level* examples (e.g. smart transportation), and global, *macro-level* examples (e.g. engineered contagions on platforms like Facebook). We've also explored how techno-social engineering creeps across contexts (e.g. electronic contracting creep spreads from websites to apps to smart televisions) and spans the different scales (e.g. single click-to-contract transaction → streams of electronic contracts governing much of our lives). These examples along with many others paint a complex picture of the slippery-sloped path that we're on and illustrate how humanity's techno-social dilemma consists of many incremental and interdependent steps.

Environmental Humanism

It's hard to know where to begin in terms of proposing solutions. As with most problems, grasping what's wrong and why things should change are important first steps. That's why we developed a framework to identify and evaluate techno-social engineering of humans, and now will take a step further.

Our general-purpose response to the problems we've identified is a call for *freedom* that encompasses two related ideals:

1. Freedom from programming, conditioning, and control engineered by others. In our modern techno-social world, we call this the *freedom to be off*.
2. Freedom of will and practical agency. In our modern techno-social world, we call this the *freedom from engineered determinism*.

Each ideal entails positive and negative liberties[2] that are contingent upon the dynamic relationships among individuals and between individuals and techno-social environments. What we're asking is for degrees of freedom engineered into our lived-in environments and thus our lives. Note the irony. It's one with an influential pedigree. In her famous reflection, "A Cyborg Manifesto," science and technology studies theorist Donna Haraway explained that such irony "is about contradictions that do not resolve into larger wholes, even dialectically, about the tension of holding incompatible things together because both or all are necessary and true."[3] In a similar way, we're calling for freedom from techno-social engineering of humans while acknowledging that such freedom needs to be engineered into our techno-social environments. In this regard, we are not suggesting that techno-social engineering can or should be eliminated. It can't be, at least not without losing our humanity. We are fundamentally techno-social animals.[4] Our lives and societies are necessarily interdependent and dependent upon the worlds and environments we collectively build.

In short, we need a new form of humanism, an *environmental humanism* that revolves around two truths: (1) what meaningfully distinguishes *homo sapiens* from all other species is our capability to imagine, conceptualize, and engineer ourselves and our environment; and (2) what matters about being human is how we exercise such power over generations to collectively produce, cultivate, and sustain shared normative conceptions of humanity. Humanity is reflected in us and our built world of imagined realities, institutions, infrastructures, and environments.

Across cultures and generations, humans have engineered themselves and their built techno-social environments to sustain capacities for thinking, the ability to socialize and relate to each other, free will, autonomy, and agency, as well as other core capabilities. Across cultures and generations, there have been variations in achievements and aspirations. Although these capabilities and values are part of our shared heritage and collective humanity, they are at risk of being whittled away through modern forms of techno-social engineering; humanity's techno-social dilemma is one of the most pressing issues of the twenty-first century.

To escape humanity's techno-social dilemma and the slippery-sloped path we are on, we need to imagine and build alternatives – alternative paths, destinations, and, ultimately, worlds. A world governed by engineered determinism is possible, but it is not inevitable.

Capabilities

Different forces and logics drive us down the slippery-sloped path toward engineered determinism. Taylorism extended, fetishized computational power, and the allure of ever more powerful "smart" systems promise efficiency and productivity along with the convenience and happiness of optimized lives. These logics determine means and ends, path and destination, and structure our world and the world we're building.[5] We thus need alternative logics to counter existing forces and momentum and provide new ways to conceive of alternatives.[6]

Fundamentally, developing a new logic requires a normative theory, an answer to the basic question we've asked repeatedly: *To what end?* Answering this social/cultural/political question requires collective action. And so, one difficulty with developing a new logic is that it must replace old ones that already have tremendous weight and influence along with significant vested interests. That's why fundamental normative issues often turn on the most basic of political questions: *Who decides?*[7]

The normative outlook we've been advancing is consequentialist in the sense that we believe techno-social engineering should be evaluated in terms of its consequences for human beings and humanity. Different types of consequences are relevant to our evaluation. Our normative baseline is pluralist, multidimensional, and focused on capabilities for human flourishing. We emphasize specific human capabilities and acknowledge the importance of others, and we stress the relevance of happiness and broader conceptions of well-being. Thus, we reject "the notion that there exists a single irreducible fundamental moral value to which all other moral values may be reduced."[8]

Our orientation to evaluating techno-social engineering resonates strongly with the capabilities approach developed and applied by economist Amartya Sen,[9] philosopher Martha Nussbaum,[10] and many others.[11] The capabilities approach is a framework for evaluating social arrangements that focuses on capabilities, which are opportunities or freedoms to realize actual, "real-life" achievements.[12] Sen, Nussbaum, and other capabilities scholars explain how society is and would be better off supporting the capabilities of individuals to be and do what they have reason to value; in Aristotelean terms, these are capabilities for human flourishing.[13] Sen emphasizes consideration of actual people situated in particular contexts, recognizing explicitly how their lives are shaped by techno-social environments. The way the capabilities approach is configured it doesn't defer to individuals' subjective beliefs and preferences. These beliefs and preferences are understood to be contextually contingent and therefore malleable. An incredibly poor person with very little opportunity in life might be subjectively happy because she has adapted to her conditions in life. Just because adaptive preferences are formed doesn't mean that society should shirk its commitment to reducing poverty or investing in building the capabilities of future generations of similarly situated people. In this regard, the capabilities approach is unabashedly normative. While happiness and preference satisfaction play a significant role in evaluating well-being within a society, the capabilities approach envisions a more complex, multidimensional model of individual and social well-being. Sen's version is decidedly open and pluralistic, admitting for variance in how different communities and cultures may value and prioritize different capabilities. We've taken a similar approach.

Experience Machines and Paternalism

We haven't limited our discussion of consequences of techno-social engineering to the subjective experiences human beings can have. Instead, we considered the consequences for humanity, conceptualized as a shared intergenerational and intercultural resource, a set of ideals reflected in the world we build, sustain, and pass on to future generations. Some will object to this move and insist that humanity matters if and only if and only to the extent that it affects subjective experiences of existing or future human beings. This debate brings us back to the experience machine thought experiments.

The transition from Nozick's experience machine to Experience Machine n.o marked a significant shift in focus, from evaluating individual well-being to evaluating humanity in a social world. How you answer the question of whether you'd plug in to the original experience machine doesn't necessarily determine how you would or should answer the question of whether you'd build Experience Machine n.o.

We hope that, upon reflection, most people, including hard-core hedonists, would decline to build Experience Machine n.o because they recognize that there is more that matters about being human than subjective feelings of happiness.[14] We can build much better worlds.[15] Free will and agency matter, above and beyond how those capabilities cash out in terms of subjectively experienced well-being. But worst case, even if most people say they would choose to build the Experience Machine n.o, that empirical attestation of their values does not provide sufficient justification. This is where liberalism and paternalism clash.[16] A confounding difficulty with liberalism and relying on individuals' existing preferences and beliefs is that such preferences and beliefs are contingent upon the techno-social environment within which they've lived their lives. It's hard to fully credit preferences and beliefs that significantly discount the constitutional value of free will and agency. After all, deferring to individuals' choices only makes sense if the individuals themselves have free will and practical agency, and, if they do, then it seems morally wrong to deny the same capabilities to future generations, to deny them access to the fundamental blessings of humanity passed on to the present generation. Still, this line of inquiry risks an endless debate that goes round-and-round, circling the same questions raised by the pair of experience machine thought experiments: Who decides what constitutes a "good life" and who decides what ends society should seek to achieve collectively?

Our take is paternalist in so far as we elevate core human capabilities above satisfying engineered preferences and beliefs. Paternalism has become a dirty word in some places, especially in the United States. Nevertheless, is our view any more paternalist than building the Experience Machine n.o and opting everyone into it? Paternalism, like techno-social engineering, is inevitable. Debates about paternalism versus liberalism[17] are political contests that seek to control baselines about how to approach the "who decides" questions.[18]

Liberalism is a powerful logic that's been driving us down the slippery-sloped path. As law professor Julie Cohen – whose arguments are complementary to our own – claims, liberal political theory and liberal individualism generate "particularly seductive" "analytical constructs" such as the "autonomous, rational, disembodied self" who naturally and seamlessly lives within the "networked information society."[19] Cohen's work has been devoted to dismantling the seductive construct of the liberal self. Drawing on a wide range of perspectives and disciplines, she defends a more sophisticated, nuanced, and contextual understanding of the self who continuously interacts with and develops within complex and evolving techno-social environments. Her view necessitates a correspondingly more sophisticated, nuanced, and contextual understanding of techno-social environments and the world we're building.

Play

In *Configuring the Networked Self*, Cohen makes a case "for a more comprehensive, structural understanding of the ways that the information environment can foster, or undermine, capabilities for human flourishing."[20] She examines the "everyday practices" of human beings situated within techno-social environments, the importance of "play" for human development and self-determination, and the role that legal and technical architectures perform in mediating everyday practices and play. Play is not coextensive with frivolous entertainment or games. According to Cohen:

> Social scientists who study play have concluded that its developmental functions extend into adulthood and remain centrally implicated in the processes by which individuals orient themselves in relation to the world. Particularly relevant to the domains with which this book is concerned are play with objects and narratives, which locates the individual in relation to

material and intellectual culture, and play with conceptions of empathy and morality, which enables individuals to form and pursue conceptions of the good. Play is both the keystone of individual moral and intellectual development and a mode of world making, the pathway by which transformative innovation and synthetic understanding emerge. It is neither inherently frivolous nor essentially single-minded, but rather a process of open-ended encounter.[21]

Thus understood, play is a critical aspect of our everyday lives as human beings situated within techno-social environments. The freedom to play is instrumental to our development and exercise of capabilities, and it is contingent upon the techno-social environment; it requires freedom from engineered determinism.[22]

Semantic Discontinuity

Cohen advances three principles to inform the design of legal and technical architectures: access to knowledge, operational transparency, and semantic discontinuity. Each is important, but we highlight the third because of how strongly it relates to our call for freedom and the need for a new countervailing logic. In her words:

> Semantic discontinuity refers to gaps and inconsistencies within systems of meaning and to a resulting interstitial complexity that leaves room for the play of everyday practice. In an increasingly networked information society, maintaining those gaps requires interventions designed to counterbalance the forces that seek to close them.[23]

Though the terminology of semantic discontinuity admittedly is opaque, the powerful concept is worth unpacking. Semantic discontinuity can be understood as a design principle for engineering techno-social systems. The idea is that sometimes techno-social engineers can and should build "gaps and inconsistencies within systems" and between systems. Despite pressure from efficiency experts, risk managers, and other optimizers, we sometimes should sustain rather than close these gaps and inconsistencies. Let's put it another way. All built systems are imperfect. System engineers seek to minimize imperfections. But perfection exists in the eye of the beholder. Often the imperfections in our techno-social systems, particularly those that shape our everyday lives and practices, afford people with room to play. These affordances can be beneficial to human beings in ways that system designers and operators may fail to appreciate. We've discussed various examples throughout the book. Recall, for instance, our analysis of fitness tracking tools. The written journal was an imperfect activity-tracking device compared to the Fitbit, but the imperfections in data collection afforded students the freedom to play and thereby practice and develop basic capabilities. Gaps in data collection leave open the possibility of inconsistencies in the meaning of the fitness data recorded and reported, and this sustains a higher degree of complexity in the intervening "space" between students, teachers, and various third parties.

Implementation of this design principle can take many forms, and we explore some examples below. For now, the critical point is that Cohen has uncovered the roots of a powerful alternative logic. Her call for semantic discontinuity is a call for freedom from engineered determinism. Such freedom sustains opportunities for human beings to play and thereby exercise self-determination, develop, and flourish as human beings.

From Logics to Strategies

Developing alternative logics involves social change at a *meta level*. Success may depend upon political movements and many other factors that are difficult to predict or account for in the space of a book. To move to less abstract and more practical levels for implementing social change, we now consider mitigation strategies for humanity's techno-social dilemma. Let's consider three:

1. Challenge conventional wisdom, ideas, and theories that perpetuate existing logics and engineer complacency.
2. Create gaps and seams between smart techno-social systems that constrain techno-social engineering and techno-social engineering creep.
3. Engineer transaction costs and inefficiencies to support human flourishing through the exercise and development of human capabilities.

Challenge Conventional Wisdom with Critical Analysis

The first strategy is a call for critical analysis. This is not a novel idea. There are plenty of critical theorists engaging in such work. Unfortunately, the persuasive power of critical analysis has dampened in recent decades. This is not the place for a diagnosis, except to say the rise of the dominant logics we've identified has drowned out critical voices and made them easy targets of unfair but sticky labels, "nostalgic," "Luddite," and "romantic." When all social problems are presumed comprehensible in the language of computation, persuasive power vests in those with the most powerful computational tools and data sets. To be persuasive in modern policy debates, one often must fight empirical data with more empirical data;[24] quantitative analysis reigns supreme. There are plenty of pros and cons to empiricism, and we're not suggesting empiricism should be abandoned. To the contrary, we've developed the techno-social engineering test framework to support empirical research. Critical analysis certainly can have empirical dimensions.

Let's be honest about empiricism as practiced in modern policy debates. The empirical turn in policy debates and the associated call for evidence-based policy-making depend upon some subtle non-empirical premises. Most obvious is the premise that what matters normatively is amenable to measurement by reliable empirical methods. Related is the often-implicit premise of commensurability among normative values – the idea that a common denominator exists. In most cases, available empirical measures are simply the best available proxies.[25] (You might be wondering: According to whom? Who decides what's the best proxy? Sometimes it's a matter of scientific consensus. Sometimes it's pure politics. Sometimes it's historical pedigree and plain inertia.)

The logics – mindsets, mental models, outlooks, or worldviews, if you prefer – set the normative baseline for analysis, define relevant problems and what's worth measuring, and determine the rules of the game, such as who bears the burden of proof in a policy debate. The logics are social constructions that serve as powerful means of social control. Thus, while we support critical empirical analyses of techno-social engineering, we also advocate critical analyses of empirical practices, including normative baselines, problem definitions, accepted forms of measurement and proxies, and rules of the game. To be frank, in many contentious policy debates ranging from antitrust to environmental protection, winners and losers are determined by who ultimately bears the burden of proof.

How does critical analysis fare when it emphasizes aspects of the problem that are incomprehensible in the language of computation? Not well. Too often, in modern discourse, it takes a testable theory and (quantitative) empirical data to beat the status quo. All that seems to matter is what's visible beneath the light of the dominant logics' lamppost. Things that lurk in the darkness beyond are dismissed as irrelevant, speculative, imaginary, or inevitable. Just ask privacy advocates who have long been told that harms that are difficult to measure don't count as real harms.

The rise of empiricism has created numerous problems for evaluating and determining public policy. Economics is a good example to consider.

Economists strongly prefer to work with formal mathematical models and quantitative data, for good reasons, but this preference introduces considerable limitations. Among other things, this preference leads many economists to isolate a specific market or two to analyze, holding others constant and assuming them to be complete and competitive. This approach can be highly distorting. Economists may cordon off various nonmarket systems and corresponding social values because such phenomena are deemed to be outside the bounds of economics.[26] Many economists recognize these potential distortions and the corresponding limits of their expertise and policy prescriptions. Nonetheless, these limits often are not apparent or well understood by policy-makers and other consumers of economic analyses, and even when the limits are understood, there are various reasons why they may be disregarded, including ideology or political pressures. J. Scott Holladay, an environmental economist, observes:

> When conducting an economic valuation of an ecosystem, we are well aware of our limitations. In a valuation study, we identify environmental services and amenities that are valuable but cannot be valued via existing economic methods, and we may assign a non-numerical value to make clear that we are not assigning a value of zero, but when the valuation study is used by policy makers, those non-numerical values may effectively be converted to a zero value and the identified environmental services and amenities truncated from the analysis. Is that a fault of the economist or the policy maker?[27]

We've examined various examples where conventional wisdom, ideas, and theories perpetuate existing logics and engineer complacency. Recall economist Richard Thaler's conversation-stopping dismissal of slippery-slope arguments. He insisted that critics evaluate nudge proposals one by one, each on its individual merits. This type of narrow incrementalism is myopic, truncates cost-benefit analyses, and precludes critical analysis of the nudge agenda. Or recall how extended mind proponents cast their analysis in descriptive terms and presume that people who use mind-extending technologies retain their autonomy. Our critical analysis cast significant doubt on the autonomy presumption and raised the complicated and contentious issue of mind control. Or recall how focusing on important privacy concerns when evaluating the fitness tracking programs in schools obscures deeper concerns about conditioning and techno-social engineering of beliefs and preferences. There are many other examples. We've only begun to scratch the surface.

Critical analysis of technology is too often and too easily dismissed as fear-mongering, in terms similar to Thaler's attack on "slope-mongering."

This is a shame. To escape humanity's techno-social dilemma and the slippery-sloped path we are on, we need a reasonable dose of rigorous technology criticism, grounded in theoretical frameworks and empirical research drawn from a wide range of disciplines.

Still, it's a mistake to cast critical analysis solely in terms of identifying and diagnosing problems. The first strategy also encompasses critically thinking about what's possible. Critical analysis must generate solutions and lead to alternative paths.[28] Often the dominant logics preclude consideration of alternative paths and solutions to social problems. Consider a rather obvious example. *Ever wonder why the United States doesn't have a single payer health care system?* The solution is simply off the table, out of bounds because of the political mindset. There are many other relevant examples, however, including the problem of fake news.

Solving the Fake News Problem with a New Social Media Platform[29]

How should we solve the problem of fake news on smart media systems? Notice how jarring this question sounds. One might think that such a problem wouldn't exist on truly smart media systems. The solution, therefore, must be to better utilize the intelligence of the media system. What would this entail? Naturally, media platforms should improve the intelligence of their data-driven algorithmic systems and exercise correspondingly better control. This line of thinking coincides with the conventional logic in policy discussions. Sure, some deny the existence of a problem. Some dispute the magnitude of any ill effects and dismiss claims that fake news sways elections, public opinion, or consumer markets. Others deny that media platforms bear responsibility, attack the idea of filter bubbles, and defend "innovation" and "markets" and so on from any form of government intervention. So, again, the first step is identifying and evaluating the scale, scope, and nature of the problem. But if we move past this first step, the conventional wisdom seems to accept the following premises.

1. Facebook is and will be the dominant social media platform. (Google is and will be the dominant search platform. Amazon . . .)[30]
2. Solutions should be private, market-driven solutions; public intervention is, at most, a threat in the background to spur private action.

Each of these premises reflects many other entrenched beliefs and assumptions. For brevity's sake, we won't unpack them. The point is that these premises are akin to a lamp-post. They shed light upon the range of plausible solutions and leave alternative paths and solutions in the dark.

Critical analysis provides a useful way to identify and diagnose the problem, and it also helps identify alternative solutions. Fake news involves at least two distinct types of problems.

The first depends on profit-making. Some fake news purveyors aim to make money. They do not necessarily care about communicating a specific message. They do not necessarily care about truth or falsity, whether the content confers benefits or harms on some audience, or whether they have an impact upon anyone or the world more generally. They're not trying to change anyone's beliefs or affect their behavior beyond manipulating them into clicking. They mainly care about generating revenue, and they typically rely on the rapid-click business model often associated with click-bait. Facebook[31] enables this business model because it coincides with their incentives as surveillance capitalists. This brief critical analysis suggests that relying on Facebook to solve the problem with more intelligence and control might not work, unless Facebook changes its own business model and/or commits substantial resources to policing its advertising system. The analysis also suggests an alternative solution: *new social media platforms with new business models*. In light of the first premise above, this solution might seem ludicrous. There is, however, some precedent. Federated social networks – like Diaspora – do not rely on advertising revenue and, by extension, the economic incentives that force Facebook and other proprietary social networks to optimize for clicks and ignore user privacy to more effectively serve ads. Federated social networks don't nudge users to over-share information or structure their sites to encourage clicks and other superficial engagements that can be analyzed. Their business model doesn't require it. Still, to date, federated social networks have only gained fringe acceptance. There are many possible reasons for this, but network effects and the high costs of switching create a significant barrier to overcome. Simply put, even if these alternatives offered significant advantages over Facebook, it's difficult to motivate people to leave the platform they've grown accustomed to and where they've already built an extensive social network. We return to the seemingly outlandish idea of a new social media platform in a moment, after we diagnose the second type of problem.

The second species of fake news problem is propaganda. Purveyors of propaganda aren't motivated by making money through superficial engagements like clicks. Instead, the goal is to affect beliefs, preferences, and attitudes by cultivating false or intentionally misleading narratives. Facebook and other platforms enable these actors because they deny that they are media companies in the traditional sense and refuse to develop or exercise editorial expertise. In some sense, Facebook has backed itself into a corner. Situations emerge where Facebook needs to act like a media company and make determinations about newsworthiness or the credibility of certain sources and articles. If Facebook starts making these decisions, a large subset of its user base falls back on Facebook's own cultivated narrative that it's just a platform and should not be making these decisions. They claim it's censorship. In short, people don't really trust Facebook to be making these decisions.

A solution must address both the perverse economic incentives and expertise issues that justifiably undermine the public's faith in networked news distribution. *What would it take to create a new, trusted social networking platform?* Surprising as it may seem, the path to an answer appears to lie in considering what the British Broadcasting Corporation would do if it created a social network. The key ingredients for a trusted media platform are an institutional structure that supports independence and a firm commitment to cultivating and exercising editorial expertise. The BBC has – some would say had[32] – these features, and, as a result, it has been widely judged a decent model of a trusted, competent public media platform. To be clear, the BBC is not perfect; it does not manage a social network; and it is not the only viable mode for imagining alternatives.[33]

1. *The BBC is deeply trusted by the public.* The public trusts the BBC to cover stories impartially, and trusts that the BBC covers a wide variety of topics. This trust translates to the role that the BBC would play as the operator of a social media platform. The BBC could curate news sections that continued its missions of covering a diverse set of issues while leveraging its impartiality. The BBC's reach and trust would allow its social media platform to help establish a baseline set of facts that make debate across ideological lines possible and pressure against the development of filter bubbles and echo chambers.

2. *The BBC has media expertise,* which it can draw from to make sound editorial judgments and create content specific to the platform – making it better situated than both federated social networks and Facebook to create and deliver news content. Media expertise is crucial for disseminating news in a networked environment. A truly peer-to-peer platform, like federated social networks, may be effective as interpersonal communication platforms, but this model does not account for the expertise required for mass-media distribution. Effective mass-media distribution requires nuanced judgments about

newsworthiness as well as identifying and critiquing propaganda narratives. Unlike Facebook, the BBC already has a seasoned staff of media experts who could – and might be willing to – focus their efforts on the broad array of judgments and decisions that attend disseminating news through a social media platform. In practice, this expertise most likely would be leveraged as an input for the BBC's own algorithms. For example, one can imagine that some randomly selected fraction of news-related content on the platform is evaluated by a BBC editor and rated for quality, and that such ratings would be incorporated into the machine-learning system.

3. *The BBC's funding model shields it from corrosive economic and political pressure.* The BBC is funded through a license model, which would insulate a BBC social media platform from having to respond to the incentives that attend online advertising. Without the market pressure to model and predict user behavior for more effective advertising, a BBC-based social media platform could respect privacy rights of users – as its funding model does not depend on user data as fuel for its advertising profit engine. Thus, the BBC could plausibly claim, "We will not surveil or profile you or in any way seek to sell you or anyone else anything about you. You are our client, and you can trust us." This independence frees up a BBC platform to select for news stories that do more than entertain and confirm the biases of its users to increase engagement and monitoring. The BBC could tailor its algorithms to promote stories that optimize for other values besides entertainment. There could still be space for news stories that entertain, but the motivations underlying news story selections could also include commitments to other core public values like diversity of information, an informed public, and non-fragmented space for public debate. The license model also insulates the BBC from unwarranted government interference. Because license fees are paid directly by the public and not funded through taxation, the BBC is not necessarily responsive to government demands about how to report events or what events require coverage.

Despite its appeal, the idea of a BBC-style social media platform remains far outside the mainstream. To take it seriously, one would have to reject the first premise and relax the second. Of the two, we suspect relaxing the second premise is the most difficult obstacle. To think critically and creatively about funding models akin to the BBC's license fee borders on taboo.[34] This example shows the power of conventional wisdom, ideas, and theories to perpetuate existing logics and engineer complacency. It also highlights the need for critical analysis of problems and solutions.

Net Neutrality and Beyond

The second strategy aims to mitigate the threat of engineered determinism, create friction on the slippery-sloped path, and illuminate alternative paths.[35] The basic idea is to engage in techno-social engineering to sustain humanity, by engineering degrees of freedom into our built world. Underdetermined techno-social environments should leave ample room for self-determination, human development and flourishing, and Cohen's "play of everyday practice." The strategy applies at various scales.

We've discussed a few ideas about how to sustain underdetermined techno-social environments. For example, we explained how the Internet evolved with the end-to-end design principle as its central tenet. This is an illustrative example of techno-social engineering that preserves degrees of freedom. End-to-end design defines a seam. It provides a general technology-and-application-independent interface between the higher and lower layers of the network. This design engineered a form of blindness – a lack of a specific type of intelligence – into the techno-social system. End-to-end design insulated end-users from market-driven restrictions on access to and use of the infrastructure. It precluded certain forms of intelligence-enabled control and thus maintained corresponding degrees of freedom from techno-social engineering. Notably, the end-to-end principle is not law. Compliance with the principle has always been voluntary. In various ways and for various reasons, network owners developed tools and business strategies to circumvent the design principle. The familiar logics of efficiency and fetishized computation pushed networks to pursue more intelligent architectures capable of differentiating and discriminating among end-uses and end-users in the name of traffic management and in pursuit of profit maximization. This led to the network neutrality debate.

Though still highly contentious, network neutrality is one example of a regulatory rule that aims to sustain the Internet as an underdetermined environment.[36] Network neutrality sustains a degree of freedom for users by preventing owners of broadband networks from prioritizing Internet traffic based on the identity of users or their activities – basically, based on who is doing what. Users decide what to do with the intellectual, relational, and many other capabilities that the Internet affords. This freedom is not absolute; nor is it free for users, who still must pay to access and use the Internet. And there are trade-offs involved. We'll not litigate the issue here, however.[37] The point is that network neutrality engineers a powerful seam that constrains broadband networks' exercise of social control and creates a substantial gap within the techno-social environment.

Yet it is important to make clear that network neutrality only operates at a specific seam, at a specific scale, on a specific set of powerful techno-social engineers, and at the interface between specific layers. It may be necessary. But it is by no means sufficient.

On one hand, powerful techno-social engineers operate within and between other higher layers, such as the applications and content layers. We've discussed examples, such as Facebook and Google. Some have called for "search neutrality" as a variation on network neutrality for search technology. The nuances of that debate are beyond the scope of this chapter, but suffice it to say that the general concerns about techno-social engineering of humans are similar (i.e. search engines are powerful techno-social engineering tools) but many details complicate the neutrality analogy. For example, search engines necessarily exercise intelligence-enabled control to sort, filter, and ultimately prioritize content.[38] As business professor and legal scholar Deven Desai emphasizes, the question of "who should decide to what someone should be exposed" is unavoidable and not answered easily by reference to neutrality, deference to markets or governments, or appeals to self-determination by individuals.[39] Alternative institutional means for resisting engineered determinism and engineering degrees of freedom into search may be required.[40]

On the other hand, we're likely to need network-neutrality-style rules in many other contexts. Frankly, we already have similar nondiscrimination rules at the infrastructural layers of many other techno-social systems, ranging from electricity to law. But as we proceed down the slippery-sloped path, infatuation with the power of smart techno-social systems will lead to recurring conflicts resembling the network neutrality debate. At least, that is our hope because recurring conflicts would mean that engineered complacency hasn't set in. Specifically, the smart grid and smart transportation systems of the near future will give rise to debates about whether to engineer (by law or architectural design principle) a seam that prevents discrimination or prioritization based on who you are or what you're doing. We illustrated this basic concern in a slightly different way when we previously presented the trolley car problem.

Neutrality rules are not the only means for engineering seams, gaps, and other forms of resistance to engineered determinism. Consider the possibility of engineered air gaps, incompatibilities, and non-interoperability between techno-social systems. Air gaps are a relatively familiar concept for security researchers. Air gap usually refers to a computer that is not connected to the Internet or any other network that is connected to the Internet. The idea is that an air-gapped computer is more secure (though not perfectly so) from hacking. Air gaps are implemented for systems that require an extra degree of security; for example, "payment and industrial control systems should only be on internal networks that are not connected to the company's business network, thus preventing intruders from entering the corporate network through the internet and working their way to sensitive systems."[41]

Engineering air gaps between techno-social systems seems a plausible way to prevent techno-social engineering creep. One can imagine designing air gaps between different smart subsystems on the emerging Internet of Things. *Does your smart toaster need to be connected to the Internet? To the smart transportation system? Who decides?* Unfortunately, it's all too easy to presume that someone else will figure it out, to defer to the market, the government, the wisdom of the crowd, the engineers. Progress down the slippery-sloped path toward ubiquitous smart systems is paved by engineered complacency comparable to what we've seen for electronic contracts. A critical outlook and critical analysis is needed. Once the importance of such gaps and seams is recognized, entrepreneurial possibilities emerge.[42] Witness free and open source software. Witness Wikipedia. Witness the powerful and sophisticated ecosystem of decentralized systems and services, ranging from federated social networks (Diaspora) to blockchain-enabled applications (Bitcoin, smart contracts)[43] to user-empowering, in-home servers (Freedom Box).[44] There is room for bottom-up resistance, but it's an uphill battle.[45] As we noted earlier with respect to Diaspora, it can be hard to overcome the network effects and inertia that glue customers to Facebook.[46] It's hard to attract consumers who've become accustomed to the simple convenience. It's hard to start from scratch.

James Vasile's Views on the Difficulties of Decentralization[47]

There's more to decentralization than seeking a straightforward technical solution and building a better social networking app. It's true that we haven't realized the grand vision of Diaspora and FreedomBox. We need enlightened policy. We need the centralized platform monopolies to behave better. Those steps, though, won't ever give people control over the means of communication. Without that control, we'll always be at the mercy of Facebook or whatever comes next.

Redecentralizing the web is hard. FreedomBox and other projects I've worked with found that delivering exciting, secure, privacy-respecting apps required starting from scratch. Every piece of centralized tech depends on a bunch of other pieces that also tend toward the efficiency of centralization. Most of it is invisible to end users but it's centralized pieces all the way down. We wanted to build a beautiful fountain but were missing basic plumbing. If you want to fundamentally change the relationships between the visible parts, you can't just skim the surface. You have to dive deep and you need to invent all the decentralized building blocks that make up a complete web service.

It's a little like switching cars from gas to electricity. You can't just aim sunbeams at your fuel tank. You have to change every moving part in the vehicle, rethink gas stations, reinvent batteries, redesign a chunk of the electric grid, adopt new regulations, grow a new supply chain, and maybe fundamentally change the average person's relationship to their car.

The internal combustion car and all the pieces of our world that relate to it benefited from billions of dollars of investment and a century of development. We're not going to shift everybody to electric cars overnight. With all the might of the car companies, it will still take decades of small changes, each one ambitious on its own. Likewise, we're not going to dislodge the Internet monopolies overnight with weekend coders and money begged on Kickstarter.

What we're going to do instead is start at the bottom and build some boring infrastructure (like https://ipfs.io or https://briarproject.org/) that makes other decentralized things possible. That piece will make new decentralized work possible (like http://ongakuryoho.com/). Those efforts will also be boring to everybody except privacy geeks. But we'll keep building and refining. Eventually we'll have a towering stack of pieces, each providing some crucial bit of decentralized functionality. They'll add up to something that, finally, some end users want.

And when that thing is built, nobody will notice. Unless you care what's under the hood, it will be boring, like a Prius. People who use it will like that it works well and respects their privacy, but they will understand decentralization about as well as they get battery chemistry or regenerative braking.

That is what we're building towards. This is a monumental task. But we should firmly reject any suggestion that we stop building just because it's hard and will take a while.

Similarly, deliberately engineered incompatibilities and non-interoperability might serve as useful air gaps and sources of friction. Economists and technologists generally celebrate compatibility and inter-operability for the social welfare gains attributable to increased efficiency, productivity, and innovation. It's often better to have things work together without a conflict and to have functional communications between techno-social systems (or components thereof). We also celebrate these technological characteristics in many contexts. But since our focus is on the smart techno-social systems that shape the environments within which we develop and live our lives, we should be wary, in these contexts, of presuming that all the gains from compatibility and interoperability will in fact materialize. We should want to know to whom such gains flow, and, critically, we need to account for the social costs.

Consider the idea of engineering noise into our intelligence-enabled control systems. This could take many forms. Finn Brunton and Helen Nissenbaum develop a bunch of obfuscation techniques and tools to enable average Internet users to disrupt surveillance, disable machine learning, and resist techno-social engineering.[48] The basic idea is to deliberately inject "ambiguous, confusing, or misleading information" into surveillance streams.[49] Anonymization of data is another example. While imperfect and too often misunderstood as impervious to re-identification efforts,[50] anonymization is a technique that can constrain techno-social engineering and enable resistance. It involves engineered noise in the (perhaps counterintuitive) sense that removing personally identifiable information is akin to overwriting such information with random characters to generate ambiguity about identity. Notably, these proposals are not costless. Obfuscation may lead to less accurate or less personal advertisements. And as Danielle Citron has argued persuasively, anonymity not only lubricates free speech and resistance, it also enables antisocial, hateful behavior that causes significant harm to others. Panaceas are pipedreams. But returning to the idea of developing new logics and alternative mindsets, let's abandon our quest for perfection and acknowledge that "messiness is a virtue."[51]

Support Human Flourishing by Engineering Transaction Costs and Inefficiencies

The third strategy is a direct challenge to existing logics. The strategy rejects the ideals of minimizing transaction costs and maximizing efficiency. These are ideals for markets, not necessarily for human beings or society in general. The strategy explicitly adopts human flourishing as the relevant end, and, further, it depends upon an identifiable set of causal relationships, specifically, that the exercise and development of specific human capabilities (i) entail transaction costs and inefficiencies, and (ii) support human flourishing. Executing the strategy thus requires knowledge about these relationships in a specific techno-social context. Various social science disciplines have developed such knowledge. We need to figure out how to integrate their knowledge into techno-social engineering practices, or, as Cohen suggests, "the design of legal and technical architectures."[52] We've explored various examples where this strategy could apply and where modern techno-social engineering pushes strongly in the opposite direction.

Our most detailed discussion along these lines was in Chapter 5, where we explained how the electronic contracting architecture seems to have been optimized to minimize transaction costs, maximize efficiency, minimize deliberation, engineer complacency, and, as a result, nudge people to behave like simple machines. We carefully raised a series of hypotheses and suggested a number of areas in need of further research. Suppose our hypotheses turn out to be accurate. *What do our proposed strategies suggest we ought to do?* First, we need to identify the human capabilities at risk. According to conventional contract law theory, contract law enables and ought to enable people to exercise their will freely in pursuit of their own ends[53] and to relate to others freely in pursuit of cooperative ends.[54] At the core of contract law are the basic human capabilities of autonomy and sociality.[55] Yet our critical analysis suggested that the electronic contracting architecture threatens the development and exercise of both capabilities. What follows is a brief exploration of legal reforms that would engineer transaction costs and inefficiencies to support human flourishing and mitigate the hypothesized (and, for purposes of this section, assumed to be empirically proven) harmful effects of techno-social engineering.

Legal Reforms for Electronic Contracting

Before considering legal reform, let's clear the deck. Some recent developments in electronic contract law aim to protect consumers. In practice, these reforms might address one problem and exacerbate another. For example, *Specht* v. *Netscape* requires conspicuous notice to protect consumers from surreptitious contracts.[56] This might overcome one problem – *surreptitious* contracts – but leave various others unaddressed and perhaps make them worse. Notice is hardly a panacea. As Judge Jack Weinstein explained in *Berkson* v. *GOGO*:[57]

> Reliable scientifically-based studies assessing the types of visual and written cues that put a representative sample of American society, i.e., the average Internet user, on actual notice of the importance and ramifications of "terms of use" have yet to appear.

Conclusion: Reimagining and Building Alternative Futures 289

Even if the average Internet user is effectively put on notice through well-studied "visual and written cues," that would not remediate electronic contract law. Neither a lack of conspicuous notice nor ineffective notice is what causes people to behave like machines. We are likely as susceptible – if not more susceptible – to techno-social engineering when we are put on notice and then prompted to proceed to click-to-contract automatically.[58]

This is tricky. Meaningful notice might mean that consumers are put on notice of salient terms, and this triggers a duty to read on the presumption that consumers then can and perhaps will deliberate about whether to read those terms. But such initial deliberation[59] will likely be short-lived; many consumers will decide not to bother reading because it would be irrational to do so, given the various design features we've discussed. And again, repeat interactions with this human-computer interface likely lead to the same conditioning. Alternative designs might increase the likelihood of actual deliberation over the terms (rather than whether to read) and/or reduce the likelihood of conditioning. Other legal reforms that reshape the electronic contracting environment will be necessary.

The doctrinal fix of conspicuous notice falls short of what consumers might need. It provides the appearance of protection through notice but that only reinforces the existing regime. As law professor Nancy Kim put it:

> Notice triggers the duty to read. The duty to read is onerous when the terms are convoluted and voluminous. It is frustrating when there is no ability to negotiate for different terms. It is troubling when the duty is triggered by notice that terms exist rather than by the terms themselves. But it is unrealistic and maybe sadistic given the burdensome nature of some standard wrap contract terms.[60]

The song remains the same. The behavior remains the same. The path we are on remains the same. In other words, the creeping phenomena – boilerplate creep, surveillance creep, nudge creep – continue to optimize the environment, our interactions (reduced to mere transactions), and ourselves.

Not only does the doctrinal intervention fail to address the fundamental problem, but, in practice, requiring conspicuous notice might even contribute to the techno-social engineering we've described.[61] It could contribute to engineered complacency by creating a false sense of security, autonomy, and participation.

Process-oriented fixes like conspicuous notice extend well beyond electronic contracting. For example, notice-and-consent plays a similar role in discussions of surveillance (privacy) and nudging. At bottom, such fixes hollow out the substance of the relevant legal regime and run the risk of doing the same to the corresponding human relationships.

Accordingly, we consider five proposals that would combat electronic contracting creep and the techno-social engineering we've posited. The first and second are extreme. Although we don't endorse them, they're worth considering. Then, we present three more modest recommendations.

Two Extreme Proposals

One straightforward reform proposal would be to eliminate electronic contracts altogether and replace the entire regime with legislation that fully determines the contours of legal relationships formed online. There are various ways to imagine such legislation.[62] The basic idea would be to replace the private ordering accomplished by electronic contracting with public ordering enacted by a legislative body or regulatory agency charged with looking out for the public good. This would eliminate the techno-social engineering we've identified. And if we assumed that it would achieve the optimal outcomes in terms of efficiency and fairness for consumers that we assumed for purposes of argument here, then this proposal would be an ideal solution. It would be substantively the same (in terms of the terms and conditions that govern the relevant legal relationships), yet without producing externalities of the type we've discussed. In the real world, this proposal potentially creates more worrisome problems than the one it solves. There are a host of well-known dilemmas associated with public ordering through legislative bodies and regulatory agencies that would lead us far from the assumed ideal, and many of the positive social gains traditionally associated with contract law, gains in autonomy and sociality, might be lost.

Another straightforward reform proposal would be to embrace electronic contracts wholeheartedly but insist upon actual consent through deliberation and a meeting of the minds. This would instantiate Radin's World A. The basic idea would be to sustain private ordering through contracts but get rid of the legal fiction that equates notice or assent with consent. This also would eliminate the techno-social engineering we've identified, but it would come at a steep cost to society. As many have observed, the transaction costs would be too high, causing electronic commerce and innovation to come to a screeching halt.

We reject both extreme proposals. Electronic contracting plays a critical role in modern society, and we do not aim to throw out the baby with the bathwater. Our aim is remediation rather than replacement of contract law as practiced, and retention of contract law's infrastructural role in promoting human autonomy and sociality.

Our Three Proposals

Our three proposals primarily respond to micro and macro design features of the electronic contracting environment and aim to mitigate the techno-social engineering we've identified. The proposals are framed in terms of preliminary recommendations and pitched at the level of principles rather than specific doctrinal reforms. Consider these proposals conversation starters offered with an understanding that more detail is necessary for them to be implemented.[63]

Our first proposal is that with respect to electronic contracting, *contract law should require some deliberation* on the part of the entity accepting contractual terms offered by another. At a foundational level, this would expand upon two bedrock contract principles: (i) voluntariness and (ii) the absence of coercion or duress. A *deliberation principle* – understood either as a newly formulated criterion or an implied but undertheorized dimension of voluntariness – would add the moral legitimacy detailed by Heidi Hurd,[64] while also going some way towards dealing with the techno-social engineering problem.

Consistent with our overall discussion, deliberation here refers generically to some substantial degree of System 2 thinking. Its existence might be difficult to prove empirically. Nevertheless, it seems reasonable to require that, at a minimum, consumers pay attention to the act of contracting and its consequences. Should courts endorse this principle, automatic contracting would be ruled out.[65] In practice, this requirement might combine meaningful notice with speed bumps designed to prompt demonstrable deliberation.

Speed bumps designed to prompt demonstrable deliberation and comprehension are also plausible interventions in other contexts where techno-social engineering interferes with humans' capacity to think critically. For example, some media platforms concerned with fake news and comment trolling have considered implementing engineered speed bumps that require people to stop, think, and demonstrate comprehension prior to posting comments.

Theoretically, requiring deliberation returns electronic contracting closer to its roots in consent. But it need not go all the way to the foundational concept of the "meeting of the minds." Nor would deliberation need to entail substantive evaluation of all terms. Instead, it might focus on the most important and salient terms. A deliberation principle would be justified in part by the notion of the "gravity" of binding oneself by contract to another and consensually contributing to their autonomy.[66] There are many detailed questions of implementation that might be quite tricky. We leave such details to be worked out by scholars and courts in the future.

Ruling out automatic contracting raises some contestable line-drawing issues. Our deliberation principle could, but need not, rule out automatic contracting that itself results from a person's initial decision to delegate. One can imagine a person deliberatively choosing to delegate future contractual decision-making to an agent, whether a lawyer, a spouse, or a bot. Such delegation could, but need not, raise the same concerns that we have considered with regard to decisions not to read and our current online contracting behavior more generally. We recognize this is a grey area. It highlights how difficult it is to establish the appropriate threshold of sufficient deliberation. After all, deliberative practices occur over at least two axes: *intensity* (e.g. quick, medium, long amounts of scrutiny) and *frequency* (e.g. once, intermittently, all the time), both of which are strongly influenced by the designed environment. Quick deliberation, for example, might be too brisk to justifiably count as critically thought-through validation. Likewise, a transfer of continuous contracting power after a single instance of deliberation would, over time, become the functional equivalent to automatic behavior. Beyond these considerations, however, is the matter of meaning. As we have hypothesized, the degree of our deliberation might vary with the perceived salience of contractual terms and the related significance of contract formation itself.

Accordingly, our second proposal picks up on the idea that *contract law should concern meaningful relationships*. The proliferation of contracts dealing with seemingly mundane and trivial matters is a product of and at the same time a contributing factor to electronic contracting creep. As we discussed, the macro effects of countless seemingly meaningless contracts could weigh heavily on our capacity to devote time and attention to deliberation and the exercise of our autonomy. Reducing the scope of contract law might be necessary to preserve its role in promoting individual and group autonomy and to avoid the slow degrading effects we've hypothesized. It might be quite difficult, as a doctrinal and policy matter, to get rid of *de minimus* contracts because, arguably, too much economic activity is governed by contract. Should every website visit or app update require a click-to-contract contract?

Doctrinally, we suspect various speed bumps could be introduced,[67] and policy-wise, we recognize that many of the relationships currently governed by standard form electronic contracts would have to be governed by alternative institutional arrangements. Such reform might be justified by the age-old principle of not troubling the legal system with trivial matters that are best handled by self-help and alternative institutional means, such as social norms, standard-setting, and consumer protection laws. Although we do not endorse the extreme proposal discussed in the previous section, we do see a role for modest legislative and regulatory interventions that established uniform commercial codes for the many low-stakes transactions that are incredibly widespread.

Our third proposal focuses on *developing better reciprocity with respect to third parties*. We advocate the following doctrinal reform: Courts should refuse to enforce "no third-party beneficiary" clauses when one of the parties is in fact a third-party beneficiary of a different but dependent contract (what we referred to as a side-agreement). This reform aims to sever the hidden, one-sided relationships brokered between consumers and various third-party strangers with whom the brokering party – typically, the website owner – has a relationship. Such a reform might be justified as a means to preserve the integrity of contract and the socializing relationships it purports to support. We advocate this reform because the illusion of free electronic goods and services seems to be an important part of the techno-social engineering. That is, the side deals struck by consumer-facing websites depend on the no third-party beneficiary clauses in part because of the nature of the hidden exchanges (e.g. selling consumers for advertising or data collection) and in part because the hidden exchanges are what subsidize the consumer-facing websites. Disabling the no third-party beneficiary clauses might force such exchanges to the surface, where notice becomes more meaningful and some degree of deliberation more likely. (Notably, a more aggressive reform would be to give consumers express third-party beneficiary rights. This has been done, for example, by the European Commission in its Standard Contractual Clauses for personal data transfers outside the European Union.[68])

The three proposals introduce friction into electronic contracting practices. Many will balk at the ideas for this reason alone. Introducing friction slows down progress. It interrupts the seamlessness of electronic contracting. It creates transaction costs and inefficiencies. These are anathema to the efficiency and productivity logics. This is, of course, the point. Stopping and thinking about when and with whom and on what terms one enters legally binding contractual relationships may be costly, but those may be costs worth paying if we are to exercise and develop our autonomy and sociality.

May 25, 2018: Time for Change

Back in 2012, a Facebook user posted a message to Facebook in his timeline. He declared "my copyright is attached to all of my personal details, illustrations, comics, paintings, professional photos and videos, etc. (as a result of the Berner Convention). For commercial use of the above my written consent is needed at all times!"[69] In a Daily News piece, "Facebook Message Claiming Users Have 'Copyright' to Photos, Timeline Posts Is a Hoax", Philip Caulfield explained why the Facebook user's attempted exercise of will was futile. The law was well settled. The user entered a contract with Facebook, and Facebook's Terms of Service provided Facebook with the licenses and consent it needed. The user post was a legally ineffective hoax.[70]

Imagine if you could bargain with websites over contractual terms. What if you could say to Facebook: "Sure, collect data about what I look at, what I click, and who I interact with on your service, but don't share that data with anyone engaged in advertising or marketing or with any data brokers." What if you could say to Google: "You can collect, store, and use my search data for 30 days, but after that, I withdraw consent completely and unequivocally." What if you could say to Amazon: "I authorize you to collect and use my browsing and transactional data only to improve the quality of my searches and only while I am logged on as an Amazon Prime customer." Alright, the transaction costs of trillions of different, idiosyncratic user-initiated contracts would be overwhelming. Like the second of the extreme proposals we described above, it would grind electronic commerce to a halt.

Doc Searls and his colleagues at Customer Commons[71] have been working for years on standardized terms for customers to use in managing their relationships with websites and other vendors.[72] The contracting tools are part of the Vendor Relationship Management toolkit, which is a set of tools that enables customers to exercise agency in the marketplace. They've made progress over the years, but uptake has been slower than they'd hoped. That may change on May 25, 2018.

On that date, the General Data Protection Regulation, or GDPR, will be enforceable by the European Union. With potential fines for non-compliance being quite substantial,[73] the GDPR will give European residents some bargaining leverage with companies and an opportunity to assert control over their personal data.[74] Among many other regulatory requirements, the GDPR strictly governs the granting and withdrawal of consent. Consent must be explicit about what data is collected and the purposes for using the specified data, and, critically, consent may be withdrawn.[75] The capability to withdraw consent makes the Facebook hoax described above less outlandish. Considering the GDPR, it's possible to imagine alternative contracting practices and more nuanced contractual relationships. Doc Searls' dream of customers systematically using contract and related tools to manage their relationships with vendors now seems feasible. It could be an important first step toward flipping the scientific-management-of-consumers script we've become so accustomed to.

Mass Media and the First Amendment

In 1978, the United States Supreme Court decided that the First Amendment of the United States Constitution did not preclude the Federal Communications Commission from restricting the public broadcast of comedian George Carlin's 12-minute "Filthy Words" monologue. The following excerpt from the Court's decision, *FCC* v. *Pacifica Foundation*, 438 U.S. 726 (1978), shows how the Justices compare different media of expression and evaluate media affordances and effects:

> We have long recognized that each medium of expression presents special First Amendment problems. And of all forms of communication, it is broadcasting that has received the most limited First Amendment protection. Thus, although other speakers cannot be licensed except under laws that carefully define and narrow official discretion, a broadcaster may be deprived of his license and his forum if the Commission decides that such an action would serve "the public interest, convenience, and necessity." Similarly, although the First Amendment protects newspaper publishers from being required to print the replies of those whom they criticize, *Miami Herald Publishing Co.* v. *Tornillo*, 418 U.S. 241 (1974), it affords no such protection to broadcasters; on the contrary, they must give free time to the victims of their criticism. *Red Lion Broadcasting Co.* v. *FCC*, 395 U.S. 367 (1969).
>
> The reasons for these distinctions are complex, but two have relevance to the present case. First, the broadcast media have established a uniquely pervasive presence in the lives of all Americans. Patently offensive, indecent material presented over the airwaves confronts the citizen, not only in public, but also in the privacy of the home, where the individual's right to be left alone plainly outweighs the First Amendment rights of an intruder. Because the broadcast audience is constantly tuning in and out, prior warnings cannot completely protect the listener or viewer from unexpected program content. To say that one may avoid further offense by turning off the radio when he hears indecent language is like saying that the remedy for an assault is to run away after the first blow. One may hang up on an indecent phone call, but that option does not give the caller a constitutional immunity or avoid a harm that has already taken place.

Second, broadcasting is uniquely accessible to children, even those too young to read. Although [the] written message [at issue in Cohen] might have been incomprehensible to a first grader, Pacifica's broadcast could have enlarged a child's vocabulary in an instant. Other forms of offensive expression may be withheld from the young without restricting the expression at its source. Bookstores and motion picture theaters, for example, may be prohibited from making indecent material available to children ...

It is appropriate, in conclusion, to emphasize the narrowness of our holding. This case does not involve a two-way radio conversation between a cab driver and a dispatcher, or a telecast of an Elizabethan comedy. We have not decided that an occasional expletive in either setting would justify any sanction or, indeed, that this broadcast would justify a criminal prosecution. The Commission's decision rested entirely on a nuisance rationale under which context is all-important. The concept requires consideration of a host of variables. The time of day was emphasized by the Commission. The content of the program in which the language is used will also affect the composition of the audience, and differences between radio, television, and perhaps closed-circuit transmissions, may also be relevant. As Mr. Justice Sutherland wrote a "nuisance may be merely a right thing in the wrong place – like a pig in the parlor instead of the barnyard." *Euclid* v. *Ambler Realty Co.*, 272 U.S. 365, 388 (1926). We simply hold that when the Commission finds that a pig has entered the parlor, the exercise of its regulatory power does not depend on proof that the pig is obscene.

Perspectives on the Turing Test

Philosopher John Searle famously challenged the second premise with his Chinese Room thought experiment,[1] which can be summarized as follows. Imagine that someone writes down a question in Mandarin Chinese, perhaps "Do you speak Chinese?," and passes the note under the bottom part of a door that leads to another room. Inside that room is a person who doesn't speak any Chinese but has an instruction manual filled with pages each containing two columns that match one set of Chinese characters to another set of Chinese characters. Whenever this person is slipped a note written in Chinese, she scans the instruction manual to find the same characters and composes a response by strictly copying the other set found on the same page. In this case, she copies characters that say, "Yes, I speak Chinese."

The main question Searle asks is whether the person following the instruction manual truly speaks Chinese. Searle's answer is no, the person doesn't understand anything that she's communicating. While the instruction manual provides the structure or syntax of Chinese communication, it doesn't convey what the communication means, its semantics. Searle believes his thought experiment refutes the second premise noted above because the person in the room can be understood as analogous to a digital computer: both follow instructions without their programming yielding comprehension to the direction-following entity. Consequently, Searle concludes that Turing is wrong to embrace a functionalist account of mind. A complicated machine can exhibit a conscious-like performance without being conscious. Put otherwise, Searle contends that Turing fails to establish that his test can demonstrate authentic conversation is occurring as opposed to a simulated form of conversation. In the end, two entirely different processes can generate identical performances. More generally, Searle argues that computers can simulate thinking but cannot think.

A significant firestorm followed the publication of this argument and to this day the debate still rages. For example, philosopher Daniel Dennett made the intriguing argument that everything Searle says about the computer also can be said about the person in the room (or, more accurately, the brain of the person in the room).[2] The person speaks English and outside observers take such speech to imply that the person understands what he or she is saying. But who knows what is truly going on inside the person's head and whether his or her brain is in fact any different from the intelligent-seeming computer? Put another way, all together, the English-speaking person and the instructions – as a system – do understand Chinese.[3] We could go around in circles, perhaps spiraling toward something, but, as we will see below, we don't need to do so because we are not interested in determining the necessary and sufficient conditions for attributing intelligence to machines that is on par with that of humans.

During the firestorm, cognitive scientist Stevan Harnad developed what he refers to as the *Total Turing Test* (TTT), which expands the locus of examination to include nonverbal behavior.[4] He claims that "our ability to interact bodily with the things in the world – and the many nonverbal ways we do – are as important to the test as our linguistic capacities." Harnad also states "it is hard to imagine, for example, that a TT candidate could chat with you coherently about the object in the world until doomsday without ever having encountered any objects directly." This idea of symbol grounding is a response to Searle's "Chinese Room."[5] Incorporating Searle's ideas, Harnad contends that there must be some connection between the symbols and what they denote to have actual thought. Without sufficient experience to make such connections, the processes would "send us round and round in endless circles, from one meaningless string of symbols to another."[6] Harnad incorporates sensorimotor performance into his TTT to escape this problem.[7]

Philosopher of technology Paul Schweizer goes further than Harnad and develops what he refers to as the *Truly Total Turing Test* (TTTT).[8] He emphasizes that neither the original TT nor the TTT are tests that, if passed, would wholly justify ascription of intelligence because they lack sufficient conditions. He explains that we do not really use just a short conversation with a person to attribute intelligence to that person. That is, we do use and rely on the conversation, but in large part because the conversation is taking place against the backdrop of "extended and multifarious interactions with human beings generally."[9] We might attribute intelligence to machines on the basis of a five-minute conversation, but these machines would have been making use of background knowledge that is relevant to a different type of entity, humans. Per the TTTT, to evaluate whether "artificial or alien cognitive structure should be regarded as possessing intelligence on a par with human beings," the type being tested would have to be capable of generating and relying on its own background knowledge. Thus, for Schweizer, "what is necessary for genuinely comparable performance is that the algorithms responsible for [a] robot's behavior not only enable it to use the languages that we have programmed into it, but rather that a community of such robots could develop these languages starting from the 'state of nature' of our pre-linguistic forebears."[10]

Our Free Will Discussion

For better or worse, our goal is to write an accessible interdisciplinary book – at least one that's more accessible than typical academic monographs. In pursuit of clarity and sharp intuitions, we took several liberties when presenting the free will debate, sometimes deliberately aiming for simplification over complexity. To set the record straight for interested readers, we'd like to identify the main shortcuts we took.

For starters, our account presupposes that consciousness exists. This view has long been attacked by behaviorists and we don't take up their arguments. If we did, one of the things we'd need to address is whether the *mens rea* criterion in law can be adequately interpreted as an inference to the best explanation that's compatible with natural determinism. Specifically, it would entail asking if *mens rea* focuses on patterns of behavior that are best explained as an intent to do X solely because deterministic possibilities aren't given their due.

Second, we presented the free will debate in binary terms: determinism vs. free will. Admittedly, this is a rather old-fashioned way of putting things. Many contemporary philosophers embrace a third alternative called compatibilism. According to this view, determinism can be reconciled with freedom – which is to say, we can be responsible for our choices even if determinism is true. Harry Frankfurt, whom we cite several times, is a seminal figure in the compatibilist debates. In this context, it's important to note that compatibilism is a metaphysical perspective, not an empirical one. For even if determinism is true, logical arguments can be made that varieties of freedom (to use a phrase from the philosopher Daniel Dennett) still exist.[1]

Third, many contemporary versions of natural determinism attempt to account for quantum uncertainty. They typically assert that at the quantum level probabilistic events occur that don't follow the rigid causal sequence of Laplace's demon. This view leads to debate about whether quantum events scale up to non-trivially influence our decisions, and, if so, whether their impact makes us beholden to forces that impact us in ways that we cannot (or cannot easily) predict in advance. Whether this line of thinking provides a basis for free will or compatibilism is beyond the scope of this book. Our arguments hold regardless.

Fourth, when we explained why determinism conflicts with our folk psychological intuitions, we emphasized the importance of having alternatives. We illustrated this view by appealing to the reader's sense that she could continue reading our chapter or stop, at least relative to certain constraints. In so doing, we omitted discussion of Frankfurt's renowned argument that having alternatives is not a necessary condition for moral responsibility.[2] Imagine discussing this chapter with us at a café. After an hour passes, you decide to continue chatting because you find the conversation fascinating or amusing. When making this choice, it turns out that the heavy door leading in and out of the café is locked and no one is around with the key; you couldn't leave if you wanted to. What Frankfurt wants us to believe is that you're still responsible for staying even though you couldn't leave anyway.

Fifth, we sometimes engaged in rhetorical slippage that allowed us to seamlessly link allegedly necessary features of free will with folk psychological commitments and mere methodological assumptions. Simply put, much of our description of free will assumes its existence instead of considering skeptical alternatives. For example, we say that if reality is naturally determined, free will would be an important illusion. But to say that we've evolved thus is to admit that we could have evolved otherwise. Similarly, when we discuss what moral responsibility requires, we sometimes are only talking about what widely held norms presuppose. We don't consider whether these norms are wrong and driven by false presumptions.

Sixth, it could be said that our account of free will – an agent's situated capability to engage in reflective self-determination about her will – prematurely puts free will in the stipulated definition. To get around this problem, we could have anchored our argument in one of the main concepts related to free will, such as "control," instead of free will itself. But shifting terminology profoundly would disrupt the flow of our narrative.

Seventh, our discussion of engineering determinism does not consider the existential possibilities that are open to humans who are stuck in environments that cause them to behave in a rigid repetitive manner. For example, existential philosopher Albert Camus' reinterpretation of the myth of Sisyphus focuses on the subjective meaning the failed boulder-pusher can add to his unchangeable external situation, i.e. viewing his imprisonment through a defiant lens and not a hopeless one. Again, this is a matter of emphasis and the shift from outer constraints to internal freedom would require a chapter-long discussion, at a minimum.[3]

In the end, we could have avoided these issues and bypassed the need for an appendix. For, as this discussion clarifies, we know exactly what's required to add nuance. Nevertheless, the fact remains that a longer discussion of free will – which, after all, is a central philosophical topic and covered in voluminous papers and books – would detract from our main and delimited objectives: (1) differentiating natural determinism from engineered determinism, and (2) discussing how an outlook on the former can influence one's perspective on the latter.

Modern Meal Times

Meals can be such a waste of time and energy. Food (fuel) should be consumed as quickly and efficiently as possible. This mindset was lampooned at least as far back as 1936 in Charlie Chaplin's *Modern Times*. In one scene, Chaplin's character, an assembly line worker in a factory, is coerced into demonstrating a Billows Feeding Machine: a contraption that binds his arms and force feeds him both efficiently and quickly. The machine was fictional, but its satirical presentation was meant to demonstrate real concern about mechanized factories turning workers into just another cog in the assembly line. In the lead-up to Chaplin's tenure as a test subject, the following sales pitch is presented.

> Don't stop for lunch: be ahead of your competitor. The Billows Feeding Machine will eliminate the lunch hour, increase your production, and decrease your overhead. Allow us to point out some of the features of this wonderful machine: its beautiful, aerodynamic, streamlined body; its smoothness of action, made silent by our electro-porous metal ball bearings. Let us acquaint you with our automaton soup plate – its compressed-air blower, no breath necessary, no energy required to cool the soup. Notice the revolving plate with the automatic food pusher. Observe our counter-shaft, double-knee-action corn feeder, with its synchro-mesh transmission, which enables you to shift from high to low gear by the mere tip of the tongue. Then there is the hydro-compressed, sterilized mouth wiper: its factors of control insure against spots on the shirt front. These are but a few of the delightful features of the Billows Feeding Machine. Let us demonstrate with one of your workers, for actions speak louder than words. Remember, if you wish to keep ahead of your competitor, you cannot afford to ignore the importance of the Billows Feeding Machine.[1]

There are two things worth emphasizing here. First, the value of adopting the Feeding Machine is purportedly only to make the work day more productive by removing the need for workers to be given a lunch hour – an outcome that they probably would reject if given a choice. Second, the worker strapped into the system is stripped of his autonomy. Once you're in the Feeding Machine, you lose control over your body. (Hopefully, this point is making you think of the discussion of outsourcing bodily control in Chapter 2.) And just as importantly, you're "unable to manage or process the abundance of goods the machine keeps pushing."[2] This point about uncontrollable consumption resonated with the Depression Era audience the film was made for.[3] As one analyst aptly put it:

> Faced with a depression of the nation's buying power, industry's challenge was to create a more prolific, efficient, and effective buyer for the goods it manufactured. When Chaplin's Tramp straps himself into the Feeding Machine – on his supervisor's orders, though presumably he's clocked out for lunch – he becomes (at least until the machine breaks down) the product that every American factory is trying to assemble: a perfect consumer. He's literally an open mouth, captive to the aggressive new machinery that American industry has designed to feed his appetites. He's passive, while the marketplace is active and (r)evolving. As metaphors for the technology of capitalism itself go, the Feeding Machine is a pretty transparent one: to live in *Modern Times* (and, by extension, in modern times) means to train yourself to consume as quickly, efficiently, and widely as possible.[4]

This vision of the value of producing hyper-efficient, commodified meals lives today. Technology companies are churning out "edible tools for the overworked drones of the tech industry: cubes of caffeine engineered to increase brainpower, without the coffee doldrums that follow, and, yes, Soylent, a liquid meal replacement for the nutrients you need to survive, without the inconvenience of eating actual food."[5] These products are some of the more ominous magnifications of the "postwar industrial food system" that pervades our work lives as well as our personal ones.[6] This system is part of the larger machinations of sprawling Taylorism, running the gamut from microwave dinners to junk food products that are designed to be addictive and offer "maximum bliss" to taste buds engineered (evolved?) to prefer artificial flavors.[7] *We can't emphasize these points enough: cheap bliss can result from techno-social engineering altering expectations, norms, and even physiological responses; and creating the conditions for regular experiences of cheap bliss links some powerful trends in techno-social engineering to hedonism.*

There are many ways to resist the plunge into cheap bliss. In this context, we're going to emphasize the practice of meal preparation as an opportunity to develop skill and character; it also looks at groups – friends, family, colleagues, neighbors, or even strangers – having a meaningful experience when gathered for a homemade meal. Philosopher of technology Albert

Borgmann develops a robust account of this perspective in his analysis of "focal things" and "focal practices."

During mealtimes, the food and its setting are the focal things. The preparation of the meal, the gathering around the table, and the customs of serving, eating, and conversing are the focal practices. Focal things and practices disclose the world about us – our time, our place, our heritage, our hopes – and center our lives. They lead us to say: "There is no place I would rather be. There is nothing I would rather do. There is no one I would rather be with."[8]

Let's unpack this observation. On the focal practice side of the equation, we have cooks engaged in food preparation. Sometimes they follow recipes (including ones with sentimental value passed down from friends and family); sometimes they improvise in the kitchen; and, sometimes they do a bit of both. These approaches are deliberately less efficient than pre-fab alternatives. Poetically, it's called preparing food with love. More prosaically, it requires some modicum of skillful activity, such as knowing which ingredients are best, how to chop, slice, dice, and cut, which pots, pans, and other kinds of equipment are appropriate, when to stir and drain, when to add more seasoning, when to adjust cooking temperature, and how to construct a multi-dish meal. These multisensory knowledges involve touch, taste, smell, and dexterous movement. Judgment also is involved, ranging from deciding when to not mechanically follow a recipe to how to make adjustments to accommodate different guests. All this knowledge and judgment takes time to cultivate, trial and error experience, and the discipline to not cut and run when things don't turn out as planned. By making food, we thus work on bettering ourselves. When we place value on acquiring the right skills to cook we recognize the intrinsic value of a reality – however mediated and hyper-mediated it may be when we experience it – that isn't designed to bend to our whim or lower its resistance when we become frustrated and anxious. We gestured to these points in chapter eight when we asked the question of what can be learned by using a smart toaster.

On the focal thing side of the equation, we have the product of the labor of love: home-cooked food and its presentation. Yes, there are different ways of setting a table and some are more formal than others. Yes, not everyone has good silverware or bowls, plates, and saucers. But when we take the time and effort to cook food for our loved ones, the presentation of the food matters. Simply choosing to not use paper plates or plastic cups can make a big difference on what mood arises. And that's one of Borgmann's main points: meals can be especially meaningful when everyone is immersed in the moment – savoring every morsel and enjoying the emergent conversation such that no one prefers to be anywhere else or with anyone else. These are the moments, Borgmann insists, where it's appropriate to say grace before eating and we should feel inclined to use our best manners – verbally, when talking with others, and physically, when adopting a conscientious posture, avoiding scarfing down the food, and being discreet about unwanted bodily functions.

It's tempting to think that this slice of the good life merely is the result of people having the pleasure of eating tasty food with good company. After all, it seems like we can enjoy other people's company to the heightened extent Borgmann describes when we're at a good restaurant with inviting decor or even at a dive joint that does a decent job of serving comfort food. Thanksgiving can still be a memorable holiday at restaurants when the folks who regularly do the cooking get a break and can be totally present to the people around them – not least when unfair gendered dynamics would dictate who spends considerable time in the kitchen. Sometimes take-out that's eaten straight from the container can even do the trick. Does this mean that self-cultivation primarily belongs on the production side of the food-making process, not extending to the consumption side? Maybe all that matters are that everyone is absorbed in the pleasure of each other's company, isn't distracted by devices like phones and televisions, and enjoys what they're eating. Then again, it seems like media can play an important role in creating memorable occasions. Think of a time when you went to a World Series, Superbowl, or Game of Thrones party, ate snacks, and said to yourself, "At this moment there isn't anywhere else I'd rather be."

Perhaps the situation is more complex. Gatherings that revolve around sporting events and shows can be fun, but they miss a crucial ingredient that Borgmann has in mind when he describes the culture of the table. During the type of meal he has in mind, the people who are sitting around the table are absorbed in each other's company in ways that go beyond merely having fun. They're catching up. They're expressing hopes. They're conveying fears. They're exchanging important information – like where a grandparent originated from or what happened to a friend who faded from sight and only recently was heard from. This careful back-and-forth is a sign of care and respect and it's hard to do in a consistent and deep way when your attention is directed elsewhere to learn which team is winning or what plot twist just occurred.

The fact is, memorable conversation that's emotionally impacting, free to spring off in multiple directions, and demonstrates interpersonal care requires skill. This is easy to overlook because we learn to communicate at an early age and spend lots of time as adults in situations where all that's required of us is shallow banter or tightly constrained discourse that revolves around single topics: going over the latest business report or getting through agenda items at a meeting. It's also easy to forget that there are different levels of listening. Attentive social listening requires that we stay undistracted, use body language to convey interest (and displaying contextually appropriate emotional responses), don't interrupt the other party or make them feel rushed, and offer cues that help the other party find the words to convey what they are hoping to say. Can we do this in restaurants? Sometimes. It depends on how close we are to other diners: intimate conversation requires a certain amount of privacy. Courtesy requires that we don't distract other patrons from having a good time. Perhaps there's music playing in the background, either enhancing or impeding a conversation. Maybe the restaurant has television sets constantly broadcasting. What about take-out? It's one thing to serve take-out at a table where people are gathered together and undistracted, but it's quite another to perceive take-out as contributing to creating an informal atmosphere where it's tempting to eat in front of the TV or with everyone's eyes fixated on their individual phone screens.

It's not a stretch to claim that some technology companies are trying to techno-socially engineer new norms that can displace the interplay between conscientious speaking and listening, making focal meals harder to experience. The public was presented with a revealing window into this ambition in 2013 when Facebook launched commercials for a product called Facebook Home. Although the interface received poor reviews, stopped receiving updates in the very same year that it launched, and can't be downloaded from the Google Play Store, the ideals it portrayed still feel as Facebook-ian as ever.

You've probably forgotten what the Facebook Ads showed. Let's start with the most egregious one: "Dinner." On the surface, it portrays an intergenerational family meal where a young woman escapes from the dreariness of her older aunt's boring cat talk by surreptitiously turning away from the feast and instead feasting her eyes on Facebook Home. The young woman is automatically, frictionlessly transported to what she perceives to be a better place full of enchanting rock music, ballerinas, and snowball fights, normal dinner companions.

But let's break Zuckerberg's spell and shift our focus away from the character we'll call Selfish Girl. Think off-camera and outside the egocentric perspective framed by the ad. Reflect instead on the people *surrounding* her.

Ignored Aunt will soon question why she's bothering to put in effort with her distant younger niece. Eventually, she'll adapt to the Facebook Home-enforced situation and stop caring. In a scene that Facebook would never run, Selfish Girl will come to Ignored Aunt for something and be ignored herself: Selfishness is contagious, after all. Once it spreads to a future scene where everyone behaves like Selfish Girl, eyes glued to their own Home screens, the Facebook ads portend the death of family gatherings.

More specifically, they depict *the end of connecting through effort*. Unlike the entertaining and lively Chatheads the ad recommends we put on our personalized network interfaces and Home screens, we don't get to choose family members. It's a dystopian situation when everyone matches our interests and we don't feel obliged to try to connect with those folks: people with whom it's initially difficult to find common ground.

So why didn't the "Dinner" ad depress every viewer? The ad is narrated in such a way as to give Selfish Girl special license: Everyone else behaves responsibly except for her. In fact, her irresponsible behavior doesn't affect what others do.

This same exceptionalism pervades "Airplane," another Facebook Home ad. Here, the Home-obsessed main character doesn't turn off his phone when a stewardess instructs him to do so. This defiance may seem like harmless self-absorption, a stand against seemingly ridiculous rules behind airplane regulations of technology that surely resonated with Facebook's target audience. But here, too, it's only because the commercial limits the self-centeredness to one person. What if everyone on board behaved as Zuckerberg's ads instruct? No plane could depart on time.

Another Facebook Home ad, "Launchday," revolves around the same, problematic exceptionalism. This one shines a spotlight on one of Zuckerberg's bearded employees who focused on his Home screen instead of listening to his famous boss rallying the troops. The narrative seems funny because Zuckerberg is on the receiving side of the rudeness. But the layer of irony hides a fundamental sleight of hand. Our positive is shaped by the other Facebook workers who attentively carry the slack and don't rat out Bearded Guy. Would the scene be so funny if organizations we cared about or invested in came to a grinding halt because nobody paid attention to their bosses and the work to be done? We doubt it.

It would be a mistake to undervalue the ideological function of the Home ads. The message of technological efficiency and frictionless sharing is increasingly being depicted as an appropriate social ethic. If Borgmann is right, then to stop the spread we need to push back against its source, not the technology per se, but rather the depressing ethic its apostles and their commercials idealize.

Accordingly, then, some convictions deserve to be innovation-proof and shouldn't be techno-socially engineered away. These convictions are fully compatible with embracing social media, even making the most of its potential. Rejecting the ethic promoted in the Home ads doesn't perpetuate the mistaken conviction that online and offline lives are largely distinct rather than interrelated experiences. Social media can only stop us from being genuinely responsive to and responsible for others if we let it undermine pro-social effort in maintaining meaningful connections. It only diminishes our characters and true social networks if we treat Selfish Girl as a role model rather than a tragically misguided soul.

Because selfishness spreads like a contagious yawn, the real hypocrisy of the Home ads is that if everyone embraced Zuckerberg's ideology, only one type of relationship would remain: fleeting entertainment buddies. The very second we become boring, the moment we make communication anything more than a self-satisfying convenience, we'd be abandoned by fair-weather friends. No explanation necessary. No apologies given. No attempt to blunt the hurt feelings. Just an easy click of the unfriend box.

Rethinking Contract Theory

No existing contract theory explains or justifies our current electronic contracting law and architecture, at least in a manner that accounts for techno-social engineering.[1] This is admittedly unfair to contract theorists, who have had no reason to consider contracts and the technological medium through which contracts are formed as tools for techno-social engineering humans.[2]

There are many contract law theories that aim to explain and justify contract law in its various forms across jurisdictions and sectors of society.[3] Per conventional contract law theory, contract law enables and ought to enable people to exercise their will freely in pursuit of their own ends[4] and to relate to others freely in pursuit of cooperative ends.[5] At the core of various theories' conceptions of contract law are the basic human capabilities of autonomy and sociality.[6]

Contract law is often justified by two different appeals to autonomy. First, consent- and promise-based theories of contract law celebrate the individual's ability to decide for herself how and with whom to form legal relationships.[7] Second, economic theories of contract law celebrate efficient private ordering in markets. While the theories diverge in various ways,[8] they *converge on the prominence of human autonomy*. It's important to recognize that, according to these theories, contract law enhances human autonomy by providing a reliable institutional means by which individuals can bind themselves to each other and thus restrict their free will in the future. Practically, this means that the institutions must be amenable to use by people, firms, lawyers, judges, and so on. This need for practical implementation in human-social systems leads to the objective theory of contract, which holds people accountable based on their interpretable actions rather than their (typically hard to interpret, decipher, or prove) subjective intentions.[9] Beyond autonomy, the theories appear to be united in their political and institutional commitments to private ordering with minimal government intervention.

Law professor Randy Barnett, for example, has written extensively about a consent-based theory of contract law. Contract law turns on an externally manifested intention to be legally bound. In short, contracts turn on consent, objectively determined.[10] According to Barnett, "Consent is the voluntary communication by one person to another person of a particular message: that one intends to alter an already existing legal relation between the parties or to create a new one."[11] Communication is a critical aspect of his theory because it enables parties to a transaction as well as third parties to identify "rightful boundaries" and "accurately ascertain what constitutes rightful conduct and what constitutes a commitment on which they can rely."[12] Barnett's theory explains and justifies the objective theory of contract because "only a general reliance on objectively ascertainable assertive conduct will enable a legal system to perform its boundary-defining function."[13]

Electronic contracting seems to fit very well with Barnett's theory. As many courts have held, the click-to-contract mechanism requires "objectively ascertainable assertive conduct" and it communicates an unequivocal message, such as "I agree." Further, many online businesses, some would say the entire Internet economy, have relied on the conduct and its message.

Yet superficial appearances can be deceiving. In the electronic contracting context, the consent theory elevates form over substance. Clicking might be assertive conduct or an affirmative action, and it could be an external manifestation ripe for objective evaluation. But what exactly is being asserted, affirmed, or manifested? Objective evaluation is required. If the consumer is clicking automatically, habitually, and without deliberation, is it reasonable to say that the consumer asserted, communicated, or manifested an intention to be legally bound or to form a legal relationship? This is fundamental to Barnett's theory. And the question is not whether, as a matter of contract doctrine, a court could so hold. Many have done so. That isn't the point.[14] The question is whether the act of clicking in fact communicates this specific intention. The answer depends on the speaker and audience and how they interpret the act. Can we reasonably say that the person clicking is speaking or communicating something significant and meaningful? Can such a message reasonably be understood to flow from human beings engineered to behave like machines? From System 1 responses rather than System 2 deliberation? We're highly skeptical.

Electronic contracting seems to undermine Barnett's core beliefs. First and foremost, autonomy – at least in contracting itself – is a pure legal fiction. The electronic contracting environment is only autonomy-preserving in the superficial sense that consumers decide whether to take it or leave it. There are two levels at which to dismiss this dangerous fiction. First, at the micro level, it isn't clear that consumers actually decide anything when they click-to-contract. Second, at the macro level, repeated engagement with the electronic contracting environment might habituate consumers and shape beliefs, preferences, and consequently social expectations and norms regarding both the contracting interface and law. At both levels, contract law and architecture appear to reduce and devalue human autonomy. One only escapes this "autonomy challenge" by saying that the time saved by the click-to-contract mechanism increases autonomy in other activities. However, this route is dangerous because all time-saving but autonomy-sacrificing technologies could be justified in this fashion, but only so long as there is enough time in the day left to exercise autonomy. Given the expanding scale and scope of boilerplate, surveillance and nudge creep, this is a dangerously slippery slope.

Second, freedom from elite control and hierarchical coercion appear to be illusory. Electronic contracting might be oppressive, and, much worse, it might be oppressive in a manner that provides the illusion of freedom. In the electronic contract context, society simply substitutes one governing agent for another. Barnett's concerns about government intervention are simply shifted to equally if not more totalizing agents with power to coerce. The fiction of market discipline is no savior.

The electronic contract context reveals how ludicrous it would be to accept Barnett's famous sealed envelope analogy as a general theory of contracting, as opposed to a theory that fits a narrower set of cases where parties have strong existing relationships. To accept the broad version would undermine the exact values Barnett's theory purports to hold dear and accelerate the engineered demise of meaningful contractual relationships and the basic institution of freedom of contract.[15]

Law professor Charles Fried's theory of contracts as promises also celebrates the individual's ability to decide for herself how and with whom to form legal relationships. Fried emphasizes the importance of human agency and contracts as expressions of and means for exercising one's will. Fried's theory is fundamentally relational.[16] It focuses on the moral and practical importance of promises we make to each other and how legal recognition of contracts serves to enable trust and cooperation among people.[17] Contracts exist as instantiations of an individual's exercise of her will on herself and others. Fundamentally, contracts exist among people. Accordingly, Fried insists upon acceptance of promises as a necessary feature of contract law.[18] And so contracts necessarily are relational social institutions that simultaneously enhance human autonomy and sociality.

Electronic contracting fits poorly with Fried's theory because the consumer isn't respected as an equal, an agent endowed with independent free will. Instead, the consumer is treated as an object, a mere resource to be mined and shaped. Further, the relationships and trust that many electronic contracts engender are fragile and often fake. Hidden side-agreements create a network of relationships that exclude the consumer from the club through "no third-party beneficiary" clauses and hidden agendas. Moreover, whatever trust consumers develop in their relationships with websites often flows from dubious sources, such as brands, herd behavior, decision fatigue, engineered complacency and sheer ignorance.[19]

A complex extension of the consent and promise theories suggests that contract law might enhance autonomy on both sides of contractual relations. My act of entering an agreement enhances the autonomy of the other party to the contract because I have agreed that the other party can now do something that the other party did not previously have the right or power to do. Law professor Heidi Hurd refers to this as "moral magic" because "consent can, by itself, turn a battery into a handshake, a sexual assault into a kiss, a trespass into a dinner party, a theft into a gift, and the commercial appropriation of a name and likeness into a biography."[20] All of Hurd's examples also work "legal magic." There are at least two important points to make about how this theory relates to our analysis of the electronic contracting environment.

First, the theory hinges on consent and decidedly not on the legal fictions, such as inquiry notice and assent, that parade as consent in the courts.[21] Thus, it matters from moral and legal perspectives that autonomy-enhancement of one party flows from the actual consent of the other. There are many reasons to doubt that such consent exists in many click-to-contract contracts. Foremost, we don't believe consent sufficient to work "moral/legal magic" can exist without some deliberation. We should be highly skeptical of environments engineered to produce such moral/legal transformations automatically, through habituation and the other mechanisms we've discussed. Moreover, even where consent exists, we still might need to further examine the extent to which such consent is itself engineered, for example, through choice architectures designed to nudge.

Second, the theory reveals power dynamics that appear quite oppressive. Consider who is the other party whose autonomy is enhanced through electronic contracting. Obviously, at first glance, it's the website or service provider, or more generally, the firm. Although the details vary considerably, the firm often gains the freedom to commodify the consumer in terms of her attention, data, and relationships. It would be a mistake, however, to focus only on the firm that is party to the contract. There are many others whose autonomy is enhanced. A network of other parties is empowered to act in ways that otherwise they could not. If one were only measuring autonomy, one might conclude that electronic contracting results in a significant increase in net autonomy because of the magical ways in which many firms gain autonomy through the backdoor of side-agreements. This moral/legal magic is quite perverse because the autonomy gains on one side of the transaction not only are based on the illusion of consent but they also perpetuate a rigged system.

Economic theories of contract law take a variety of forms, but the core idea is that contract law is a means to efficient markets, which are means to the ultimate end of maximizing social welfare. Superficially, electronic contracting appears to fit rather well with economic theories of contract. The legal and technical architecture is, after all, optimized to minimize transaction costs and significantly expand the scale and scope of market transactions. Given the incredible growth in the number of contracts executed electronically, in part because of the incredible growth in the number of digital goods and services, it seems quite natural to conclude that electronic contracting is efficient and welfare maximizing. Nonetheless, a closer and deeper examination might tip the applecart. There are a host of conventional economic considerations one might turn to, for example, by considering whether electronic contracting enables or retards competition, or whether electronic contracting has caused specific market failures.[22] But these conventional considerations seem to be a distraction. The better types of economic questions to ask would concentrate on two major themes: (1) comparative institutional analysis and (2) social goods and how to value the preservation of basic human capabilities, or, more generally, humanity.

The first set of issues would require a careful and comparative analysis of electronic contract enabled mass markets with alternative approaches to enabling mass market provisioning of various goods and services. It's by no means obvious, and should not be accepted as natural or inevitably true, that governing trillions of mundane and trivial transactions by electronic contracts is efficient when compared with alternatives, such as standards or consumer product regulation. First, there might be tremendous negative externalities (social costs) associated with information overload, decision fatigue, and the various other effects that follow from overextending contract.[23] Second, extending contract to many of the areas where it is not necessary can distort social institutions and markets.[24] In conventional economic terms, it could be seen as a form of unnecessary government intervention into markets that otherwise would function well. Nearly costless contract formation might distort rather than enable efficient markets because the flood of contracts overwhelms institutions and individuals. (A similar argument has been made about copyright law and the social costs associated with the elimination of copyright formalities).[25] Conversely, one might argue that it is a form of market intervention into government because it routinely allows companies to replace public ordering with private ordering.[26] Either or both ways, one would need to comparatively evaluate alternative institutional regimes. To our knowledge, no one has done this type of work.[27]

The second set of issues is more fundamental. We tackle some of them in this book. The analysis moves well beyond the conventional law and economic approach to contract law. And thus, we leave a deep dive for separate work. At one level, such analysis triggers a classic debate about normative ends and the function of contract law as a means. Law and economics tend to focus on maximizing social welfare as the relevant end, and thus consider autonomy and sociality as means. Yet, to do the comparative evaluation of alternative social arrangements (both legal and technological), we would have to be able to value autonomy and sociality in terms of welfare. And that turns out to be an incredibly difficult, if not impossible, task. It's much akin to the old debates about Taylorism, which tended to pit efficiency versus human dignity, and modern legal debates that pit efficiency versus fairness. Yet, at another level, such analysis triggers a debate about social versus technological determinism and the comparative power of contract law and contracting technologies to engineer human beings. Put simply, it's a chicken and egg problem. *Which comes first? What structural factors are driving the creep phenomena? Are the human beings pushing the human-computer interface design, or is it the other way around?* These questions move well outside contract law and theory. Yet they become integral to the analysis once we introduce the possibility that contract law and architecture might be tools for techno-social engineering humans.

The bottom line with respect to the law and economic theories of contract law is that even if electronic contracting perfected markets by lowering transaction costs and improving efficiency, society might nonetheless be much worse off.[28]

The bottom line more generally is that existing contract theories fail to explain and justify electronic contracting practices. The existing theories are ill-equipped for identifying or evaluating the consequences of techno-social engineering. They may even perpetuate the Taylorist logic of electronic contracting and contribute to engineered complacency.

We don't aim to remediate contract theory. We could develop a new theory to explain and justify electronic contracting practices, but such a theory would have to shift away from contract law's historical purposes of supporting human autonomy and sociality. Instead, we advocate reforming electronic contracting law and practice.

Notes

Introduction

1. Manjoo (2017).
2. Manjoo (2017).
3. Cohan (2017).
4. Madhdawi (2017).
5. Oremus (2016).
6. Manjoo (2017).
7. Opam (2014).
8. Madhdawi (2017).
9. Manjoo (2017).
10. Calvin (2017).
11. Manjoo (2017).
12. The foundational book on persuasive technology is B. J. Fog's *Persuasive Technology: Using Computers to Change What We Think and Do*. Fog (2002).
13. For more on the power of anthropomorphizing technology, see Darling (2016). For more on how Amazon is trying to endow Alexa with a "more natural voice experience," see Carman (2017).
14. For a great overview of the privacy issues associated with "always-on" devices, see Gray (2016).
15. Anderson and Rainee (2014).
16. By "theirs," we don't mean to suggest that the tools are alive or sentient or have emotions and intentions of their own. The tools simply may serve the interests of others, e.g. technology companies. See, e.g., Rushkoff (2016): 91.
17. We realize "fake news" is a fraught term. For a good analysis of why this is the case, see Oremus (2016).
18. The distinctions may matter in specific settings. For example, consumer protection laws may treat influence favorably but manipulation unfavorably. Manipulation implies unfairness, information asymmetry, dishonesty, and unequal bargaining or power relationships. See, e.g., Calo (2014); Calo and Rosenblat (2017).
19. Readers may be familiar with the concept of "social engineering." Some claim that organized religion is a form of social engineering because it promotes "adherence to moral conventions and rules that can facilitate social order." Gelfand et al. (2011): 1101. However, the term "social engineering" is most often associated with centralized planning through political or economic

318

processes that tightly regulate how citizens behave in order to mold society into a particular structure or get it to function in a particular way. This ideal of social engineering has an ancient pedigree. It dates all the way back to antiquity when the Greek philosopher Plato provided a recipe for creating an ideal city, "the republic," that's organized and run by an anti-democratic "philosopher king" (approximately 380 BC). In our time, technology plays an equally important and arguably illiberal role in engineering society – hence, our hyphenated wordsmithing. Plato's *Republic* (2017).

20. Baumeister and Tierney (2011).
21. Alter (2017).
22. Researchers also contend that the annoyance factor has a lot to do with how people feel about being in the presence of others who can't keep their eyes off their phones. See Baym (2010).
23. It's akin to the techno-social engineering by casinos. See Schüll (2012).
24. Conventional wisdom gets many things wrong. Conventional wisdom focuses on the immense, obvious, and clear benefits of technology at the expense of taking seriously nuanced and complicated problems. Conventional wisdom also dims the power of contemporary techno-social engineering because it has a hard time appreciating power dynamics that don't fit the simple story of malicious exploiters taking advantage of powerless people and organizations. To be sure, today's techno-social engineering can manipulate our vulnerabilities and capitalize on asymmetric relations. But it also occurs in situations where we receive benefits that we really want – even if we don't like all of the strings that get attached. Conventional wisdom underplays how, under conditions of neo-liberalism, the lines dividing government, technology corporations, and educational institutions continue to shrink, as does the space separating personal and professional lives. As a result of boundary collapse, governance mechanisms are diffuse, spread thinly across contexts, making effective regulation exceedingly difficult. Conventional wisdom also creates the false impression that deep problems aren't flying under the radar due to the heightened scrutiny of legal review and professional ethics audits. Unfortunately, both forms of protection have substantial blind spots, including secondary effects and many unintended consequences. Finally, conventional wisdom accepts too much of the hype surrounding big data and artificial intelligence; a profound shift is occurring in how social control is administered, experienced, and contested.
25. A reviewer asked if we had in mind an ideal time in history when the set of techno-social conditions were optimal. We don't. We enjoy the present and hope for an even better future. We don't idealize the past. This book develops a framework for identifying and evaluating techno-social engineering of humans that, at least in theory, could be applied at any moment in time. We focus on the present and future because we're most interested in understanding the world we're living in and the world we're building.
26. Nozick (2013).

27. There are two main criticisms of thought experiments in general. The first is that they aren't helpful because people supposedly are inclined to rebel against the proposed hypothetical conditions. In the case of the "experience machine," the worry is that people will focus on elements of the set-up that Nozick found irrelevant. For example, folks will be anxious about the machine malfunctioning and get stuck, mentally, on that concern. We concede that such fixation is possible. But as all good teachers can confirm, it's easy to get students past that initial reaction by doing two things: explaining why it isn't relevant and then emphasizing what matters. The second criticism is that analysts who propose thought experiments tend to cheat. They act as if their submitted scenarios are merely models that drill a problem down to its essential components, when actually they embed hidden normative values (that analysts endorse) into the description. We hope to avoid that problem by reviewing and proposing many thought experiments throughout the book. This way, our arguments don't depend on any particular one and the biases (including implicit ones) it contains.

28. Allenby and Sarewitz (2011).

29. Frischmann and Selinger (2016): 372–391.

30. Biotech is another set of technologies that makes substantial promises about engineering humans in various ways. We recognize the importance of biotech yet devote much less attention to it. The main reason is that the techno-social dilemma we posit doesn't seem to fit the biotech trajectory. That is, biotech will be used to engineer humans and in ways that require careful evaluation, but the biotech path does not seem to point in the direction of machine-like humans. We might be wrong about that, and, if so, we hope our book could be usefully extended to biotech.

31. Several complications arise when making the analogy between the tragedy of the commons and humanity's techno-social dilemma. One is that it's hard to identify the widely shared environmental resource that can be jeopardized by techno-social engineering. If it's our humanity, the question arises as to what that term actually means. We offer thoughts about what matters about being human in Part III of the book where we propose techno-social engineering tests. Also, while in the tragedy of the commons the agents, actions, and resources are reasonably well-delineated, the lines between these categories are not as easily drawn in the tragedy of techno-social engineering: the agents include both engineers and humans being engineered; the actions involve treating human agents as (and possibly transforming them into) resources; and the shared resource is socially constructed and sustained, not a given or natural. Even describing the negative externalities is more complex. Instead of overgrazing sheep with externalities described in terms of the limited capacity of the pasture, we need to unpack the nuanced and complex relationships between technologies and humanity.

32. This is not a new concern. As discussed in Chapter 4, it has been raised often over the past century. Also, the notion of power being imposed upon us as

well as something that we choose to impose upon ourselves is well developed by Michel Foucault in his analysis of the "repressive" and "productive" aspects of power.

33. In the late nineteenth century and the early twentieth century, Frederick Taylor developed his theory of scientific management of humans in the workplace. "Taylorism" refers to his management theory and associated techniques. We discuss Taylorism in Chapter 4.

34. We're not making any claims whatsoever about how sophisticated machines presently are or might become someday. Nor are we weighing in the heated debate about whether machines eventually will turn on us. Our attention is solely being directed at problems that techno-social engineering can pose to humans. Nor are we taking a position on the computational theory of mind. That is, we don't take a position on whether or not the human mind is, at its core, just a really complex machine, like a neural net.

35. Within artificial intelligence, robotics, machine learning, and other adjacent fields, the race to cross this line has been on since Turing published his article. Many experts have lamented this racing behavior. Today, few researchers in these fields focus on passing the Turing test. See Chapter 10 for more details.

36. We're not the first to analyze the human side of the line. Others have articulated at length what they believe fundamentally distinguishes humans from machines, how that difference can be engineered away, and why we should resist becoming too mechanized. Perhaps the most famous polemic on the topic is Karl Marx's nineteenth-century writing about how repetitive factory jobs alienate workers. Wendling (2009). There's been a lot written since Marx's day about the implications of compelling and incentivizing humans to behave like simple automatons. Indeed, many analysts have come to address the dehumanization caused by post-industrial forms of technology within and well beyond the workplace. We've learned much from their work. More importantly, though, we work with and within a stream of critical thinking that bridges generations of people and various disciplines. Many theorists have influenced how we view the central subjects in this part of the book. For the sake of brevity, we'll only mention a few here; we note various others in the bibliography at the end of the book. Philosopher Hubert Dreyfus, like Weizenbaum before him, made a compelling case that the more rule-following computers are viewed as ideal problem-solvers, the easier it becomes to promote educational programs and business systems that encourage humans to behave like rule-governed machines. Dreyfus (1992). Sociologist Harry Collins and philosopher Martin Kusch opened our eyes to crucial mistakes that have been made when programmers have tried to replicate human behavior without adequately accounting for how humans internalize, transmit, and update social norms. Collins and Kusch (1999).

Chapter 1 Engineering Humans

1. Historian and philosopher of technology Lewis Mumford observes that top-down techno-social engineering took place in ancient civilizations. When the pharaohs ruled Egypt, they created complex projects, like building pyramids, which had vast amounts of people behaving like coordinated, simple machines. Mumford (1971).

2. Philosopher Helen Nissenbaum developed a rigorous theory of privacy that uses her "contextual integrity framework" to identify and evaluate "appropriate information flows." Nissenbaum (2009). With respect to the Oral Roberts controversy, even though the new information practices do not appear to violate existing norms in that context, Nissenbaum's framework still would require normative evaluation of the practice in terms of "high-level moral and political values, such as autonomy and freedom." Sanfilippo, Frischmann, and Strandburg (2017: 6). Whether such evaluation ordinarily would extend to the techno-social engineering we describe is unclear, but in the future, we hope it will.

3. Sanders (1997): 108.

4. Sanders (1997): 108.

5. Goffman (1959).

6. Exercising this capability depends on knowing who might see the record. Transparency is thus important here as well.

7. Billing someone for work performed, reporting news, disclosing the contents of products one is selling, and many other activities depend upon social performances that demonstrate trustworthiness and build social capital.

8. When it comes to commute time, one of us admits that he usually understates how long he's on the train. This is partly to make himself feel better and partly to suggest to others that he's a little better off than he actually is.

9. We realize there are ways to manipulate Fitbit data and that determined students will seize those opportunities. That's why our discussion focuses on the different affordances of automatic and non-automatic modes of recording exercise accomplishments. For more on Fitbit manipulation, see CBS News (2017): Fitbit users find creative ways to cheat the system.

10. We recognize that this raises an important (and, we think, interesting) empirical question about how much time, effort, and judgment students exercise in different contexts with different tools, and so for now we proceed upon the hypothesis that the analog tool (handwritten journal) involves greater time, effort, and judgment than the digital tool (Fitbit). On the broader issue of what empirical studies have to say about the limited utility of fitness trackers, it's worth noting that there are limited long-term studies and that the "handful of short-term studies" have yielded "mixed results." Ross (2016).

11. Mueller and Oppenheimer (2014).

12. Adults can easily oversimplify the systems, too. Case in point: Authorities used Fitbit data to contradict the testimony given by a man who was accused of murdering his wife. Lartey (2017).

13. Schneier (2010).
14. Sherman (2017).
15. Sherman (2017). For an ethnographic look at the growing wearable technology market, see Schüll (2016).
16. For a great discussion of "hidden curriculum," see Turow (2017): 13–14.
17. Thaler and Sunstein (2008).
18. Marcus (2012).
19. For a look at the more general trend toward "data-driven micronudging" in the health sector, see Schüll (2014); Schüll (2016).
20. Erisman and Gautschi (2015).
21. Morozov (2014a).
22. Our belief that reforms like the ones we just described are possible and meaningful distinguishes the trajectory we take in this book from French philosopher Michel Foucault's writing on "discipline" and surveillance. To be sure, Foucault's ideas have deeply influenced our conception of techno-social engineering. To give but two examples that are relevant to this chapter, when Foucault detailed the structure of our so-called disciplinary society, he characterized teachers as "technicians of behavior" and "engineers of conduct" "who have absorbed . . . a set of disciplinary norms which they, in turn, impose upon their charges." Furthermore, as Foucault saw it, "it is not so much that 'we go to school'; it is more that we only *emerge from* school – there having been no 'us' prior to institutional manufacture." Leask (2012): 60. While these are important and timely insights, the pessimism they can inspire needs to be tempered by due consideration of alternative pedagogies and administrative policies. We agree with the scholars who admire Foucault but worry that if the cluster of ideas related to discipline are embraced too strongly the theoretical prism they create can distort empirical reality: rinse-wash-repeat explanations of power dynamics involving technology and technique can obscure the more nuanced micro-, meso- and macro-level ways power is both expressed and resisted.
23. Hull and Pasquale (2017).

Chapter 2 Cogs in the Machine of Our Own Lives

1. Carr (2015).
2. Dreyfus and Kelly (2011).
3. Judith Donath describes the history of eighteenth century road infrastructure and social change from wayfaring to map-reading; she notes that "maps let us navigate asocially" and she further notes how modern navigation through GPS, guidebooks, and maps can make travel "an isolated experience." Donath (2014): 39. For an interesting take on maps, see Weinberger (2007): 156–158.
4. Stockton (2015).
5. For further discussion of this issue, see Ihde (2008).
6. Merleau-Ponty (2012).

7. Haraway (2000).
8. Bostrom (2005).
9. Eugenios and Kurzweil (2015). See Ford (2015): 233–241 (discussing the Singularity).
10. De Schrijver (2015): 45–48.

Chapter 3 Techno-Social Engineering Creep and the Slippery-Sloped Path

1. There is much more to say about the pros and cons of education technology, and the complicated future of education. We return to the topic in subsequent chapters.
2. For more on the Google controversy, see Singer (2017). For more on the problem of branding in schools, see Sandel (2012).
3. The path to non-branded goods, services, and technology in educational settings is unclear. Open source options exist and are growing. We've not assessed their quality.
4. Selinger (2015d).
5. Our view of quantified self technologies is influenced by Morozov (2012).
6. Apodaca (2015).
7. Nathan Fisk – author of *Framing Internet Safety: The Governance of Youth Online* – puts the point this way:

    > A lot of the issues that get framed as being about Internet safety are not about the Internet at all. They're more about the ways we bound off a generation's disempowered childhood and how these decisions give rise to Internet safety problems. For example, if I was to talk to someone concerned about the persistence of cyberbullying I would ask: Have you looked into how schools operate and try, or fail to try, to come up with ways to reduce surveillance and give kids spaces that are free from adult supervision? As you can imagine, it's difficult to translate this idea into the policy space. At this time, people don't want to hear the message that kids need more freedom, more autonomy, and more mobility.

    Nathan Fisk expresses this in his interview with Evan Selinger. Selinger (2016).
8. See generally Volokh (2003): 1028–1137.
9. Thaler (2010).
10. Or consider, once more, the use of activity watches in elementary schools. One might dismiss our concerns by noting that children have always been and will be subject to social engineering and surveillance during school whether or not a school decides to use activity watches to nudge children to be more active. Their beliefs and preferences about surveillance and nudging are shaped to some degree by the school environment, one way or another. So stick to analyzing the activity watch program on its own terms and don't worry so much about creep or speculative slippery slopes.

The description of the background environment – existing conditions involving some degree of surveillance and social engineering – doesn't undermine our claim that using activity watches may condition children to uncritically embrace 24/7 bodily surveillance. Nor does it undermine our creep hypothesis. Deployment of the activity watch is plausibly a first step along a slippery-sloped path that makes a second step easier and more palatable than it would be if the first step wasn't taken. Our argument is neither wildly speculative nor rooted in bathmophobia.

11. Sunstein (2014a): 31 (Maguire et al. (2000) and Rebonato (2014).
12. This is a fictional extension of the activity watch program.
13. Upgrades to activity watches or other worn devices may be replaced with other technologies, such as a neural implant, that perform the same function.
14. We don't mean to imply uniformity by our use of the terms "society" and "path." Rather, we argue that there are discernable general trends that boil down to a path.

Chapter 4 Tools for Engineering Humans

1. It's ambitious to discuss how tools have engineered humans in a single chapter. Entire books are written on the subject. Our approach is modest and limited by two organizational principles. First, we only aspire to provide a window into the complex ways that technology can enhance or diminish our skills and aptitudes. Second, we highlight work from three thinkers who have influenced our view of techno-social engineering: the historian Yuval Noah Harari, the computer scientist Joseph Weizenbaum, and the mechanical engineer Frederick Winslow Taylor. The bibliography at the end of the book lists many other sources.
2. Ihde (1998): 48–49 ("*[T]here are no human cultures which are pre-technological . . .* ").
3. See, e.g., Shumaker, Walkup, and Beck (2011). On the minds and communication capabilities of other species, see Cheney and Seyfarth (1992).
4. Ihde (2008).
5. Crosby (2002).
6. The actual history of fishing tools is much more complex. See Sahrhage and Lundbeck (2012).
7. The relative utility of the different tools varies based on culture, context, and access.
8. Technological progress also may affect socio-economic conditions. For example, the socio-economic conditions may be quite different when individuals and families fish for subsistence than when fishing is industrialized. Harari makes the following bold claim: "[A]ll of the upheavals [brought about by the Industrial Revolution] were dwarfed by the most momentous social revolution that ever befell humankind: the collapse of the family and the local community and their replacement by the state and the market." Harari (2014): 355. We do not examine this relationship fully in this chapter.

9. Selinger (2015c).
10. Culkin (1967). Donath (2014: 13) explains the power of architectural design:

> The online world is a synthetic universe – entirely human-made and designed. The design of the underlying system shapes how we appear and what we see of other people. It determines the structure of conversations and who has access to what information. Winston Churchill once said, "We shape our buildings; thereafter they shape us." Architects of physical cities determine the paths people will take and the vistas they will see. They affect people's mood by creating cathedrals that inspire awe, schools that encourage playfulness, and jails that evoke dread. Architects, however, do not control how the inhabitants of those buildings present themselves or see each other – the social experience of their users. They determine whether we see each other's faces or instead know each other only by name. They can reveal the size and makeup of the audience, or provide the impression that one is writing intimately to only a few, even if millions are in fact reading. They can make worlds ephemeral, disappearing forever once they leave the screen, or eternal, by permanently archiving them, amassing a history of a person's views and reactions.

11. Searle (1984): 44.
12. Weizenbaum (1976): 17.
13. Harari (2014): 21–22.
14. As Wittgenstein argued, language is necessarily social and communal; there is no such thing as an inherently private language.
15. Harari (2014): 28.
16. Harari (2014): 104–105.
17. Harari (2014): 102–110.
18. Harari (2014): 121–122.
19. Harari (2014): 122–123.
20. Harari (2014): 249–259.
21. Harari (2014): 255.
22. Harari (2014): 256.
23. Weizenbaum (1976): 18.
24. Weizenbaum (1976): 18.
25. Weizenbaum (1976): 18.
26. Our basic understanding of and relationship with other species, e.g. fish, is shaped by the tools we use. Anecdotally, one of us spoke with a relative who is an avid fly fisherman. He explained how fly fishing has led him to develop a deep respect for and "almost spiritual" relationship with the fish. He suggested that people who eat but don't catch fish are "the ones who are out of touch." While his argument didn't persuade us about the morality of fishing, it did illustrate how tool use shaped his reality.
27. Weizenbaum (1976): 21.
28. Weizenbaum (1976): 21.
29. Mumford (1963): 15.
30. Weizenbaum (1976): 23.
31. Weizenbaum (1976): 25.
32. Weizenbaum (1976): 34–35.
33. Or: "A person falling into a manhole is rarely helped by making it possible for him to fall faster or more efficiently." Weizenbaum (1976): 34–35.

34. Weizenbaum (1976): 252.
35. B. F. Skinner (1904–1990) was a famous (or infamous, depending on your point of view) psychologist. His research, which came to be called radical behaviorism, focused on reinforcement and operant conditioning. Skinner's influence persists in many walks of life today, including technological development. The Pavlok bracelet (http://pavlok.com), for example, sends a shock (i.e. bad stimulus) when you are participating in a bad habit. In principle, "your brain associates the stimulus with the bad habit, creating an aversion" to the behavior.
36. Weizenbaum (1976): 255.
37. Unfortunately, his "criticism largely fell on deaf ears in the United States. Years later his ideas would receive a more positive reception in Europe, where he moved at the end of his life." Markoff (2015): 174.
38. Weizenbaum (1976): 257. The problem of instrumental reason displacing alternative social and ethical values and logics preoccupied an entire philosophical tradition: Frankfurt School Critical Theory. It would take us too far beyond the scope of our analysis to review that tradition, but we'd be remiss if we didn't include this seminal remark made by Herbert Marcuse, one if its founding fathers:

> There is no personal escape from the apparatus which has mechanized and standardized the world. It is a rational apparatus, combining the utmost expediency with utmost convenience, saving time and energy, removing waste, adapting all means to the end, anticipating consequences, sustaining calculability and security. (Marcuse (1982).)

39. As Blaise Pascal wrote:

> It is in this manner that we may at the present day adopt different sentiments and new opinions, without despising the ancients and without ingratitude, since the first knowledge which they have given us has served as a stepping-stone to our own, and since in these advantages we are indebted to them for our ascendency over them; because being raised by their aid to a certain degree, the slightest effort causes us to mount still higher, and with less pains and less glory we find ourselves above them. Thence it is that we are enabled to discover things which it was impossible for them to perceive. Our view is more extended, and although they knew as well as we all that they could observe in nature, they did not . . . know it so well, and we see more than they.

Blaise Pascal, *Thoughts, Letters, and Opuscules*, 548 (O. W. Wight trans., Boston, Houghton, Mifflin and Company 1893) (1859) (emphasis omitted).
40. The phrase – we stand on the shoulders of giants – "often used to emphasize the cumulative nature of cultural or scientific progress, . . . also reflects an understanding of intergenerational dependence. Each generation is both dwarf and giant; the current generation stands on the shoulders of the past and also serves as the shoulders for the future." Frischmann and McKenna (2011). What's often left unexamined, however, is the path the giant is on and the direction in which the giant is marching. "Surely the dwarf (present generation) perched on the giant's shoulders (past generations' blessings) sees more if the giant walks along some path than if the giant stays still. But

that does not tell us about the relative value of different paths … "
Frischmann and McKenna (2011): 126–127.

Various scholars have studied the intellectual history of the metaphor and
how its usage has evolved over time. While the modern usage may elevate the
dwarf (or pygmy) to stress the superiority of the present, historical usage, for
example in the Middle Ages, revered the accomplishment of the ancients. See,
e.g., Rebecca Moore Howard, *Standing in the Shadow of Giants: Plagiarists,
Authors, Collaborators,* (1999): 65–66, (discussing the historical instability of
the metaphor); Robert K. Merton, *On the Shoulders of Giants: A Shandean
Postscript* (1965).

41. Weizenbaum (1976) develops this argument over the course of his book. Early
    pioneers of computability theory, including Alonzo Church, Kurt Gödel, and
    Alan Turing, developed the fundamental thesis about the scope of what is
    computable. See Church (1936); Church (1937); Gödel (1934); Turing (1937);
    Turing (1938).

42. Further, as Shannor Vallor emphasized in reviewing this chapter: "it's unclear
    that these baselines can be [accurately] represented computationally, rooted as
    they are in an ever-changing social context that evolves unpredictably and is
    produced by interactions between countless complex personal psychologies."

43. Weizenbaum (1976): 258–259.

44. See Taylor (1903).

45. Kanigel (1997): 1.

46. Some would call it "technique" and reserve "technology" for systems of
    applied knowledge that employ a material component. We do not have
    such a limited definition in mind, however, and this is not the place to
    debate the issue.

47. See OECD (2015): *Data Driven Innovation: Big Data for Growth and Well-
    Being.*

48. See, e.g., Ajunwa, Crawford, and Schultz (2017) (describing this evolution).

49. Other scholars have noticed and explored these developments. See Foucault
    (1977); Kanigel (1997): 10.

50. Kanigel (1997): 10.

51. According to James O'Connell, "Taylor and his assistants declare: 'Give us
    big physical men and we will do the thinking for them.' The scheme tends to
    wipe out all the manhood and genius of the American workman and make
    him into a mere machine, to be driven at a high speed until he breaks down,
    and then to be thrown in the scrap heap." Kanigel (1997): 448–449.

52. Kanigel (1997): 438.

53. Charlie Chaplin's famous comedy, *Modern Times* (1936), provides
    a memorable picture.

54. Tolliday and Zeitlin (1987): 1–2.

55. Autonomous clocks added a persistent set of stimuli that directly affected –
    one might say regulated – human behavior. There are many other examples of

such environment-altering technologies. Mass media and smartphones are two prominent and powerful examples. See Chapter 7.

56. Harari (2014): 352.
57. There is a rich history and debate surrounding the example of workplaces in which automation and management practices dehumanize workers and treat them like machines. See, e.g., Noble (1984); Head (2005).
58. Kanigel (1997): 498.
59. Michel Foucault made similar observations in his discussions of discipline. For example, he claimed the Panopticon shapes surveillance practice by providing people with an architectural blueprint that could be transformed in different ways.
60. Harari (2014): 352–353.
61. Au (2011): 25.
62. Kanigel (1997): 498. See also Lobel (2013): 20–21, 134–135.
63. The Japanese automobile industry is one famous example. See, e.g., Cusumano (1985); Fujimoto (1999).
64. Kanigel (1997): 14.
65. Ajunwa, Crawford, and Schultz (2017).
66. It remains to be seen whether future management will consist of humans with AI-enhanced intelligence or of pure AI-based systems. See R. Hoffman (2016).
67. See Chapter 2.

Chapter 5 Engineering Humans with Contracts

1. We don't want to overgeneralize. As David Hoffman emphasizes, "not all mass market contracts are the same." Hoffman (2017b): 53. Some contractual arrangements may be liberating for consumers. Hoffman discusses "examples of innovative fine print that appears to really communicate with and manage users." These examples seem to be exceptions to the basic story we tell in this chapter because the platforms Hoffman studies don't seem to use the electronic contracting architecture to nudge consumers to just click. Rather, the platforms seek to engage consumers as participating users, to develop relationships and trust. Yet the nature of those relationships and the legitimacy of the engendered trust are themselves engineered and require evaluation; they likely vary considerably across platforms and business models. After all, Hoffman describes the platforms' adhesive contracts as instructions, means for shaping and controlling user behavior. In future work, we'd like to explore whether these "relational contracts of adhesion" reflect an alternate means for engineering humans with contracts.
2. There are a few exceptions. See Kim (2013); D. Hoffman (2017a). In addition to these contract scholars, various privacy scholars have examined the relationships between privacy preferences, interface design, human behavior,

and other contextual variables. Acquisti, Brandimarte, and Loewenstein (2015) and Böhme and Köpsell (2010) are two excellent, representative articles with useful reference lists.

3. See Chapter 4.

4. Cf. Kennedy (1982). We thank Lauren Henry Scholz, who commented on our draft at the 2016 Privacy Law Scholars Conference, for pointing out the connection between our chapter and Duncan Kennedy's seminal work.

5. Radin (2013).

6. Or, depending on your perspective, it could be Bizarro World. See Wikipedia – *Bizarro World*.

7. Radin discusses the proliferation of boilerplate in terms of standardization and tacit collusion. Radin (2013). We introduce the term "boilerplate creep," because it is quite similar to surveillance creep.

8. Radin (2013). Some contract scholars would dispute whether boilerplate has expanded; they note that adhesive boilerplate has been around since at least the early 1900s and was widespread by the 1950s. See, e.g., D. Hoffman (2017a)(tracing this history and longstanding debates among contract scholars about boilerplate). This might be true, in which case we might need to revise our description slightly, perhaps using the term "contract creep" instead of boilerplate creep.

9. Choice architects are everywhere, "from alarm clock makers to exercise and health professionals to retirement planners to bureaucrats in government agencies. Choice architects should identify the biases that can be detrimental in select circumstances and then create devices (e.g. alarm clocks), plans (e.g. dietary regimens and retirement schemes), and government policies that work with the biases to advantage those who have choices to make. Thaler and Sunstein call this activity 'nudging' and define a nudge as any aspect of design 'that alters people's behavior in a predictable way without forbidding any options or significantly changing their economic incentives.' Nudges are changes in the decision-making context that work with cognitive biases, and help prompt us, in subtle ways that often function below the level of our awareness, to make decisions that leave us and usually our society better off." Selinger and Whyte (2011).

10. With few exceptions, our online experience fits Radin's World B. Our offline experience might as well. See, e.g., Slawson (1971): "Standard form contracts probably account for more than ninety-nine percent of all contracts now made. Most persons have difficulty remembering the last time they contracted other than by standard form; except for casual oral agreements, they probably never have. But if they are active, they contract by standard form several times a day. Parking lot and theater tickets, package receipts, department store charge slips, and gas station credit card purchase slips are all standard form contracts."

11. See Radin (2013): 12 (listing seven explanations why people don't read boilerplate); Marotta-Wurgler (2011): 179–181; Bakos, Marotta-Wurgler, and Trossen (2014) (finding that "only one or two of every 1,000 retail software shoppers access the [software] license agreement and that most of those who do access it read no more than a small portion"); see also Masnick (2010).

12. Hillman and Rachlinski (2002): 429. Hillman and Rachlinski examine the similarities and differences between "virtual and paper contracting environments" and conclude that the existing contract law framework could accommodate many of the new challenges posed by the electronic contracting environment. See Hillman and Rachlinski (2002): 429. Many others trace the legal, technological, and practical changes. See, e.g., D. Hoffman (2017a) (describing changes in contract practices); Kim (2013); Moringiello (2005); Lemley (2006) (reviewing history of shrink-wrap and browse-wrap contract law and practice); Hartzog (2011): 1642–1645 (review of "loose [judicial] consensus in applying standard-form doctrine to online agreements"); Ben-Shahar and Schneider (2011). For a recent judicial summary, see *Berkson* v. *GOGO*, 97 F.Supp.3d 359 (E.D.N.Y. 2015).

The law and economics explanation for contract law evolution seems to make the most sense. Simply, contract law might have loosened traditional doctrines, e.g. formation doctrines, to minimize transaction costs and enable efficient mass market transactions. See, e.g., *ProCD, Inc.* v. *Zeidenberg*, 86 F.3d 1447, 1452 (7th Cir. 1996) (J. Easterbrook) (Zeidenberg's position, which Easterbrook rejected, "would drive prices through the ceiling or return transactions to the horse-and-buggy age"); *Hill* v. *Gateway 2000, Inc.*, 105 F.3d 1147, 1149 (7th Cir. 1997) (finding it impractical to require full disclosure of terms prior to purchase). See generally Radin (2013); Bix (2012). Some courts have begun to tighten up the formation doctrine, although mostly by focusing on notice rather than actual assent. See, e.g., *Specht* v. *Netscape*, 306 F.3d 17 (2nd Cir. 2002); *Long* v. *Provide Commerce, Inc.*, 245 Cal. App. 4th 855 (2016); *Sgouros* v. *TransUnion Corp.*, No. 15–1371, 2016 WL 1169411 (7th Cir. 2016). These shifts intended to protect consumers might have the opposite effect because they create the illusion of sufficient protection, reinforcing the functional role of electronic contracts as tools for techno-social engineering.

13. Hartzog (2011) (quoting Calabresi (1982)). See Radin (2013) (describing World B).

14. See, e.g., McDonald and Cranor (2008) (documenting the huge numbers of privacy policies and costs associated with reading them); Ben-Shahar and Schneider (2014): 94–106 (defending consumer decision aversion based on the quantity of disclosures, in terms of an "accumulation problem" – overwhelming numbers of disclosures – and an "overload problem" – each disclosure is "too copious for the discloser to handle"); Hartzog (2011) ("With online agreements on a number of websites, the 74% of Americans online each day could enter into dozens of contracts that impact the flow of their

personal information"); Kim (2005) ("The increase in online commercial transactions and consumer purchases of software has resulted in a rise in the use of 'shrinkwrap' and 'clickwrap,' or 'click,' agreements. Each day, more consumers of varying ages and educational backgrounds use the Internet for a wide array of important activities such as banking, investing, shopping, and paying bills."). See also Slawson (1971); Korobkin (2003): 1203 ("[N]early all commercial and consumer sales contracts are form driven."); Leff (1970): 141 n. 35 (arguing that there was "no empirical evidence that the frequency of this type of [consumer standard form contract] transaction has increased, over, say, the last fifty years or so. But most people seem to assume so ... and it seems certainly reasonable (given the increase in market concentration) to believe that it did.").

15. See D. Hoffman (2017a); Radin (2013); Ben-Shahar and Schneider (2014): 94–106.

    A related hypothesis would be that the number of "rolling contracts" has increased. Electronic contracts are an extension of rolling contracts, which involve provision of some terms but only "after initial agreement on basic terms." Bix (2012): 28. Examples of rolling contracts include purchasing insurance (based on general type of policy and price with detailed terms arriving later) or buying tickets to a sporting event or for a cruise. See Bix (2012): 28. Bix explains that "[a]lthough 'rolling contracts' had once been peripheral, they are becoming increasingly common." Bix (2012): 29.

16. The default contract law of sales generally applies to mundane sales transactions. Firms often modify Uniform Commercial Code defaults with boilerplate, such as product warnings. See generally R. Anderson (1963); White, Summers, and Hillman (2010).

17. *Empirical Query*: The fact that we enter into many offline contracts without carefully reading all of the terms or negotiating fine details doesn't mean that we don't deliberate at all. We usually deliberate over the most salient terms – price, quality of service, timing of delivery, and so on. Many of the finer details, some of which may very well be substantively important, escape our attention. This is the nature of "rolling contracts" as we note above. But we must emphasize how this phenomenon is different from the one we discuss in the text; in the typical offline rolling contracts context, we aren't nudged to employ System 1; we deliberate and employ System 2. This is our hypothesis, at least, and an empirical claim in need of testing.

18. For some data on these questions, see D. Hoffman (2017a). In their book critiquing mandated disclosure, Ben-Shahar and Schneider make a similar point by telling *The Parable of Chris Consumer*, which describes a day in the life of a consumer who reads all of the disclosures he encounters. See Ben-Shahar and Schneider (2014): 94–100.

19. *Empirical Query*: We could be wrong. This is an empirical question. It might be the case that the overall number of contracts didn't change much, and the most significant difference would be between the number of written versus

oral agreements. Past generations may have had roughly the same number of contracts with a larger portion being oral contracts. We thank David Hoffman for raising this possibility.

20. Macaulay (2004).

21. Radin (2013) (explaining how automatic and ubiquitous contracts would replace public ordering with private ordering); Kessler (1943): 640 (same). See also Macneil (1980). Macneil distinguished between discrete and continuous relational contracts; electronic contracting online blurs them. On one hand, a simple click of a button (or swipe of a thumb) reinforces the feeling of a small, discrete transaction; on the other, the services provided and hidden terms of trade (data, relational capital) are more lasting.

22. *Empirical Query*: There is little empirical evidence about how people feel when performing different actions to manifest assent to different contracts. The best is D. Hoffman (2017a) (finding about an 8% difference in signing a form versus clicking a button with respect to the same transaction). The intuitive claim we make in the text is based on personal experience and anecdotes.

23. *Empirical Query*: Most people don't read, much less understand, most of the terms and conditions of complex contracts such as mortgages, employment contracts, or insurance agreements. This doesn't undermine the points we advance here, however. We make a similar observation regarding electronic contracts and emphasize how the design of the electronic contract and contracting environment is designed to nudge people to manifest consent without reading or understanding, but, critically, we go further.

   We argue that repeated interactions with this environment architected to nudge us affects us in important ways, above and beyond outcomes directly associated with the contract itself. We couldn't, and thus don't, make a similar claim about highly significant but rarely encountered contracts. Most people haven't and don't consistently interact with mortgages, employment contracts, or insurance agreements. Moreover, as we note below, when people do engage with such contracts, they deliberate over the most salient terms even if they do not read most of the terms. In other words, people who don't read contracts offline still do some System 2 thinking. This is one more empirical claim to test.

24. Those side-agreements usually have "No Third Party Beneficiary" clauses, which means you really have no contractually relevant relationship with those third parties. This is an important, designed feature. Cf. Hartzog (2009) (proposing better leveraging of the concept of third-party beneficiaries).

25. Radin argues that as contract law has evolved to accommodate the mass market and electronic contracting, the meaning of consent has been devalued. Radin (2013): 33. She points to specific practices in contracting that compel parties to consent to less than favorable conditions and ultimately deprive parties of rights under contract. For example, choice of forum clauses that force litigation to occur far from parties, exculpatory clauses, adhesion

contracts, offsite terms, and shrink-wrap licenses all heighten the imbalance of power for consumers. Radin (2013): 6, 10–11.

26. These design choices have regulatory implications. See Lessig (1999); Reidenberg (1998).

27. Many others have argued that some loss of privacy is the price users pay for free or cheap internet services. For extensive analysis, see Hoofnagle and Whittington (2014). See also Kim (2013): 76–78.

28. Radin (2013): 15–16, 19–52 (extensive analysis of "normative degradation" and "democratic degradation").

29. See, e.g., Roshkoff (2016): 32; Hachman (2015); Angwin and Singer-Vine (2012). See generally Hoofnagle and Whittington (2014): 629–634 (discussing examples). Michael Risch makes the following observation about the role of contracts and third parties in the context of virtual worlds: "In virtual worlds, where 20 million people spend $200 million each year [based on figures from 2005], rules of life are governed by contract, and three-party transactions are ubiquitous; every exchange of virtual cash, property, sound, pictures, and even conversation introduces a third-party into the contractual relationship between user and virtual-world provider." Risch (2009b).

30. See Risch (2009b). Not surprisingly, new economic models and a host of buzzwords have developed to explain why this state of affairs is efficient, innovative, and optimal. Multi-sided markets efficiently managed by intermediary platforms, complex ecosystems of innovation, and so on generally hide the human beings, assuming them to be rational or bounded rational consumers. On their own terms, these models might make sense, although elsewhere one of us has expressed doubts. Frischmann (2012): Ch. 13 (critiquing multi-sided market models of the Internet). Here, we reject their terms and focus directly on the human.

31. Arguably, "sheer ignorance" is engineered. Radin (2013): 21–22, 31.

32. An issue to confront may be the difference between voluntary and deliberate in the context of contract formation. Supposedly, contracts are voluntary. But should contracts also be the product of at least some modicum of deliberation? Are purely impulsive actions – or reactions to stimuli designed to induce – voluntary? Contract law has long recognized the absence of meaningful consent in situations of coercion or duress. The techno-social engineering we discuss here seems to fall short of these concepts, however. Radin (2013): 22–32. Radin describes well the gradual "devolution or decay of the concept of voluntariness." She explains that "consent is degraded to assent, then to fictional or constructive or hypothetical assent, and then further to mere notice . . ., until finally we are left with only a fictional or constructive notice of terms." Radin (2013): 30. This process relates to the concept of boilerplate creep. We suspect a very similar dynamic in other examples of "creep phenomena," such as nudge creep and surveillance creep.

33. *Empirical Query*: This is an empirical claim that requires testing. It is based upon anecdote and informal surveys of students and audiences. For two studies that provide some support, see D. Hoffman (2017a); Böhme and

Köpsell (2010) ("new evidence supporting the hypothesis that ubiquitous EULAs have trained even privacy-concerned users to click on 'accept' whenever they face an interception that reminds them of a EULA").

34. Radin (2013): 27. Radin notes how status quo and other heuristic biases undermine consent. Radin (2013): 27. See also Kim (2013): 59 ("Due to the ubiquitous nature of wrap agreements, consumers may become habituated to them and take less notice or care of their terms"); Böhme and Köpsell (2010) ("new evidence supporting the hypothesis that ubiquitous EULAs have trained even privacy-concerned users to click on 'accept' whenever they face an interception that reminds them of a EULA"); Hillman (2007): 85 (suggesting consumers may not "attach appropriate significance to a mouse click and therefore may fail to appreciate the seriousness of their actions").

35. See, e.g., Radin (2013): 27 (describing how status quo bias encourages individuals to "stick with what we've done before," making the act of accepting a contract by clicking "I agree" completely rational); Ayres and Schwartz (2014) (suggesting that optimism bias – specifically, misplaced optimism about terms and conditions – may affect consumers); Bar-Gill (2013): 21–22 ("Myopic consumers care more about the present and not enough about the future ... Myopia is common. People are impatient, preferring immediate benefits even at the expense of future costs."); Kim (2013): 85–87 (discussing various cognitive biases that affect contracting behavior). See note 38 below (citing studies of habits). See also Waldman (2016) (examining a series of ways in which Facebook designs its platform to take advantage of heuristics and thereby create the illusion of trust and encourage data-sharing).

36. To paraphrase John Tierney, no matter how much you might wish to rationally deliberate over the electronic contracts you enter into, you can't make decision after decision without paying a biological price. Fatigue, ego depletion, and decision aversity are three of various descriptions of the psychological toll. See, e.g., Tierney (2011) ("No matter how rational and high-minded you try to be, you can't make decision after decision without paying a biological price."; discussing and citing studies); Baumeister (2003): 3–16 (making choices in a deliberative manner can deplete limited internal resources and will; decision fatigue can impair self-regulation and lead to irrational decisions); Schaub et al. (2015) (describing privacy notice fatigue).

Ben-Shahar and Schneider suggest people are not "homo arbiter"; rather, people are decision averse. "Decision aversion occupies a long continuum – from declining to decide, to delegating decisions, to keeping options open, to postponing decisions, to deliberating sketchily, to making decisions loathing every step." Ben-Shahar and Schneider (2014): 62. Ben-Shahar and Schneider explain various factors that lead to consumer decision aversion. Many of the factors are products or features of the environment, which raises an interesting question about their description of human nature. Are we so intensely

decision averse because that is human nature or because of the modern
techno-social environment we've built and relentlessly continue to expand?

37. Cf. McDonald and Cranor (2008): 19 (estimating $781B in lost productivity if
individuals actually read privacy policies, at 244 hours a year).

38. See Aarts, Verplanken, and van Knippenberg (1997): 1–2 ("[W]hen the same
behavior is performed many times, one does not need to weigh pros and cons,
or to check one's attitude to arrive at a choice. When habits are formed,
subsequent behavior may be associated with, and automatically triggered by,
the specific situational cues that normally precede it" (p. 2). "Habits are
characterized by a goal-directed type of automaticity; habitual behaviors are
instigated by a specific goal-directed state of mind in the presence of triggering
stimulus cues, for instance kissing one's spouse when coming home from
work, or ... taking the bicycle to travel to the university. Once evoked by
the very goal to act, decisions on courses of action and their subsequent
execution may be enacted without much deliberation, and are therefore
relatively independent of reasoned considerations." In short, "[o]nce evoked
by the very goal to act, decisions on courses of actions and their subsequent
execution may be enacted without much deliberation, and are therefore
relatively independent of reasoned considerations."); Ouellette and Wood
(1998): 54–57 ("In domains in which habits can develop, frequent
performance in the past reflects habitual patterns that are likely to be
repeated automatically in future responses. In domains in which habits are
unlikely to develop, behavior is likely to be controlled by deliberative reasoning
processes, and the effects of past behavior on future behavior are mediated by
intentions."); Aarts and Dijksterhuis (2000) ("[M]uch effort is devoted to
trying to explain various, if not all, actions by studying the relations among
attitude, intentions, and behavior. We believe, however, that although the
emphasis on more reasoned behavior and deliberative processes is helpful for
an understanding of certain behaviors, it is not the only useful concept for
insight into behavior in general. Much of what people do in daily life becomes
highly automated. In these cases, consciousness has delegated the onset and the
proceeding of behavior to the unconscious"); Barnes, Gartland, and Stack
(2004) (explaining that behavioral lock-in "occurs when the behavior of the
agent (consumer or producer) is 'stuck' in some sort of inefficiency or sub-
optimality due to habit, organizational learning, or culture").

39. In their explanation of why mandated disclosure fails, Ben-Shahar and
Schneider describe subjects replying "Whatever" to disclosures, and they
argue that the attitudes reflected in this "verbal rolling of the eyes" show
why mandated disclosure – and the meaningful engagement and informed
consent associated with mandated disclosure – fails. Ben-Shahar and
Schneider (2014): 59–61.

40. For those fans of nudging who feel we are being unfair, please hold off
judgment, consider our arguments, and keep in mind that not all nudges
implemented currently or likely to be implemented in the future necessarily
conform fully to the careful constraints of liberal paternalism. See Sunstein

(2014b); Sunstein (2015); see also Hurd (2015). Consequently, we are skeptical of holding the "classic/ideal nudge" as a benchmark when many if not most real-world nudge-like practices fall short of the ideal. The real world is and will increasingly be full of carefully designed choice architectures that are "sort of a nudge" because the range of actual, situated choices is narrower than the ideal. Three related thoughts are worth noting. First, even ideal nudges may affect the humans being nudged in a manner that makes them more susceptible to non-ideal nudges. Second, the ideal nudges of today may be low-hanging fruit on the metaphorical nudge tree. Third, and related to the prior, we're thinking about how boilerplate creep, surveillance creep, and nudge creep interrelate. One might also have a reasonably well-articulated conception of ideal surveillance that properly balances values in the same manner that liberal paternalism does for nudging, but nonetheless, in practice (and in theory once you think of it in terms of creep and systemic evolutionary effects), evaluation of surveillance practices necessarily focuses mostly on non-ideal forms of surveillance. The same should be the case for evaluating nudging practices.

41. The dynamic reinforcing relationships among these phenomena are beyond the scope of this paper.

42. *Empirical Query*: This is an empirical claim that requires testing. We do not yet have empirical evidence to support the claim. It is based entirely upon anecdotes and informal surveys of students and audiences. We should expect some people to deviate from the script in some contexts.

43. *Empirical Query*: This presents a very difficult empirical claim. As Matthew Tokson helpfully pointed out in an email:

> One big challenge here is separating out people's rational reaction to the high costs of reading online contracts from the habit/fatigue/learned helplessness effect that you're positing. Both lead to the same behavior. Even if there was no habituation as a result of the choice architecture, a rational actor would presumably always choose to ignore online boilerplate, because the cost of reading it outweighs any benefits. [Even if] you're right about the learned helplessness effect, it may be difficult to show with empirical data.

44. Again, the behavior of not reading contract terms is not new. For example, bank and insurance contracts are notoriously long and filled with incomprehensible legal jargon, and, consequently, customers tend to sign them without thoroughly reading or understanding them. Additionally, electronic contracting on the Internet has led to the development of creative ways to get parties to agree to terms they have never seen. Radin points to the "unwitting contract," where websites have a link to a separate webpage containing terms of service.

> If one were to click on it, which most users don't (in fact, most probably don't even notice the link), one would see pages of boilerplate open out, telling the user that she is bound to these terms, that she has agreed to them simply by the act of looking at the site, and moreover the owner may change the terms from time to time and that the user will then be bound by the new terms as well.

Radin (2013): 11–12. Moreover, the frequency of consumer engagement with electronic contracts is one important distinguishing feature.

45. Radin (2013) (explaining why the objective theory of contract fails for boilerplate).
46. Consumers may believe firms are unlikely to insist on egregious terms. See, e.g., Van Loo (2015).
47. See Surowiecki (2005).
48. In a sense, this view admits some pre-programming or scripting and simply disputes *who* authored the script. This also is a deep issue we deal with in our book.
49. Evaluating whether you in fact decide for yourself is a difficult empirical question, which is not answered simply by asking for your own self-assessment. The empirical question is complicated by the fact that the optimized environment may be architected to make you feel as though you have chosen in a deliberate manner. This is one difficulty with evaluating techno-social engineering from an internal, subjective perspective; self-reporting and evaluation by those within the environment and subject to engineering is not exactly trustworthy. This is a significant problem for many methods of valuation.
50. One reviewer suggested that electronic contracting architecture bears a close resemblance to the Magician's Choice.
51. *Empirical Query*: This is an empirical claim that requires testing. We do not yet have empirical evidence to support the claim. For promising work in this vein, see D. Hoffman (2017a).
52. See Barnett (2002). *But what justifies such trust?*
53. The terms System 1 and System 2 thinking originate in "dual process" theories of cognition, recently popularized by Daniel Kahneman, the Nobel Prize winning behavioral economist. See Kahneman (2011). Dual process theory explains how an experience can occur as a result of two different cognitive processes, or two different systems: System 1 experiences are "fast, automatic, effortless, associative, and often emotionally charged"; System 2 ones are "slower, serial, effortful, and deliberately controlled." Kahneman (2002).
54. One study measured "response latency" to distinguish between systematic (System 2) processing and heuristic (System 1) processing when subjects responded to consent dialogues concerning a security update. See Böhme and Köpsell (2010).
55. The parenthetical string of n winners includes the third-party beneficiaries to the contract.
56. In another context, the relevant human capability being engineered (by the techno-social environment) and examined (by us) might be cognitive processing associated with emotions (emotional responses to stimuli or emotional states). Emotions may be associated with System 1 rather than System 2. The capability to experience emotions is important for human beings, and so we would be concerned if the techno-social environment systematically nudges us to rely exclusively on System 2. Thus, in that context, System 2 thinking is what we would associate with behaving like

a simple machine, and System 1 (emotional) thinking is what we would associate with being human.

57. On instrumental rationality and decision-making, see Stanovich (2013); Kahneman (2011). On different conceptions of rationality, see Stein (1996).

58. Kahneman (2011).

59. We initially thought this claim would be uncontroversial. However, reviewers consistently express wonder at the idea that, offline, people deliberate at all. Hence, we resort to price, the one factor that usually attracts attention and some modicum of deliberation.

60. This presents a challenge to Barnett's consent theory of contracts. Barnett (2002).

61. Taylor (1903).

62. We do not cast blame on web designers. The power dynamics and economic and technological forces that led to our current electronic contracting environment differ in important ways from the application of Taylorism in work environments; the struggle between producers and consumers differs from the struggle between management and labor, although some market fundamentalists might disagree. We leave such complications aside for purposes of this work.

63. There is plenty of work focused on privacy and security notices and warnings, and some on contracts and end-user licensing agreements. See, e.g., Böhme and Köpsell (2010) (discussing literature). In addition, there are some law review articles, books, and judicial opinions that trace the evolution of electronic contracts, but these sources do not directly address the questions we have raised. See, e.g., sources cited in previous notes.

64. See, e.g., Loranger and Nielsen (2006); Nielsen and Tahir (2001); Krug (2014).

65. We did not conduct formal interviews. We considered them unnecessary considering our preliminary, informal conversations with folks at conferences (e.g. we presented this chapter in draft form at the Privacy Law Scholars Conference, prompting plenty of discussion during our session and afterwards) and workshops. These informal conversations consistently told the simple story we tell in the text, which fits rather well with the absence of published materials. Simply put, while "time and motion" studies influenced web design generally, designers of electronic contracting interfaces mostly took what they generally knew about website design and applied it to contract-related pages. There could be a more complicated story that we've failed to uncover, but it seems unlikely.

66. Yes, we are being a bit cynical. As Böhme and Köpsell suggest, some human-computer interface researchers have attempted to design interfaces that attract user attention and improve comprehension. Böhme and Köpsell (2010). Yet they note that such efforts are stymied by users who already appear to be habituated. Böhme and Köpsell (2010).

67. Donath (2014): 42.

68. Electronic contracting pages are not designed to add to the user experience or communicate messages or ideas, yet designers don't want to detract from the user's overall experience with the website. As we describe, the electronic contracting pages are speed bumps placed in front of the user's desired destination, and one objective is thus to minimize any negative experiences associated with the speed bump itself.

69. Terms and conditions of electronic contracts suffer from bloat because the marginal costs of adding more is incredibly low for digital contracts, unlike paper contracts. Moreover, it is relatively cheap to find and copy terms and conditions from other sites. There has been much standardization of terms, which can have benefits and costs. But it is worth noting that one potentially significant social cost is the absence of competition in terms themselves. Some law and economics scholars like to characterize terms and conditions, licenses, and so on as "product features" that provide an additional basis for competition. See, e.g., Baird (2005): 933; *ProCD, Inc.* v. *Zeidenberg*, 86 F.3d 1447, 1453 (7th Cir. 1996). The reality of electronic contracts doesn't seem to include such competition.

70. See, e.g., *Specht* v. *Netscape*, 306 F.3d 17 (2nd Cir. 2002); *ProCD, Inc.* v. *Zeidenberg*, 86 F.3d 1447, 1453 (7th Cir. 1996).

71. In this chapter, we are not concerned with browse-wrap agreements, which consist of posted terms that a user purportedly consents to by simply using the site or receiving services. See *Berkson* v. *GOGO*, 97 F. Supp.3d 359 (E.D.N.Y. 2015) ("Browsewrap exists where the online host dictates that assent is given merely by using the site. Clickwrap refers to the assent process by which a user must click 'I agree,' but not necessarily view the contract to which she is assenting. Scrollwrap requires users to physically scroll through an Internet agreement and click on a separate 'I agree' button in order to assent to the terms and conditions of the host website. Sign-in-wrap couples assent to the terms of a website with signing up for use of the site's services."); Kim (2013). We are highly skeptical of them, but not for the same reasons.

72. There are exceptions. Some contracts are written in more readable language. See, e.g., D. Hoffman (2017b) (discussing case studies).

73. Some interfaces draw the user's attention to specific terms, such as arbitration and forum selection clauses. For example, for its recent Windows 10 operating system update, Microsoft prominently displays the following text at the top of a scroll (with terms to be read if the user scrolls) above two buttons (decline and agree) that can be clicked without scrolling:

> Last updated July 2015
> MICROSOFT SOFTWARE LICENSE TERMS
> WINDOWS OPERATING SYSTEM
> IF YOU LIVE IN (OR IF YOUR PRINCIPAL PLACE OF BUSINESS IS IN) THE UNITED STATES, PLEASE READ THE BINDING ARBITRATION CLAUSE AND CLASS ACTION WAIVER IN SECTION 10. IT AFFECTS HOW DISPUTES ARE RESOLVED.
> Thank you for choosing Microsoft!

74. We will use click-to-contract and focus on websites. Everything we say can be extended to smartphones, tablets, and app contracts, as well as to smart TVs and other contexts. There are additional nuances and we leave them for future work.

75. As law professor Nancy Kim and many others have explained, this practice followed and built upon earlier practices with so-called "shrink-wrap." See, e.g., Kim (2013): 36–39.

76. Kim (2013): 39.

77. Kim (2013): 41. On the objective theory of contract, see below.

78. See, e.g., Böhme and Köpsell (2010); Egelman, Cranor, and Hong (2008); Schaub et al. (2015) (survey of literature and examination of the design space for privacy notices); see also Plaut and Bartlett (2012) (showing that design manipulations can improve readership rates and comprehension).

79. As Nancy Kim noted in an email, "Wrap contracts are really about using an efficient vehicle [the standard form contract] in the most aesthetically pleasing way."

80. As noted, even that feature was not always part of the design; contract law gradually imposed constraints on architects, for example, requiring conspicuous notice of terms and manifestation of consent through some action above and beyond browsing a site. See, e.g., *Specht* v. *Netscape*, 306 F.3d 17 (2nd Cir. 2002).

81. Budiu (2013).

82. Budiu (2013) ("Their relative importance may depend on the user – for example, dyslexic users may have a harder time reading than clicking around, whereas users with motor impairments may find clicking more difficult. They also depend on the device – a page load on a desktop connected to a high-speed network may be insignificant, but a page load on a mobile device may take forever if the cellular coverage is slow.")

83. We don't make any claims about deception. Woody Hartzog discusses the problem of "malicious interface" design, suggests a taxonomy, and considers legal approaches to addressing the problem. See Hartzog (2011): 1666–1668. Hartzog notes: "eleven categories of malicious design techniques have been identified by Conti and Sobiesk: coercion, confusion, distraction, exploiting errors, forced work, interruption, manipulating navigation, obfuscation, restricting functionality, shock, and trick." Hartzog cites Conti and Sobiesk (2010) (arguing that security and human-computer interaction committees need to come together to fix deceptive designs).

84. One probably could make a similar point about paper boilerplate contracts, where relevant action might be getting a signature, getting a box checked, or simply generating awareness of proposed terms prior to receipt of services. Cf. Hillman and Rachlinski (2002): 435–437 (examining paper boilerplate practices and the relevant interaction costs).

85. For an interesting study comparing the effectiveness of labels and architectural design remedies in the context of online search, see Hyman and Franklyn (2015) (finding that the architecture (i.e. the way search results

are graphically arranged on the page) is far more important than any labels that might appear on that page).

86. On the eye-tracking tendencies of the average internet user and the quantity of information read and processed, see e.g., Nielsen (2006) (eye-tracking heat map study: "[A]reas where users looked the most are colored red; the yellow areas indicate fewer views, followed by the least-viewed blue areas. Gray areas didn't attract any fixations."); Nielsen (2008) (empirical analysis finding that internet users on average read approximately 20% of the words on a webpage during an average visit). See generally Nielsen and Pernice (2009).

87. See Nielsen (2009) ("From 0.1 seconds to 10 years or more, user interface design has many different timeframes, and each has its own particular usability issues."). According to Neilsen, "0.1 second is the response time limit if you want users to feel like their actions are directly causing something to happen on the screen." Thus, in eye-tracking studies, most of the fixations tracked last little more than 0.1 seconds. Nielsen (2009). Other interesting observations made by Neilsen (based on his group's human-computer interface and web usability studies) include: (i) "The average page visit lasts about 30 seconds, but the more experienced the users are, the less time they allocate to each Web page. People are impatient on the Internet. Instantly gratify them, or they're out." (ii) "Most website visits last about 2–4 minutes." (iii) "10 minutes would be a long visit to a website." and (iv) "People complete most Web tasks in less than an hour." Nielsen (2009). See also Haile (2014) ("Chartbeat looked at deep user behavior across 2 billion visits across the web over the course of a month and found that most people who click don't read. In fact, a stunning 55% spent fewer than 15 seconds actively on a page."). On how computer response times affect user experience and behavior, see, e.g., Card, Robertson, and Mackinlay (1991): 181–188; Miller (1968): 267–277; Myers (1985): 11–17; Böhme and Köpsell (2010) (response latency study).

88. Kim (2013): 61–62; Tasker and Pakcyk (2008) (discussing many examples).

89. Others have stated this hypothesis. Kim (2013): 61; Hillman (2006b) (suggesting the Internet likely promotes impulsive purchases). But, to our knowledge, it remains an open empirical question.

90. According to the Second Circuit in *Specht*, "[r]easonably conspicuous notice of the existence of contract terms and unambiguous manifestation of assent to those terms by consumers are essential if electronic bargaining is to have integrity and credibility." *Specht* v. *Netscape*, 306 F.3d 17, 35 (2nd Cir. 2002). As one New York court explained:

> When e-commerce transactions are involved, the same general [contract] rules apply, with a twist. Under an evolving and still-developing body of federal and state law, an e-commerce merchant can condition its sales upon a mandatory forum selection provision through various means, including an exchange of e-mails, a click-through agreement, or other circumstances allowing for the "incorporation by reference" of conspicuous "terms of sale." But if the "terms of sale" are simply buried or "submerged" in multiple layers of web-pages, and such terms are not specifically brought to the buyer's attention, the "forum selection" clause will not be deemed part of the parties' agreement. (*Jerez* v. *JD Closeouts, LLC*, 36 Misc.3d 161 (2012).)

91. Cf. Kennedy (1982). We thank Lauren Henry Scholz, who commented on our draft at the 2016 Privacy Law Scholars Conference, for pointing out the connection between our chapter and Duncan Kennedy's seminal work.

92. There is some evidence, in fact, that the terms online are better than the terms offline. See, e.g., Mann and Siebeneicher (2008) (finding that terms evaluated then were generally benign).

93. We focus mostly on autonomy in this chapter. But the techno-social engineering may affect other human capabilities, such as our ability to relate to each other and create meaningful social relationships. Our beliefs and moral intuitions about and preferences for various social relationships are shaped by our built techno-social environment, and, as some scholars have begun to explore, our experience with the electronic contracting environment may shape our beliefs and moral intuitions about our contractual and moral commitments. Cf. Wilkinson-Ryan and Hoffman (2015): 1270 ("[T]he law itself (or, at least, what the parties believe the law to be) affects transactional decision making and parties' commitments to their interpersonal obligations").

94. See Chapter 12.

95. On the virtuous cycle, see FCC (2015): Open Internet Order.

96. See Chapter 11.

97. See Chapter 9.

Chapter 6 On Extending Minds and Mind Control

1. Brooks (2007).

2. We challenge this instrumental view of technology throughout the book. There is a rich literature on the topic. See, e.g., Ellul (1964); Shallis (1984); Postman (1992).

3. Selinger and Engstrom (2007). Likewise, Heersmink discusses the advantages of using "anthropotechnology" instead of enhancement. Heersmink (2017).

4. For a different and more normative view of technology as an extension of our bodies, see Nicholas Carr's contrast between farmers using a scythe and a combine.

5. Feenberg (2006): 192–193.

6. Buccafusco and Fromer (2017): 1.

7. Buccafusco and Fromer (2017): 2. "Many features of garment design – line, shape, texture, color, and print – exploit features of human visual perception and optical illusions to influence the way in which the wearer's body is perceived." Buccafusco and Fromer (2017): 12. See also Horn and Gurel (1981): 314; Fan (2004): 1 ("Few people have a perfect body. Most people would like to improve their appearance with appropriate clothing, by camouflaging their less desirable attributes and highlighting the most attractive aspects of their bodies.").

8. In their analysis of how copyright law treats fashion design, Buccafusco and Fromer argue "aspects of a design [that] affect the perception of the wearer, for example, by making him or her look taller, slimmer, broader, curvier, or lengthier, . . . must be treated as functional and excluded from copyright protection." Buccafusco and Fromer (2017): 2. The authors distinguish "fashion design features that 'look good on,' as compared to [features that] merely 'look good.'" The latter category refers to designs that are beautiful independent of the wearer.

9. Feenberg (2006): 192.

10. Feenberg (2006): 193.

11. Feenberg (2006): 193.

12. Giere (2002): 228.

13. Giere (2002): 231.

14. Giere (2002): 229.

15. In his 1991 paper "Cognitive Artifacts," Donald Norman examines this kind of cognitive processing, noting the differences between a system-level analysis (i.e. looking at the person-plus-pen-and-paper) and a person-level analysis (i.e. looking at just the person themselves and how they relate to the objects in their environment). His key insight is that the material culture enhances cognitive performance at the system level but that it does so not by enhancing performance at the person level but, rather, by changing the cognitive tasks that the person has to perform. Norman suggests that cognition is distributed but not according to a simple "sharing" model; rather, it does so by changing a whole cognitive ecology. His view thus accords with our own. Norman (1991).

16. Boden (2006): 1450.

17. Mey (1996): 230.

18. Norman (1991).

19. Sterelny (2004); Zhang and Patel (2006).

20. Clark and Chalmers (1998): 8.

21. Ibid.

22. Note that we can describe the Otto scenario in terms of distributed cognition and cognitive technology theories. The tools (notebook, pen) provide rather limited opportunities for other people to exercise any control over the cognitive system; Otto retains control. The cognitive technology is enabling in general, and especially so for Otto.

23. Cf. D. Robinson (2013): 11–12 (examining the criteria in the case of Otto and his notebook, Clark and Chalmers' paradigm example). In *Feeling Extended*, Robinson offers an interesting twist to the extended mind theory. He suggests that humans extend their minds not only to and with things but also to and with other humans through social interactions and the sharing of qualia. This twist folds into the common-sense reverse Turing test developed in the previous chapter.

24. Clark (2011).

25. Clark and Chalmers (1998); Clark (2011); D. Robinson (2013); Malafouris (2013).

26. Douglas Robinson suggests that "there are some important ways in which the feeling that [the mind 'literally' extends to tools and other epistemic artifacts] enhances our cognitive processes." D. Robinson (2013).

27. Not all, however. Philosophers, such as John Danaher, Richard Heersmink, and Neil Levy consider some of the normative implications of mind-extending technologies. Danaher makes the same move as we do and notes: "What matters is whether the extension of the mind into technological artifacts is ethically significant." Danaher (2016): 1–16. Even Clark has recognized that cognitive enhancement is not necessarily neutral. In a 2007 article, he says: "It is our basic, biologically grounded nature (or so I have suggested) to be open to a wide variety of forms of technologically mediated enhancements [...] not all change is for the better, and hybridization (however naturally it may come to us) is neutral rather than an intrinsic good. Uncritical talk of human 'enhancement' thus threatens to beg philosophically, culturally, and politically, important questions." Clark (2007): 278. Moreover, there is an extensive literature on biological enhancement that addresses these issues: see, for example, Danaher (2016); as we noted earlier, we have not aimed to mine that vein.

28. We might use a term other than machine. "Slave" and "zombie" implicate different concepts.

29. Clark (2010): ix.

30. Obviously, this isn't literally the case. Chalmers is sincere. He's an intellectual maverick, not a corporate shill.

31. McLuhan (1964): 73.

32. Chalmers (2014).

33. Someone could "hack" Otto's notebook. But the probability of this is low because doing so is unethical and not a motivation encouraged by the affordances of the object.

34. Carr (2015).

35. Lin (2014) ("your robot car decides to take a new route, driving you past a Krispy Kreme Doughnut shop").

36. We are not evaluating this practice in terms of efficiency. It may or may not be to the long-term benefit of all users participating in this system to sacrifice in the short term, and the sacrifice could be negligible. Our point concerns our general question – Who is doing the thinking? – and more specifically – Who is in charge of the cognitive tasks? Who decides what routes to take? Who evaluates the cost-benefit trade-off? etc.

37. Danaher (2016).

38. Rushkoff (2016): 90.

39. He also considers: Inequality, Overload, Alienation, Narrowing, Deceit, Degradation, and Disembodiment. For the sake of brevity, we do not address these specters or his rebuttals. We certainly raise the specters of Alienation and Degradation, but, in the end, the main force of his response

to such concerns boils down to pay attention and educate yourself: "Know Thyself: Know Thy Technologies." Clark (2004): 183. While we agree with the advice, it falls well short, particularly where our capabilities to know are contingent and shaped by the technologies we're tasked with understanding, and where autonomy is itself contingent and constrained.

40. Clark (2004): 169.
41. Clark (2004): 174.
42. Clark (2004): 174–175.
43. Clark (2004): 175.
44. Solon (2017).
45. Solon (2017).
46. Solon (2017).
47. Dreyfus and Kelly (2011): 214–215.
48. Sunstein (2014a): 29 (citing Maguire et al. (2000): 4399).
49. Heersmink (2017): 28–29.
50. This approach doesn't address the desirability of maintaining so-called "intrinsically valuable" skills against degradation. Heermsink (2017). Whether intrinsically valuable skills really exist or are instead a mischaracterized version of instrumentally valuable skills is an important issue that Heersmink does not consider. It's beyond the scope of the present analysis for us to resolve that debate.
51. Brumfiel (2016).
52. Brumfiel (2016).

Chapter 7 The Path to Smart Techno-Social Environments

1. *What is the cheapest way to make large numbers of human beings perfectly happy?* By the gradual deployment over decades of the sort of techno-social tools we're highlighting, consumer expectations may be set so low that the techno-social system need only meet or barely surpass expectations. As hedonists know and often are prone to emphasize, people adapt to their conditions and their corresponding happiness levels typically adjust too. The goal might very well be to engineer beliefs, preferences, and expectations in a manner that makes supplying happiness cheap and easy. In the end, cheap satiation might constitute optimal happiness. We return to this argument in the penultimate chapter. In this chapter, we consider mass media as techno-social engineering tools. As Desai (2015: 549) (quoting Webster 1995) notes:

> The general concern that provision of information via a new medium possibly harms public life by turning people inward and limiting action is not new. Newspapers, publishing houses, radio and television stations and networks, bookstores, and many other purveyors of information performed filter functions in the past and still do so today. As far back as 1933 – and throughout the decades since – theorists have been concerned that information power and new media supported consumer capitalism over all else. That way of life was thought to be "home-centered to the detriment of civic relations." The claim and fear was that "people [would be] predominantly passive" and "hedonism and self-engrossment predominate and [would] find

encouragement" while "public virtues such as neighborliness, responsibility, and social concern" languish. Today, those ideas have been resurrected on the theory that because information media are now digital, there is a new urgency about sorting, organizing, and controlling what people see, read, and hear.

As we explain in this and the next chapter, digital media are only part of the story (albeit an important one).

2. For a more extensive discussion, see Frischmann (2012): Ch. 5.

3. For a more extensive discussion, see Frischmann (2012): Ch. 5.

4. Cohen (2012) put it succinctly and explained it thoroughly and persuasively.

5. Drawn from Frischmann (2012).

6. Kleinman (2011): 117.

7. As Edmund Carpenter and Marshall McLuhan suggested:

> English is a mass medium. All languages are mass media. The new mass media – film, radio, television – are new languages, their grammars as yet unknown. Each codifies reality differently; each conceals a unique metaphysics. Linguists tell us it's possible to say anything in any language if you use enough words or images, but there's rarely time, and the natural course is for a culture to exploit its media biases. (Carpenter and McLuhan (1956): 46–52.)

8. Kleinman (2011): 116.

9. While a stump or even a stage enables a performer to reach a larger audience, the tool might not be mass media, although this might depend upon how massive an audience must be to fit the somewhat amorphous definition.

10. Kleinman (2011): 117. The causes for convergence of various media are complex, and a full examination is beyond the scope of this chapter. However, considering a few factors reveals details about our current path and possible future.

11. Our description is abbreviated by necessity.

12. Media theorist Marshall McLuhan emphasized how each medium is an extension of human senses. See, e.g., McLuhan (1964).

13. Cohen (1996).

14. Carpenter and McLuhan (1956), above (comparing manuscript, book, newspaper, and magazine media in terms of these and other biases).

15. Carpenter and McLuhan (1956): 49.

16. McLuhan (1964): 7–9.

17. See, e.g., *FCC* v. *Pacifica Foundation*, 438 U.S. 726 (1978) ("We have long recognized that each medium of expression presents special First Amendment problems. And of all forms of communication, it is broadcasting that has received the most limited First Amendment protection.").

18. Radio and television borrowed the serial model from print, but the serial shows differed, in part, because of the different affordances the media provided to content producers.

19. Strandburg (2013): 107 (citing Anderson and Coate (2005): 950–952).

20. She considers alternative theories and assumptions. Strandburg (2013): 107 (citing Anderson and Coate (2005): 950–952).

21. Strandburg (2013): 129. There are extensive debates and analyses of this phenomena. See, e.g., Turow (2012).
22. McLuhan (1964).
23. Kellner and Share (2007): 60.
24. Ihde (2016): 100.
25. The same can be said for many if not most other countries. For a survey of different media systems and histories around the world, see Oates (2008).
26. Bernays (1947): 114.
27. Herman and Chomsky (1988).
28. Advertising may be an obvious form of techno-social engineering aimed at shaping customers' beliefs and preferences, but Herman and Chomsky (1988) suggested that, among other things, advertising-based mass media enabled elites to shape news media and thereby engineer cultural and political beliefs.
29. We use the Internet as a focal point for our discussion. We could instead refer to networked computers. Even if we put too much weight on the Internet as the infrastructure that brings the various technologies and techniques together, we believe our basic arguments still hold. But see Morozov (2012): 17–62 (strongly criticizing Internet-centrism). As we hope is clear from the text, we don't believe there is anything predetermined or inevitable about the Internet, mass media, or any other of the techno-social engineering tools we discuss.
30. The following paragraphs are drawn from Frischmann (2012): Ch. 13.
31. There are two versions of the end-to-end arguments. See Van Schewick (2010): 96–105.
32. Van Schewick (2010): 116–123 (describing how the Internet Protocol implements the two versions of end-to-end arguments). Internet Protocol: DARPA Internet Program Protocol Specification, IETF RFC 791 (September 1981), http://www .ietf.org/rfc/rfc0791.txt?; number=791 (formally describing IP).
33. IBM – *What is Big Data?*
34. Others trace the origins of big data to the post-World War II rise of computing and note that we have witnessed similar transformative data-driven revolutions in the past. See, for example, Ambrose (2014). On the "digitization of just about everything," see Brynjolfsson and McAfee (2014).
35. In his book chapter titled "*So Open It Hurts,*" Evgeny Morozov describes "digital sunburn." "As more of our personal information finds its way into easily accessible databases – an unfortunate consequence of ever-growing demands for more transparency, more sunlight, more disinfection – the risks of digital sunburn have substantially increased, while awareness of such risks seems still to be quite rudimentary." Morozov (2012): 63.
36. Zuboff (2015).
37. Filmmaker Oliver Stone discussed surveillance capitalism while promoting his biopic on Edward Snowden. Sounding a loud alarm, Stone made a starkly dystopian prediction about where surveillance capitalism will lead: "You'll see a new form of frankly a robotic society." Rottenberg (2016).

38. Ed Felten, Professor of Computer Science and Public Affairs at Princeton University, made this point during an IoT reading group at Princeton's Center for Information Technology Policy IoT Reading Group Workshop, Center for Information Technology Policy, Princeton University (April 26, 2017).
39. Bartholomew (2017): 31.
40. Kramer, Guillory, and Hancock (2014): 8788–8790.
41. Kramer, Guillory, and Hancock (2014): 8788.
42. Kramer, Guillory, and Hancock (2014): 8790.
43. Kramer, Guillory, and Hancock (2014): 8790.
44. For a collection of sources, see Grimmelmann (2014a). To get a sense of the debate, browse the sources listed under *Journalism* or *Commentary*.
45. Goel (2014).
46. Facebook has created its own internal Research Review process. For details, see Molly Jackman and Lauri Kanerva, Evolving the IRB: Building Robust Review for Industry Research, 72 *Wash. & Lee L. Rev. Online* 442 (2016).
47. See Cohen (2012): 252 (describing how the United States system of consumer protection against invasions of privacy revolves around a "purely proceduralist" model of notice and consent).
48. Some scholars insist that preferences are not shaped; instead, they believe preferences are latent and are discovered over time, revealed to oneself and the world through one's actions and exposure to advertising, marketing, and information that better helps one to understand what one truly prefers. For a discussion of different views within economics, see Hodgson (2002): 159.
49. Our claim is not that Facebook has eliminated privacy preferences. Many people, including young people, care about privacy and take steps to protect their privacy, for example, by managing privacy settings. Boyd and Hargittai (2010).

Chapter 8 Techno-Social Engineering of Humans through Smart Environments

1. Cohen (2000).
2. It is the *Field of Dreams* phenomena: "If you build it, they will come." Gordon and Robinson (1989): *Field of Dreams*.
3. There are many communications between machines that enable the Internet to function effectively, and there are even higher-layer communications generated by computer programs. These are usually examples of communications that are either inputs that facilitate human communications at higher layers or constitute communications of the human who wrote or is running the program. Besides, as we move toward the Internet of Things, it will be the case that the Internet as we know it changes and perhaps becomes the Internet as we like to remember it.
4. The Internet of Everything metaphor is equally suggestive. It certainly doesn't hide the ambitions of scale, scope, and power.

5. Department of Commerce (2017): 6.
6. Such questions may be unnecessary if one embraces the extended mind philosophy and assumes human participants retain their autonomy.
7. Matyszczyk (2016). Samsung may have changed its privacy policy and data collection practices, and it could do so again in the future (to be more or less privacy protective).
8. Are smart home devices like vampires? There are two ways in which smart home devices are like vampires. First, to feed their thirst for intelligence generation – that is, to be smart – smart devices must suck up data. Second, smart devices cannot enter the home unless invited. Thus, any claims of intrusion or invasion shall be met with an invocation of consent. According to some sources, vampires also could exert mind control over their victims.
9. Lin (2015); Hevelke and Nida-Rumelin (2015); Goodall (2014).
10. Some folks might protest that accidents are not inevitable because a truly smart system will prevent all accidents. This view is fundamentally flawed, however, on many levels. See, e.g., Goodall (2014). The most basic flaw is the hubris of human engineered perfection. In the Conclusion, we explain how the logics and mindset that perpetuate this hubris need to be replaced.
11. Coeckelbergh (2016): 748–757.
12. See, e.g., Calo and Rosenblat (2017) (discussing promises and pitfalls of the sharing economy).
13. Zuboff (2016).
14. "Network neutrality" emerged from Wu (2003) and Wu (2004). See also Wu & Lessig (2003).
15. Isenberg (1997).
16. For a detailed examination of the social value of shared infrastructures, see Frischmann (2012).
17. As Frischmann (2012) explains, managing infrastructure as a commons – meaning, in a manner that does not discriminate or prioritize on the basis of who you are or what you are doing – sustains an underdetermined environment and allows individuals and groups to engage in self-determination with different outcomes, depending on the context and changing conditions. In this fashion, infrastructures afford users room for play.
18. Frischmann (2012).
19. For a lengthier explanation of why intelligently managing infrastructure to deal with congestion and related problems does not conflict with the idea of network-neutrality-style non-discrimination rules, see Frischmann (2012).
20. Laris and Halsey (2016).
21. Parker (2017).
22. Facebook – *Community Standards*.
23. Galperin and Ben Hassine (2015).
24. Youtube Help – *Restricted Mode*.
25. Eordogh (2017).
26. Shahani (2016).

Chapter 9 #RelationshipOptimization

1. Ruse (1994): 144.
2. Ruse (1994): 147.
3. Goldman (2016).
4. Goldman (2016).
5. Descartes (1985).
6. Dvorsky (2015).
7. Companies aren't just using software to try to create digital representations that behave just like real people. In 2012, Apple acquired a patent for "Techniques to Pollute Electronic Profiling" which might be used to develop a "cloning service." Such a service would study a user's behavior and create automated transactions that look like the person herself initiated them. The goal is to, in some cases, predict how a user would behave and act accordingly, and, in other instances, initiate behaviors that differ from the user's typical patterns. By introducing information that becomes associated with the user but is an inaccurate portrayal of the user's proclivities, surveillance data becomes "polluted" and, this, in turn, as Finn Brunton and Helen Nissenbaum note, minimizes "the value of profiles gathered from the data." Brunton and Nissenbaum (2015): 37.
8. Patent 8589407 (2013).
9. Apple – *Our Smartest Keyboard Ever.*
10. Apple – *Our Smartest Keyboard Ever.*
11. Boyle (2015).
12. Levy (2007). See also Markoff (2015): 222–26; Turkle (2011).
13. The related themes of robot lovers and sex robots have been explored in lots of literary, cinematic, and televisual treatments. Indeed, the very premise of an artificial object of desire dates at least as far back as the ancients when Ovid told the story of Pygmalion falling in love with an ivory statue that the goddess Aphrodite brought to life. For more on the Pygmalion theme, see Sullins (2012).
14. Wilson (2009).
15. See generally Donath (2014).
16. See Levy (2007).
17. Any beliefs, preferences, or desires that we might attribute to Android Ash are fully determined by others – its programmers and the material and social cultures that serve as inputs for its programs. Android Ash is effectively mindless. It has no mind of its own. Or, if one were to insist otherwise, the mind of Android Ash always would be fully extended in the sense that all of the thinking relevant to being human or a person would be done by others.
18. Johnson and Cureton (2017).
19. Yan (2015).
20. Philosopher of mind Patricia Churchland thus gives the following answer to an interviewer who asks whether she finds neuroscience unsettling: "I'd have to say no. It takes some getting used to, but I'm not freaked out by it.

I certainly understand the ambivalence people have. On one hand, they're fascinated because it helps explain their mother's Alzheimer's, but on the other, they think, 'Gosh, the love that I feel for my child is really just neural chemistry?' Well, actually, yes, it is. But that doesn't bother me." Lawton (2013).

21. De Boer, Van Buel, and Ter Horst (2012). ("Love is More Than Just a Kiss: A Neurobiological Perspective on Love and Attraction"); see generally CNS Charité Neuroscience – June 2014 Newsletter.

22. Although we are making a distinction about pre-cleaning compulsions, we are not denying that Roombas evoke strong anthropomorphic tendencies. The tendencies are so strong that people actually name their devices and develop emotional attachments to them. Biever (2014) (interview with CEO of Roomba, Colin Angle) ("Once, a woman called and explained that her [Roomba] had a defective motor. I said, 'Send it back. We'll send you a new one.' She said, 'No, I'm not sending you Rosie.'") ("If you ask people who doesn't [sic] own Roombas if they would name them, they almost violently say, 'No, why would I name my vacuum cleaner?' Yet once they own one, more than 80 percent of people do.") There's no evidence that such sensibilities will extend this far for most people. (This article is from Slate and is an interview with the CEO of Roomba: http://www.slate.com/articles/he alth_and_science/new_scientist/2014/03/roomba_vacuum_cleaners_have_na mes_irobot_ceo_on_people_s_ties_to_robots.html.)

23. Abramian-Mott (2007) ("'There's a part of me that just doesn't want her to think I'm a slob ... She's a stranger, but it still matters for some reason.'"). (LA Times, "Cleaning for the cleaning lady." http://articles.latimes.com/20 07/nov/22/home/hm-clean22.)

24. Bulajewski (2014).

25. Goffmann (1959).

26. John Sullins argues that a perpetual affirmation machine wouldn't possess key elements of *eros* that Plato describes in *The Symposium*. Lacking these capacities, Sullins contends such a robot couldn't impose the type of demands that inspire us to develop the virtues required for living a meaningful and good life. See Sullins (2012). Charles Ess expands on Sullins's arguments and contends that while robots can offer "good sex" they cannot offer "complete sex," a practice that is central for maintaining an ethical commitment to a partner who is, in a Levinasian sense, Other, and for whom our experience of passion and attraction fluctuates. See Ess (2017).

27. Bruce Feiler, "For the Love of Being 'Liked'". http://www.nytimes.com/2014/ 05/11/fashion/for-some-social-media-users-an-anxiety-from-approval-seeking .html?_r=1

28. Aristotle's *Nicomachean Ethics* (2011).

29. See Sartre (1991); see also Zweig (2014); see generally Selinger (2014) (connecting Zweig and Sartre: https://www.wired.com/2014/06/you-are-worth-more-than-just-likes-faves-and-retweets/).

30. In fact, one of us accidently ran an experiment on his friends and family. A few years ago, annoyed by dozens of pithy messages on his birthday and the

idea that Facebook required that data to be shared, I changed the birthdate displayed on my Facebook profile. I did this a few days after my actual birthday; I picked a random day in the opposite season. Then I forgot about it. About five months later, my email inbox was flooded with Facebook notifications indicating the presence of dozens of pithy Happy Birthday messages on my Facebook page. I shrugged as this confirmed that most people simply respond automatically to Facebook's prompts without really thinking about what to say, much less whether to say something. I was surprised, however, when two of my close relatives posted messages, and one of them had spoken to me on my actual birthday over the phone.

31. Meyer (2015).
32. Meyer (2015).
33. Meyer (2015).
34. Meyer (2015).
35. Rose (2015).
36. Rose (2015): 90.
37. Habermas (1985): 325.
38. Dor Tal Portfolio – *Predictables*; see also Designboom – *Predictables App*.
39. Parts of this chapter previously appeared in or were adapted from Evan Selinger's "The Black Box Within: Quantified Selves, Self-Directed Surveillance, and the Dark Side of Datification".
40. Dormehl (2014): 15.
41. Dormehl (2014): 38.
42. Dormehl (2014): 38.
43. There are lots of important methodological questions to raise about how "Angela" tracked her data and interpreted it, as well as why she was motivated to use a mood-tracking program. Dormehl offers scant details, but one of us critically explores some possibilities. See Selinger (2015a).
44. If this sounds like an implausible thought experiment, think again. This example is adapted from an actual person's story and the claims he made to one of us when explaining why he uses the app. That person re-purposed an app designed for women to use to gain more control over their own reproductive health. This is a recurring theme in consumer technology, and it's hard to see how it won't have a role to play in the future of techno-social engineering. Consumers often find creative ways to put technology to new uses, and they've readily embraced technologies that are developed to add subversive functionality. Take Snapchat, for example. This app was created so people could send ephemeral information – such as pictures that automatically get deleted shortly after being seen. But after a wave of hype and widespread enthusiasm for the service, a number of apps were developed that archive screenshots of Snapchat images. Many view the tools that produce these enduring copies as undermining their choice to communicate over a transient channel. But that concern hasn't stopped the image-preserving apps from becoming popular downloads and users who don't know they exist from making regrettable choices.
45. Hesse (2010).

46. See Eveleth (2014).
47. Eveleth (2014). Also, for more on Glow and related issues, see Levy (2015).
48. Oaklander (2015).
49. Conversation with Lara Freidenfelds.
50. Jaggar (2002): 137.
51. James (2000): 29.
52. A recent meta-study of PMS suggests that, if it exists, it's not a generalized phenomenon. See Romans et al. (2012).
53. Freidenfelds (2009).
54. Freidenfelds (2009). Also, as Karen Levy rightly pointed out, in conversation, after reading a draft version of this chapter, it's important not to push the delegation of self-management motif too far. As Levy emphasized, women still have to know when their periods are coming and do intimate bodily things like apply their own tampons. She further suggested that much of the affect-related management encouraged by the technologies under consideration involves trying to ameliorate the effects of a woman's period on aspects of her partner's life.
55. One reason not to extend the analysis would be to focus on consent. The relationship between loving partners is different from the other relationships in many important ways, and perhaps consent between partners is a differentiating factor. However, we suspect that consent is an illusory limiting principle and a weak crutch to lean on.

Chapter 10 Turing Tests and the Line between Humans and Machines

1. Many commentators contend that Turing did not intend the TT to be an operational definition of intelligence that provides necessary and sufficient conditions. This, however, doesn't mean that "passing" isn't a sufficient condition for intelligence. Dennett (1980): 429–430. Some commentators maintain that the test is merely a procedure for getting good evidence about whether a machine is intelligent. Moor (2001); Schweizer (1998).
2. Moor (2001): 82.
3. Turing (1950): 433–460.
4. Shieber (2008): 686–713.
5. Hayes and Ford (1995): 972–977.
6. Hayes and Ford (1995): 977.
7. We address this position in Chapter 12.
8. Many experts in the various fields affected by the Turing Test have lamented this racing behavior, for it is by no means clear that this is the best race to run; resources might have been better focused elsewhere, for example. See, for example, Hayes and Ford (1995). In fact, today, researchers in these fields no longer focus on passing the Turing test as a *goal*, for various reasons, including that most recognize that intelligence is much more than verbal communication.

9. Turing (1950).
10. One of us asked a colleague how he would feel about being a mere brain in a vat with his happiness optimized by some technical system. He responded, "Extremely happy, I guess." For him, the stipulation of optimal happiness made it easy; he suggested that intuitions derived from the hypothetical just tend to fight the hypothetical and its stipulation. The concerns many people have about the hypothetical may have more to do with doubts about it being possible or whether there is something hidden in the stipulation of optimal happiness. We think there are reasons to be concerned with the hypothetical and its stipulation. But our conversation reminded us that what may be of the highest concern is not the endpoint itself but what happens during the race to get there.
11. It is analogous to an argument Frischmann made about price discrimination. Truly perfect price discrimination may be socially valuable; everyone should love it. But it does not and cannot exist in reality. Imperfect price discrimination is much more ambiguous; it is sometimes good, sometimes bad. Frischmann explained how the path to perfect price discrimination is fraught with peril for society, yet we continue down the path deluded by the siren's song of perfection. Frischmann (2012): Ch. 5.
12. The TT has usually been used to answer the question "at what point can we say that a non-thinking thing (machine) is acting like a thinking thing (human)?," but it also can be used to ask "at what point can we say that a thinking thing is acting like a non-thinking thing?"
13. We might add religiously, in the sense that acting with or as a result of blind religious faith can be and has been set in sharp contrast with rational or scientific thought. This may be a can of worms or adders not worth opening.
14. This discussion implicates the line between machines and other living non-human beings that experience many of these mental states. Darwin (1872); Goodall (2000); Cheney and Seyfarth (1992); Braitman (2014). Regarding animals' experience of emotions, Braitman suggests "A number of recent studies have gone far beyond our closest relatives to argue for the possible emotional capacities of honeybees, octopi, chickens, and even fruit flies. The results of these studies are changing debates about animal minds from 'Do they have emotions?' to 'What sorts of emotions do they have and why?'" Braitman (2014): 24.
15. Segal (2014).

Chapter 11 Can Humans Be Engineered to Be Incapable of Thinking?

1. Some reviewers have suggested that we don't need to rely on games at all. The Imitation Game has been seriously criticized, they say, and the underlying concerns about the construction of humans to be machine-like can be addressed more directly. We're not so sure about this position, however. We believe the value of the Turing test is not necessarily limited to the particular machine-environment (i.e. the Imitation Game) he constructed; the method matters, as do the underlying sets of questions it invokes.

2. For a more recent study of the confederate effect, see Warwick and Shah (2017).

3. Shieber (1994).

4. Warwick and Shah (2017): 287–297.

5. But cf. Christian (2011) (explaining how human "confederates" act strategically, trying to appear human to the human observers).

6. "Simple" has a specific meaning in this context, as described in the text.

7. Per Brian Christian: "I learned from reading the Loebner Prize transcripts that there are two types of [human] judges: the small-talkers and the interrogators. The latter are the ones that go straight in with word problems, spatial-reasoning questions, deliberate misspellings … [tests that are] extraordinarily hard for programmers to prepare [for]." He goes on to describe his experience with "a small-talk, stranger-on-a-plane judge." Christian (2011): 100–103.

8. See, e.g., Loebner Competition – *Rules*; Christian (2011).

9. E.g. the capacity to feel and understand the feeling of hot/cold, hunger, etc., or to see and understand the color red. We considered developing a techno-social engineering test focused on phenomenological experience, such as sensing, understanding, and experiencing temperature or color. It could be based on an adaptation of Frank Jackson's famous Black-and-White Mary thought experiment to examine phenomenological experience and technological manipulation of the human capacity to feel. Jackson (2007); Jackson (1982). For further detail, see Appendix B.

10. "To be human," writes Dan Falk, "is to be aware of the passage of time; no concept lies closer to the core of our consciousness." "Without it, there would be no planning, no building, no culture; without an imagined picture of the future, our civilization would not exist." Falk (2010): 3, 99.

11. Goodall (2000): 188. Humans have the capability to use language to express ideas about objects and events that are not present. Although chimpanzees and other intelligent primates have complex communication systems, they do not have the ability to communicate about things that are not present. This uniquely human capacity enables people to plan for future events and recall past events. Most importantly, per Goodall, human language allows members of a group to discuss ideas and share a "collective wisdom." See also Cheney and Seyfarth (1992) (explaining how monkeys' "inability to examine [their] own mental states or to attribute mentality to others severely constrains the ability of monkeys to transmit information, deceive, or feel empathy with one another. It also limits the extent to which monkey vocalization can be called semantic … Unlike our language, … the vocalizations of monkeys are not given with the intent to modify the mental states of others.").

12. Wagenaar (1972): 65–72; Brugger (1997): 627–661; Towse and Neil (1998): 583–591.

13. Gandy (2010): 29–42.

14. Gandy (2010): 29–42.

15. Stein (1996).

16. Stanovich (2013): 1–26.
17. Stanovich (2012): 435.
18. Though the observer generally could distinguish humans and machines on the basis of plain computational errors, for example in performing mathematics, we would prefer to rule out such instances. Similarly, we would prefer to rule out instances of nonsensical responses by humans that might be described as completely irrational or just insane.
19. Allais (1953) : 503–546.
20. Ariely (2008). "A substantial research literature – one comprising literally hundreds of empirical studies conducted over several decades – has firmly established that people's responses sometimes deviate from the performance considered normative on many reasoning tasks. For example, people assess probabilities incorrectly, they test hypotheses inefficiently, they violate the axioms of utility theory, they do not properly calibrate degrees of belief, their choices are affected by irrelevant context, they ignore the alternative hypothesis when evaluating data, and they display numerous other information processing biases." Stanovich (2013) (collecting studies).
21. I use the phrase "can be seen" to refer to a plausible observation by the observer conducting the tests and experiments.
22. It might be better (less controversial) to describe the human responses in terms of bounded rationality rather than irrationality. Some will argue that many responses that deviate from the rational choice model or instrumental rationality are in fact rational; for example, some would argue that it is rational to contextualize problems as humans do but machines don't. It reminds me of Tolstoy's ruminations on reason and faith: "Either that which I called reason was not so rational as I supposed, or that which seemed to me irrational was not so irrational as I supposed." Tolstoy (1988). Again, though it may seem like we're cheating, we wish to avoid these types of debates, at least for the purposes of this discussion. We recognize that in future works, it might be necessary to specify in more detail the rational choice experiments that our observer will employ.
23. Stanovich (2012); Stewart (2009): 1041–1062.
24. Jolls and Sunstein (2006): 199–241; Jolls (2009).
25. Stanovich (2012): 433–455.
26. Stanovich (2013): 1–26. See also Stanovich (2012): 433–455.
27. Stanovich (2013), citing various sources.
28. Stanovich (2005): 249.
29. We examine this idea in other work focused on free will and autonomy as well as an environment game.
30. Sunstein and Thaler (2008); Ariely (2008); Amir and Lobel (2008).
31. We don't mean to judge, much less attack, the behavioral law and economics agenda that aims to implement nudging or debiasing policies to improve human decision-making in contexts where humans tend to act irrationally or contrary to their own welfare. Jolls (2007); Sunstein and Thaler (2008); Ariely (2008); Amir and Lobel (2008). We do, however, intend to cast that agenda in

a slightly different light and provide a different way to discuss their prescriptions. Incremental changes through nudging may make a lot of sense when evaluated in isolation, but that doesn't mean we shouldn't also examine and investigate (i) how those changes are implemented in light of and comparison with alternatives, and (ii) the path set by the agenda and where it may take us. Jolls and Sunstein discuss how debiasing through law can raise substantial autonomy concerns, and they explain how the "nature and force" of the concerns "depend on the setting and the particular [debiasing] strategy involved." We agree. Jolls and Sunstein (2006): 199–241.

32. Rebonato (2014): 357–396.

33. For purposes of the thought experiment only, the means chosen by government are not specified and thus are unimportant. That is, whether the government constructs the nudging environment through the legal system or through technological architecture is not germane to the thought experiment. Of course, in reality, the means do matter. Sunstein and Thaler are careful in prescribing gentle means that seem empowering (rather than constraining) in the sense that they generally enable people to make more informed, unbiased decisions. Sunstein and Thaler (2008).

34. We can substitute other contexts for the workplace. Consider the classroom, grocery store, sidewalk, or public park, if you prefer.

35. This presumption is made for purposes of argument only and is by no means an empirical or theoretical claim we wish to defend. There are certainly reasons to doubt the presumption in various real-world workplaces where, for example, human creativity and emotion impact productivity.

36. Schumacher (2010).

37. Erion (2001): 33.

38. Erion (2001): 36.

39. Erion (2001): 36.

40. Erion notes that "it is everyday knowledge that is hardest to convey to a computer" and concludes that accordingly the Cartesian (common-sense) test is a rather high bar for machines. One might wonder whether big data and networked machines will undermine this view. IBM's WATSON computer or even SIRI may seem to exhibit common sense because of the computers' ability to interpret questions in context and respond in ways that seem to correspond to common sense. Of course, any such responses are derivative of human-generated data. For example, if a computer evaluates observed human responses to being lost (suppose the iPhone tracks user behavior and makes the data available to SIRI) and determines what is common sense based on the frequency of response (and perhaps subsequent behavior as well as a measure of success), does the computer possess common sense? Note that we have not directly conveyed everyday knowledge to the computer; instead, we have provided the computer with the tools for identifying and then responding with the statistically deduced response. But does the computer actually possess everyday knowledge? Can the computer apply the knowledge to reason or "to act through reason?"

Of course, this brings us back to Searle's Chinese language experiment and the basic mind-body problem – Does the computer know anything? As Erion suggested, an observer with sufficient time probably would be able to determine that such a computer was in fact just a computer. Erion (2001): 36. See also the classic by Hubert Dreyfus, *What Computers Still Can't Do*. Dreyfus (1992).

41. Erion (2001): 36.

42. Other species may possess common sense. Chimps seem to have a weaker version in the sense that they solve problems and share solutions; other animals are social and cooperate in ways that suggest some means for sharing knowledge. But it is not clear that any animals other than humans combine language, reasoning, and social skills to generate common sense, at least as we have defined it. Cheney and Seyfarth discuss these issues, document various ways in which non-human primates communicate and develop "social knowledge," and cite various studies. Cheney and Seyfarth (1992).

43. It would be interesting to examine such a shift in the health care context, where the relationships between common sense, technology, and medical treatment are evolving rapidly.

44. Morozov (2014b).

45. The missing step is important: It is difficult to say how "close" or "far" from the Turing line we might be at any given time, although it seems likely that we remain quite distant. Perhaps we can posit that we are progressing toward the line, but even then, at what rate? What is the shape of the "progress curve" or path? Would such a curve be linear or nonlinear? Would there be a tipping point? (A phased transition as we approach the boiling point?) As suggested earlier, we might be concerned with changes or losses along the way, even if we never truly cross the Turing line.

46. Another example our reviewer raised regarding the research competency of younger generations:

> I think my students are savvier researchers as college freshman than my generation was. They've spent their whole lives evaluating online info. They'd never have survived to adulthood if they believed everything they read. They have a researcher's common sense that in my generation we really didn't develop that acutely until graduate school.

47. Here is how Lee put it at the Being Human seminar in Princeton University on March 9, 2017:

> In the case of a machine, there are often measures in place to ensure the continuous operation of a system, but in humans, this is often precisely the instinctive state, often accompanied by common sense. The question is, therefore, not so much based on what the ideal state is (for which a human may indeed begin to approximate a machine) but rather the ability to tolerate suboptimal conditions with resourcefulness. In the example with Alice being lost, being able to pull out a phone and call an Uber may seem technologically [determined], but it represents only a small fraction of the likely possibilities. Perhaps her phone is running low on battery, or it doesn't have signal. Perhaps there simply are no Ubers available in her area. Even if the immediate technology fails her, we have an expectation of a general human to be able to navigate, ask for directions, and by whatever means get home . . . Humans are

supposed to be able to inform others about in what ways they are experiencing difficulty and to process outside information as necessary. I have personally never been so lost in a city that I had to ask complete strangers for help, but I know that it is always an available option. Even if the most obvious options were exhausted, I have retained the ability to sit down and come up with more ideas. This ability to rely on common sense to recover from a failure state (in this case, being lost) is critical to humanity. (Lee (2017).)

48. Note that since common sense is dependent on shared core knowledge, uneven distribution or deployment of common-sense-destroying technology could have distributional impacts.

Chapter 12 Engineered Determinism and Free Will

1. Mawson (2011): 115. Contemporary versions of natural determinism account for quantum uncertainty and hold the view not that the past rigidly determines a specific, well-defined future, but merely that the future will be determined by our present physical state acted upon by (at bottom, broadly statistical) physical laws and not by any causal agents or forces acting independently of those laws. Quantum indeterminacy does not impact our arguments or analysis. Accordingly, for simplicity, we discuss Laplacian determinism.

2. Laplace (1998): 2.

3. Determinism is often classified as an empirical thesis: a view about the nature of reality that can be confirmed or disproven by scientific inquiry. Either the universe is entirely physical and every event that occurs is determined by antecedent physical conditions, or it isn't. Currently, the consensus is that quantum physics demonstrates that reality is indeterminate, but only at the micro level. Some, however, view determinism as a metaphysical thesis. They take this position because they believe that metaphysical commitments (acknowledged or implicit) guide empirical investigation into the building blocks of reality.

4. See Chapter 2; Weizenbaum (1976).

5. It is also referred to as causal determinism.

6. Mawson (2011): 115.

7. Although as the literature on "moral luck" suggests, we might not give appropriate consideration to the role that luck plays in moral outcomes. Nelkin (2013).

8. Empirical claims purporting to prove otherwise are not trustworthy; see below for a brief discussion of free will empiricism. As Samuel Johnson said, "All theory is against the freedom of will; all experience for it." Boswell (1986). T. J. Mawson suggests that the burden of persuasion falls on determinists for various reasons, most important of which seems to be the fact that freedom fits better with our common sense. See Mawson (2011). It is also worth noting that the Introduction to his book provides an excellent thought experiment involving the People's Republic of Freedom that in interesting ways is similar to our experience machine n.0 thought experiment. Mawson (2011): Introduction.

9. As Ray Kurzweil notes, "Attempts to prove its existence, or even to define it, may become hopelessly circular, but the reality is that almost everyone believes in the idea. Very substantial portions of our higher-level neocortex are devoted to the concept that we make free choices and are responsible for our actions. Whether in a strict philosophical sense that is true or even possible, society would be far worse off if we did not have such beliefs." Kurzweil (2012): 235.

10. Pascal (1958): 233.

11. We're aware that, in making this claim, we're separating James' general views on pragmatism (i.e. truth is what works) from his analysis of Pascal's Wager in "The Will to Believe." James (1912). There James contends that Pascal's "logic of the gaming table" is a rationalization whereby a deep personal conviction gets presented in seemingly objective terms by formulating it in mathematical terms. James (1912). Our sense of where James stands on free will is anchored in his *The Dilemma of Determinism*. James (2010).

12. Parallels can be made to P. F. Strawson's seminal paper on reactive attitudes, "Freedom and Resentment." A key difference, however, is that Strawson focuses on natural attitudinal reactions and not on a pragmatic wager based on comparative consequences. Strawson (1963): 1–25.

13. Some will fight us here and insist that the truth of natural determinism is knowable, that reason and empirical study can, does, or will reveal the truth. As Hawking and Mlodinow put it:

> Recent experiments in neuroscience support the view that it is our physical brain, following the known laws of science, that determines our actions, and not some agency that exists outside those laws. For example, a study of patients undergoing awake brain surgery found that by electrically stimulating the appropriate regions of the brain, one could create in the patient the desire to move the hand, arm or foot, or to move the lips and talk. It is hard to imagine how free will can operate if our behaviour is determined by physical law, so it seems that we are no more than biological machines and that free will is just an illusion.

Hawking and Mlodinow (2010): 32. The epistemology of determinism is itself hotly contested. We do not engage that debate, except to express our skepticism and note that some of the existing experiments that purport to offer proof tend to be isolated and contextual examples that are too often and too easily misinterpreted and overextended to make generalized claims. Libet's work on the relationship between conscious intention and physical action appears to present a challenge to free will. Libet (1985): 529–566. Libet identified the readiness potential in subjects' brains that led to a specific motor function (e.g. tapping a button). It turned out that unconscious brain activity occurred prior to conscious awareness by the subject. The subjects may have believed that they consciously chose to push the button and thus exercised their own free will, but the study suggested that their conscious intention arose afterwards. Some have argued that this suggests free will is an illusion. Like many others who have rejected this argument, we don't see much of a challenge. That some subconscious processes govern some human behavior doesn't undermine free will or autonomy. Our minds (selves) encompass both conscious and subconscious processes, which interact and integrate in complex ways to provide our various capabilities, including our capacity for self-reflection and determination. See, for example, Dennett (2003). Some have suggested that motor control is an inappropriate focus because the time scales are so short, and there is substantial unconscious action involved: " ... free will cannot be squeezed into time frames of 150–350 ms; free will is a longer term phenomenon; it is a higher level activity that 'cannot be captured in a description of neural activity or of muscle activation ... '" Gallagher (2009): 119–121. More recent work has shown that subjects can veto movements for which readiness potential signals have been detected if the subjects become aware of the action at least 200 milliseconds before movement onset. Schultze-Kraft et al. (2016): 1080–1085.

14. Pascal's wager is more complicated than meets the eye. For an overview of the literature, see Hájek (2012).
15. It's worth noting that due to the role of infinity the specific probabilities don't matter at all in Pascal's wager: .0001 percent probability of infinity still gives you an expected value of infinity.
16. Our argument is similar to one made by philosopher Saul Smilansky in his book, *Free Will and Illusion*. Smilansky suggests that free will is a socially valuable and necessary illusion. Smilansky (2000). See also Kurzweil (2012): 235.
17. Eagleman (2011).
18. See Chapter 2.
19. Caruso (2016): 43.
20. E.g. ideas about punishment in criminal justice system due to bad choices people had the free will to make, repentance (religious and non-religious) for wrongs freely committed, medical autonomy, etc.
21. Hart observed that, under traditional contract law, a contract could be voided by presenting defenses related to either the lack of or fraudulent knowledge possessed by the defendant, the compromised will of the defendant in creating the contract, and defenses which overlapped with both knowledge and will to contract such as intoxication. Hart (1959): 145–166.
22. Grim (2007): 190.
23. Again, recall Weizenbaum, or substitute techno-social engineers for Laplace's divine intelligence.
24. Heidegger (1977).
25. Dreyfus (1996).
26. Dreyfus (1996).
27. Even if our world is naturally determined, that wouldn't explain or justify engineered determinism. Some might argue that we already and inevitably live in a world of engineered determinism, but that would attribute free will or autonomy to the engineers, and thus undermine their premise. Others might dismiss the problem of engineered determinism as a symptom of natural determinism where the perception of engineering is itself an illusion. But that

would seem to border on fatalism because the same move could be made with respect to all sorts of techno-social engineering, including legal systems and social norms. Most firm believers in natural determinism and the corresponding illusion of free will do not turn to fatalism.

28. Latour (2008): 151–152.
29. Latour (2008): 152.
30. boyd (2014): 65.
31. Verbeek (2010): 10.
32. Spinoza (1996).
33. Risch (2009a): Virtual Rule of Law, 2.
34. Risch (2009a): Virtual Rule of Law, 2.
35. Frankfurt (1971): 5–20. There is a rich and complex literature on this topic. As noted in Appendix C, we focus on the key concepts that help explain the position we take, but we do not – because we cannot, given our commitment to brevity and clarity in this book – delve fully into existing debates. We also note that Frankfurt's theory of free will is compatible with determinism. Frankfurt (1971): 20. See generally Frankfurt (1971): 15, 18–19 (good citation of others' ideas on the subject).
36. Frankfurt (1971): 5–20. We can have conflicting preferences and perhaps resolve internal conflicts through reflection and reason. Once more, language is important. We have language with which to reflect and reason about what we want and what we want ourselves to want. Even if we do so silently within our own heads, self-reflection about preferences (or beliefs or values) is an internal dialogue dependent, at least to a significant degree, on access to and use of language.
37. Jeffrey (1974); Sen (1974); Sen (1977); Sen (2004).
38. Sayre-McCord and Smith (2014): 129.
39. Frankfurt distinguishes among different types of addicts. One type might want to not want to drink while another, the "wanton" type, might not care about the addictive desire. This distinction is not critical to our analysis, but we note that it is a topic of debate in the literature. McKenna and Coates (2016).
40. They may or may not be depending upon the person and context. For example, the person may have a longstanding desire to cease drinking and be unsuccessful because of various environmental factors that stimulate the immediate desire for a drink that is stronger in the moment. Both desires may be sufficiently robust to be the agent's own. It would be different if the person has a fleeting (non-robust/fragile) desire to stop drinking.
41. E.g. a taste for fatty foods.
42. E.g. heuristics.
43. E.g. Western traditional gender roles.
44. Buss (2016); Christman (2015). Some focus on the desires, preferences, or beliefs that motivate people to act. Some distinguish different orders of such mental states (e.g. second-order preferences about first-order preferences that are acted upon). Some focus on how responsive to reasons an agent might be,

while others focus on the reasoning process itself. Some focus on self-rule or governance. Sneddon (2013).

45. We recognize this is a bit obtuse, but we've not been able to settle on a clearer way to explain the point. Intentions are a mental state that is part belief, part desire, and part value. My intention to do something – say to write the explanatory text in this note or to eat an apple – entails (1) beliefs about the action, (2) desire to act, and (3) some sense of value attributable to the act.

46. While many experts may reject our view as insufficiently respectful of the nuances between these concepts, others have similarly conflated free will and autonomy. For example, Jackson's hierarchical mesh theory is often discussed as a theory of autonomy.

47. Stanovich (2005).

48. Dennett (2003).

49. Stanovich (2005): 13.

50. Genetic determinism is a causal thesis that applies to biological creatures and not the universe itself.

51. This suggests a very different illusion than that suggested by the Spinoza quote.

52. Cohen (2000): 1424.

53. Cohen (2000): 1424.

54. Sartre (1993): 700 (theorizing that a "slave in chains is as free as his master").

55. Frankfurt (1971) (discussing categories of *wantons* and *addicts*).

56. We do not mean to raise or discuss the underlying existential and epistemic questions of how do we really know that the simple machine lacks free will and autonomy (or that we have it). Again, we assume a baseline.

57. Nor should we get off course by focusing on how machines of debatable complexity can be built to exhibit conflicts between first- and second-order preferences. One could design a program that interprets a subroutine as a first-order preference, a potential overriding subroutine as a second-order preference, and interpret some responses as conflicts between the two.

58. Howell (2014): 389–415 (Google Morals, Virtue, and the Asymmetry of Deference).

59. Howell (2014): 389.

60. Tsalatsanis et al. (2015): 1–2.

61. Tsalatsanis et al. (2015): 1–2.

62. Carr (2015).

63. Bernard Harcourt suggests that "Many others of us are lulled into giving away our most sensitive data." Harcourt (2015): 181. He goes on: "And after a few moments of doubt, when we flinch at the disclosure, most of us nevertheless proceed, feeling that we have no choice, not knowing how not to give our information, whom we could talk to, how to get the task done without the exposure." Ibid. (at 182).

64. In "Preference, Deliberation and Satisfaction," philosopher Philip Pettit provides an excellent explanation of how deliberation relates to self-determination of one's will:

Deliberation is the enterprise of seeking out higher-order beliefs with a view to imposing further checks on one's fact-construing and goal-seeking processes. Not only do we human beings show ourselves to be rational agents, as we seek goals, construe facts, and perform actions in an appropriate fashion. We also often deliberate about what goals we should seek, about how we should construe the facts in the light of which we seek them, and about how therefore we should go about that pursuit: about what opportunities we should exploit, what means we should adopt, and so on. We do this when we try to ensure that we will form suitably constraining higher-order beliefs about the connections between candidate goals and candidate facts.

The fact that we human beings reason or deliberate in this sense means that not only can we be moved by goal-seeking and fact-construing states – by the belief that p or the desire that q – in the manner of unreasoning, if rational, animals. We can also reflect on the fact, as we believe it to be, that p, asking if this is indeed something we should believe. And we can reflect on the goal we seek, that q, asking if this is indeed something that we should pursue. We will interrogate the fact believed in the light of other facts that we believe, or other facts that perceptions and the like incline us to believe, or other facts that we are in a position to inform ourselves about; a pressing question, for example, will be whether or not it is consistent with them. We may interrogate the goal on a similar basis, since the facts we believe determine what it makes sense for us to pursue. Or we may interrogate it in the light of other goals that also appeal to us; in this case, as in the case of belief, a pressing question will be whether or not it is consistent with such rival aims.

Nor is this all. Apart from drawing on deliberation to interrogate the facts we take to be the case, and the goals we seek, we can ask after what actions or other responses we ought to adopt in virtue of those facts and goals. Not only can we ask after whether they give us a reliable position at which to stand; we can ask after where they would lead us, whether in espousing further facts or goals, or in resorting to action. We may be rationally led in the manner of non-human animals, . . . But we can also reason or deliberate our way to that action – we can reinforce our rational inclination with a deliberative endorsement – by arguing that the facts, as we take them to be, are thus and so, the goals such and such, and that this makes one or another option the course of action to take; it provides support for that response. (Pettit (2006): 141–142.)

65. Singer (1997): In Singer's hypothetical scenario, university students are walking to class and see a child drowning in a pond. The child can be saved without harm coming to the student, except for getting the student's clothes wet such that they would miss class. Should the child be saved if it will cost the student to miss a class? If yes, then the moral obligation to save the child outweighs the relatively small difficulties associated with missing class. What if the drowning child is, instead, a child in need but across the world? If such little difficulty could be undertaken to help said foreign child, for instance, a relatively small monetary donation, should it be undergone? But why should the moral imperative to save any child be only if the cost is low enough?

66. Keep in mind that simple machines serve only as a baseline for evaluating techno-social engineering of humans. We are not especially interested in more complex machines that can be programmed to do the more complex semantic analysis and risk estimation necessary to modify the numeric trade-off presented. We could build these more complex machines. Perhaps that might be interesting for future variations of the techno-social engineering tests we're developing. But, for now, the main objective is to design a baseline against which to evaluate human behavior.

Chapter 13 To What End?

1. Other baselines are possible. We chose simple machines. Others might choose other species. We leave consideration of alternatives for future work.
2. Their convictions may be rooted in religion, reason, or both. We adopt a reasonably accommodating pluralist approach in the sense that the capabilities we focus on tend to fall within an area of overlapping consensus. Divergence, however, tends to arise when one attempts to prioritize commitments and justify them.
3. In this and the fourth bullet point, we use singular words (people, society) where we could use plural words (peoples, societies). We do so only for ease of reading. As we develop further in the text that follows, different groups of peoples and different societies can and do choose to possess and commit themselves to sustaining different values and capabilities. They can and do decide, in different ways, that they owe different obligations to past, present, and future generations.
4. Rousseau (2010): 5.
5. We realize that many will either be confused or appalled by our description of humanity as a resource. The word "resource" is often taken to mean commodity, asset, or thing to be consumed or exploited for value. As we develop further in the text that follows, we adopt a more liberal interpretation.
6. Zimbardo (2007).
7. Sartre (2007). For example, in an email commenting on this chapter, John Breen noted: "I don't believe anyone ever loses their humanity. Their humanity may be diminished but never totally lost. Mao and Stalin and Hitler were human even as they committed the most heinous atrocities. If humanity – or rather human nature – is a given, then it can't be lost entirely. It can only be more or less actualized. 'Humanity' is not a commodity that one possesses. It isn't a physical thing that can be acquired and then given away. It is an innate quality that one always possesses simply by virtue of being human."
8. Critics, we hope, will still find much of what we have to say relevant and important, even if they happen to disagree about the definitions or rhetoric we use.
9. United Nations – *Universal Declaration of Human Rights*. According to Article 1, "All human beings are born free and equal in dignity and rights."
10. Harari (2014): 3–25 (explaining how *homo sapiens* existed along with other humans, such as *homo neanderthalensis* and *homo erectus*).
11. Harari (2014).
12. Harari (2014): 11 (explaining the significance of *homo sapiens* moving from the middle to the top of the food chain).
13. Some reviewers have asked how our approach relates to transhumanism. According to Joanna Kavenna, transhumanism was "defined by evolutionary biologist Julian Huxley in 1957 as the belief that the human species can and should transcend itself "by realizing new possibilities" of and for human nature." Kavenna (2017). According to philosopher Nick

Bostrum, "Transhumanists view human nature as a work-in-progress, a half-baked beginning that we can learn to remold in desirable ways." Kavenna (2017) (citing Bostrom (2005)). We are transhumanists in the sense that we believe (i) human beings have and exercise the capability to imagine, conceptualize, and engineer ourselves and (ii) humanity involves a set of ideals that evolve over time. We part ways with many in the transhumanist camp at death's door; we do not aspire to escape death or live in a world where we escape our bodies by extending our minds into the digital networked environment.

14. Breen (2008): 340.

15. "[C]ulture itself is an environmental concept." Frischmann (2007a): 1083. While writing this book, we considered developing and defending the concept of environmental humanism as a needed replacement for (or upgrade to) humanism. For the sake of brevity, focus, and avoiding too many new concepts, we decided to leave this task for future work. We welcome collaborators.

16. By focusing on the state of human affairs, we do not mean to overinflate the position of human beings. However, this book does have a particular focus: it is about the relationships between humans and the technologies we create and use. Of course, as Peter Singer has argued, the suffering of other species caused by humans and our technologies is important. Nevertheless, consideration of this issue would bring us beyond the scope of this book.

17. The set could include more than characteristics and capabilities. One could focus on knowledge and moral virtues, for example.

18. While debates have raged for millennia over what matters about being human and what constitutes a good human life, there are persuasive philosophical accounts that identify several basic human capabilities. See Sen (2005): 151–166; Sen (1985); Sen (2001); Nussbaum and Sen (2004); Nussbaum (2011): 33–34 (2011); Rachels (2014): 15–32 (making the case for universal values that exist across all societies).

19. Some might criticize our approach because it allows for too much variation and cultural contingency. This objection presupposes too much for the reasons stated in the text. Others might criticize us for not being as sensitive to diversity as we aspire to be. After all, appeals to culture risk focusing on shared values at the expense of recognizing differences in race, class, and gender, as well as commonalities found in subcultures (of which there are many) and norms that only make sense in specific contexts (e.g. what's acceptable at work might not be at home). Our straightforward response to this charge is that we're using culture broadly to refer to any group that's constituted, even if only temporarily, by shared commitments, values, experiences or yearnings.

20. For an interesting take on moral floors, see Nussbaum (2007): 126 ("any minimally just society will make available to all citizens a threshold level of ten central capabilities, as core political entitlements."); Nussbaum (2011): 33–34.

21. For the same reasons that we reject technological determinism, we reject corresponding notions of moral determinism. Moral progress and regress are possible.

22. Throughout history, different cultures have built diverse worlds that allowed different values to become pre-eminent or techno-socially engineered into existence. In *The Order of Things*, philosopher Michel Foucault contends that fundamental values like what constitutes "humanity" have been constantly redefined throughout history to suit a variety of agendas and powerful actors. Foucault (1994). Indeed, it's hard to deny that the confluence of power and prejudice – racism, sexism, classism, and ableism, amongst other pernicious "isms" – has had an oversized influence in determining who gets to count as being sufficiently similar to ingroups to qualify as human. Moreover, formulations of humanity and the imagined worlds that support these conceptions can lose their hold on us, just like perceptions of the gods do – a shift that's aptly illustrated by polytheism being displaced by monotheism in large parts of the world. We could create a laundry-list of the features that have differentiated worlds across human history.

23. This section draws from Frischmann's article "Some Thoughts on Shortsightedness and Intergenerational Equity." See generally Frischmann (2005).

24. Lincoln (1838):

> We find ourselves in the peaceful possession, of the fairest portion of the earth, as regards extent of territory, fertility of soil, and salubrity of climate. We find ourselves under the government of a system of political institutions, conducing more essentially to the ends of civil and religious liberty, than any of which the history of former times tells us. We, when mounting the stage of existence, found ourselves the legal inheritors of these fundamental blessings. We toiled not in the acquirement or establishment of them – they are a legacy bequeathed us, by a once hardy, brave, and patriotic, but now lamented and departed race of ancestors. Their's [sic] was the task (and nobly they performed it) to possess themselves, and through themselves, us, of this goodly land; and to uprear upon its hills and its valleys, a political edifice of liberty and equal rights; 'tis ours only, to transmit these, the former, unprofaned by the foot of an invader; the latter, undecayed by the lapse of time and untorn by usurpation, to the latest generation that fate shall permit the world to know. This task [of] gratitude to our fathers, justice to ourselves, duty to posterity, and love for our species in general, all imperatively require us faithfully to perform.

25. Jaffa (1959): 228 (citing Lincoln (1863) ("The 'people' is no longer conceived in the Gettysburg Address, as it is in the Declaration of Independence, as a contractual union of individuals in the present; it is as well a union with ancestors and with posterity; it is organic and sacramental.")).

26. Lincoln (1838). See also Deganawide (1977) (often referred to as "The Iroquois' Law of Seven Generations"); Morris (1995) (discussing the "centuries-old Haudenosaunee philosophy that all major decisions of a nation must be based on how those decisions will affect at least the next seven generations").

27. Swift (1947): 4 (describing the Athenian Ephebic Oath translation by Clarence A. Forbes).

28. The analogy to unjust enrichment is imperfect. Unlike unjust enrichment – where two parties look to the past, and the beneficiary, to whom a benefit has been conferred, compensates the person who provided the benefit – the dynamic we describe involves three parties (past, present, and future generations) and looks to the future. We thank John Breen for pointing this out.

29. On the boiling frog metaphor, see Wikipedia – *Boiling Frog*. Frogs do not actually behave as the story suggests. Nonetheless, as Eugene Volokh noted, the metaphor is useful conceptually, regardless of how frogs actually behave. Volokh (2003): 1026–1137.

30. Quinn (1996): 258.

31. Oreskes and Conway (2010).

32. For some, the boiling frog story could be utopian. Some people would choose to stay in the pot even when informed about the warming trend and their eventual demise. That is, some people may be and/or may want to be satiated frogs.

33. To make his objections vivid, Nozick introduced the experience machine thought experiment (1974 and revisited in 1989), a hypothetical scenario that bears a striking resemblance to Ray Bradbury's earlier short story, "The Happiness Machine" (1957). Weijers (2011).

34. For an extended discussion of this issue, see Grau (2005).

35. Haybron (2016). Haybron provides a sophisticated survey of different mental state approaches to well-being, including different types of hedonism. For thorough account of the intellectual and philosophical history of hedonism, see Moore (2013).

36. Weijers (2014); Kolber (1994). There is a debate among philosophers and experimentalists about whether thought experiments like Nozick's are amenable to empirical study. Smith (2011); De Brigard (2010).

37. Bramble (2016). This may be an empirical claim worth exploring. We are unaware of a definitive study and are not certain that empirical testing would work well.

38. Susan Wolf offers compelling examples that illustrate why thinkers like Nozick don't reduce meaningful experiences to instances where we strive for pleasure or even necessarily experience it.

> The mother who stays up all night to finish her son's Halloween costume in time for the parade does not see herself as doing this because she will be happier this way, nor does she just happen to prefer finishing her son's costume to getting enough sleep. She stays up sewing for her son's sake – it is his happiness, or the place of the costume in his preference-ranking that provides her, to her mind, with a reason. The philosopher who struggles over an article that she is trying to write, disregarding draft after draft in the attempt to get it right is trying to attain clarity and understanding and to express it in an effective and perspicuous way because that is good philosophy, and, as such, she believes, intrinsically worthwhile. Wolf (2015): 51.

39. Ben Bramble observes: "Hedonism has few contemporary advocates. This is mainly due to a single, highly influential objection to it, widely considered to be decisive: Robert Nozick's experience machine. Discussions of well-being – whether in scholarly journals, academic conferences, or university lecture halls – often begin with a quick dismissal of hedonism by reference to Nozick's objection before turning to 'more interesting matters' (usually the question of which desire-based or hybrid theory of well-being is true)." Bramble (2016): 136.

40. Weijers (2011).

41. Weijers (2014): 3.

42. In an email exchange, a hedonist criticized us for suggesting that hedonism and the experience machine raised ethical, moral, or normative concerns. We are baffled by this criticism. It seems wrong and, worse, misleading to say that what constitutes a good life, well-being, and welfare are merely descriptive. These concepts are baseline criteria for evaluating public policy, social arrangements, and social welfare. How the concepts are defined and measured dramatically affects evaluation, in large part by virtue of what's left out of the definition and what's not measured. Further, the long intellectual history of hedonism unambiguously demonstrates its roots in moral and ethical theory. Of course, hedonic theorists are free to narrowly define their pursuits, such as Roger Crisp's careful delimitation in "Hedonism Reconsidered." In that article, Crisp specifies precisely the "kind of hedonism [he] wants to discuss," which happens to be hedonism as a theory of well-being. Crisp distinguishes other kinds of hedonism, including moralistic kinds like hedonistic utilitarianism, but he doesn't deny that they exist. Crisp (2006). See also Bronsteen, Buccafusco, and Masur (2014) (focusing on hedonism as a theory of well-being); Haybron (2016) (same).

    The criticism reminded us of similar moves made in other academic contexts. For example, economists often disclaim normativity and insist their work is purely descriptive. In 2008, one of us debated economist Harold Demsetz about whether or not his seminal work on property rights advanced a normative theory. Frischmann (2007b); Demsetz (2008) (insisting his work advanced only a descriptive theory); Frischmann (2009) (responding in part to Demsetz's essay). A reviewer suggested the move is also quite similar to one made by some folks who argue in favor of an "originalist" approach to interpreting the US Constitution. Not all originalists take this position, but many hide their normative arguments under the "mere description/ interpretation/definition veil." Rather than belabor the point, we'll close by referring the interested reader to *The Stanford Encyclopedia of Philosophy*, which provides a thorough account of the intellectual and philosophical history of hedonism. See Moore (2013).

43. Mendola (2006): 441–477; Layard (2005). See also Bronsteen, Buccafusco, and Masur (2014): 172–175 (suggesting that the experience machine thought experiment pumps "inadmissible intuitions").

44. Hypothesis: People who admit that they would plug in are more likely to believe in natural determinism and that free will is an illusion. Someone who believes in natural determinism is less likely to be concerned about engineered determinism. See Chapter 12. So far, our anecdotal observations support this hypothesis. It would be interesting to explore it further.

45. Nozick seems to have tilted the scales in favor of hedonism by guaranteeing optimal happiness. Yet he probably did this to show why hedonism, even in its most tempting form, is repugnant once you think carefully about it. By making the lives on and off the machine equivalent, we adjust the extreme framing of the trade-offs. This might eliminate speculation about optimal happiness and elevate status quo bias as a factor.

46. Crisp (2006): 635–636. "According to hedonism, [the lives on and off the machine] have exactly the same level of well-being. And that is surely a claim from which most of us will recoil." Crisp goes on to argue that our beliefs about the value of accomplishment (and by extension free will) might be "an example of a kind of collective bad faith, with its roots in the spontaneous and largely unreflective social practices of our distant ancestors." Perhaps. But perhaps he has it backwards.

47. These are hypotheses and intuitions, in need of empirical testing.

48. This hypothesis needs empirical testing. If we eliminate framing effects and other cognitive biases, hedonists should be indifferent and willing to flip a coin.

49. De Brigard (2010): 43–57.

50. In fact, even if we stack the deck in further in favor of unplugging, for example by guaranteeing a much better and authentic life, we suspect most people would decline the offer.

51. We are not committed to identifying multinational companies as the architects. Governments, public-private partnerships, and others would also presumably be involved. As we explain elsewhere, the point is not to allocate blame to any particular master planner.

52. As Amartya Sen argued long ago in his critique of welfarism, an incredibly poor person with very little opportunity in life might be subjectively happy because she has adapted to her conditions in life, but that cannot mean that society should not be committed to reducing poverty or investing in building the capabilities of her daughters and sons or of future generations of similarly situated people. Sen (1985); Sen (2001); Nussbaum and Sen (2004).

53. Mill (1962): 9.

54. Historically, not everyone has had the means to experience Mill's higher pleasures. Significant distributional and class-based concerns challenge appeals to higher pleasures. Further, strong commitment to individualism triggers concerns about paternalism – *who's to say what is higher?* We don't address these concerns, except to note that perhaps Experience Machine n.0 could level the playing field. Of course, it is not clear how such leveling would affect humanity.

55. Of course, if we're wrong, then that would tell us something about people's baseline normative values.
56. Kahneman (2002).
57. We originally included a chapter on nudging titled "Do Choice Architects Dream of Programmable Humans?" But we disagreed about some of the details and decided to save the chapter for future work. On nudging, see Thaler and Sunstein (2008); Sunstein (2014b).
58. OECD – Use of Behavioural Insights in Consumer Policy.
59. Hansen and Jespersen (2013).
60. Apparently, some tech industry insiders are starting to recognize and regret their contributions to humanity's techno-social dilemma. See James Vincent, "Former Facebook Exec Says Social Media Is Ripping Apart Society," *The Verge*, Dec. 11, 2017, at https://www.theverge.com/2017/12/11/16761016/former-facebook-exec-ripping-apart-society
61. Morozov (2014a).
62. Pasquale (2015).
63. Or: Who speaks for humanity? There is no Lorax for humanity.

Chapter 14 Conclusion: Reimagining and Building Alternative Futures

1. Genetic determinism holds that evolutionary biology fully determines what humans do. It is distinguishable from natural determinism because it is a causal thesis that applies to biological creatures and not the universe itself.
2. "Negative liberty is the absence of obstacles, barriers or constraints. One has negative liberty to the extent that actions are available to one in this negative sense. Positive liberty is the possibility of acting – or the fact of acting – in such a way as to take control of one's life and realize one's fundamental purposes." Carter (2016); Berlin (1969); Berlin (1978). "[I]n the first case liberty seems to be a mere absence of something (i.e. of obstacles, barriers, constraints or interference from others), whereas in the second case it seems to require the presence of something (i.e. of control, self-mastery, self-determination or self-realization)." Carter (2016). See generally Berlin (1969): 121–122 (Negative liberty is relevant when one answers the following question: "What is the area within which the subject – a person or group of persons – is or should be left to do or be what he is able to do or be, without interference by other persons?" Positive liberty is relevant when one answers the following question: "What, or who, is the source of control or interference that can determine someone to do, or be, this rather than that?"). There is a close connection to our discussion of free will, autonomy, and engineered determinism. See Chapter 12.
3. Haraway (1991): 149.
4. Or, as Haraway argued, we are cyborgs.

5. Haraway similarly described how communications technologies and biotechnologies translate the world into "a problem of coding, a search for a common language in which all resistance to instrumental control disappears and all heterogeneity can be submitted to disassembly, reassembly, investment and exchange." Haraway (1991): 164.

6. Haraway also criticized the dominant logics and called for new ones that embraced the irony and reality of being cyborgs. Haraway (1991): 164. We build upon her work and ideas but, for reasons explored in Chapter 6, we do not fully adopt the cyborg metaphor.

7. Frankly, we don't engage sufficiently in the political and economic work needed to answer the latter question, but we have engaged with the normative question. If we were to do so, we probably would explore the connections between environmental humanism and cultural environmentalism. On cultural environmentalism, see Cohen (2012); Frischmann (2007a); Benkler (2006); Boyle (2003, 1997, 1996).

8. Alexander (2013); Alexander (2009).

9. Sen (2005); Sen (1985); Sen (2001). See also Alkire (2002).

10. Nussbaum and Sen (2004); Nussbaum (2011).

11. Frankly, it resonates with a few other logics and analytical paradigms. We considered engaging more directly with the literature on cultural environmentalism because of its strong connections to some of our prior work and to the concept of environmental humanism. For brevity, we decided to leave such exploration for future work.

12. The capabilities approach has been used effectively in a variety of disciplines to develop moral prescriptions and tools for evaluation. In the past two decades, it has emerged as the dominant approach to human development policy and led to the creation of the United Nations' Human Development Index. The HDI provides a useful measurement tool that captures various aspects of human development and capabilities related to education, health and income. The HDI is used in the Human Development Reports produced by the United Nations Development Program and provides an alternative measure to GDP and other output-based metrics. The CA also has inspired other capabilities-based indices, such as the Gender Empowerment Index and the Human Poverty Index. An incredibly rich, interdisciplinary literature has developed involving economics, philosophy, political science, health policy and other social sciences.

13. Cohen (2012); Sunder (2012); Vallor (2016).

14. See Chapter 13.

15. This is an important caveat. Suppose the Experience Machine n.0 thought experiment framed the choice in binary terms as follows: (1) Build the Experience Machine n.0; or (2) Retain our current world as it currently exists. This choice presents a more difficult decision. The first option might sacrifice actual free will, but it would provide the illusion of free will and tremendous welfare gains in terms of much longer and happier lives for billions of people. The second choice might sustain free will, but it would

sacrifice the opportunity for massive social welfare gains. If these are the only choices, the trade-off might be very difficult. It is critical, in our view, to recognize that these are not the only choices.

16. Paternalism kicks in where there is good reason to conclude that people don't know what's best for them; liberalism is skeptical of any such alleged state of affairs. The battle usually devolves into the core political question of Who Decides?

17. For the sake of brevity, we focus on this debate and put aside (for future work) the more interesting but much longer discussion of liberalism versus republicanism.

18. After reviewing the manuscript, legal scholar Michael Madison sent us a note making the following argument about baselines:

> There's a deep "legal system" or "modern Western government" baseline that you're using that we usually spend so much time taking for granted that even specifying it explicitly can sound a little silly. Basically, the idea is that "law" (in a formal sense) means: rule of law – abstract, universal statements adopted by accountable citizen-supported institutions that govern human activity; violations of the rules are sanctioned via systems defined by due process and all that entails. We contrast that with what "law" meant before it meant "rule of law" (i.e., before the late 18th and early 19th century, more or less): "law" meant the King (or the monarch) and the King's men, and basically if you broke "the law," you had virtually no recourse and you went to jail (or worse). The transition from "the King's law" to "rule of law" (basically: self-governance by "citizens," via well-defined political systems) was massive both conceptually and operationally. "Techno-social engineering" threatens to undermine some of its basic philosophical and psychological commitments, in ways that citizen self-governance does not. How can we engage in meaningful self-governance if we are not, at some foundational level, choice-processing individuals? The modern risk, of course, is not that we go back to rule by the monarch; instead, we end up with rule by the Fabulous Five.

19. Cohen (2012). Bernard Harcourt also suggests that humanism was eclipsed by economic liberalism. Harcourt (2015): 166–183.

20. Cohen (2012).

21. Cohen (2012): 53–54.

22. Legal scholar Neil Richards has developed a complementary theory of intellectual privacy that also resonates strongly with our analysis. Richards defines intellectual privacy as "the ability, whether protected by law or social circumstances, to develop ideas and beliefs away from the unwanted gaze or interference of others." He goes on to explain that "Surveillance or interference can warp the integrity of our freedom of thought and can skew the way we think, with clear repercussions for the content of our subsequent speech or writing. The ability to freely make up our minds and to develop new ideas thus depends upon a substantial measure of intellectual privacy." Richards (2008): 389.

23. Cohen (2012): 224–225.

24. For example, behavioral economics powerfully challenged neoclassical economics in large part because of experimental studies finding people do not behave much like *homo economicus* in rational actor models. Kahneman (2011); Thaler and Sunstein (2008); Kahneman (2002).

25. For a discussion of proxies used to value environmental resources, see Frischmann (2012): 233–234:

> Economists use a range of sophisticated methods, such as stated preference methods and revealed preference methods, to approximate preferences. Although used in many policy and resource management settings, these methods are, at best, incomplete proxies for measuring the social value of environmental resources. Even if economists could accurately measure everyone's current preferences, the resulting valuation would nonetheless be skewed in a manner that undervalued the environment's "true" contribution to human well-being.
> . . .
> Despite inevitable trade-offs and reasonable appeals for marginal valuation, we should not pretend that such proxies accurately capture the social value humans derive from environmental resources. If individuals' willingness to pay is systematically biased against making trade-offs that would improve their own welfare and the welfare of future generations, we must resist approaches that rely on aggregating individuals' willingness to pay to guide valuation and management decisions, and we must develop better approaches.

26. Frischmann (2012).
27. Frischmann (2012): 366, n. 2.
28. For the sake of brevity, we decided not to include a discussion of a set of alternatives grouped loosely around the concepts of the commons, peer collaboration, trusted communities, and digital distributism. See, e.g., Strandburg, Madison, and Frischmann (2017); Rushkoff (2016); Chase (2015); Frischmann, Madison, and Strandburg (2014); Benkler (2006); Ostrom (2005); Ostrom (1990).
29. This section is adapted from Frischmann and Verstraete (2017) and based upon Frischmann (2017).
30. Some people reject this premise because they do not believe these companies are dominant. For example, some argue that the companies compete for attention, advertising, etc. Some people reject the premise because they believe competition and disruptive innovation will eventually topple any dominant player. We don't wish to engage in a debate about the premise. Our basic arguments hold even if you disagree with the first premise.
31. Our analysis applies to other platform intermediaries besides Facebook.
32. It is possible that the modern BBC does not quite live up to the ideals noted in the text, and the views of the public in the United Kingdom also may have shifted in recent years. Frischmann wrote a short paper commissioned by the BBC in October 2015. Frischmann (2017).
33. We use this example to illustrate a different mental model and not (yet) as a full-fledged policy proposal.
34. Compare Pasquale (2015): 208–210.
35. The allure of seamlessness across and within techno-social systems – of zero transaction costs, instantaneous information flow and consumer satiation, and efficient allocation and management of all resources – greases the slope. But seamlessness is dangerous, for the many reasons we've discussed. It can lead to incredible overdependence. The Irish Potato Famine is a famous agricultural example. We thank Guy Jarvis for pointing out this example.

36. Network neutrality is often criticized as overbearing government intervention into markets. This criticism rests on (deliberate/mistaken) oversimplifications. Network neutrality is better understood as an institutional means for sustaining an infrastructure commons that corrects for both market and government failures. Frischmann (2012): Chs. 4, 5 and 13. See also Van Schewick (2010).
37. Frischmann (2012): Ch. 13.
38. There is an extensive literature. Desai (2015); Grimmelmann (2014b); Pasquale (2010); Grimmelmann (2010); Odlyzko (2009).
39. Desai (2015): 561.
40. See, for example, the preceding discussion of the BBC-style social network. That discussion did not center on neutrality per se.
41. Kim Zetter, "Hacker Lexicon: What Is an Air Gap?," *Wired*, Dec. 8, 2014, at https://www.wired.com/2014/12/hacker-lexicon-air-gap/
42. The history of free and open source software, creative commons, and related movements demonstrates the potential of decentralized, commons-based peer production. Benkler (2006). We shouldn't take Wikipedia or Linux or the (hundreds of) thousands of successful open source software projects for granted. These incredibly successful ventures demonstrate the possibility of sidestepping to an alternative path. (We use the sidestepping metaphor because we're not confident that commons-based peer production is sufficient. It might be.)
43. Wright and De Filippi (2018); Narayanan et al. (2016).
44. "FreedomBox is a 100% free software self-hosting web server to deploy social applications on small machines." https://wiki.debian.org/FreedomBox
45. Barabas, Narula, and Zuckerman (2017).
46. Barabas, Narula, and Zuckerman (2017).
47. Excerpt of an email communication from James Vasile.
48. Brunton and Nissenbaum (2015). See also Richards and Hartzog (2017).
49. Brunton and Nissenbaum (2015).
50. Anonymizing data is no panacea for surveillance or techno-social engineering because data subjects can often be re-identified when the anonymized data set is combined with other sources of data. The costs of re-identification may be quite high and thus prohibitive in some cases, and so de-identification of data can be useful. For relevant research, we recommend reading some of the work by Arvind Narayanan and colleagues. It's available at randomwalker.info.
51. OK, we intentionally messed up the quote. "Messiness as a virtue" is the title of Ch. 9 in David Weinberger's classic, *Everything Is Miscellaneous: The Power of the New Digital Disorder* (2007). For Weinberger's critical analysis of perfection, see Ch. 4 of his earlier book, *Small Pieces Loosely Joined* (2002). On the perils of pursuing optimality and perfect price discrimination, see Frischmann (2012): Ch. 5.
52. Cohen (2012).
53. Cohen (1933): 575 ("According to the classical view, the law of contract gives expression to and protects the will of the parties, for the will is something

inherently worthy of respect."); Fried (2015); see generally Markovits (2015) (summarizing contract theories).

54. Fried (2015): 137 ("Contract as Promise sought to assert the coherence of standard contract doctrine as providing the structure by which actors could determine for themselves the terms of their interaction and cooperation – whether in commercial or personal relations."). Fried recognizes the commitment to autonomy in his formulation while focusing it on cooperation and relationships. Fried (2015): 136. He also emphasizes that the contract-as-promise theory also "depends on the deeper morality of trust and respect for persons." Fried (2015): 138. "We start with respect, which allows trust, which allows language, which finally allows the institution of promising [and contract]." Markovits (2004): 1417–1518.

55. There is one major caveat to this characterization. Welfare-based theories – beginning with the classic utilitarian Jeremy Bentham and progressing to the law and economics scholars of today – view contract law as a means for maximizing social welfare. This view typically relies on private ordering in markets, which, at least theoretically, depends upon individual autonomy and cooperation.

56. *Specht* v. *Netscape*, 306 F.3d 17 (2d Cir. 2002).

57. *Berkson* v. *GOGO*, 97 F.Supp.3d 359 (E.D.N.Y. 2015).

58. Wilkinson-Ryan (2016).

59. We distinguish initial deliberation because deliberation about whether to read serves as a necessary precursor to deliberation about the contractual terms.

60. Kim (2013). On the duty to read, see Calamari (1974): 341–342; Ayres and Schwartz (2014): 548–549.

61. Hillman (2006a): 837–840, 854–856 (arguing that mandatory website disclosure of standard terms might backfire "because it may not increase reading or shopping for terms or motivate businesses to draft reasonable ones, but instead, may make heretofore suspect terms more likely enforceable."). Like Hillman, we also worry that our proposals might backfire, and so we acknowledge the need for comparative analysis of potential solutions. See Hillman (2006a): 837–856.

62. For a historical review of important model codes such as the Uniform Commercial Code and the Uniform Computer Information Transactions Act, see O'Rourke (1999).

63. We suggest three. These might be inadequate, infeasible, and highly controversial. And there could be many other possibilities. Kim (2013): 174–210 (discussion of various reforms). Many people will critique our proposals on economic grounds, suggesting, for example, that commerce (or the economy, or even the Internet) will grind to a halt if courts intervened and disrupted [*insert one of the following buzzwords*: competition, the market, the innovation ecosystem, two-sided markets, many-sided markets]. First, nod, then laugh, and finally, ask for proof. If a more serious answer is required, remind them that the proposed reform is no more a government intervention than any other doctrine in contract or for that matter contract law itself.

64. We discuss Hurd's explanation of moral magic in Appendix E.
65. This relates to a more general problem with process-based approaches to governing surveillance and nudging practices. Voluntariness and lack of duress/coercion principles guard against manipulation, but it's important to recognize that manipulation captures a set of risks and harms but ignores others.
66. There are many criticisms. First, deliberation may lead to worse outcomes for consumers. Second, deliberation is costly. Third, designing for deliberation is costly. Etc. At this stage, our primary reply to such criticisms is to agree with them in general, and note that, nonetheless, the costs might be worth bearing.
67. Sprigman (2004): 485–568 (explaining how copyright formalities served as a useful speed bump).
68. European Commission Decision 2001/497/EC; European Commission Decision of 27 December 2001 on standard contractual clauses for the transfer of personal data to processors established in third countries, under Directive 95/46/EC.
69. Caulfield (2012).
70. Frischmann used the hoax as an example problem back in 2012. The challenge was for law students to make the best possible case for the Facebook user.
71. http://customercommons.org/
72. Searls (2016).
73. The fine can be up to 20,000,000 EUR or up to 4% of the annual worldwide turnover of the preceding financial year in case of an enterprise, whichever is greater. GDPR, Article 83, paras 5 and 6.
74. The GDPR demonstrates pluralism in action. In the US and the EU, most people share many of the same basic normative commitments, particularly concerning the fundamental blessings of humanity. Privacy is important on both sides of the Atlantic. But it is conceptualized, valued, implemented, and prioritized differently in the US and the EU. In the US, privacy is often conceptualized instrumentally and valued in terms of its contribution to welfare. There are exceptions, as in the context of health care. By contrast, in the EU, privacy is conceptualized as a fundamental human right. Privacy is the identity and integrity of individuals as human beings, and, thus, it is given higher priority than in the US.
75. GDPR, Article 7.

Appendix B Perspectives on the Turing Test

1. Searle (1980): 417–424.
2. Dennett (1980): 429–430.
3. Dennett (1991): 439.
4. Harnad (1991): 43–54.
5. Harnad (1991): 43–54.
6. Harnad (1991): 43–54.
7. Harnad (1991): 43–54. See also, Harnad (1990): 335–346; Erion (2001): 29–39.

8. Schweizer (1998): 263–272.
9. Schweizer (1998): 266.
10. Schweizer (1998): 268.

Appendix C Our Free Will Discussion

1. Dennett (2003).
2. Frankfurt (1969).
3. Camus (1955).

Appendix D Modern Meal Times

1. *Modern Times* (1936).
2. Leland (2013).
3. Leland (2013).
4. Leland (2013).
5. Sax (2016).
6. Sax (2016).
7. Sax (2016).
8. Borgmann (2000): 421.

Appendix E Rethinking Contract Theory

1. Before considering whether our chapter raises deep soul-searching questions for contract law theory, we should address one easy way out of such consideration. It is to marginalize the electronic contracts we've discussed, to cast them as outliers or exceptions. This has sometimes been the response to critical analysis of boilerplate. To do so would be a major mistake and ultimately a concession that would only return us, after a quick roundabout, to where we are and need to be. To marginalize electronic contracts seems foolish given their ubiquity and persistence in our daily lives. Even if at some point in history electronic contracts were exceptional, they are now quite common.

   A second way out would be to argue that electronic contracting online is not really so different from written contracts offline. We presumed that offline, people might not always read but they generally deliberate over salient terms, such as price and quality. Our presumption is based in part on the different business models off- and online, and the prevalence of freemium models online. Our arguments are not contingent on this presumption. Suppose the problem we've identified exists offline as well, where written contracts offline also techno-socially engineer humans, in the sense that their design (e.g., verbosity, incomprehensible jargon, presentation, non-negotiable terms) often leads people to behave automatically. Then, the problem is simply broader in scope than we've suggested.

2. Some contract scholars have compared media and identified similarities and differences in how people behave. Hillman and Rachlinski (2002): 429–495. Hillman and Rachlinski examine the similarities and differences between "virtual and paper contracting environments"; identify rational, cognitive, and social reasons why consumers may not read electronic contracts; and conclude that the existing contract law framework could accommodate many of the new challenges posed by the electronic contracting environment. However, they do not consider whether or how the designed human-computer interface of electronic contracting conditions consumers, nor do they develop a theoretical account that could justify techno-social engineering.

3. For further discussion, see Radin (2013): 55–109.

4. Cohen (1933): 575 ("According to the classical view, the law of contract gives expression to and protects the will of the parties, for the will is something inherently worthy of respect."); Fried (2015); Markovits (2015) (summarizing contract theories).

5. Fried (2015): 137 ("Contract as Promise sought to assert the coherence of standard contract doctrine as providing the structure by which actors could determine for themselves the terms of their interaction and cooperation – whether in commercial or personal relations."). Fried recognizes the commitment to autonomy in his formulation while focusing it on cooperation and relationships. Fried (2015): 136. He also emphasizes that the contract-as-promise theory also "depends on the deeper morality of trust and respect for persons." Fried (2015): 138. "We start with respect, which allows trust, which allows language, which finally allows the institution of promising [and contract]." Markovits (2004): 1417–1518.

6. There is one major caveat to this characterization. Welfare-based theories – beginning with the classic utilitarian, Jeremy Bentham and progressing to the law and economics scholars of today – view contract law as a means for maximizing social welfare. This view typically relies on private ordering in markets, which, at least theoretically, depends upon individual autonomy and cooperation.

7. Consent- and promise-based theories differ in many important respects. Barnett (2017).

8. The divergences are beyond the scope of this discussion.

9. Barnett (2017): 5–6 ("[I]t has long been recognized that a system of contractual enforcement would be unworkable if it required a subjective inquiry into the putative promisor's intent. Where we cannot discern the actual subjective intent or will of the parties, there is no practical problem since we may assume it corresponds to objectively manifested intentions … Not surprisingly, despite the oft-expressed traditional sentiment that contracts require a 'meeting of the minds,' the objective approach has largely prevailed. A rigorous commitment to a will theory conflicts unavoidably with the

practical need for a system of rules based to a large extent on objectively manifested states of mind.").

10. Barnett (2017): 9–10; see generally Barnett (1986): 269–321.
11. Barnett (2017)
12. Barnett (2017): 13.
13. Barnett (2017): 14.
14. As Nancy Kim observes: "Consent is supposed to reveal intent; instead, courts have imputed meaning to acts to create consent, divorcing the act from the state of mind that should be attributable to it." Kim (2013): 139.
15. See Kennedy (1982): 569–570.
16. Fried (2015): 45.
17. There is a recursive relationship because contract depends upon trust and cooperation as well. Fried (2015): 138.
18. Fried (2015): 43.
19. Waldman (2016) (examining a series of ways in which Facebook designs its platform to take advantage of heuristics and thereby create (the illusion of) trust and encourage data-sharing).
20. Hurd (2017).
21. Radin (2013): 22–32.
22. For example, Kim argues that wrap contracts contribute to market failures associated with consumers making uninformed decisions, "acting in ignorance" of actual costs and benefits in various online transactions, and behavioral lock-in, and also that "[w]rap contracts were instrumental in creating norms that led to [a] market failure in online privacy." Kim (2013): 76–79. See generally Hillman and Rachlinski (2002): 429–495 (examining and comparing market failures in paper and electronic contracting).
23. There is a growing literature documenting the adverse effects of choice proliferation or "too much choice." See Korff and Böhme (2014).
24. Cf. Kennedy (1982): 569 (suggesting that freedom of contract as an institution exists only to the extent and so long as "the decision maker maintains his balance between the two extremes of non-intervention and over-intervention in the affairs of civil society").
25. Sprigman (2004): 485–568.
26. Radin (2013); Kim (2013).
27. There is a rich literature on comparative institutional analysis. See, e.g., Komesar (1994). See also Kennedy (1982): 569–570.
28. It is well understood that perfectly competitive markets fail to maximize social welfare in various ways. See Frischmann (2012).

Bibliography

Aarts, Henk and Dijksterhuis, Ap (2000). Habits as Knowledge Structures: Automaticity in Goal-Directed Behavior. *Journal of Personality and Social Psychology, 78*(1), 53–63.

Aarts, Henk, Verplanken, Bas, and van Knippenberg, Ad (1997). Habit and Information Use in Travel Mode Choices. *Acta Psycholgica, 96*(1), 1–14.

Abramian-Mott, Alexandria. (2007, November 22). Cleaning for the Cleaning Lady. *Los Angeles Times.* Retrieved from http://articles.latimes.com/2007/nov/22/home/hm-clean22

Acquisti, Alessandro, Brandimarte, Laura, and Loewenstein, George (2015). Privacy and Human Behavior in the Age of Information, *Science, 347*(6221).

Acquisti, Alessandro and Grossklags, Jens (2004). Losses, Gains, and Hyperbolic Discounting: An Experimental Approach to Personal Information Security Attitudes and Behavior. In J. Camp and R. Lewis (eds.), *The Economics of Information Security,* New York, NY: Kluwer.

Ajunwa, Ifeoma, Crawford, Kate, and Schultz, Jason (2017). Limitless Worker Surveillance. *California Law Review, 105,* 101–142.

Alexander, Gregory S. (2009). The Social-Obligation Norm in American Property Law, *Cornell Law Review, 94,* 745.

Alexander, Gregory S. (2013). Ownership and Obligations: The Human Flourishing Theory of Property, *Hong Kong Law Journal, 43*(2).

Allais, M. (1953). Le comportement de l'homme rationnel devant le risque: Critique des postulats et axioms de l'e'cole americaine. *Econometrica, 21*(4), 503–546.

Allenby, Braden R. and Sarewitz, Daniel (2011). *The Techno-Human Condition.* Cambridge, MA: Massachusetts Institute of Technology Press.

Alkire, Sabina (2002). *Valuing Freedoms: Sen's Capability Approach and Poverty Reduction.* New York, NY: Oxford University Press.

Alter, Adam (2017). *Irresistible: The Rise of Addictive Technology and the Business of Keeping Us Hooked.* New York, NY: Penguin Press.

Ambrose, Meg L. (2014). From the Avalanche of Numbers to Big Data: A Comparative Historical Perspective on Data Protection in Transition. In M.-H. Kieron O'Hara, Carolyn Nguyen, and Peter Haynes (eds.), *Digital Enlightenment Foundation Yearbook* (pp. 49–74). Amsterdam: IOS Press.

Amir, On and Lobel, Orly (2008). Stumble, Predict, Nudge: How Behavioral Economics Informs Law and Policy. *Columbia Law Review, 108*(8), 2098–2137.

Anderson, Janna and Rainee, Lee (2014, May 14). The Gurus Speak. *Pew Research Center*. Retrieved from http://www.pewinternet.org/2014/05/14/the-gurus-spe ak-2/

Anderson, Ronald A. (1963). *Anderson on the Uniform Commercial Code*. Rochester, NY: Lawyers Co-operative Publishing Co.

Anderson, Simon and Coate, Stephen (2005). Market Provision of Broadcasting: A Welfare Analysis. *The Review of Economic Studies, 72*(4), 947–972.

Angwin, Julia and Singer-Vine, Jeremy. (2012, April 7). Selling You on Facebook. *The Wall Street Journal*. Retrieved from http://www.wsj.com/articles/ SB10001424052702303302504577327744009046230

Apodaca, Patrice (2015, June 6). Apodaca: Drone Parents Swoop Onto the Scene. *Los Angeles Times*. Retrieved from http://www.latimes.com/tn-dpt-me-0607-patrice-apodaca-column-20150606-story.html

Apple. *Our Smartest Keyboard Ever*. Retrieved from https://www.apple.com/my/ ios/whats-new/quicktype/

Ariely, Dan (2008). *Predictably Irrational: The Hidden Forces that Shape Our Decisions*. New York, NY: Harper.

Aristotle's *Nicomachean Ethics* (2011). (Robert C. Bartlett and Susan D. Collins, trans.). (Chicago, IL: University of Chicago Press.

Au, Wayne (2011). Teaching under the New Taylorism: High-Stakes Testing and the Standardization of the 21st Century Curriculum, *Journal of Curriculum Studies, 43*(1), 25–45.

Ayres, Ian and Schwartz, Alan (2014). The No-Reading Problem in Consumer Contract Law. *Stanford Law Review, 66*(3), 545–610.

Baird, Douglas G. (2005). The Boilerplate Puzzle. *Michigan Law Review, 104*(5), 933–952.

Bakos, Yannis, Marotta-Wurgler, Florencia, and Trossen, David R. (2014). Does Anyone Read the Fine Print? Consumer Attention to Standard Form Contracts. *Journal of Legal Studies, 43*(1), 1–35.

Barabas, Chelsea, Narula, Neha, and Zuckerman, Ethan (2017). Defending Internet Freedom Through Decentralization: Back to the Future? The Center for Civic Media & The Digital Currency Initiative MIT Media Lab. http://dci .mit.edu/assets/papers/decentralized_web.pdf

Bar-Gill, Oren (2013). *Seduction by Contract: Law, Economics and Psychology in Consumer Markets*. New York, NY: Oxford University Press.

Barnes, William, Gartland, Myles, and Stack, Martin (2004). Old Habits Die Hard: Path Dependency and Behavioral Lock-In. *Journal of Economic Issues, 38*(2), 371–377.

Barnett, Randy E. (1986) A Consent Theory of Contract. *Columbia Law Review, 86*(2), 269–321.

Barnett, Randy E. (2002). Consenting to Form Contracts. *Fordham Law Review, 71*(3), 627–645.

Barnett, Randy E. (2017). Contract is Not Promise; Contract is Consent. *Suffolk University Law Review*. [In Press]. Retrievable from: http://ssrn.com/abstract=1792586

Bartholomew, Mark (2017). *Adcreep: The Case Against Modern Marketing*. Stanford, CA: Stanford University Press.

Baumeister, Roy F. (2003). The Psychology of Irrationality. In Isabelle Brocas and Juan D. Carrillo (eds.), *The Psychology of Economic Decisions: Rationality and Well-being* (pp. 3–16). New York, NY: Oxford University Press.

Baumeister, Roy F. and Tierney, John (2011). *Willpower: Recovering the Greatest Human Strength*. New York, NY: Penguin Books.

Baym, Nancy (2010). *Personal Connections in the Digital Age*. Malden: Polity Press.

Benkler, Yochai (2006). *The Wealth of Networks: How Social Production Transforms Markets and Freedom*. New Haven, CT: Yale University Press.

Bennett, Collin J. (2015). Trends in Voter Surveillance in Western Societies: Privacy Intrusions and Democratic Implications. *Surveillance and Society*, *13* (3–4), 370–384.

Ben-Shahar, Omri and Schneider, Carl E. (2011). The Failure of Mandatory Disclosure. *University of Pennsylvania Law Review*, *159*(3), 647–749.

Ben-Shahar, Omri and Schneider, Carl E. (2014). *More Than You Wanted to Know: The Failure of Mandated Disclosure*. Princeton, NJ: Princeton University Press.

Berkson v. *GOGO*, 97 F.Supp.3d 359 (E.D.N.Y. 2015).

Berlin, Isaiah (1969). Two Concepts of Liberty, in I. Berlin, *Four Essays on Liberty*. London: Oxford University Press. New ed. in Berlin 2002.

Berlin, Isaiah (1978). From Hope and Fear Set Free, in I. Berlin, *Concepts and Categories. Philosophical Essays*, ed. H. Hardy. London: Hogarth Press; Oxford: Oxford University Press, 1980. Reprinted in Berlin 2002.

Bernays, Edward (1947). The Engineering of Consent. *The Annals of the American Academy of Political and Social Science*, *250*(1), 113–120.

Biever, Celeste (2014, March 23). My Roomba's Name is Roswell. *Slate*. Retrieved from http://www.slate.com/articles/health_and_science/new_scientist/2014/03/roomba_vacuum_cleaners_have_names_irobot_ceo_on_people_s_ties_to_ro bots.html

Bix, Brian H. (2012). *Contract Law: Rules, Theory, and Context*. New York, NY: Cambridge University Press.

Boden, Margaret (2006). *Mind as Machine: A History of Cognitive Science* (Vols. 1 and 2). New York, NY: Oxford University Press.

Böhme, Rainer and Köpsell, Stefan (2010). Trained to Accept?: A Field Experiment on Consent Dialogs. *Proceedings from the SIGCHI Conference on Human Factors in Computing Systems, 2010*. New York, NY: ACM. Retrieved from https://www.wi1.uni-muenster.de/security/publications/BK2010_Traine d_To_Accept_CHI.pdf

Borgmann, Albert (2000). The Moral Complexion of Consumption. *The Journal of Consumer Research*, *26*(4), 418–422.

Bostrom, Nick (2003). Transhumanist Values. In Frederick Adams (ed.), *Ethical Issues for the 21st Century* (pp. 3–14). Charlottesville, VA: Philosophical Documentation Center Press.

Bostrom, Nick (2005). A History of Transhumanist Thought. *Journal of Evolution and Technology 14*(1).

Boswell, James (1986). *Life of Samuel Johnson.* Christopher Hibbert, (ed.). New York, NY: Penguin. (Originally published 1791.)

boyd, danah (2014). *It's Complicated: The Social Lives of Networked Teens.* New Haven, CT: Yale University Press.

boyd, danah and Hargittai, Eszter (2010). Facebook Privacy Settings: Who Cares? *First Monday.* Retrieved from http://firstmonday.org/ojs/index.php/fm/article/view/3086/2589

Boyle, Josh (2015, May 4). A Crystal Ball for Email and Communication. *Venture Fizz.* Retrieved from https://venturefizz.com/blog/crystal-ball-email-and-communication

Braitman, Laurel (2014). *Animal Madness: How Anxious Dogs, Compulsive Parrots, and Elephants in Recovery Help Us Understand Ourselves.* New York, NY: Simon & Schuster.

Bramble, Ben (2016). The Experience Machine. *Philosophy Compass, 11*(3), 136–145.

Breen, John M. (2008). John Paul II, The Structures of Sin and The Limits of Law. *Saint Louis University Law Journal, 52*, 317–374.

Bronsteen, John, Buccafusco, Christopher, and Masur, Jonathon S. (2014). *Happiness and the Law.* Chicago, IL: Chicago University Press..

Brooks, David (2007, October 26). The Outsourced Brain. *The New York Times.* Retrieved from http://www.nytimes.com/2007/10/26/opinion/26brooks.html

Brugger, Peter (1997). Variables that Influence the Generation of Random Sequences: An Update. *Perceptual and Motor Skills, 84*(2), 627–661.

Brumfiel, Geoff (2016, February 22). U.S. Navy Brings Back Navigation By The Stars for Officers. *National Public Radio.* Retrieved from http://www.npr.org/2016/02/22/467210492/u-s-navy-brings-back-navigation-by-the-stars-for-officers

Brunton, Finn and Nissenbaum, Helen (2015). *Obfuscation: A User's Guide for Privacy and Protest.* Cambridge, MA: Massachusetts Institute of Technology Press.

Brynjolfsson, Erik and McAfee, Andrew (2014). *The Second Machine Age: Work, Progress, and Prosperity in a Time of Brilliant Technologies.* New York, NY: W. W. Norton & Co.

Buccafusco, Christopher and Fromer, Jeanne C. (2017). Fashion's Function in Intellectual Property Law. *Notre Dame Law Review, 93*, 1–52.

Budiu, Raluca (2013, August 31). Interaction Cost – Definition. *Nielsen Norman Group.* Retrieved from https://www.nngroup.com/articles/interaction-cost-definition/

Bulajewski, Mike (2014, October 22). The Man Who Loved His Laptop. *Boundary 2 Online*. Retrieved from http://boundary2.org/2014/10/22/the-man-who-loved-his-laptop/

Buss, Sarah (2016). Personal Autonomy. In *Stanford Encyclopedia of Philosophy* online. Retrieved from http://plato.stanford.edu/entries/personal-autonomy/

Calabresi, Guido (1982). *Common Law for the Age of Statutes*. Cambridge, MA: Harvard University Press.

Calamari, John D. (1974). Duty to Read – A Changing Concept. *Fordham Law Review, 43*(3), 341–362.

Calo, Ryan (2014). Digital Market Manipulation. *George Washington Law Review, 82*(4), 995–1051.

Calo, Ryan and Rosenblat, Alex (2017). The Taking Economy: Uber, Information, and Power. *Columbia Law Review, 117*.

Calvin, Aaron P. (2017, March 30). Can Amazon's Alexa Be Your Friend? *Digg*. Retrieved from http://digg.com/2017/amazon-alexa-is-not-your-friend

Camus, Albert (1955). *The Myth of Sisyphus and Other Essays* (Justin O'Brien, trans.). New York, NY: Vintage-Random House. (Originally published 1942.)

Card, S. K., Robertson, G. G., and Mackinlay, J. D. (1991). The Information Visualizer: An Information Workspace. *Proceedings from the SIGCHI Conference on Human Factors in Computing Systems, 1991*. New York, NY: ACM. Retrieved from http://www2.parc.com/istl/groups/uir/publications/items/UIR-1991-01-Card-CHI91-IV.pdf

Carman, Ashley (2017, May 2). Amazon's Alexa Can Now Whisper, Bleep Out Swear Words, and Change Its Pitch. *The Verge*. Retrieved from https://www.theverge.com/circuitbreaker/2017/4/28/15475070/amazon-alexa-speech-synthesis-markup-language

Carpenter, Edmund and McLuhan, Marshall (1956). The New Languages. *Chicago Law Review, 10*(1), 46–52.

Carr, Nicholas (2015). *The Glass Cage: How Our Computers Are Changing Us*. New York, NY: W. W. Norton & Co.

Carter, Ian (2016). Positive and Negative Liberty. In *The Stanford Encyclopedia of Philosophy* (Fall 2016 Edition), Edward N. Zalta (ed.), URL = https://plato.stanford.edu/archives/fall2016/entries/liberty-positive-negative/

Caruso, Gregg (2016). Free Will Skepticism and Criminal Behavior: A Public Health-Quarantine Model. *Southwest Philosophy Review, 32*(1), 25–48.

Caulfield, Philip (2012) Facebook Message Claiming Users Have "Copyright" to Photos, Timeline Posts Is a Hoax. *New York Daily News* (Nov. 26). http://www.nydailynews.com/news/world/copyright-facebook-message-hoax-article-1.1208028

CBS News (2017, June 8). Fitbit users find creative ways to cheat the system [Television broadcast]. New York, NY: Columbia Broadcasting Service. Retrieved from http://www.cbsnews.com/news/fitbit-users-find-creative-hacks-to-cheat-the-system/

Chalmers, David (2014, March). How Do You Explain Consciousness?. *TED Talk 2014*. Retrieved from https://www.ted.com/talks/david_chalmers_how_do_you_explain_consciousness

Chase, Robin (2015). *Peers Inc: How People and Platforms Are Inventing the Collaborative Economy and Reinventing Capitalism*. London: Headline.

Cheney, Dorothy L. and Seyfarth, Robert M. (1992). *How Monkeys See the World*. Chicago, IL: University of Chicago Press.

Christian, Brian (2011). *The Most Human Human: What Talking with Computers Teaches Us About What It Means to Be Alive*. New York, NY: Doubleday.

Christman, John (2015). Autonomy in Moral and Political Philosophy. In *Stanford Encyclopedia of Philosophy* online. Retrieved from http://plato.stanford.edu/entries/autonomy-moral/

Church, Alonzo (1936). An Unsolvable Problem of Elementary Number Theory. *American Journal of Mathematics*, *58*(2): 345–363. JSTOR 2371045. doi:10.2307/2371045.

Church, Alonzo (1937). Review: A. M. Turing, On Computable Numbers, with an Application to the Entscheidungsproblem. *Journal of Symbolic Logic*, *2*(1): 42–43. doi:10.2307/2268810.

Churchland, Paul M. (2013). *Matter and Consciousness*. Cambridge, MA: Massachusetts Institute of Technology Press.

Citron, Danielle Keats (2014). *Hate Crimes in Cyberspace*. Cambridge, MA: Harvard University Press.

Clark, Andy (2004). *Natural-Born Cyborgs: Minds, Technologies, and the Future of Human Intelligence*. New York, NY: Oxford University Press.

Clark, Andy (2007). Re-Inventing Ourselves: The Plasticity of Embodiment, Sensing, and Mind. *Journal of Medicine and Philosophy*, *32*(3), 263–282.

Clark, Andy (2010). *Supersizing the Mind: Embodiment, Action, and Cognitive Extension*. New York, NY: Oxford University Press.

Clark, Andy (2011). Finding the Mind. *Philosophical Studies*, *152*(3), 447–461.

Clark, Andy and Chalmers, David (1998). The Extended Mind. *Analysis*, *58*(1), 7–19.

CNS Charité Neuroscience (2014, June). *2014 International Graduate Program Medical Neurosciences Newsletter*, *7*(2).

Coeckelbergh, Mark (2016). Responsibility and the Moral Phenomenology of Using Self-Driving Cars. *Applied Artificial Intelligence*, *30*(8), 748–757.

Cohan, Peter (2017, March 31). Race to $1 Trillion: Apple Will Get There First But Buy Amazon. *Forbes*. Retrieved from https://www.forbes.com/sites/petercohan/2017/03/31/race-to-1-trillion-apple-will-get-there-first-but-buy-amazon/#679c484ce862

Cohen, Julie E. (1996). A Right to Read Anonymously: A Closer Look at "Copyright Management" in Cyberspace. *Connecticut Law Review*, *28*, 981–1039.

Cohen, Julie E. (2000). Examined Lives: Informational Privacy and the Subject as Object. *Stanford Law Review*, *52*, 1373–1438.

Cohen, Julie E. (2012). *Configuring the Networked Self: Law, Code, and the Play of Everyday Practice*. New Haven, CT: Yale University Press.

Cohen, Morris R. (1933). The Basics of Contract. *Harvard Law Review*, 46(4), 553–592.

Collins, Harry (1990). *Artificial Experts: Social Knowledge and Intelligent Machines*. Cambridge, MA: Massachusetts Institute of Technology Press.

Collins, Harry, and Kusch, Martin (1999). *The Shape of Actions: What Humans and Machines Can Do*. Cambridge, MA: Massachusetts Institute of Technology Press.

Conti, Gregory, and Sobiesk, Edward (2010). *Malicious Interface Design: Exploiting the User. Proceedings of the 19th International Conference on the World Wide Web, 2010*. New York, NY: ACM. Retrieved from http://www.ru mint.org/gregconti/publications/201004_ malchi.pdf

Crisp, Roger (2006). Hedonism Reconsidered. *Philosophy and Phenomenological Research*, 73(3), 619–645.

Crosby, Alfred (2002). *Throwing Fire: Projectile Technology Through History*. New York, NY: Cambridge University Press.

Culkin, John (1967, March 18). A Schoolman's Guide to Marshall McLuhan. *The Saturday Review*. Retrieved from http://www.unz.org/Pub/SaturdayRev-1967 mar18-00051

Cusumano, Michael A. (1985). *The Japanese Automobile Industry: Technology and Management at Nissan and Toyota*. Cambridge, MA: Council on East Asian Studies/Harvard University Press.

Danaher, John (2016). Why Internal Moral Enhancement Might Be Politically Better than External Moral Enhancement. *Neuroethics*. Retrieved from https://link.springer.com/article/10.1007/s12152-016–9273–8

Darling, Kate (2016). Extending Legal Protection to Social Robots: The Effects of Anthropomorphism, Empathy, and Violent Behavior Towards Robotic Objects. *Proceedings of the We Robot Conference; 2012 April 1; Miami*. Miami, FL: Edward Elgar. Retrieved from https://papers.ssrn.com/sol3/papers.cfm?abstract_id=2044797

Darwin, Charles (1872). *The Expression of the Emotions in Man and Animals*. London: John Murray.

De Boer, Antina, van Buel, E. M., Ter Horst, G. J. (2012). Love is More Than Just a Kiss: A Neurobiological Perspective on Love and Affection. *Neuroscience, 201*, 114–124.

De Brigard, Felipe (2010). If You Like It, Does It Matter If It's Real? *Philosophical Psychology 23*(1), 43–57.

De Filippi, Primavera and Wright, Aaron (forthcoming 2018). *Blockchain and the Law: The Rule of Code*. Boston, MA: Harvard University Press.

De Schrijver, Georges (2015). *Imagining the Creator God: From Antiquity to Astrophysics*. Manila: Anteneo De Manila University Press.

Deganawide (1977). *The Great Law of Peace of the Longhouse People (Iroquois, League of Six Nations) Kaianerekowa, Hotinonsionne*. Rooseveltown, NY: Akwesasne Notes.

Demsetz, Harold (2008). Frischmann's View of "Toward a Theory of Property Rights." *Review of Law and Economics, 4*(1), 127–132.

Dennett, Daniel C. (1980). The Milk of Human Intentionality. *Behavioral and Brain Sciences 3*(3), 428–430.

Dennett, Daniel C. (1991). *Consciousness Explained*. Boston, MA: Little, Brown and Co.

Dennett, Daniel C. (2003). *Freedom Evolves*. New York, NY: Viking.

Department of Commerce (DOC) (2017, January 12). Green Paper: Fostering the Advancement of the Internet of Things. Retrieved from https://www.ntia.doc.gov/other-publication/2017/green-paper-fostering-advancement-internet-things

Desai, Deven R. (2015). Exploration and Exploitation: An Essay on (Machine) Learning, Algorithms, and Information Provision, 47 *Loyola University Chicago Law Journal* 541–581.

Descartes, René (1985). *Discourse on Method* (John Cottingham, Robert Stoothoff, and Dugold Murdoch, trans.). In *The Philosophical Writings of Descartes* (vol. 1) (pp. 109–151). New York, NY: Cambridge University Press. (Original work published 1637.)

Design Boom. (2013, March 3). *Dor Tal Forecasts the Future with Wearable Predictables App*. Retrieved from https://www.designboom.com/technology/dor_tal-forecasts-the-future-with-wearable-predictables-app-03-03-2013/

Donath, Judith (2014). *The Social Machine*. Cambridge, MA: Massachusetts Institute of Technology Press.

Dormehl, Luke (2014). *The Formula: How Algorithms Solve All Our Problems . . . and Create More*. New York, NY: Perigree.

Dreyfus, Hubert (1992). *What Computers Still Can't Do: A Critique of Artificial Reason*. Cambridge, MA: Massachusetts Institute of Technology Press.

Dreyfus, Hubert (1996). Being and Power: Heidegger and Foucault. *International Journal of Philosophical Studies, 4*(1), 1–16.

Dreyfus, Hubert and Kelly, Sean D. (2011). *All Things Shining: Reading the Western Classics to Find Meaning in a Secular Age*. New York, NY: Free Press.

Dvorsky, George (2015, August 21). This Social Network Turns Your Personality Into an Immortal Artificial Intelligence. *Gizmodo*. Retrieved from http://io9.com/this-social-network-turns-your-personality-into-an-immo-1725618358

Eagleman, David (2011). The Brain on Trial. *The Atlantic*. Retrieved from https://www.theatlantic.com/magazine/archive/2011/07/the-brain-on-trial/308520/

Egelman, Serge, Cranor, Lorrie F., and Hong, Jason (2008). You've Been Warned: An Empirical Study of the Effectiveness of Web Browser Phishing Warnings. *Proceedings from SIGCHI Conference on Human Factors in Computing Systems, 2008* (pp. 1065–1074). New York, NY: ACM.

Ellul, Jacques (1964). *The Technological Society*. New York, NY: Vintage.

Eordogh, Fruzsina (2017, April 5). Why Youtube's Unfixed Restricted Mode Algorithm Is Still The Bigger Story. *Forbes*. Retrieved from https://www.forbes.com/sites/fruzsinaeordogh/2017/04/05/why-youtubes-unfixed-restricted-mode-algorithm-is-the-bigger-story/#21e4163038b2

Erion, Gerald (2001). The Cartesian Test for Automatism. *Minds and Machines, 11* (1), 29–39.

Erisman, Albert and Gautschi, David (eds.) (2015). *The Purpose of Business: Contemporary Perspective from Different Walks of Life.* New York, NY: Palgrave Macmillan.

Ess, Charles (2017). What's Love Got to Do With It? Robots, Sexuality, and the Arts of Being Human. In Marco Nørskov (ed.), *Social Robots: Boundaries, Potentials, and Challenges* (pp. 57–82). New York, NY: Routledge.

Eugenios, Jillian (2015, June 3). Ray Kurzweil: Humans Will Be Hybrids by 2030. *CNN.* Retrieved from http://money.cnn.com/2015/06/03/technology/ray-kurzweil-predictions/

Eveleth, Rose (2014, December 15). How Self-Tracking Apps Exclude Women. *The Atlantic.* Retrieved from http://www.theatlantic.com/technology/archive/2014/12/how-self-tracking-apps-exclude-women/383673/

Facebook. *Community Standards.* Retrieved from https://www.facebook.com/communitystandards

Falk, Dan (2010). *In Search of Time: The History, Physics, and Philosophy of Time.* New York, NY: Thomas Dunne Books.

Fan, J. (2004). Perception of Body Appearance and Its Relation to Clothing. In J. Fan, W. Yu, and L. Hunter (eds.), *Clothing, Appearance, and Fit: Science and Technology* (pp. 1–14). New York, NY: Woodhead Publishing Ltd.

FCC v. *Pacifica Foundation*, 438 U.S. 726 (1978).

Federal Communications Commission (FCC) (2015, March 12). Open Internet Order. Retrieved from https://apps.fcc.gov/edocs_public/attachmatch/FCC-15-24A1.pdf.

Feenberg, Andrew (2006). Active and Passive Bodies: Don Ihde's Phenomenology of the Body. In Evan Selinger (ed.), *Postphenomenology: A Critical Companion to Ihde* (pp. 189–196). Albany, NY: State University of New York Press.

Fog, B. J. (2002). *Persuasive Technology: Using Computers to Change What We Think and Do.* San Francisco, CA: Morgan Kaufmann.

Foucault, Michel (1977). *Discipline and Punish: The Birth of the Prison.* New York, NY: Pantheon Books.

Foucault, Michel (1994). *The Order of Things: An Archaeology of the Human Sciences.* New York, NY: Vintage Books.

Ford, Martin (2015). *Rise of the Robots: Technology and the Threat of a Jobless Future.* New York, NY: Basic Books.

Frankfurt, Harry G. (1969). Alternate Possibilities and Moral Responsibility. *The Journal of Philosophy, 66*(23), 829–839.

Frankfurt, Harry G. (1971). Freedom of the Will and the Concept of the Person. *The Journal of Philosophy, 68*(1), 5–20.

Freidenfelds, Lara (2009). *The Modern Period: Menstruation in Twentieth-Century America.* Baltimore, MD: The Johns Hopkins University Press.

Fried, Charles (2015). *Contract as Promise.* New York, NY: Oxford University Press.

Frischmann, Brett M. (2005). Some Thoughts on Shortsightedness and Intergenerational Equity. *Loyola University Chicago Law Journal, 36*(2), 457–467.

Frischmann, Brett M. (2007a). Cultural Environmentalism and the Wealth of Networks. *University of Chicago Law Review, 74*, 1083–1911.

Frischmann, Brett M. (2007b). Evaluating the Demsetzian Trend in Copyright Law. *Review of Law and Economics, 3*(3), 649–677.

Frischmann, Brett M. (2009). Spillovers Theory and Its Conceptual Boundaries. *William & Mary Law Review, 51*(2), 801–824.

Frischmann, Brett (2012). *Infrastructure: The Social Value of Shared Resources.* New York, NY: Oxford University Press.

Frischmann, Brett M. (2017). Understanding the Role of the BBC as a Provider of Public Infrastructure (January 11). *Cardozo Legal Studies Research Paper No. 507.* Available at https://ssrn.com/abstract=2897777 or http://dx.doi.org/10.2139/ssrn.2897777.

Frischmann, Brett M. and McKenna, Mark P. (2011). Intergenerational Progress. *Wis. L. Rev.*, 123.

Frischmann, Brett M., Madison, Michael J., and Strandburg, Katherine J. (eds.) (2014). *Governing Knowledge Commons.* New York, NY: Oxford University Press.

Frischmann, Brett M. and Selinger, Evan (2016). Utopia?: A Technologically Determined World of Frictionless Transactions, Optimized Production, and Maximal Happiness. *UCLA Law Review, 64*, 372–391.

Frischmann, Brett M. and Verstraete, Mark (2017). We Need Our Platforms to Put People and Democratic Society Ahead of Cheap Profits. *RECODE*, June 16.

Fujimoto, Takahiro (1999). *The Evolution of a Manufacturing System at Toyota.* New York, NY: Oxford University Press.

Gaiman, Neil (2001). *American Gods.* New York, NY: William Morrow and Co.

Gallagher, Shaun (2009). Where's the Action? Epiphenomenalism and the Problem of Free Will. In Susan Pockett, William P. Banks, and Shaun Gallagher (eds.), *Does Consciousness Cause Behavior?* Cambridge, MA: Massachusetts Institute of Technology Press.

Galperin, Eva and Ben-Hassine, Wafa (2015, December 18). Changes to Facebook's "Real Names" Policy Still Don't Fix the Problem. *Electronic Frontier Foundation.* Retrieved from https://www.eff.org/deeplinks/2015/12/changes-facebooks-real-names-policy-still-dont-fix-problem

Gandy, Oscar H., Jr. (2010). Engaging Rational Discrimination: Exploring Reasons for Placing Regulatory Constraints on Decision Support Systems. *Ethics and Information Technology, 12*(1), 29–42.

Gelfand, Michele; Raver, Jana L.; Nishii, Lisa; Leslie, Lisa M.; Lun, Janetta; Lim, Beng Chong; Duan, Lili; Almaliach, Assaf; Ang, Soon; Arnadottir, Jakobina; Aycan, Zeynep; Boehnke, Klaus; Boski, Pawel; Cabecinhas, Rosa; Chan, Darius; Chhokar, Jagdeep; D'Amato, Alessia; Ferrer, Montse; Fischlmayr, Iris C.; Fischer, Ronald; Fülöp, Marta; Georgas, James; Kashima, Emiko S.; Kashima, Yoshishima; Kim, Kilbum; Lempereur, Alain; Marquez, Patricia; Othman, Rozhan; Overlaet, Bert; Panagiotopoulou, Penny; Peltzer, Karl;

Perez-Florizno, Lorena R.; Ponomarenko, Larisa; Realo, Anu; Schei, Vidar; Schmitt, Manfred; Smith, Peter B.; Soomro, Nazar; Szabo, Erna; Taveesin, Nalinee; Toyama, Midori; Van de Vliert, Evert; Vohra, Naharika; Ward, Colleen; Yamaguchi, Susumu (2011). Differences Between Tight and Loose Cultures: A 33-Nation Study. *Science, 332*(6033), 1100–1104.

Giere, Ronald N. (2002). Models as Parts of Distributed Cognitive Systems. In Lorenzo Magnani and Nancy J. Nersessian (eds.), *Model-Based Reasoning: Science, Technology, Values* (pp. 227–241). New York, NY: Springer Science & Business Media.

Gödel, Kurt (1934). On Undecidable Propositions of Formal Mathematical Systems. Reprinted in Martin Davis (ed.) (1965). *The Undecidable: Basic Papers on Undecidable Propositions, Unsolvable Problems and Computable Functions*, New York, NY: Raven; Reprint, Dover, 2004.

Goel, Vindu (2014, August 13). Under the Microscope. *New York Times*, p. B–1.

Goffman, Erving (1959). *The Presentation of Self in Everyday Life*. New York, NY: Anchor Books.

Goldman, Jason (2012, October 17). Is Language Unique to Humans? BBC. Retrieved from http://www.bbc.com/future/story/20121016-is-language-unique-to-humans

Goodall, Jane (2000). *Reason for Hope: A Spiritual Journey*. New York, NY: Grand Central Publishing.

Goodall, Noah J. (2014). Machine Ethics and Automated Vehicles. In Gereon Meyer and Sven Beiker (eds.), *Road Vehicle Automation*. Springer International Publishing. https://doi.org/10.1007/978–3-319–05990-7_9

Google Patent 8589407 (2013). Retrieved from https://www.google.com/patents/US8589407

Gordon, Lawrence, Gordon, Charles, and Robinson, Phil (1989). *Field of Dreams* [Motion picture]. United States of America: Universal Pictures.

Graham-Rowe, Duncan. (2008, May 15). Fifty Years of DARPA: Hits, Misses and Ones to Watch. *New Scientist*. Retrieved from https://www.newscientist.com/article/dn13907-fifty-years-of-darpa-hits-misses-and-ones-to-watch/

Grau, Christopher (ed.) (2005). *Philosophers Explore* The Matrix. New York, NY: Oxford University Press.

Gray, Stacey (2016, April). Always On: Privacy Implications of Microphone-Enabled Devices. *Future of Privacy Forum Report*. Retrieved from https://fpf.org/wp-content/uploads/2016/04/FPF_Always_On_WP.pdf

Grim, Patrick (2007). Free Will in Context: A Contemporary Philosophical Perspective. *Behavioral Sciences and the Law, 25*(2), 183–201.

Grimmelmann, James (2010). Some Skepticism About Search Neutrality. In Berin Szoka and Adam Marcus (eds.), *The Next Digital Decade: Essays on the Future of the Internet* (p. 435). Washington, DC: TechFreedom.

Grimmelmann, James (2014a). The Facebook Emotional Manipulation Study: Sources. *The Laboratorium*. Retrieved from http://laboratorium.net/archive/2014/06/30/the_facebook_emotional_manipulation_study_source

Grimmelmann, James (2014b). Speech Engines, 98 *MINN. L. REV.* 868.

Habermas, Jürgen (1985). *The Theory of Communicative Action* (Vol. 2) (Thomas McCarthy, trans.). Boston, MA: Beacon Press. (Original work published in 1981.)

Hachman, Mark (2015, September 23). The Price of Free: How Apple, Facebook, Microsoft and Google Sell You to Advertisers. *PC World*. Retrieved from http://www.pcworld.com/article/2986988/privacy/the-price-of-free-how-apple-facebook-microsoft-and-google-sell-you-to-advertisers.html

Haile, Tony (2014, March 9). What You Think You Know About the Web Is Wrong. *Time*. Retrieved from http://time.com/12933/what-you-think-you-know-about-the-web-is-wrong/

Hájek, Alan (2012). *Pascal's Wager*. Retrieved from http://plato.stanford.edu/archives/win2012/entries/pascal-wager/

Hansell, Michael Henry (2005). *Animal Architecture*. New York, NY: Oxford University Press.

Hansen, Pelle and Jespersen, Andreas (2013). Nudge and the Manipulation of Choice: A Framework for the Responsible Use of the Nudge Approach to Behaviour Change in Public Policy. *European Journal of Risk Regulation, 1*, 3–28.

Harari, Yuval Noah (2014). *Sapiens: A Brief History of Humankind*. New York, NY: Vintage.

Haraway, Donna (1991). A Cyborg Manifesto: Science, Technology, and Socialist-Feminism in the Late Twentieth Century. In *Simians, Cyborgs and Women: The Reinvention of Nature* (pp. 149–181). New York, NY: Routledge.

Haraway, Donna (2000). A Cyborg Manifesto: Science, Technology, and Socialist-Feminism in the Late Twentieth Century. In David Bell and Barbara M. Kennedy (eds.), *The Cybercultures Reader* (pp. 291–324). New York, NY: Routledge.

Harcourt, Bernard E. (2015). *Exposed: Desire and Disobedience in the Digital Age*. Cambridge, MA: Harvard.

Harnad, Stephen (1990). The Symbol Grounding Problem. *Physica D: Nonlinear Phenomena, 42*(1), 335–346.

Harnad, Stephen (1991). Other Bodies, Other Minds: A machine Incarnation of an Old Philosophical Problem. *Minds and Machines, 1*(1), 43–54.

Hart, H. L. A. (1959). The Ascription of Responsibility and Rights. In Anthony Flew (ed.), *Essays on Logic and Language (First Series)* (pp. 145–166). Oxford: Basil Blackwell.

Hartzog, Woodrow (2009). Promises and Privacy: Promissory Estoppel and Confidential Disclosures in Online Communities. *Temple Law Review, 82*: 891–928.

Hartzog, Woodrow (2011). Website Design as Contract. *American University Law Review, 60*(6), 1635–1671.

Hauser, Larry. Chinese Room Argument. *Internet Encyclopedia of Philosophy*. Retrieved from http://www.iep.utm.edu/chineser/

Hawking, Stephen and Mlodinow, Leonard (2010). *The Grand Design*. New York, NY: Bantam Books.

Haybron, Daniel M. (2016). Mental State Approaches to Well-Being. In Matthew D. Adler and Marc Fleurbaey (eds.), *The Oxford Handbook of Well-Being and Public Policy* (pp. 347–378). New York, NY: Oxford University Press.

Hayes, Patrick and Ford, Kenneth (1995). Turing Test Considered Harmful. *Proceedings of the Fourteenth International Joint Conference on Artificial Intelligence, 1995.* Montreal: Morgan Kaufmann Publishers, Inc. Retrieved from https://www.ijcai.org/Proceedings/95-1/Papers/125.pdf

Head, Simon (2005). *The New Ruthless Economy: Work and Power in the Digital Age.* New York, NY: Oxford University Press.

Heersmink, Richard (2017). Extended Mind and Cognitive Enhancement: Moral Aspects of Cognitive Artifacts. *Phenomenology and the Cognitive Sciences, 16*(1), 17–32.

Heidegger, Martin (1977). *The Question Concerning Technology and Other Essays.* New York, NY: Garland Publishing.

Herman, Edward S. & Noam Chomsky (1988). *Manufacturing Consent: The Political Economy of the Mass Media.* New York, NY: Pantheon.

Hesse, Monica (2010, April 22). "Code Red": iPhone/iPad App for Men Who Need to Track Women's Menstrual Cycles. *Washington Post.* Retrieved from http://www.washingtonpost.com/wp-dyn/content/article/2010/04/21/AR2010 042104578.html

Hevelke, Alexander and Nida-Rumelin, Julian (2015). Responsibility for Crashes of Autonomous Vehicles: An Ethical Analysis. *Science and Engineering Ethics, 21*(3), 619–630. doi:10.1007/s11948-014-9565-5.

Hill v. *Gateway 2000, Inc.*, 105 F.3d 1147 (7th Cir. 1997)

Hillman, Robert A. (2006a). Online Boilerplate: Would Mandatory Website Disclosure of E-Standard Terms Backfire? *Michigan Law Review, 104*(5), 837–856.

Hillman, Robert A. (2006b). Online Consumer Standard Form Contracting Practices: A Survey and Discussion of Legal Implications. In Jane K. Winn (ed.), *Consumer Protection in the Age of the Information Economy* (pp. 283–312). Burlington, VT: Ashgate Publishing Co.

Hillman, Robert A. (2007). Online Boilerplate: Would Mandatory Web Site Disclosure of E-Standard Terms Backfire? In Omri Ben-Shahar (ed.), *Boilerplate: The Foundation of Market Contracts* (pp. 83–94). New York, NY: Cambridge University Press.

Hillman, Robert A. and Rachlinski, Jeffrey J. (2002). Standard-Form Contracting in the Electronic Age. *New York University Law Review, 77*(2), 429–495.

Hodgson, Geoffrey M. (2002). Reconstitutive Downward Causation: Social Structure and the Development of Individual Agency. In Edward Fullbrook (ed.), *Intersubjectivity in Economics: Agents and Structures* (pp. 159–180). New York, NY: Routledge.

Hoffman, David (2017a). From Promise to Form: How Contracting Online Changes Consumers. *New York University Law Review, 91*, 1595–1650.

Hoffman, David (2017b). Relational Contracts of Adhesion. *University of Chicago Law Review*, forthcoming. Available at SSRN: https://ssrn.com/abstract= 3008687

Hoffman, Reid (2016, June 14). Using Artificial Intelligence to Humanize Management and Set Information Free. *MIT Sloan Management Review, 58* (Fall). Retrieved from http://sloanreview.mit.edu/article/using-artificial-intelli gence-to-humanize-management-and-set-information-free/

Hoofnagle, Chris J. and Whittington, Jan (2014). Free: Accounting for the Costs of the Internet's Most Popular Price. *UCLA Law Review, 61,* 606–670.

Horn, Marilyn J. and Gurel, Lois M. (1981). *The Second Skin: An Interdisciplinary Study of Clothing.* New York, NY: Houghton Mifflin.

Horwitz, Morton J. (1987). History and Theory. *Yale Law Journal, 96*(8), 1825–1835.

Howell, Robert J. (2014). Google Morals, Virtue, and the Asymmetry of Deference. *Nous, 48*(3), 389–415.

Hull, G., and Pasquale, F. (2017). Toward a Critical Theory of Corporate Wellness. BioSocieties. https://doi.org/10.1057/s41292-017-0064-1

Hurd, Heidi M. (2015). Fudging Nudging: Why "Libertarian Paternalism" Is the Contradiction It Claims It's Not. *Georgetown Journal of Law and Public Policy.* Retrieved from http://ssrn.com/abstract=2688636.

Hurd, Heidi M. (2017). The Normative Force of Consent. In P. Schaber (ed.), *The Routledge Handbook on The Ethics of Consent.* New York, NY: Routledge Press. Retrieved from https://papers.ssrn.com/sol3/papers.cfm?abstract_id=2643657

Hyman, David A. and Franklyn, David J. (2015). Search Bias and the Limits of Antitrust: An Empirical Perspective on Remedies. *Jurimetrics Journal, 55*(3), 339–380.

IBM. *What is Big Data?* Retrieved from https://www-01.ibm.com/software/data/ bigdata/what-is-big-data.html

Ihde, Don (1998). *Philosophy of Technology: An Introduction.* New York, NY: Paragon House Publishers.

Ihde, Don (2008). The Designer Fallacy and the Technological Imagination. In Peter Kroes, Pieter E. Vermaas, Andrew Light, and Steven A. Moore (eds.), *Philosophy and Design: From Engineering to Architecture* (pp. 51–59). Dordrecht: Springer Science & Business Media.

Ihde, Don (2016). *Acoustic Technics.* New York, NY: Lexington Books.

Isenberg, David S. (1997). The Rise of the Stupid Network. *Computer Telephony,* (August 1997), pp. 16–26.

Jabr, Ferris (2013, April 11). The Reading Brain in the Digital Age: The Science of Paper Versus Screens. *Scientific American.* Retrieved from http://www.scientifi camerican.com/article.cfm?id=reading-paper-screens

Jackson, Frank (1982). Epiphenomenal Qualia. *Philosophical Quarterly 32*(127), 127–136.

Jackson, Frank (2007). The Knowledge Argument, Diaphonousness, Representationalism. In Torin Alter and Sven Walter (eds.), *Phenomenal Concepts and Phenomenal Knowledge: New Essays on Consciousness and Physicalism* (pp. 52–64). New York, NY: Oxford University Press.

Jaffa, Harry V. (1959). *Crisis of the House Divided: An Interpretation of the Issues in the Lincoln-Douglas Debates.* Chicago, IL: University of Chicago Press.

Jaggar, Alison M. (2002). Feminism and the Objects of Justice. In James P. Sterba (ed.), *Social and Political Philosophy: Contemporary Perspectives* (pp. 251–269). New York, NY: Routledge.

James, Susan (2000). Feminism in Philosophy of Mind: The Question of Personal Identity. In Miranda Fricker and Jennifer Hornsby (eds.), *The Cambridge Companion to Feminism in Philosophy* (pp. 29–48). New York, NY: Cambridge University Press.

James, William (1912). *The Will to Believe*. Retrieved from https://www.gutenberg.org/files/26659/26659-h/26659-h.htm

James, William (2010). *The Dilemma of Determinism*. Whitefish, MT: Kessinger Publishing, LLC.

Jeffrey, Richard C. (1974). Preference Among Preferences. *Journal of Philosophy, 71* (13), 377–391.

Jerez v. JD Closeouts, LLC, 36 Misc.3d 161 (2012).

Johnson, Robert and Cureton, Adam (2017). Kant's Moral Philosophy. *The Stanford Encyclopedia of Philosophy* (Fall 2017 Edition), Edward N. Zalta (ed.), URL = https://plato.stanford.edu/archives/fall2017/entries/kant-moral/.

Jolls, Christine (2009). Behavioral Law and Economics. *Yale Law & Economics Research Paper No. 342*. Retrieved from http://ssrn.com/abstract=959177

Jolls, Christine and Sunstein, Cass R. (2006). Debiasing Through Law. *Journal of Legal Studies, 35*(1), 199–241.

Kahneman, Daniel (2002). Maps of Bounded Rationality: A Perspective on Intuitive Judgment and Choice, Nobel Lecture. *Nobel Prize Award Ceremony, 2002*. Retrieved from http://nobelprize.org/nobel_ prizes/economics/laureates/2002/kahnemann-lecture.pdf

Kahneman, Daniel (2011). *Thinking, Fast and Slow*. New York, NY: Farrar, Straus and Giroux.

Kanigel, Robert (1997). *The One Best Way: Frederick Winslow Taylor and the Enigma of Efficiency*. New York, NY: Viking.

Kavenna, Joanna (2017, July 5). Who Do We Think We Are? *New Scientist*. Retrieved from https://www.newscientist.com/article/2139809-who-do-we-think-we-are/

Kellner, Douglas and Share, Jeff (2007). Critical Media Literacy Is Not an Option. *Learning Inquiry, 1*(1), 59–69.

Kennedy, Duncan (1982). Distributive and Paternalistic Motives in Contract and Tort Law: With Special Reference to Compulsory Terms and Unequal Bargaining Power. *Maryland Law Review, 41*, 563–658.

Kessler, Friedrich (1943). Contracts of Adhesion – Some Thoughts About Freedom of Contract. *Columbia Law Review, 43*(5), 629–642.

Kim, Nancy S. (2005). Evolving Business and Social Norms and Interpretation Rules: The Need for a Dynamic Approach to Contract Disputes. *Nebraska Law Review, 84*(2), 506–570.

Kim, Nancy S. (2013). *Wrap Contracts: Foundations and Ramifications*. New York, NY: Oxford University Press.

Kleinman, Sharon (2011). *The Media and Communication Dictionary: A Guide for Students, Educators, and Professionals.* New York, NY: Peter Lang Publishing, Inc.

Kolber, Adam J. (1994). Mental Statism and the Experience Machine. *Bard Journal of Social Sciences, 3,* 10–17.

Komesar, Neil K. (1994). *Imperfect Alternatives: Choosing Institutions in Law.* Chicago, IL: University of Chicago Press.

Korff, Stefan and Böhme, Rainer (2014). Too Much Choice: End-User Privacy Decisions in the Context of Choice Proliferation. *Proceedings from: 2014 Symposium on Usable Privacy and Security.* Menlo Park, CA: USENIX. Retrieved from https://www.usenix.org/system/files/soups14-paper-korff.pdf

Korobkin, Russel (2003). Bounded Rationality, Standard Form Contracts, and Unconscionability. *University of Chicago Law Reform, 70*(4), 1203–1295.

Kramer, Adam D. I., Guillory, Jamie E., and Hancock, Jeffrey T. (2014). Experimental Evidence of Massive-Scale Emotional Contagion Through Social Networks. *Proceedings of the National Academy of Sciences of the United States of America, 111*(24), 8788–8790.

Krug, Steve (2014). *Don't Make Me Think, Revisited: A Common Sense Approach to Web Usability.* Berkeley, CA: New Riders Press.

Kurzweil, Ray (2012). *How to Create a Mind: The Secret of Human Thought Revealed.* New York, NY: Penguin.

Laplace, Pierre Simon (1998). *Philosophical Essay on Probabilities.* (Andrew I. Dale, trans.). New York, NY: Springer-Verlag. (Original work published 1825.)

Laris, Michael and Halsey, Ashley (2016, October 18). Will Driverless Cars Really Save Millions of Lives? Lack of Data Makes it Hard to Know. *Washington Post.* Retrieved from https://www.washingtonpost.com/local/trafficandcommuting/will-driverless-cars-really-save-millions-of-lives-lack-of-data-makes-it-hard-to-know/2016/10/18/6a678520-8435-11e6-92c2-14b64f3d453 f_story.html?utm_term=.c3443f3e621b

Lartey, Jamiles (2017, April 25). Man Suspected in Wife's Murder after Her Fitbit Data Doesn't Match His Alibi. *The Guardian.* Retrieved from https://www.theguardian.com/technology/2017/apr/25/fitbit-data-murder-suspect-richard-dabate

Latour, Bruno (2008). Where Are the Missing Masses? The Sociology of a Few Mundane Artifacts. In Deborah J. Johnson and Jameson M. Wetmore (eds.), *Technology and Society: Building Our Sociotechnical Future* (pp. 151–180). Cambridge, MA: Massachusetts Institute of Technology Press.

Lawton, Graham. (2013, November 27). The Benefits of Realising You're Just a Brain. *New Scientist.* Retrieved from https://www.newscientist.com/article/mg22029450-200-the-benefits-of-realising-youre-just-a-brain/

Layard, Richard (2005). *Happiness: Lessons from a New Science.* New York, NY: Penguin Group.

Leask, Ian (2012). Beyond Subjection: Notes on the Later Foucault and Education. *Educational Philosophy and Theory, 44*(1), 57–73.

Lee, Clement (2017, March 9). Note Submitted to Brett Frischmann. *Being Human Seminar*. Princeton University.

Lee, Gwanhoo (2016). IoT Innovation and Deployment: A Blueprint for U.S. and Korean Leadership. *U.S.-Korea Business Council*. Retrieved from https://www.uschamber.com/sites/default/files/final_accelerating_iot_growth_and_deployment_uskbc.pdf

Leff, Arthur A. (1970). Contract as Thing. *American University Law Review*, *19*(2), 131–157.

Leland, Jacob (2013, January 2). Fast, Cheap, and Out of Control: Modernists Go Off-Menu. *The Paris Review*. Retrieved from https://www.theparisreview.org/blog/2013/01/02/fast-cheap-and-out-of-control-modernists-go-off-menu/

Lemley, Mark A. (2006). Terms of Use. *Minnesota Law Review*, *91*(2), 459–483.

Lessig, Lawrence (1999). *Code and Other Laws of Cyberspace*. New York, NY: Basic Books.

Levy, David (2007). *Love and Sex With Robots: The Evolution of Human-Robot Relations*. New York, NY: Harper Collins.

Levy, Karen (2015). Intimate Surveillance. *Idaho Law Review*, *51*(3), 679–693.

Libet, Benjamin (1985). Unconscious Cerebral Initiative and the Role of Conscious Will in Voluntary Action. *Behavioral Brain Science*, *8*(4), 529–566.

Lin, Patrick (2014). What If Your Autonomous Car Keeps Routing You Past Krispy Kreme? *The Atlantic*. http://www.theatlantic.com/technology/archive/2014/01/what-if-your-autonomous-car-keeps-routing-you-past-krispy-kreme/283221 (2014). Accessed September 15, 2017.

Lin, Patrick (2015). Why Ethics Matters For Autonomous Cars. In M. Maurer et al. (eds.), *Autonomes Fahren (Autonomous Driving)*. Springer.

Lincoln, Abraham (1838, January 27). The Perpetuation of Our Political Institutions, Address Before the Young Men's Lyceum of Springfield, Illinois (January 27, 1838). Retrieved from http://Federalistpatriot.us/histdocs/Lincoln lyceum.html

Lloyd, Seth (2012). A Turing Test for Free Will. *Philosophical Transactions: Mathematical, Physical and Engineering Sciences*, *370*(1971), 3597–3610.

Lobel, Orly (2013). *Talent Wants to Be Free*. New Haven, CT: Yale University Press.

Loebner. *Contest Rules*. Retrieved from http://www.loebner.net/Prizef/2010_Contest/Loebner_Prize_Rules_2010.html

Long v. *Provide Commerce, Inc.*, 245 Cal. App. 4th 855 (2016).

Loranger, Hoa and Nielsen, Jakob (2006). *Prioritizing Web Usability*. Berkeley, CA: New Riders Press.

Macaulay, Stewart (2004). Freedom from Contract: Solutions in Search of a Problem? *Wisconsin Law Review*, 777–820.

Macneil, Ian R. (1980). *The New Social Contract: An Inquiry into Modern Contractual Relations*. New Haven, CT: Yale University Press.

Madhdawi, Arwa (2017, June 20). It's Not Just Amazon Coming for Whole Foods – Silicon Valley Is Eating the World. *The Guardian*. Retrieved from

https://www.theguardian.com/commentisfree/2017/jun/20/amazon-whole-foo
ds-silicon-valley-global-domination

Maguire, Eleanor A.; Gadian, David G.; Johnsrude, Ingrid S.; Good, Catriona
D.; Ashburner, John; Frackowiak, Richard S. J.; and Frith, Christopher D.
(2000). Navigation-Related Structural Changes in the Hippocampi of Taxi
Drivers. *Proceedings of the National Academy of* Sciences, *97*(8), 4398–4403.

Malafouris, Lambros (2013). *How Things Shape the Mind: A Theory of Material
Engagement.* Cambridge, MA: Massachusetts Institute of Technology Press.

Manjoo, Farhad (2017, May 10). Tech's Frightful Five: They've Got Us. *New York
Times.* Retrieved from https://www.nytimes.com/2017/05/10/technology/tech
s-frightful-five-theyve-got-us.html?smid=tw-share

Mann, Ronald J. and Siebeneicher, Travis (2008). Just One Click: The Reality of
Internet Retail Contracting. *Columbia Law Review, 108*(4), 984–1012.

Marcus, Ruth (2012, June 5). Bloomberg's Soda Ban and the Rise of Noodge
Government. *Washington Post.* Retrieved from https://www.washingtonpost
.com/opinions/bloombergs-soda-ban-and-the-rise-of-noodge-government/201
2/06/05/gJQAhfJxGV_story.html?utm_term=.c4577e70bfff

Marcuse, Herbert (1982). Some Social Implications of Modern Technology. In
Andrew Arato and Eike Gebhardt (eds.), *The Essential Frankfurt School Reader*
(pp. 138–162). New York, NY: Bloomsbury Academic.

Markoff, John (2015). *Machines of Loving Grace: The Quest for Common Ground
between Humans and Robots.* New York, NY: HarperCollins.

Markovits, Daniel (2004). Contract and Collaboration. *Yale Law Journal, 113*,
1417–1518.

Markovits, Daniel (2015). Theories of the Common Law of Contracts. In *Stanford
Encyclopedia of Philosophy* online. Retrieved from http://plato.stanford.edu/arc
hives/fall2015/entries/contracts-theories/

Marotta-Wurgler, Florencia (2011). Will Increased Disclosure Help? Evaluating
the Recommendations of the ALI's "Principles of the Law of Software
Contracts." *University of Chicago Law Review, 78*(1), 165–186.

Masnick, Mike (2010, October 22). Supreme Court Chief Justice Admits He
Doesn't Read Online EULAs or Other "Fine Print." *Techdirt.* Retrieved from
https://www.techdirt.com/articles/20101021/02145811519.shtml

Matyszczyk, Chris (2016, May 19). Samsung's Warning: Our Smart TVs Record
Your Living Room Chatter. *CNET.* Retrieved from https://www.cnet.com/ne
ws/samsungs-warning-our-smart-tvs-record-your-living-room-chatter/

Mawson, T. J. (2011). *Free Will: A Guide for the Perplexed.* New York, NY:
Continuum.

McDonald, Alecia M. and Cranor, Lorrie F. (2008). The Cost of Reading
Privacy Policies. *I/S: A Journal of Law and Policy for the Information Society*,
4, 1–22.

McKenna, Michael and Coates, D. Justin (2016). Compatibilism. In *The Stanford
Encyclopedia of Philosophy* online. Retrieved from https://plato.stanford.edu/ar
chives/win2016/entries/compatibilism/

McLuhan, Marshall (1964). *Understanding Media: The Extensions of Man*. New York: McGraw Hill.

Mendola, Joseph (2006). Intuitive Hedonism. *Philosophical Studies: An International Journey for Philosophy in the Analytic Tradition*, *128*(2), 441–477.

Merleau-Ponty, Maurice (2012). *Phenomenology of Perception*. New York, NY: Routledge.

Mey, Jacob L. (1996). Cognitive Technology? Technological Cognition. *AI and Society*, *10*(3–4), 226–232.

Meyer, Robinson (2015, February 13). The Robot That Knows When To Swipe Right. *The Atlantic*. Retrieved from http://www.theatlantic.com/technology/ archive/2015/02/the-tinder-bot-that-knows-when-to-swipe-right/385446/

Mill, John S. (1962). *Utilitarianism: On Liberty*. London: Collins.

Miller, Robert B. (1968). Response Time in Man-Computer Conversational Transactions. *Proceedings from the AFIPS Fall Joint Computer Conference, 1968*. New York, NY: ACM. Retrieved from http://theixdlibrary.com/pdf/Mil ler1968.pdf

Moor, James H. (2001). The Status and Future of the Turing Test. *Minds and Machines*, *11*(1), 77–93.

Moore, Andrew (2013). Hedonism. In *The Stanford Encyclopedia of Philosophy* online. Retrieved from https://plato.stanford.edu/archives/win2013/entries/ hedonism/

Moringiello, Juliet M. (2005). Signals, Assent and Internet Contracting. *Rutgers Law Review*, *57*(4), 1307–1349.

Morozov, Evgeny (2012). *To Save Everything Click Here: The Folly of Technological Solutionism*. New York, NY: Public Affairs.

Morozov, Evgeny (2014a). The Rise of Data and the Death of Politics. *The Guardian*, July 19. Retrieved from https://www.theguardian.com/technology/ 2014/jul/20/rise-of-data-death-of-politics-evgeny-morozov-algorithmic-regulation

Morozov, Evgeny (2014b). Every Little Byte Counts, *The New York Times*, May 18. Retrieved from https://www.nytimes.com/2014/05/18/books/review/the-nake d-future-and-social-physics.html

Morris, Glenn (1995). *For the Next Seven Generations: Indigenous Americans and Communalism. Fellowship for Intentional Community*. Retrieved from http:// www.ic.org/wiki/next-seven-generations-indigenous-americans-communalism/ (last visited Jan. 6, 2005).

Mueller, Pam A. and Oppenheimer, Daniel M. (2014). The Pen Is Mightier Than the Keyboard: Advantages of Longhand Over Laptop Note Taking. *Psychological Science*, *25*(6), 1159–1168.

Mumford, Lewis (1963). *Technics and Civilization*. New York, NY: Mariner Books.

Mumford, Lewis (1971). *The Myth of the Machine* (vols. 1–2). Philadelphia, PA: Harvest Books.

Myers, Brad A. (1985). The Importance of Percent-Done Progress Indicators for Computer-Human Interfaces. *Proceedings from the SIGCHI Conference on Human Factors in Computing Systems, 1985*. New York, NY: ACM.

Nagel, Thomas (1974). What Is It Like to Be a Bat? *Philosophical Review*, *83*(4), 435–350.

Narayanan, Arvind; Bonneau, Joseph; Felten, Edward; Miller, Andrew; and Goldfeder, Steven (2016). *Bitcoin and Cryptocurrency Technologies: A Comprehensive Introduction*. Princeton, NJ: Princeton University Press.

Nelkin, Dana K. (2013). Moral Luck. In *The Stanford Encyclopedia of Philosophy* online. Retrieved from https://plato.stanford.edu/archives/win2013/entries/moral-luck/

Newman, Judith. (2014, October 17). To Siri, with Love: How One Boy with Autism Became BFF with Apple's Siri. *The New York Times*. Retrieved from http://www.nytimes.com/2014/10/19/fashion/how-apples-siri-became-one-autistic-boys-bff.html

Nichols, Shaun (2011, November 1). Is Free Will an Illusion? *Scientific American*. Retrieved from https://www.scientificamerican.com/article/is-free-will-an-illusion/

Nielsen, Jakob (2006, April 17). F-Shaped Pattern for Reading Web Content. *Nielsen Norman Group*. Retrieved from https://www.nngroup.com/articles/f-shaped-pattern-reading-web-content/

Nielsen, Jakob (2008, May 6). How Little Do Users Read?. *Nielsen Norman Group*. Retrieved from https://www.nngroup.com/articles/how-little-do-users-read/

Nielsen, Jakob (2009, October 5). Powers of 10: Time Scales in User Experience. *Nielsen Norman Group*. Retrieved from https://www.nngroup.com/articles/powers-of-10-time-scales-in-ux/

Nielsen, Jakob and Pernice, Kara (2009). *Eyetracking Web Usability*. Berkeley, CA: New Riders Press.

Nielsen, Jakob and Tahir, Marie (2001). *Homepage Usability: 50 Websites Deconstructed*. Berkeley, CA: New Riders Publishing.

Nissenbaum, Helen (2009). *Privacy in Context: Technology, Policy, and the Integrity of Social Life*. Redwood City, CA: Stanford University Press.

Noble, David F. (1984). *Forces of Production: A Social History of Industrial Automation*. New York, NY: Knopf.

Norman, Donald (1991). Cognitive Artifacts. In John M. Carrol (ed.), *Designing Interaction: Psychology at the Human-Computer Interface* (pp. 17–37). New York, NY: Cambridge University Press.

Nozick, Robert (2013). *Anarchy, State, and Utopia*. New York, NY: Basic Books.

Nussbaum, Martha (2007). The Capabilities Approach and Ethical Cosmopolitanism: A Response to Noah Feldman. *Yale Law Journal Pocket Part*, *117*, 123–129.

Nussbaum, Martha (2011). *Creating Capabilities: The Human Development Approach*. Cambridge, MA: Harvard University Press.

Nussbaum, Martha and Sen, Amartya K. (2004). *The Quality of Life*. Oxford: Oxford University Press.

Oaklander, Mandy (2015, June 9). A Period Tracker App Is Coming To Your iPhone. *Time*. Retrieved from http://time.com/3914121/period-tracker-app/

Oates, Sarah (2008). *Introduction to Media and Politics*. London: Sage.

Odlyzko, Andrew (2009). Network Neutrality, Search Neutrality, and the Never-ending Conflict between Efficiency and Fairness in Markets. *Review of Network Economics*, *8*(1), 1–21.

OECD (2015, October 6). *Data Driven Innovation: Big Data for Growth and Well-Being*. Retrieved from http://dx.doi.org/10.1787/9789264229358-en

OECD (2016, October 19). *Use of Behavioural Insights in Consumer Policy*. Retrieved from http://www.oecd-ilibrary.org/industry-and-services/use-of-behavioural-insights-in-consumer-policy_c2203c35-en

Opam, Kwame (2014, January 18). Amazon Plans to Ship Your Packages Before You Even Buy Them. *The Verge*. Retrieved from: https://www.theverge.com/2014/1/18/5320636/amazon-plans-to-ship-your-packages-before-you-even-buy-them

Oremus, Will (2016, December 6). Stop Calling Everything "Fake News". *Slate*. Retrieved from http://www.slate.com/articles/technology/technology/2016/12/stop_calling_everything_fake_news.html

Oremus, Will (2017, June 16). Amazon's Whole Foods Purchase Isn't Just About Groceries. It's About Everything. *Slate*. Retrieved from http://www.slate.com/blogs/moneybox/2017/06/16/amazon_buying_whole_foods_isn_t_just_about_groceries_it_s_about_everything.html

Oreskes, Naomi and Conway, Erik (2010). *Merchants of Doubt*: Bloomsbury Press.

O'Rourke, Maureen A. (1999). Progressing towards a Uniform Commercial Code for Electronic Commerce or Racing towards Nonuniformity, 14 Berkeley Tech. L.J. 635.

Ostrom, Elinor (1990). *Governing the Commons*. Cambridge: Cambridge University Press.

Ostrom, Elinor (2005). *Understanding Institutional Diversity*. Princeton, NJ: Princeton University Press.

Ouellette, Judith A. and Wood, Wendy (1998). Habit and Intention in Everyday Life: The Multiple Processes by Which Past Behavior Predicts Future Behavior. *Psychological Bulletin*, *124*(1), 54–74.

Parker, Kathleen (2017, April 18). The Facebook Murder Was Inevitable. *Washington Post*. Retrieved from https://www.washingtonpost.com/opinions/the-facebook-murder-was-inevitable/2017/04/18/3d1fb75a-2475-11e7-b503-9d61 6bd5a305_story.html?utm_term=.8a82f76d0b22

Pascal, Blaise (1958). *Pascal's Pensées*. New York, NY: E. P. Dutton & Co., Inc. Retrieved from http://www.gutenberg.org/files/18269/18269-h/18269-h.htm

Pasquale, Frank (2010). Beyond Innovation and Competition: The Need for Qualified Transparency in Internet Intermediaries. 104 NW. U. L. REV. 1.

Pasquale, Frank (2015), The Black Box Society: The Secret Algorithms That Control Money and Information. *Business Ethics Quarterly*, *26*(4), 568–571.

Pettit, Philip (2006). Preference, Deliberation and Satisfaction. In Serena Olsaretti (ed.), *Preferences and Well-Being* (pp. 131–153). Cambridge: Cambridge University Press.

Plato's *The Republic* (2017). (Bloom, Allan, trans.). New York, NY: Basic Books.

Plaut, Victoria and Bartlett, Robert P. (2012). Blind Consent? A Social Psychological Investigation of Non-Readership of Click-Through Agreements. *Law and Human Behavior, 36*(4), 293–311.

Post, David G. (2002). Against "Against Cyberanarchy." *Berkeley Technology Law Journal, 17*(4), 1365–1387.

Postman, Neil (1992). *Technopoly: The Surrender of Culture to Technology.* New York: Knopf.

ProCD, Inc. v. *Zeidenberg*, 86 F.3d 1447 (7th Cir. 1996)

Protecting and Promoting the Open Internet, 80 Fed. Reg. 19737 (June 12, 2015) (codified at 47 C.F.R. pts. 1, 20, and 8). Retrieved from https://apps.fcc.gov/edocs_public/attachmatch/FCC-15-24A1.pdf

Quinn, Daniel (1996). *The Story of B.* New York, NY: Bantam Books.

Rachels, James (2014). The Challenge of Cultural Relativism. In Stuart Rachels (ed.), *Elements of Moral Philosophy* (pp. 15–32). New York, NY: McGraw-Hill Education.

Radin, Margaret J. (2013). *Boilerplate: The Fine Print, Vanishing Rights, and the Rule of Law.* Princeton, NJ: Princeton University Press.

Rebonato, Riccardo (2014). A Critical Assessment of Libertarian Paternalism. *Journal of Consumer Policy, 37*(3), 357 396.

Reidenberg, Joel R. (1998). Lex Informatica: The Formulation of Information Policy Rules Through Technology. *Texas Law Review, 76*(3), 553–593.

Richards, Neil (2008). Intellectual Privacy. *Yale Law Journal, 87*(2), 387.

Richards, Neil M. and Hartzog, Woodrow (2017). Privacy's Trust Gap. 126 *Yale Law Journal* 1180.

Risch, Michael (2009a). Virtual Rule of Law. *West Virginia Law Review, 112*(1), 1–52.

Risch, Michael (2009b). Virtual Third Parties. *Santa Clara High Technology Law Journal, 25*(2), 415–425.

Robinson, Collin (2013). The Return of Centralised Energy Planning. *Economic Affairs, 33*(3), 312–326.

Robinson, Douglas (2013). *Feeling Extended: Sociality as Extended Body-Becoming-Mind.* Cambridge, MA: Massachusetts Institute of Technology Press.

Romans, Sarah; Clarkson, Rose; Einstein, Gillian; Petrovic, Michelle; Stewart, Donna (2012). Mood and the Menstrual Cycle: A Review of Prospective Data Studies. *Gender Medicine, 9*(5), 361–384.

Rose, David (2014). *Enchanted Objects: Design, Human Desire, and the Internet of Things.* New York, NY: Scribner.

Rose, Nikolas and Abi-Rached, Joelle M. (2013). *Neuro: The New Brain Sciences and the Management of the Mind.* Princeton, NJ: Princeton University Press.

Ross, Erin (2016, September 20). Weight Loss On Your Wrist? Fitness Trackers May Not Help. National Public Radio. Retrieved from http://www.npr.org/

sections/health-shots/2016/09/20/494631423/weight-loss-on-your-wrist-fitness-trackers-may-not-help

Rottenberg, Josh (2016, July 24). Oliver Stone Calls "Pokemon Go" Surveillance Capitalism. *Los Angeles Times*. Retrieved from http://www.latimes.com/entertainment/la-et-hc-comic-con-updates-oliver-stone-calls-pokemon-go-14691309 80-htmlstory.html

Rousseau, Jean-Jacques (2010). *The Social Contract*. New York, NY: Simon & Schuster. (Originally published 1762.)

Ruse, Michael (1993). The New Evolutionary Ethics. In Matthew Nitecki and Doris Nitecki (eds.), *Evolutionary Ethics* (pp. 133–162). Albany, NY: State University of New York Press.

Rushkoff, Douglas (2016). *Throwing Rocks at the Google Bus*. New York, NY: Penguin.

Sahrhage, Dietrich and Lundbeck, Johannes (2012). *A History of Fishing*. Berlin: Springer-Verlag.

Sandel, Michael (2012). *What Money Can't Buy: The Moral Limits of Markets*. (New York, NY: Farrar, Straus and Giroux).

Sanders, John T. (1997). An Ontology of Affordances. *Ecological Psychology*, *9*(1), 97–112.

Sanfilippo, Madelyn, Frischmann, Brett M., and Strandburg, Katherine J. (2017). *Privacy as Commons: Case Evaluation Through Governing Knowledge Commons Framework* (2017). Working Paper.

Sartre, Jean-Paul (1991). *The Transcendence of the Ego: An Existentialist Theory of Consciousness*. (Forrest Williams and Robert Kirkpatrick, trans.). New York, NY: Hill and Wang.

Sartre, Jean-Paul (1993). *Being and Nothingness*. (Hazel E. Barnes, trans.). New York, NY: Washington Square Press.

Sartre, Jean-Paul (2007). *Existentialism Is a Humanism*. (Carol Macomber, trans.). New Haven, CT: Yale University Press.

Sax, David (2016, October 17). The Real Soylent Sickness. *The New Yorker*. Retrieved from http://www.newyorker.com/business/currency/the-real-soylent-sickness

Sayre-McCord, Geoffrey and Smith, Michael (2014). Desires . . . and Beliefs . . . of One's Own. In Manuel Vargas and Gideon Yaffe (eds.), *Rational and Social Agency* (pp. 129–151). New York, NY: Oxford University Press.

Schaub, Florian; Balebako, Rebecca; Durity, Adam L.; and Cranor, Lorrie F. (2015). A Design Space for Effective Privacy Notices. *Proceedings from 2015 Symposium on Usable Privacy and Security*. Ottawa: USENIX. Retrieved from https://www.usenix.org/system/files/conference/soups2015/soups15-paper-schaub.pdf

Schneier, Bruce (2010). Security and Function Creep. *IEEE Security and Privacy*, 8 (1), 88.

Schüll, Natasha Dow (2012). *Addiction by Design: Machine Gambling in Las Vegas*, Princeton, NJ: Princeton University Press.

Schüll, Natasha Dow (2014). Obamacare Meets Wearable TECHNOLOGY. *MIT Technology Review*, 6 May.

Schüll, Natasha Dow (2016). Data for Life: Wearable technology and the design of self-care. *BioSocieties* 1–17.

Schultze-Kraft, Matthias; Birman, Daniel; Rusconi, Marco; Allefeld, Carsten; Görgen, Kai; Dähne, Sven; Blankertz, Benjamin; and Haynes, John-Dylan (2016). The Point of No Return in Vetoing Self-Initiated Movements. *Proceedings of the National Academy of Sciences of the United States of America*, *113*(4), 1080–1085. Retrieved from http://www.pnas.org/content/113/4/1080.full.pdf

Schumacher, E. F. (2010). Buddhist Economics. In *Small Is Beautiful: Economics As If People Mattered*. New York, NY: Harper Perennial.

Schweizer, Paul (1998). The Truly Total Turing Test. *Minds and Machines*, 8(2), 263–272.

Searle, John R. (1980). *Minds, Brains, and Programs. Behavioral and Brain Sciences* 3(3), 417–424.

Searle, John R. (1984). *Minds, Brains and Science*. Cambridge, MA: Harvard University Press.

Searls, Doc (2016). Time for THEM to Agree to OUR Terms. *Medium*. Mar. 29, 2016. https://medium.com/@dsearls/time-for-them-to-agree-to-our-terms-263ee87e9f41

Segal, David (2014, May 24). The Computerized Voice that Wasn't. *The New York Times*. Retrieved from https://www.nytimes.com/2014/05/25/your-money/the-haggler-the-computerized-voice-that-wasnt.html?_r=0

Selinger, Evan (2014, June 9). You've Been Obsessing Over Your Likes and Retweets Way Too Much. *Wired*. Retrieved from https://www.wired.com/2014/06/you-are-worth-more-than-just-likes-faves-and-retweets/

Selinger, Evan (2015a). The Black Box Within: Quantified Selves, Self-Directed Surveillance, and the Dark Side of Datification. *Los Angeles Review of Books*, February 17. Retrieved from https://lareviewofbooks.org/article/black-box-within-quantified-selves-self-directed-surveillance-dark-side-datification/

Selinger, Evan (2015b). Automating Walking Is the First Step to a Dystopian Nightmare. *Wired UK*, May 20. Retrieved from http://www.wired.co.uk/news/archive/2015-05/20/the-future-of-walking

Selinger, Evan (2015c). Bursting the Optimistic Technology Bubble. *Los Angeles Review of Books*, July 31. Retrieved from: https://lareviewofbooks.org/article/bursting-the-optimistic-technology-bubble/

Selinger, Evan (2015d). How Obsessive Self-Tracking Is Eroding Privacy for Everyone. *Christian Science Monitor*, September 23. Retrieved from http://www.csmonitor.com/World/Passcode/Passcode-Voices/2015/0923/How-obsessive-self-tracking-is-eroding-privacy-for-everyone

Selinger, Evan (2016, November 28). What Parents Don't Get about Cyberbullying. *Christian Science Monitor*. Retrieved from http://www.csmonitor.com/World/Passcode/Passcode-Voices/2016/1128/What-parents-don-t-get-about-cyberbullying

Selinger, Evan and Engstrom, Timothy (2007). On Naturally Embodied Cyborgs: Identities, Metaphors, and Models. *Janus Head, 9*(2), 553–584.

Selinger, Evan and Frischmann, Brett M. (2015, August 10). Will the Internet of Things Result in Predictable People? *The Guardian.* Retrieved from http://www.theguardian.com/technology/2015/aug/10/internet-of-things-predict able-people.

Selinger, Evan and Whyte, Kyle (2011). Is There a Right Way to Nudge? The Practice and Ethics of Choice Architecture. *Sociology Compass, 5*(10), 923–935.

Sen, Amartya K. (1974). Choice, Orderings and Morality. In Stephan Körner (ed.), *Practical Reason* (pp. 54–67). Oxford: Basil Blackwell.

Sen, Amartya K. (1977). Rational Fools: A Critique of the Behavioral Foundations of Economic Theory. *Philosophy and Public Affairs, 6*(4), 317–344.

Sen, Amartya K. (1985). *Commodities and Capabilities.* Amsterdam: North-Holland.

Sen, Amartya K. (2001). *Development as Freedom.* Oxford: Oxford University Press.

Sen, Amartya K. (2004). *Rationality and Freedom.* Cambridge, MA: Harvard University Press.

Sen, Amartya K. (2005). Human Rights and Capabilities. *Journal of Human Development, 6*(2), 151–166.

Sen, Amartya, K. (2011). *Development as Freedom.* New York, NY: Anchor Books.

Sgouros v. *TransUnion Corp.*, No. 15–1371, 2016 WL 1169411 (7th Cir. 2016)

Shahani, Aarti (2016, September 10). With "Napalm Girl," Facebook Humans (Not Algorithms) Struggle to Be the Editor. National Public Radio. Retrieved from http://www.npr.org/sections/alltechconsidered/2016/09/10/493454256/with-napalm-girl-facebook-humans-not-algorithms-struggle-to-be-editor

Shallis, Michael (1984). *The Silicon Idol: The Micro Revolution and Its Social Implications.* Oxford: Oxford University Press.

Shaviro, Steven (2010). The Universe of Things. *Proceedings from: Object-Oriented Ontology Symposium.* Georgia Institute of Technology, Atlanta, Georgia. Retrieved from http://www.shaviro.com/Othertexts/Things.pdf

Sherman, Bill (2017, March 20). Fitbit Fitness Monitoring Program a Hit at ORU. *Tulsa World.* Retrieved from http://m.tulsaworld.com/homepagelatest/Fitbit-fitness-monitoring-program-a-hit-at-oru/article_eae41a5e-830a-5270-98de-c1aa62aac28d.html?mode=jqm

Shieber, Stuart (1994). Lessons from a Restricted Turing Test. *Communications of the Association for Computing Machinery, 37*(6), 70–78.

Shieber, Stuart (2008). The Turing Test as Interactive Proof. *Nous, 41*(4), 686–713.

Shumaker, Robert W., Walkup, Kristina R., and Beck, Benjamin B. (2011). *Animal Tool Behavior: The Use and Manufacture of Tools by Animals.* Baltimore, MD: Johns Hopkins University Press.

Singer, Natasha (2017, May 13). How Google Took Over the Classroom. *New York Times.* Retrieved from https://mobile.nytimes.com/2017/05/13/technology/google-education-chromebooks-schools.html?rref=collection%2Fbyline%2Fnatasha-singer&action=click&contentCollection=undefined&region=strea

m&module=stream_unit&version=latest&contentPlacement=1&pgtype=colle
ction&_r=0&referer=https://www.nytimes.com/by/natasha-singer

Singer, Peter (1997). Thought Experiment. *Utilitarian*. Retrieved from https://
www.utilitarian.net/singer/by/199704–.html

Singer, Peter (1997, April 5). The Drowning Child and the Expanding Circle. *New
Internationalist*. Retrieved from https://newint.org/features/1997/04/05/
drowning

Slawson, W. David (1971). Standard Form Contracts and Democratic Control of
Lawmaking Power. *Harvard Law Review*, *84*(3), 529–566.

Smilansky, Saul (2000). *Free Will and Illusion*. New York, NY: Clarendon Press.

Smith, Basil (2011). Can We Test the Experience Machine? *Ethical Perspectives*, *18*
(1), 29–51.

Sneddon, Andrew (2013). *Autonomy*. New York, NY: Bloomsbury Academic.

Solon, Olivia (2017, February 15). Elon Musk Says Humans Must Become
Cyborgs to Stay Relevant. Is He Right? *The Guardian*. Retrieved from http
s://www.theguardian.com/technology/2017/feb/15/elon-musk-cyborgs-robots-
artificial-intelligence-is-he-right?CMP=Share_iOSApp_Other

Specht v. *Netscape*, 306 F.3d 17 (2nd Cir. 2002).

Spinoza, Benedict (1996). *Ethics*. New York, NY: Penguin.

Sprigman, Christopher (2004). Reform(aliz)ing Copyright. *Stanford Law Review*,
57, 485–568.

Stanovich, Keith E. (2005). *The Robot's Rebellion: Finding Meaning in the Age of
Darwin*. Chicago, IL: University of Chicago Press.

Stanovich, Keith E. (2012). On the Distinction Between Rationality and
Intelligence: Implications for Understanding Individual Differences in
Reasoning. In Keith J. Holyoak and Robert G. Morrison (eds.), *The Oxford
Handbook of Thinking and Reasoning* (pp. 433–455). New York, NY: Oxford
University Press.

Stanovich, Keith E. (2013). Why Humans Are (Sometimes) Less Rational Than
Other Animals: Cognitive Complexity and the Axioms of Rational Choice.
Thinking and Reasoning, *19*(1), 1–26.

Stein, Edward (1996). *Without Good Reason: The Rationality Debate in Philosophy
and Cognitive Science*. New York, NY: Oxford University Press.

Sterelny, Kim (2004). Externalism, Epistemic Artifacts, and the Extended Mind.
In Richard Schantz (ed.), *The Externalist Challenge* (pp. 239–254). New York,
NY: Walter De Gruyter.

Stewart, Neil (2009). Decision by Sampling: The Role of the Decision
Environment in Risky Choice. *Quarterly Journal of Experimental Psychology*,
62(6), 1041–1062.

Stockton, Nick (2015, April 20). Scientists are Using Electrodes to Remote-
Control People. *Wired*. Retrieved from http://www.wired.com/2015/04/scien
tists-using-electrodes-remote-control-people/

Strandburg, Katherine J. (2013). Free Fall: The Online Market's Consumer
Preference Disconnect. *University of Chicago Legal Forum*, *2013*(5). Retrieved
from http://chicagounbound.uchicago.edu/uclf/vol2013/iss1/5.

Strandburg, Katherine J., Madison, Michael J., and Frischmann, Brett M. (eds.) (2017), *Governing Knowledge Commons*. Cambridge: Cambridge University Press.

Strawson, Peter (1963). Freedom and Resentment. In Gary Watson (ed.), *Proceedings of the British Academy, Volume 48* (1962), 1–25. New York, NY: Oxford University Press.

Sullins, John (2012). Robots, Love, and Sex: The Ethics of Building a Love Machine. *IEEEE Transactions of Affective Computing, 3*(4), 398–409.

Sunder, Madhavi (2012). *From Goods to a Good Life: Intellectual Property and Global Justice*. New Haven, CT: Yale University Press.

Sunstein, Cass (2014a). Choosing Not to Choose. *Duke Law Journal, 64*(1), 1–52.

Sunstein, Cass (2014b). *Why Nudge?* New Haven, CT: Yale University Press.

Sunstein, Cass (2015). *Choosing Not to Choose: Understanding the Value of Choice*. New York, NY: Oxford University Press.

Surowiecki, James (2005). *The Wisdom of Crowds*. New York, NY: Anchor.

Swift, Fletcher H. (1947). *The Athenian Ephebic Oath of Allegiance in American Schools and Colleges*. Los Angeles, CA: University of California Press.

Tal, Dor. *Predictables*. Retrieved from http://dordesign.com/

Tasker, Ty and Pakcyk, Daryn (2008). Cyber-Surfing on the High Seas of Legalese: Law and Technology of Internet Agreements. *Albany Law Journal of Science & Technology, 18*(1), 79–149.

Taylor, Frederick Winslow (1903). *Shop Management*. New York, NY: American Society of Mechanical Engineers.

Taylor, Josh (2007). Why Robert Nozick Should Have Played More Video Games. *Comparative Humanities Review, 1*(1), 70–76.

Thaler, Richard H. (2010, April 7). Fear of Falling. *Cato Institute*. Retrieved from https://www.cato-unbound.org/2010/04/07/richard-thaler/fear-falling

Thaler, Richard H. and Sunstein, Cass R. (2008). *Nudge: Improving Decisions About Health, Wealth, and Happiness*. New Haven, CT: Yale University Press.

Tierney, John (2011, August 17). Do You Suffer From Decision Fatigue? *New York Times Magazine*. Retrieved from http://www.nytimes.com/2011/08/21/magazine/do-you-suffer-from-decision-fatigue.html

Tolliday, Steven and Zeitlin, Jonathon (1987). *The Automobile Industry and Its Workers: Between Fordism and Flexibility*. New York, NY: St. Martin's Press.

Tolstoy, Leo (1988). *A Confession and Other Religious Writings* (Jane Kentish, trans.). New York, NY: Penguin Classics. (Original work published 1879.)

Towse, John N. and Neil, Derek (1998). Analyzing Human Random Generation Behavior: A Review of Methods Used and a Computer Program for Describing Performance. *Behavior Research Methods, Instruments, & Computers, 30*(4), 583–591.

Tsalatsanis, Athanasios; Hozo, Iztok; Kumar, Ambuj; and Djulbegovic, Benjamin (2015). Dual Processing Model for Medical Decision-Making: An Extension to Diagnostic Testing. *PLOS ONE, 10*(8). Retrieved from http://journals.plos.org/plosone/article?id=10.1371/journal.pone.0134800

Turing, Alan (1937). On Computable Numbers, with an Application to the Entscheidungsproblem, *Proceedings of the London Mathematical Society*, 2 (42), 230–265, doi:10.1112/plms/s2-42.1.230.

Turing, Alan (1938). On Computable Numbers, with an Application to the Entscheidungsproblem: A Correction. *Proceedings of the London Mathematical Society*, 2 (43) 544–546 (published 1937), doi:10.1112/plms/s2-43.6.544.

Turing, Alan (1950). Computing Machinery and Intelligence. *Mind*, 59(236), 433–460.

Turkle, Sherry (2011). *Alone Together: Why We Expect More from Technology and Less from Each Other*. New York, NY: Basic Books.

Turkle, Sherry (2015). *Reclaiming Conversation: The Power of Talk in a Digital Age*. New York, NY: Penguin Press.

Turow, Joseph (2012). *The Daily You: How the New Advertising Industry Is Defining Your Identity and Your Worth*. New Haven, CT: Yale University Press.

Turow, Joseph (2017). *The Aisles Have Eyes: How Retailers Track Your Shopping, Strip Your Privacy, and Define Your Power*. New Haven, CT: Yale University Press.

United Nations. *Universal Declaration of Human Rights*. Retrieved from http://www.un.org/en/universal-declaration-human-rights/

United States Government Accountability Office – Center for Science, Technology, and Engineering (2017, May 15). *Internet of Things: Status and implications of an increasingly connected world*. Retrieved from https://www.gao.gov/assets/690/684590.pdf

Vallor, Shannon (2016). *Technology and the Virtues: A Philosophical Guide to a Future Worth Wanting*. New York, NY: Oxford University Press.

Van Gulick, Robert (2017). Consciousness. In *Stanford Encyclopedia of Philosophy* online. Retrieved from https://plato.stanford.edu/archives/sum2017/entries/consciousness/

Van Loo, Rory (2015). Helping Buyers Beware: The Need for Supervision of Big Retail. *University of Pennsylvania Law Review*, 163, 1311–1392.

Van Schewick, Barbara (2010). *Internet Architecture and Innovation*. Cambridge, MA: MIT Press.

Verbeek, Peter-Paul (2010). *What Things Do: Philosophical Reflections on Technology, Agency, and Design*. University Park, PA: Pennsylvania State University Press.

Volokh, Eugene. (2003). The Mechanisms of the Slippery Slope. *Harvard Law Review*, 116(4), 1026–1137.

Wagenaar, Willem A. (1972). Generation of Random Sequences by Human Subjects: A Critical Survey of Literature. *Psychological Bulletin*, 77(1), 65–72.

Waldman, Ari E. (2016). Manipulating Trust on Facebook. *Loyola Consumer Law Review*, 29, 175–198.

Warwick, Kevin and Shah, Huma (2014). Human Misidentification in Turing Tests. *Journal of Experimental & Theoretical Artificial Intelligence*, 27(2), 123–135.

Warwick, Kevin and Shah, Huma (2017). Taking the Fifth Amendment in Turing's Imitation Game. *Journal of Experimental & Theoretical Artificial Intelligence*, *29*(2), 287–297.

Webster, Frank (1995), *Theories of the Information Society* (John Urry, ed., 3rd edn., 2006). Abingdon/New York: Routledge.

Wegner, Daniel M. and Gray, Kurt (2016). *The Mind Club: Who Thinks, What Feels, and Why It Matters*. New York, NY: Viking.

Weijers, Dan (2011). A Review and Assessment of the Experience Machine Objection to Hedonism. Retrieved from http://www.danweijers.com/pdf/A%20Review%20and%20Assessment%20of%20the%20Experience%20Machine%20Objection%20to%20Hedonism%20-%20Dan%20Weijers.pdf

Weijers, Dan (2014). Nozick's Experience Machine Is Dead, Long Live the Experience Machine. *Philosophical Psychology*, *27*(4), 513–535.

Weinberger, David (2002). *Small Pieces Loosely Joined: A Unified Theory of the Web*. New York, NY: Basic Books.

Weinberger, David (2007). *Everything Is Miscellaneous: The Power of the New Digital Disorder*. New York, NY: Holt.

Weizenbaum, Joseph (1976). *Computer Power and Human Reason: From Judgment to Calculation*. New York, NY: W. H. Freeman & Co.

Wendling, Amy (2009). *Karl Marx on Technology and Alienation*. New York, NY: Palgrave Macmillan.

White, James J., Summers, Robert S., and Hillman, Robert A. (2010). *Uniform Commercial Code*, Practitioner Treatise Series. St. Paul, MN: Thomson West.

Wikipedia. *Bizarro World*. Retrieved from https://en.wikipedia.org/wiki/Bizarro_World

Wikipedia. *Boiling Frog*. Retrieved from https://en.wikipedia.org/wiki/Boiling_frog

Wikipedia. *Internet of Things*. Retrieved from https://en.wikipedia.org/wiki/Internet_of_Things

Wilkinson-Ryan, Tess (2016). Contracts Without Terms. *University of Pennsylvania Institute for Law & Economic Research*. Retrieved from http://ssrn.com/abstract=2738567

Wilkinson-Ryan, Tess and Hoffman, David A. (2015). The Common Sense of Contract Formation. *Stanford Law Review*, *67*(6), 1269–1301.

Wilson, Mark. (2009, March 5). Robot Programmed to Love Traps Woman in Lab, Hugs Her Repeatedly. *Gizmodo*. Retrieved from http://gizmodo.com/5164841/robot-programmed-to-love-traps-woman-in-lab-hugs-her-repeatedly

Winchcomb, Tim, Massey, Sam, and Beastall, Paul (2017, March 7). Review of Latest Developments in the Internet of Things. *Ofcom*. Retrieved from https://www.ofcom.org.uk/research-and-data/telecoms-research/general/review-of-latest-developments-in-the-internet-of-things

Wolf, Susan R. (2015). *The Variety of Values: Essays on Morality, Meaning, and Love*. New York, NY: Oxford University Press.

Wood, David Murakami and Ball, Kirstie (2013). Brandscapes of Control? Surveillance, Marketing and the Co-Construction of Subjectivity and Space in Neo-Liberal Capitalism. *Marketing Theory*, *13*(1), 47–67.

Wu, Tim (2003). Network Neutrality, Broadband Discrimination. 2 *Journal on Telecommunications & High Technology Law* 141.

Wu, Tim (2004). The Broadband Debate: A User's Guide. 3 *Journal on Telecommunications & High Technology Law* 69.

Wu, Tim, and Lessig, Lawrence (2003), Letter to Marlene H. Dortch, Secretary, FCC, CS Docket No. 02–52 (Aug. 22), available at http://faculty.virginia.edu/timwu/wu_lessig_fcc.pdf

Yan, Laura (2015, September 11). Sex Dolls with Artificial Intelligence to Ease Your Loneliness (and Maybe Shoot You a Text). *PSFK*. Retrieved from http://www.psfk.com/2015/07/sex-dolls-life-sized-realdoll-realbotix-ai-powered-animatronic-head.html

YouTube. *Restricted Mode*. Retrieved from https://support.google.com/youtube/answer/174084?co=GENIE.Platform%3DDesktop&hl=en

Zhang, Jiajie and Patel, Vimla L. (2006). Distributed Cognition, Representation, and Affordance. *Pragmatics and Cognition*, *14*(2), 333–341.

Zimbardo, Philip (2007). *The Lucifer Effect: Understanding How Good People Turn Evil*. New York, NY: Random House.

Zuboff, Shoshana (2015). Big Other: Surveillance Capitalism and the Prospects of an Information Civilization. *Journal of Information Technology*, *30*(1), 75–89.

Zuboff, Shoshana (2016, March 5). The Secrets of Surveillance Capitalism. *Frankfurter Allgemeine Zeitung*. Retrieved from: http://www.faz.net/aktuell/feuilleton/debatten/the-digital-debate/shoshana-zuboff-secrets-of-surveillance-capitalism-14103616.html

Zweig, David (2014). *Invisibles: The Power of Anonymous Work in an Age of Relentless Self-Promotion*. New York, NY: Penguin.

Index